Experiencing and Explaining Disease

Edited by Basiro Davey and Clive Seale

Published by Open University P PRESS

Produced by The Open Universit delphia

Health and Disease Series, Book

The U205 *Health and Disease* Course Team

The editors have collaborated with the authors in writing this book, and have commented extensively on it during its production. We accept collective responsibility for its overall academic and teaching content.

Basiro Davey (Course Team Chair, Senior Lecturer in Health Studies, Department of Biological Sciences, The Open University)

Clive Seale (Professor of Medical Sociology, Department of Sociology, Goldsmiths' College, University of London)

The following people have contributed to the development of particular parts or aspects of this book, or of the second edition on which it is based.

Duncan Banks (critical reader), Lecturer in Biomedical Sciences, The Open University

Sandra Budin (BBC production assistant)

Sheila Dunleavy (editor)

Rebecca Graham (editor)

Celia Hart (picture researcher)

Pam Higgins (designer)

Patti Langton (BBC producer)

Jean Macqueen (indexer)

Jennifer Nockles (designer)

Rissa de la Paz (BBC producer)

Denise Rowe (course secretary)

John Taylor (graphic artist)

Joy Wilson (course manager)

Authors

The following people have acted as single or joint authors for the chapters listed below.

Chapters 1, 4, 5, 7 and 8

Basiro Davey, Senior Lecturer in Health Studies, Department of Biological Sciences, The Open University.

Chapters 2, 7 and 8

Clive Seale, Professor of Medical Sociology, Department of Sociology, Goldsmiths' College, University of London.

Chapter 3

Gareth Williams, Professorial Fellow, School of Social Sciences, Cardiff University; Ray Fitzpatrick, Professor of Public Health and Primary Care, Nuffield College, University of Oxford; Alex J. MacGregor, Arthritis Research Campaign Senior Fellow and Honorary Consultant Rheumatologist, St Thomas' Hospital, London; and Alan S. Rigby, Senior Lecturer in Statistics and Epidemiology and Chartered Statistician, Sheffield Children's Hospital, University of Sheffield.

Chapter 4

Graham Hart, Professor and Associate Director, MRC Social and Public Health Sciences Unit, University of Glasgow.

Chapter 5

Bill Bytheway, Senior Research Fellow, School of Health and Social Welfare, The Open University.

Chapter 6

Jacqueline Atkinson, Senior Lecturer, Department of Public Health, University of Glasgow; and Daniel Nettle, Lecturer in Biological Psychology, Department of Biological Sciences, The Open University.

External assessors

Course assessor for third editions

Professor John Gabbay, Professor of Public Health Medicine, University of Southampton, and Director of the Wessex Institute of Health Research and Development.

We gratefully acknowledge the contributions made by the external assessors for the previous edition of this book:

Professor Michael Bury, Professor of Sociology, Department of Social Policy and Social Sciences, Royal Holloway University of London.

Professor James McEwen, Henry Mechan Chair of Public Health and Head of Department of Public Health, University of Glasgow.

Acknowledgements

The Course Team and the authors wish to thank the following people who, as critical readers or contributors to previous editions of this book, made a lasting impact on the structure and philosophy of the present volume.

Nick Black, David Boswell, Gerald Elliott, Anna Furth, Alastair Gray, Robin Harding, David Jones, David Kelleher, Donald Lane, Julian Leff, Kevin McConway, Tim Rhodes, Roland Littlewood, Sean Murphy, Jennie Popay, Steven Rose, Patrick Wall, Ian Williams, Simon Williams.

Cover images

Background: Nebulae in the Rho Ophiuchi region (Source: Anglo-Australian Observatory/Royal Observatory Edinburgh). *Middleground*: Globe (Source: Mountain High Map™, Digital Wisdom, Inc). *Foreground: Mother at her Child's Sickbed* by Christian Krohg, painted in 1884 (Source: Photo, J. Lathion, © 1996, Nasjonalgalleriet, Oslo)

Dedication

This book is dedicated to the life of

Phillip Michael Strong (1945–1995)

whose scholarship, vision and humour were imprinted so deeply on the
original *Health and Disease* series that his contribution remains clearly visible
in the later editions. The Open University course team associated with this series
acknowledge our debt to Phil on behalf of over 20 000 adult students
who have already studied the course he inspired.

Open University Press, Celtic Court, 22 Ballmoor,
Buckingham, MK18 1XW.

e-mail: enquiries@openup.co.uk

website: www.openup.co.uk

and

325 Chestnut Street, Philadelphia, PA 19106, USA.

First published 1985. Completely revised second edition
published 1996.

This full-colour completely revised third edition published
2002.

A catalogue record of the book is available from the
British Library.

Library of Congress Cataloging-in-Publication Data is
available.

Edited, designed and typeset by the Open University.

Printed and bound in the United Kingdom by the
Alden Group, Oxford.

ISBN 0335 20837 1

This publication forms part of an Open University level 2
course, U205 *Health and Disease*. The complete list of texts
which make up this course can be found on the back
cover. Details of this and other Open University courses
can be obtained from the Course Advice and Information
Centre, PO Box 724, The Open University, Milton Keynes
MK7 6ZS, United Kingdom: tel. +44 (0)1908 653231,
e-mail ces-gen@open.ac.uk

Alternatively, you may visit the Open University website
at http://www.open.ac.uk where you can learn more
about the wide range of courses and packs offered at all
levels by the Open University.

3.1

CONTENTS

A note for the general reader

Experiencing and Explaining Disease is a multidisciplinary account of the major factors influencing the ways in which states of wellness or illness are explained by professionals and experienced by lay people. These explanations and experiences are not fixed, even for the same disease condition, but vary from person to person and between different times and places. They are profoundly affected by the state of scientific and medical knowledge, which may be comprehensive or negligible; by the political and economic climate of the society in which they occur; by the personal circumstances of the individuals caught up in the condition, either as patients, family or carers; and by the nature of the condition itself, for example whether it is contagious or disfiguring, self-limiting or chronically disabling, readily identified or difficult to diagnose and treat.

This book contains eight chapters. The first introduces the framework of competing narratives that shape the meanings ascribed to different illness conditions, and which have a profound influence on the way the condition is experienced. Chapter 2 discusses the concepts of stigma and normality as powerful forces in social interactions and examines the ways in which stigmatisation is 'managed' by individuals and societies. These two chapters are the foundation of five case studies in Chapters 3–7, each focusing on a medically recognised disorder, yet each subject to conflicting interpretations and uncertainties.

Each of the conditions discussed in Chapters 3–7 includes an analysis of its incidence and prevalence in the population and its distribution between different groups (the domain of epidemiology and demography), together with a description of the underlying biology of the condition and its medical treatment, so far as these are known and understood. No less important is the sociological perspective, which sheds light on the experience of the condition by investigating the meanings attached to it, and how these may vary in different societies. The conditions are: rheumatoid arthritis (Chapter 3), HIV and AIDS (Chapter 4), asthma (Chapter 5), schizophrenia (Chapter 6), and chronic pain (Chapter 7).

These case studies have been chosen to reflect the range of conditions affecting people in developed and developing countries in the twenty-first century. We have included a chronic degenerative condition that primarily affects people after middle age (rheumatoid arthritis); a virus infection that damages the immune system and increases susceptibility to other potentially fatal infections, and is predominantly found in young adults (HIV and AIDS); a respiratory condition that can be chronic but may involve acute life-threatening emergencies (asthma); a mental disorder characterised by problems in the perception of reality (schizophrenia), and the physical and emotional suffering caused by a wide range of disorders and injuries (chronic pain).

In Chapter 8, we revisit the main themes of the book to demonstrate that they can be generalised to many other states of ill-health and disability. It concludes with a short reflection on the series of eight books in the *Health and Disease* series.

The book is fully indexed and referenced and contains a list of abbreviations and an annotated guide to further reading and to selected websites on the Internet. The list of further sources also includes details of how to access a regularly updated collection of Internet resources relevant to the *Health and Disease* series on a searchable database called ROUTES, which is maintained by the Open University. This resource is open to all readers of this book.

Experiencing and Explaining Disease is the last in a series of eight books on the subject of health and disease. The book is designed so that it can be read on its own, like any other textbook, or studied as part of U205 *Health and Disease*, a level 2 course for Open University students. General readers do not need to make use of the Study notes, learning objectives and other material inserted for OU students, although they may find these helpful. The text also contains references to a collection of previously published material and specially commissioned articles (*Health and Disease: A Reader*, Open University Press, third edition 2001) prepared for the OU course: it is quite possible to follow the text without reading the articles referred to, although doing so will enhance your understanding of the contents of *Experiencing and Explaining Disease*.

Abbreviations used in this book

ACR	American College of Rheumatology
AIDS	acquired immune deficiency syndrome
AIMS	Arthritis Impact Measurement Scales
APHEA	Air Pollution and Health: a European Approach
ARC	Arthritis Research Campaign
CBT	cognitive behavioural therapy
CHD	coronary heart disease
COAD	chronic obstructive airways disease
CPR	cardiopulmonary resuscitation
DMARDs	disease-modifying anti-rheumatic drugs
DNA	deoxyribonucleic acid
DSM IV	*Diagnostic and Statistical Manual of Mental Disorders*, 4th revision
ECRHS	European Community Respiratory Health Survey
ECT	electroconvulsive therapy
EE	expressed emotion
FCE	finished consultant episode
GDP	Gross Domestic Product
HAQ	Health Assessment Questionnaire
HAART	highly active anti-retroviral therapy
HIV	human immunodeficiency virus
ICD–10	International Classification of Diseases, 10th revision
IDU	injecting-drug user
IgE	immunoglobulin E
IPSS	International Pilot Study of Schizophrenia

ISAAC	International Study of Asthma and Allergies in Childhood
ME	myalgic encephalomyelitis
MIND	National Association for Mental Health
MRI	magnetic resonance imaging
MS	multiple sclerosis
MSM	men who have sex with men
NSAIDs	non-steroidal anti-inflammatory drugs
NSF	National Service Frameworks
OPCS	Office of Population Censuses and Surveys
PCP	*Pneumocystis carinii* pneumonia
PPI	Present Pain Index
PRI	Pain Rating Index
PSE	Present State Examination
RA	rheumatoid arthritis
RNA	ribonucleic acid
SANE	Schizophrenia: A National Emergency
SFAF	San Fransisco AIDS Foundation
SIGN	Scottish Intercollegiate Guidelines Network
SIV	simian immunodeficiency virus
STI	sexually transmitted infection
TB	tuberculosis
TENS	transcutaneous electrical nerve stimulation
TNF	tumour necrosis factor
UA survey	unlinked anonymous survey
UN/AIDS	United Nations Programme on HIV/AIDS
WHO	World Health Organisation

Study guide for OU students

(total of around 64 hours, spread over 4 weeks)

Chapters 1 and 8 are quite short, but you should allow time for the consolidation exercise (on audiotape) associated with Chapter 8; however, there is no TMA associated with this book. Chapters 2 and 7 are of medium length, and Chapters 3, 5 and 6 are slightly longer; Chapter 4 is the longest in the book.

1st week

Chapter 1	**Making sense of illness** optional Reader article by Hardey (1991)
Chapter 2	**Stigma and normality** Reader article by Goffman (1969); optional Reader articles by Sontag (1979) and Jeffery (1979); TV programme 'More than meets the eye'
Chapter 3	**Rheumatoid arthritis** revise TV programme 'Why me? Why now?'

2nd week

Chapter 4	**HIV and AIDS** Reader articles by Garrett (1998), Finkel (2000) and Piot (2000); TV programme 'A future with AIDS'; revise video 'South Africa: Health at the Crossroads'

3rd week

Chapter 5	**Asthma** Reader article by Nocon and Booth (1990); optional Reader article by Macintyre and Oldman (1977); audiotape 'Reflections on asthma'
Chapter 6 (start)	**Schizophrenia** audiotape 'Hearing voices'

4th week

Chapter 6 (complete)	**Schizophrenia** Reader article by Helman (2000); optional Reader article by Philo (1999)
Chapter 7	**Pain and suffering** Reader article by Macintyre and Oldman (1977); audiotape 'Being in pain'
Chapter 8	**Experiencing and explaining disease: some conclusions** optional Reader article by Morris (1991); audiotape 'Living with epilepsy'

Experiencing and Explaining Disease is the final book in the *Health and Disease* series and takes a global and multidisciplinary perspective in dealing with the case studies it presents. The structure of the book is outlined in 'A note for the general reader' (p. 6) and is described further in Chapter 1.

Study notes are given at the start of every chapter. These primarily direct you to important links to other components of the course, such as the other books in the course series, the Reader, and audiovisual components. Major learning objectives are listed at the end of each chapter, along with questions that will enable you to check that you have achieved these objectives. The index includes key terms in orange type (also printed in bold in the text), which can be looked up easily as an aid to revision as the course proceeds. There is also a list of further sources for those who wish to pursue certain aspects of study beyond the scope of this book, either by consulting other books and articles or by logging on to specialist websites on the Internet.

The time allowed for studying *Experiencing and Explaining Disease* is around 64 hours spread over 4 weeks. The schedule (left) gives a more detailed breakdown to help you to pace your study. You need not follow it rigidly, but try not to let yourself fall behind. Depending on your background and experience, you may well find some parts of this book much more familiar and straightforward than others. If you find a section of the work difficult, do what you can at this stage, and then return to reconsider the material when you reach the end of the book.

There is no tutor-marked assignment (TMA) associated with this book because it falls too late in the academic year to enable marked scripts to be returned to you before the final examination.

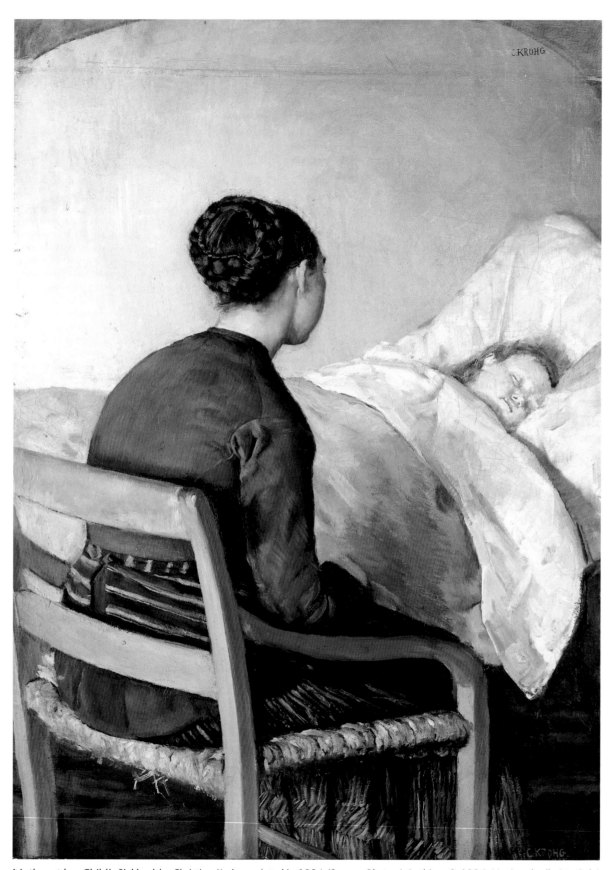

Mother at her Child's Sickbed *by Christian Krohg, painted in 1884 (Source: Photo, J. Lathion, © 1996, Nasjonalgalleriet, Oslo)*

CHAPTER 1

Making sense of illness

Study notes for OU students

This chapter introduces the final book in the *Health and Disease* series. The connections between this chapter and the first book in the series, *Medical Knowledge: Doubt and Certainty* (Open University Press, second edition 1994; colour-enhanced second edition 2001), are particularly strong. An article entitled 'Doctor in the house: the Internet as a source of lay health knowledge and the challenge to expertise' by Michael Hardey appears in *Health and Disease: A Reader* (Open University Press, third edition 2001) and is optional reading for Section 1.3. The author of this chapter, Basiro Davey, chairs the Course Team that produced this series; she is Senior Lecturer in Health Studies in the Department of Biological Sciences at The Open University.

1.1 Illness and culture

Suppose for a moment that you develop a persistent cough, or notice intermittent pain in one leg, or find yourself regularly waking at 3 a.m. feeling troubled and unable to sleep — or imagine any other departure from your familiar physical, mental or emotional states. In Western industrialised societies, events such as these are overwhelmingly interpreted as possible symptoms of illness, indicators of an underlying pathological change in the structure or function of a specific part of the body which, with the help of modern medicine, can often be detected and restored to 'health'. In the past and in some other cultures today, alternative explanations might have been considered — witchcraft perhaps, or the phase of the moon, an imbalance in opposing energies in the body (such as *yin* and *yang*), or in the flow of the four humours which dominated European understanding of the human body from ancient Greece until at least the sixteenth century.

Those of you who are reading this book as the final part of an Open University course will recognise that this is where we began — on a journey around different understandings of what constitutes health and illness, disability and disease.[1] We hope you are convinced that these states are 'contested' rather than 'fixed', in that they are each capable of sustaining a range of meanings, within certain boundaries imposed by the culture in which the term is being used. People experience an illness or disability not as isolated states, but in a social context. The same apparent condition may carry quite different meanings in different times and places — for example, epilepsy is attributed to brain malfunction in some cultures but to demon possession in others. In this sense, the condition and the meanings attached to it are, in part, *socially constructed* and *culturally relative*, and the nature of this construction can profoundly alter the experience of the condition for everyone who is affected by it.

● How does the social construction of 'hysteria' at different times or places illustrate this process?

■ Hysteria has variously been constructed as a physical affliction caused by the womb rising in the body, as an excess of sexual frustration, as evidence of witchcraft, as an abnormality in the function of the brain, as a reaction to the stifling of creativity among middle-class women, and as a psychological disturbance rooted in childhood trauma. Each of these 'meanings' has had a very different impact on people labelled as 'hysterical', and on the treatments or punishments prescribed for them.

In this book we revisit this contested territory by drawing on a wide range of personal and professional accounts of what it means to be disabled by illness.

---

[1] The social construction of health and illness, disability and disease, is discussed in the first book in this series, *Medical Knowledge: Doubt and Certainty* (Open University Press, 2nd edn 1994; colour-enhanced 2nd edn 2001), partly through the medium of three case studies, on tuberculosis, hysteria and blood.

1.2 Grand narratives

Among many other influences, we begin by examining certain widely known professional explanations of ill health, generated by several distinct disciplines of knowledge. In trying to 'make sense' of illness or disability, everyone in Western industrialised societies has very probably been influenced at some time by the professional disciplines listed in Box 1.1. Each of these professional disciplines approaches the explanation of health and ill health in different ways. One of the aims of this book is to illustrate their relative contributions and their interactions in five contrasting case studies — on rheumatoid arthritis, HIV/AIDS, asthma, schizophrenia and chronic pain. (Later in this chapter, we will justify this choice of case studies.)

> **Box 1.1 Professional disciplines that influence modern Western ideas of illness and disability**
>
> - *Biomedicine*, the system of medical knowledge based on scientific research into the biological structure and function of the human body, including the brain and mental processes;
> - *Epidemiology*, the statistical study of the distribution of disease in human populations, from which hypotheses about the causes of disease can be derived;
> - *Sociological studies* of health and illness, which investigate health issues in the context of human social relationships and interactions;
> - *Psychological theories*, which interpret human thoughts, feelings and actions as a dynamic interplay between conscious and unconscious mental processes.

Box 1.1 is more than simply a reminder of the distinctive domains of interest of these influential disciplines. It is also a way of introducing an important theme running through many of the following chapters — the existence of what social scientists refer to as **grand narratives**. This term can be applied to any system of knowledge and/or belief that has become institutionalised in a society and commands (or once commanded) widespread allegiance and respect from a large section of the population. Using this definition, the great religions of the world can be thought of as grand narratives, and so can the major political ideologies such as capitalism and socialism, nationalism and imperialism, among many other examples. They have all been generated and sustained by many people over long periods of time; one way of thinking of them is as 'collective stories' on a grand scale.

● Look back at the list of disciplines in Box 1.1 from which we have drawn professional explanations of disease and disability in writing this book. Which do you think most obviously qualify as a 'grand narrative' in modern Western culture?

■ Biomedicine is the most compelling as a grand narrative, since the majority of the population of Western societies give it their allegiance and respect, the training and practice of biomedicine is highly institutionalised and constrained by law, and medical terms and images abound in the popular media (for example, Figure 1.1). You might also have identified psychological theories as a grand narrative, given the widespread and generally unquestioned belief in Western culture in the 'unconscious', the rise of psychoanalysis and psychotherapy as recognised professions, and the extent to which terms such as 'ego', 'repression', 'inferiority complex' and 'Freudian slip' crop up in everyday speech (Figure 1.2).

Figure 1.1 *Biomedicine became one of the most powerful 'grand narratives' from the second half of the twentieth century onwards, commanding widespread allegiance among lay people, as evidenced by its unrivalled popularity as a source of news and entertainment; for example, the BBC's long-running TV serial, 'Casualty'. (Photo: BBC Photo Library)*

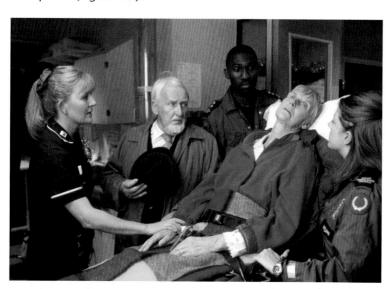

Figure 1.2 *Sigmund Freud's belief that events in the past unconsciously influence thoughts, feelings and actions in the present day has become so widespread in Western society that psychological theories as explanations for health and illness have achieved the status of a grand narrative. (Photo: The Freud Museum, London)*

Grand narratives such as biomedicine and psychological theories are an important source of the knowledge and beliefs that lay people in Western cultures draw on when faced with an unexplained physical or mental symptom. To go back to the start of this chapter, the person with the persistent cough will almost certainly consider biomedical or psychological ideas at some point in seeking an explanation for his or her symptoms, even if these ideas are later discarded in favour of more persuasive alternatives: for example, the cough may be attributed to bacteria infecting the lungs, inflammation due to cigarette smoke, or to a nervous manifestation of underlying anxieties. Other grand narratives may also contribute to the increasingly rich edifice of explanation for an illness or disability, which grows in the affected person's mind: religious beliefs may lead some individuals to wonder if they are 'being tested by God', punished for transgressions or given a divine opportunity.

> In the last 18 months I have found real peace of mind, a wonderful joy and a continuing deep contentment … In many ways I am glad to have weak legs because it makes me rely on God and I can use His strength … When I look back I can see how He helped and guided me. (Person with multiple sclerosis, quoted in Robinson, 1990, p. 1181)

1.3 Medical narratives

The weight that most lay people commonly give to the opinions of health professionals in reaching a stable understanding of their illness is part of the pressure on doctors (in particular) to offer a convincing **medical narrative** to their patients. A medical narrative can be loosely defined as a coherent 'story' about the causes, consequences or treatment of a health problem, which is generally accepted within the medical profession as a reasonable description of 'the way things are'. These accounts are passed on directly to patients by doctors, but often have a far wider currency as a result of the publicity they get in the media. For example, in the 1970s, doctors in the UK began to advise patients to quit cigarette smoking because it posed a serious risk to health. This medical narrative took about 20 years to penetrate all sectors of society, but was eventually accepted as 'true' by almost everyone, including most smokers.

Medical narratives are relayed between professionals in a technical language that lay people generally find impenetrable. Terms derived from biology, chemistry and physics are intermingled with anatomical names, physiological processes and medical diagnoses and procedures, many of which also have 'shorthand' labels or acronyms (for example, PTSD, post-traumatic stress disorder; CPR, cardiopulmonary resuscitation). Although doctors in training are warned not to use medical 'jargon' in consultations with patients, it nevertheless slips into these interactions, and the more common terms are popularised in medical documentaries and dramas.

● Can you think of a recent development that is accelerating the incorporation of elements of medical narratives into lay accounts of illness and disability?

■ In the twenty-first century, the use of the Internet as a source of medical information for lay people is rapidly increasing, and this is having an impact on the terminology in common use and on the 'prior knowledge' that patients bring to the consultation.[2]

Another social trend has also tended to bring medical narratives and lay accounts closer together: the tension between 'doubt' and 'certainty' in medicine has shifted over time, as medical culture increasingly places a value on open disclosure. Patients understandably want certainty in the explanations given to them by doctors, and in the past the medical profession was frequently accused of downplaying any

[2] Open University students may wish to read an optional article entitled 'Doctor in the house: the Internet as a source of lay health knowledge and the challenge to expertise', by Michael Hardey, in *Health and Disease: A Reader* (Open University Press, 3rd edn 2001).

uncertainty as though it were an embarrassment. However, in an increasingly litigious world, the paternalistic tradition in Western medicine that 'doctor knows best' has somewhat eroded, and medical narratives have begun to acknowledge difficulties in reaching an unequivocal diagnosis, in accurately predicting the prognosis, or in choosing the optimum treatment. Thus, patient and doctor are now more likely to share the burden of uncertainty in making sense of the illness and its consequences.

However, there are important differences in their approach to the medical narrative. The doctor's aim is to diagnose and treat a *disorder*, whereas the patient additionally strives to achieve a personally meaningful understanding of the *illness*. Moreover, Western doctors are trained in a scientific tradition that values the *objectivity* of measurable signs and symptoms, such as blood test results or a persistent cough, and which encourages them to note only these objective features as medically significant when they 'take a history' from the patient. Doctors therefore listen *selectively* to the patient's story about why medical help has been sought, sifting through details that have personal meaning for the patient but which seem irrelevant to reaching a medical diagnosis.

As a consequence of these different agendas, the doctor is unlikely to be able to answer some of the patient's most pressing questions, such as 'Why me? Why now? What next?'. Since all predictions are made on the basis of population averages, the doctor cannot know the extent to which this particular patient's future will depart from the average pattern. The doctor is dealing in probabilities whereas the patient has a need for personal certainty. Advocates of a more patient-centred approach accuse modern medical narratives of substituting 'science' for empathy in the hierarchy of clinical skills. As a result:

> At its most arid, modern medicine lacks a metric for existential qualities such as the inner hurt, despair, hope, grief, and moral pain that frequently accompany, and often indeed constitute, the illnesses from which people suffer. (Greenhalgh and Hurwitz, 1999, p.50)

The greater the uncertainty about diagnosis or prognosis, the greater the gap between professional knowledge and personal experience, which the patient has somehow to bridge. Lay people generally attempt this reconciliation by making a journey into their personal history to collect meaningful evidence.

1.4   Personal illness narratives

Sociologists refer to the process of 'making up a meaningful story to explain my illness' as constructing a **personal illness narrative**, which is unique to that individual and which attempts to make sense of the illness as an understandable event occurring at that point in the person's life. These stories about illness do much more than repeat 'the facts' as they unfolded over time — they also encompass the feelings and perceptions of everyone involved. The strands from which these narratives can be woven are extremely varied and grand narratives such as medicine, psychological theories and religion are only a part of the source material.

● Think back to a time in the past when you felt ill and try to recall the sources of information you drew on when deciding what your symptoms 'meant'.

■ We can only guess, but you may have used information from previous contacts with 'healers' from orthodox or alternative traditions, reports in the news media,

TV documentaries and dramas, conversations with friends and family, books and educational courses, 'folklore' about the possible causes of your condition, traditional remedies handed down from generation to generation, and so on.

Each personal account describes a dynamic state of *illness* (as distinct from 'wellness'), which incorporates a rich variety of information and a wealth of detail that the storyteller sees as important factors in his or her experience. The emerging narrative is unique because the 'ingredients' vary between individuals and because it tends to incorporate past events in that person's life which *now* come to seem significant in the light of present symptoms. For example, to the person who wakes up with a chest infection, a recent walk home in the damp night air may suddenly seem important, and this in turn may prompt the narrator to reach further back to a childhood spent in a damp inner-city flat. Consider a fragment from the personal illness narrative of a woman who was ultimately diagnosed as having multiple sclerosis (MS):

> I lived at home with either my mother or my father being ill. I decided I had to leave because I was becoming ill, and did, but then my mother developed nephrosis in both her kidneys … I went back to look after her and after a while had an old-fashioned nervous breakdown … I nursed her until she died … Sometime after I kept having peculiar symptoms but I thought it was probably all the stress I had been under … Then my husband insisted that I get medical advice, and later he was told I had MS, 4 months after we were married. (Quoted in Robinson, 1990, p. 1184)

In looking back over her life, she is reconsidering certain events and giving them a new meaning as they become woven into her explanation of 'Why me? Why now?'. The sociologist Gareth Williams (one of the authors of this book), refers to this process as **narrative reconstruction**; you will meet examples of it in later chapters.[3]

● Which of the 'grand narratives' in Box 1.1 appear to have been woven into the personal illness narrative of the woman quoted above?

■ She has drawn on the 'grand narrative' of biomedicine when she says that her mother 'developed nephrosis in both her kidneys', and possibly also on psychological theories when she says she had 'an old-fashioned nervous breakdown'.

The purposes of constructing a personal illness narrative may be as obvious as they are varied. We feel in greater control of events if we can 'see where they came from'; thinking the sequence through may enable us to prevent the illness in the future or reduce its impact now; perhaps our story will help us to counter accusations of blame for our ill health; or it may reinforce our faith in (for example) medicine or religion, which will sustain us in difficult times ahead if the condition worsens.

> Seen in this light, the medical consultation becomes an opportunity for dialogue between different stories: the patient's biographical one and the doctor's professional one. (Launer, 1999, p. 119)

[3] A TV programme entitled 'Why me? Why now?' for Open University students accompanies *Medical Knowledge: Doubt and Certainty* (Open University Press, 2nd edn 1994; colour-enhanced 2nd edn 2001), and explores the methods used by sociologists to analyse personal illness narratives. Research by Gareth Williams is featured in the programme.

Within a certain culture and period there is some stability in the dominant themes that emerge in a wide variety of personal illness narratives, and some may even come to characterise a period. For example, 'stress' has become an increasingly prevalent element in explanations of illness since the 1990s,[4] as illustrated by the last extract from the woman with multiple sclerosis.

For an individual who has constructed a reasonably satisfactory personal account of their illness or disability, the dominant themes generally remain relatively stable over time. But variations may emerge in response to cultural shifts; for example, the prominence of genetic explanations increased dramatically when the first draft of the human genome was published in 2000. The account may also contain different elements depending on the 'audience': some themes in the narrative may be given more prominence in public settings where the storyteller has to establish his or her credentials among relative strangers, than they are in the private accounts told to close confidants.[5]

Discontinuities between our private beliefs, the views of the 'experts' we encounter and the 'common knowledge' about a condition that prevails in a society, help to sustain a tension between stability and variability in the meaning ascribed to an illness. If personal explanations of causes and symptoms integrate very easily with those of health professionals, then the stability of the personal narrative is reinforced. But what happens when the personal and professional perspectives are impossible to reconcile? Think for a moment of the dedicated smoker with a wheezy cough who wants to reject the medical narrative that smoking greatly increases the risk of bronchitis. Maintaining a personal narrative that excludes the role of cigarettes may be a tough proposition in the anti-smoking culture that currently prevails in the UK.

1.5 Five case studies

Everything that you have read thus far has been laying a foundation for the rest of the book, and in particular it informs our choice of case studies.

The most intense struggles to 'make sense' of what is going on are revealed in disorders that display the greatest uncertainty, not only among the patients and their family and friends, but also among the professionals who try to define, treat, predict or prevent these conditions. With this in mind, we chose five highly contrasting disorders (Box 1.2), which have uncertainty as their shared feature.

All of these conditions illustrate the contribution of professional narratives from a range of disciplines, including biomedicine, epidemiology and sociology, in attempting to reach an understanding of these complex states of ill health. They also demonstrate the power of personal illness narratives to deflect the 'world shattering' impact of an uncertain prognosis by 'making sense' of the condition.

All of them affect significant numbers of people around the world and cause considerable suffering. Four of the major physiological systems of the body are represented: the musculo-skeletal, immune, respiratory and nervous systems. They

---

[4] A discussion of stress and health, particularly among adults in the workplace, occurs in another book in this series, *Birth to Old Age: Health in Transition* (Open University Press, 2nd edn 1995; colour-enhanced 2nd edn 2001), Chapter 8.

[5] A discussion of the difference between 'public' and 'private' accounts occurs in another book in this series, *Studying Health and Disease* (Open University Press, 2nd edn 1994; colour-enhanced 2nd edn 2001), Chapter 3.

Box 1.2   Case studies for this book

- *Rheumatoid arthritis* — a chronic, painful, intermittently progressive and often permanently disabling condition, primarily affecting the joints (Chapter 3);

- *HIV and AIDS* — a viral infection that gradually destroys the immune system, leading to other, usually fatal infections unless costly drugs are available (Chapter 4);

- *Asthma* — a fluctuating respiratory disorder which is usually self-managed, but may relapse into an acute attack requiring emergency treatment (Chapter 5);

- *Schizophrenia* — a severe disturbance of thought processes which alters the perception of reality and may include delusions (Chapter 6);

- *Chronic pain* — a disabling state of suffering experienced in a range of illnesses and injuries (Chapter 7).

can also affect people of any age, although the onset of rheumatoid arthritis and chronic pain is commonest beyond middle age, whereas the other conditions are generally first diagnosed in younger adults or in children. They are all chronic conditions, in that people with these diagnoses must currently learn to live with the condition for years, indeed generally for the rest of their lives. Their symptoms classically 'relapse and remit', but some conditions (notably asthma and AIDS) may flare up in acute life-threatening episodes. All can lead to premature death, but there is a wide range in their fatality rates.

These case studies also illustrate a sort of hierarchy in the 'professional status' attached to certain diseases, which is only dimly visible to people outside the professions. For example, rheumatology (the branch of medicine concerned with arthritis and other rheumatic conditions) and pain management have never been 'fashionable' specialties, attracting the huge amounts of research funding and prestigious professorial appointments associated in recent years with HIV and AIDS. The focus on asthma has been rising since the 1990s, whereas it could be said that schizophrenia was attracting most attention in the 1960s and 1970s. This is but one example of the many ways in which the experience of health and disease can be affected by factors in the wider social fabric. You will encounter many others in the course of this book.

But before commencing on the case studies, we want you to consider another important aspect of the tension between personal experiences of illness and disability and professional explanations of disease. In Chapter 2, 'Stigma and normality', we examine the forces at work in a culture that often lead people to shun the 'sick' and identify themselves with the 'well'. Why is it that some diseases are so stigmatising that people who are affected by them must cope not only with the physical manifestations of their illness and its direct impact on their lives, but also with the rejection of those who consider themselves 'normal'? In this book, AIDS and schizophrenia are examples of highly stigmatised conditions, whereas people with rheumatoid arthritis, asthma or chronic pain experience far less exclusion from 'normal' society.

Finally, a health warning: it is the explicit intention of the authors of this book to take you into awkward territory, where definitions are contested and strategies are the subject of controversy, where personal experiences are often painful and the medical profession frequently finds itself unable to alter the course of a disease. We do not expect to provide simple answers to complex questions, for there are few enough. Our aim is to promote a greater understanding of the complexity of human health, disease, disability and illness, and thereby to strengthen the case for multidisciplinary and collaborative approaches to prevention and treatment.

OBJECTIVES FOR CHAPTER 1

When you have studied this chapter, you should be able to:

1.1 Define and use, or recognise definitions and applications of, each of the terms printed in **bold** in the text.

1.2 Give examples of ways in which the experience of an illness or disability can be affected by the social construction of the condition at that time and place.

1.3 Discuss the interactions and potential conflicts between grand narratives (such as biomedicine, psychological theories and religion) as explanations for disease and suffering, and personal illness narratives.

QUESTIONS FOR CHAPTER 1

1 (*Objective 1.2*)

What changes took place in the social construction of coronary heart disease (CHD) in the UK during the twentieth century? (Open University students should refer to *Dilemmas in UK Health Care*, Open University Press, 3rd edn 2001, Chapter 8.) How have these changes influenced attitudes to treatment?

2 (*Objective 1.3*)

What grand narrative does this man appear to be drawing on when constructing the following personal illness narrative, and how has he 'made sense' of his diabetes?

> It's an enemy I've made an ally of. Really, I don't think I'd still be here, if I hadn't been diabetic. It's like the paradox of the return of the prodigal son. It kicked me out of Eden alright, having to, you know, be on my best behaviour so much and think about when to shoot up and all that. But it was what I needed. (Quoted in Charmaz, 1997; an edited version of this article appears in *Health and Disease: A Reader*, Open University Press, 3rd edn 2001.)

CHAPTER 2

Stigma and normality

Study notes for OU students

During your study of Section 2.1 you will be asked to read an article entitled 'The insanity of place' by Erving Goffman, which appears in *Health and Disease: A Reader* (Open University Press, third edition 2001). Two other Reader articles, 'Illness as metaphor' by Susan Sontag and 'Normal rubbish: deviant patients in casualty departments' by Roger Jeffery, are optional reading. A TV programme on the experience of facial disfigurement, called 'More than meets the eye', is closely associated with this chapter. Before starting this chapter, you may also find it useful to review the discussion of the sick role given in the first book in this series *Medical Knowledge: Doubt and Certainty*, (Open University Press, second edition 1994; colour-enhanced second edition 2001), Chapter 8. This chapter was written by Clive Seale, Professor of Medical Sociology at Goldsmiths' College, University of London.

As Sicknesse is the greatest misery, so the greatest of sicknes is solitude; when the infectiousnes of the disease deterrs them who should assist, from comming; even the Phisician dares scarse come ... it is Outlawry, an Excommunication upon the patient ... (John Donne, 'Devotions upon emergent occasions', 1627, quoted in Sontag, 1991, p. 120)

2.1   Introduction

The term *stigma* was coined originally by the Greeks to describe the practice of branding slaves to indicate their status. Just as such marks on the body were once used to indicate inferiority or unusual status (Figure 2.1), so some illnesses have been used from time to time to mark people out as set apart from 'normal' people. **Stigma**, in the modern sense, involves the deliberate exclusion of certain categories of person, a type of inflicted social pain. However, just as some people specialise in caring for individuals with pain, so some make it their business to champion the cause of people who are stigmatised.

Figure 2.1   *Marks on the body have signified unusual status in many cultures since ancient times. Christ shows the stigmata (marks of the crucifixion) as proof of his resurrection, in a seventeenth-century painting,* The Doubting Thomas, *by Leendert van der Cooghen. (Source: Courtesy of the Royal Cabinet of Paintings, Mauritshuis, The Hague, Netherlands)*

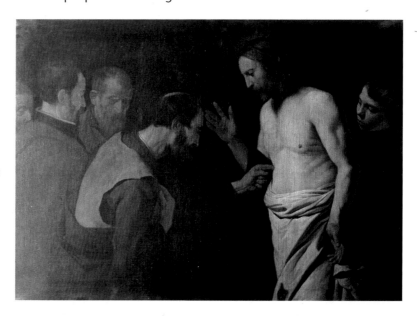

Several of the diseases that you will read about in this book have been used, at one time or another, as marks of stigma. Perhaps the best known of these currently is HIV and AIDS, where affected people have been subjected to a variety of discriminatory practices, but also have attracted a number of champions to their cause. Schizophrenia too — indeed mental illness generally — has often been the occasion for struggle over imputations of a discredited or shameful identity. The sociologist Erving Goffman, whose work on stigma will be discussed later in the chapter, wrote an article published in 1969 called 'The insanity of place', in which he explores differences between physical and mental illnesses. An extract appears in *Health and Disease: A Reader* (Open University Press, 3rd edn 2001). (Open University students should read this now and then consider the following questions.)

● According to Goffman, how does mental illness differ from physical illness in its effect on a person's relationships with others?

■   With a physical illness, people are more likely to indicate to others that, but for their illness, they would be playing their normal part in family and work life. The symptoms of mental illness, on the other hand, are more likely to be construed as an *offence* against normal codes of behaviour.

●   What is the effect of this in families, according to Goffman?

■   Family members are likely to seek actively to define the person as mentally ill in order to validate their own view of normal family life. Factions may develop, where the 'patient' is watched and the patient may feel conspired against. Outsiders are drawn in to sustain a definition of the patient as ill. As Goffman puts it, 'The family is turned inside out'.

The illness conditions that give rise to stigma vary from one culture to another. At different times and in different cultures certain illnesses have been stigmatised that in other social contexts are unremarked upon. To understand why this is so it is necessary to explore the psychosocial forces that underlie the phenomenon. Particular stigmas depend on particular definitions of what it is to be normal. The roots of the desire to be normal, and the source of changing standards of normality are explored in the first section of the chapter.

We then turn to a detailed discussion of the problems faced by people suffering from stigmatised conditions.[1] There are different varieties of stigma, and Goffman's work is central to understanding how this variety affects interaction between people. Finally, the chapter considers the contribution of health-care workers to stigma. For example, organised medicine can play a powerful role in creating and sustaining stigmatised identities; on the other hand, medicine has the capacity to challenge these identities. First, though, let us examine briefly the nature of normality, and the roots of the desire to be considered normal. This will involve a diversion into some more general considerations, before returning to the specific problems of illness.

2.2 Being normal

2.2.1 Normality as an agreement

Human social life is based upon fundamental agreements between people about what is to be counted as normal. This is reflected in even the most apparently routine interactions, as is demonstrated by the following dialogue between two people who have just seen each other:

> S: (*waving his hand cheerily*) How are you?
>
> E: How am I in regard to what? My health, my finance, my school work, my peace of mind, my …
>
> S: (*red in the face and suddenly out of control*) Look! I was just trying to be polite. Frankly, I don't give a damn how you are.
>
> (Adapted from Garfinkel, 1963, p. 222)

---

[1] Open University students will find it useful to watch the TV programme 'More than meets the eye' close to their study of this section. Please consult the notes in the *Audiovisual Media Guide* before watching the programme.

The American sociologist Harold Garfinkel conducted experiments, of which this was one, in which he deliberately ignored rules of normal conduct and observed the effects. The resultant disruption revealed the remarkable extent to which human social life depends on taken-for-granted assumptions about normal behaviour. Much humour depends on exploiting this fact.

● What causes the following interaction to be funny?

> *A*: Where are you going?
>
> *B*: I'm going quietly round the bend.
>
> (Giddens, 1989, p. 96)

■ B has deliberately 'misunderstood' the normal meaning of A's question in order ironically to convey his state of mind.

Norms of conduct can be as basic as sustaining mutual agreements about the meanings of words, or they may involve larger matters, such as conforming to a particular set of moral principles. The concept of **membership** is useful here. In recognising mutually agreed norms people are demonstrating their membership of the social group to which — at least for that moment — they belong. Naturally, the breaking of rules can threaten claims to membership. This may at times be deliberate, as in the following interaction between a parent and a teenager:

> *P*: Where are you going?
>
> *T*: Out.
>
> *P*: What are you going to do?
>
> *T*: Nothing.
>
> (Giddens, 1989, p. 96)

2.2.2 The variability of social norms

The designation of a particular state as stigmatised involves drawing a boundary between membership and non-membership of a social group on the basis of conformity to standards of normality. These standards, which sociologists call **social norms**, influence whom we regard as a legitimate, creditable member of the group in which we claim membership; they are constructed as a matter of tacit social agreement. People lay claim to their own membership of the group, and police the claims of others according to standards which are in part 'handed down', and which are in part subject to negotiation and change. Inevitably, this means that definitions of what it is to be 'normal' vary across different social groups. Stigmatised qualities, as representations of the abnormal, must therefore also be variable.

For example, you will learn in Chapter 6 that there is variability in the social norms defining mental illness. Some people argue that the norms applied by Western psychiatrists to diagnose schizophrenia in African-Caribbean males are culturally inappropriate. What may be acceptable in West Indian culture as a form of religious possession, appears to some psychiatrists as schizophrenia.[2]

---

[2] This argument is also proposed in an article by Cecil Helman, entitled 'Cross-cultural psychiatry', in *Health and Disease: A Reader* (Open University Press, 3rd edn 2001), which Open University students will study with Chapter 6.

Although social norms are culturally variable they are not, however, simply selected at random. The norms subscribed to in a particular society evolve over a long period of time, and reflect underlying social forces. For example, the way in which our modern habits, now interpreted as having a 'hygienic' rationale, have evolved over several centuries is shown in the extract in Box 2.1 from European books on manners, presented with dates of authorship.

Box 2.1   Trends in the social construction of hygienic behaviour

Thirteenth century: When you blow your nose or cough, turn around so that nothing falls on the table.

1558: It does not befit a modest, honourable man to prepare to relieve nature in the presence of other people … Similarly, he will not wash his hands on returning to decent society from private places, as the reason for his washing will arouse disagreeable thoughts in people.

1560: It is a far too dirty thing for a child to offer others something he has gnawed, or something he disdains to eat himself, unless it be to his servant … he must not lift the meat to his mouth now with one hand and now with the other … he should always do so with his right hand, taking the bread or meat decently with three fingers only …

1672: If everyone is eating from the same dish, you should take care not to put your hand in it before those of higher rank do so.

1714: Wherever you spit, you should put your foot on the saliva … At the houses of the great, one spits into one's handkerchief.

1859: Spitting is at all times a disgusting habit, I need say nothing more than — never indulge in it. Beside being coarse and atrocious, it is very bad for the health.

(From various books on manners, quoted in Elias, 1978, pp. 91, 92, 131, 143, 154, 156)

All except the first and last of these extracts describe behaviour that today would be considered abnormal, marking out a person as socially inferior, blameworthy and in need of correction. Yet they are presented as models of good behaviour, whereby readers who followed them could gain acceptability in privileged social circles. It is easy to see that the direction to which these extracts point is towards modern standards, nowadays often justified on the grounds of hygiene. Yet they were formulated before there was a general acceptance that dirt contains germs that lead to disease, representing moments in historical negotiations about standards of behaviour.

The extracts in Box 2.1 were collected by a sociologist called Norbert Elias who was interested in the historical development of social norms, and in particular how these reflected what he came to call a **civilising process** (Elias, 1978, 1982). Elias describes how many aspects of 'manners' have changed, covering — in addition to the matters outlined above — attitudes to public nakedness, to sleeping in the same bed and towards defecating in the view of others, the use of forks, and taboos on the use of knives at table. Changes in the social norms governing all of these behaviours, he argues, have been in the same general direction: the threshold at which shame and disgust are elicited has shifted so that many behaviours once considered acceptable now give offence. Children undergo a personal 'civilising process' as part of their upbringing, the purpose of learning such 'manners' being to show sensitivity towards the feelings of others by encouraging a feeling of shame about certain bodily behaviours. Elias uses the concept of *sociogenesis* to summarise his belief that these mass psychological changes are social in origin, rather than the product of some innate change in human nature. He links the civilising process to the growing complexity of modern society compared with feudal medieval societies.

In the past, for example, power was gained and defended by force of arms, and there were no very powerful sources of central authority. As these developed, however, social advancement came increasingly to depend on skills of diplomacy and the calculation of likely consequences of actions, involving intensive study of others' feelings and prediction of their likely reactions. Whereas in the past, other people could be simply divided into enemies and friends, now all people were, potentially, both. Interpersonal relationships thus became vastly more complex. Cults of refined sensibility, which arose at first in courtly society, spread gradually to other social groups in the towns, resulting today in a degree of social stratification of manners which now indicate class distinctions.

'Manners' serve to indicate membership of particular groups, drawing boundary lines between those who belong and those who do not. They may be used deliberately to gain strategic advantage, as is seen in the social climber who, insecure of his or her position, invests considerable energy in demonstrating the inferiority of those who have not yet mastered rules of refined behaviour. Illness presents quite fundamental challenges to membership and normality which, if not *legitimised* by a medical label indicating that the person has a right to enter the *sick role*,[3] may be resented by people who expect the person to play a normal part in social life. Illness labels may also be used to designate inferiority in other people, bolstering the security of 'normals' in their own claims to membership. This is what is meant by the stigma of illness. Paradoxically, sick people may themselves be particularly concerned to draw firm boundaries between legitimate and illegitimate sickness in order to sustain the 'value' of the currency from which their own label is drawn. The parallel here is the social climber who displays a particular aptitude for exposing other social climbers.

2.2.3 Defending against anxiety

We turn now to the psychological roots of the desire to claim membership of a group. It is helpful to think of this as sustaining a sense of **ontological security**. 'Ontology' refers to the philosophical study of *being*. 'Ontological security' indicates a primary and basic sense of security about being in the world, which underlies a person's capacity to engage in the business of living. For most of us, a basic sense of optimism about continuing in life is inculcated at a very early stage in human development by the experience of trust. This in turn generates the perception that, rather than living in a world of purposeless chaos, there is an order and a meaning to life. The sociologist Anthony Giddens describes this first stage in the formulation of self-identity as:

> … a sort of emotional inoculation against existential anxieties —
> a protection against future threats and dangers which allows the

---

[3] The sick role, and the role of doctors in guarding entry to it, is discussed in *Medical Knowledge: Doubt and Certainty* (Open University Press, 2nd edn 1994; colour-enhanced 2nd edn 2001), Chapter 8. The sick role consists of a series of obligations which, it is argued, people who claim the right to be called 'sick' need to fulfil.

> individual to sustain hope and courage in the face of whatever
> debilitating circumstances she or he might later confront. (Giddens,
> 1991, p. 39)

Young children experience some fundamental anxieties that centre on trust: when a parent leaves the room, for example, the baby must 'trust' that he or she will return and often experiences difficulty in doing so. The psychic processes involved in dealing with these primary anxieties about one's place in the world are dealt with, in part, by a psychological mechanism known as **projection**, described here by Sigmund Freud as a:

> … particular way of dealing with any internal excitations which
> produce too great an increase of unpleasure. There is a tendency
> to treat them as though they were acting, not from the inside,
> but from the outside, so that it may be possible to bring [a] shield
> … into operation as a means of defence against them. (Freud,
> 1920, p. 32)

Psychoanalytic theory suggests that an individual's sense of self is made up of thoughts, wishes and feelings which are often in conflict with one another.[4] Angry feelings about the people whom we love, for example, produce an unpleasant contradiction between the two emotions, resulting in a sensation of guilt. This is an 'unpleasure' which some people deal with by blaming the loved person for creating the conflict, resulting in accusations of bad behaviour that the other person feels are false. Thus, in projection, uncomfortable parts of the self which, if acknowledged, would create unpleasant feelings about ourselves, are attributed to (projected onto) outside objects, commonly other people. These others then become 'bad' for causing our discomfort.

To take the projection one stage further, we may imagine the other person feels aggression towards us; at its extreme, this can become paranoia. As a further twist, *good* parts of the self may also be projected into others, so that people come to **idealise** these others and imagine they have admirable qualities. Sometimes this is due to an over-compensation for hostile feelings towards the person thus idealised.

2.2.4 Sustaining membership through ritual

Ontological security in everyday social life is routinely threatened and repaired, most of the time occasioning no reflective thought at all. Garfinkel's experiments reveal the potential for chaos that exists from moment to moment, but which is hardly ever realised. This is because of the mundane nature of much social interaction and the ready availability of strategies for repair. Occasionally, however, major events occur which offer more serious threats to ontological security and require 'answers'. Chief among these are illness and death, which serve as frightening reminders of human fragility.

Stigma in relation to illness can be understood as a response to the threat it poses to ontological security. Firstly, an ontological 'offence' is experienced as the display of disease or deformity reminds the onlooker of the capacity of their own body or mind to deteriorate. Secondly, as the 'unpleasure' that this provokes is experienced, the onlooker projects this bad feeling onto the ill or disfigured person, 'accusing' them of behaviour that has caused this discomfort or 'offence' to the

---

[4] This 'psychodynamic' view of the conscious and unconscious inner world is explored more fully in *Birth to Old Age: Health in Transition* (Open University Press, 2nd edn 1995; colour-enhanced 2nd edn 2001), Chapter 6.

onlooker. These accusations may involve the imputation of moral deficiencies in the person stigmatised. This, however, is secondary to the original ontological 'offence' of displaying disease.

For most of human history people have turned to religious explanations for answers to the major events that threaten ontological security. Religious rituals in their original forms were not just matters of affirming belief, but occasions where members of a social group gathered to generate emotional energy which bound them together in the face of potential threats. They involved the veneration of sacred objects or symbols, which were invested with the values of the community involved. Religious ceremonies were of particular importance at times when individuals were undergoing major transformations, such as birth, marriage or death, which threatened changes to the routine ordering of social life. They also became important when the group was threatened by an outside enemy. The night before a battle occasioned much praying, as did the beds of the sick, who were threatened by a different sort of enemy.

A notable feature of traditional societies, and of religious followings, is that they are apt to make firm divisions between people who are enemies and people who are friends. This leads to the formation of a distinct group or 'tribal' identity that serves to preserve *solidarity*, a feeling of togetherness in the face of threat. One of the peculiar features of the modern vantage point, where it is possible to survey a variety of groups and to review a series of religions, all of which may lay claim to represent the one true faith, is the possibility of seeing the apparent contradictions of the claims made by different social groups. These reveal a shared underlying motive.

2.2.5 Stigma and modern society

Modern societies differ from traditional societies in ways that make fixed definitions of normality difficult to sustain. A variety of systems of belief compete with each other for people's allegiance. For example, commitment to a *single* religious system is no longer widespread in the UK: religion becomes a matter of belief or non-belief, rather than a part of an unquestioned background assumption about the nature of the world. Science competes with religion, and there are many critics of science as well. In short, such *grand narratives*,[5] which make the individual's anxieties feel manageable (sometimes called *containing* the anxiety), and which explain to him or her how to behave, are less available in modern societies. This can contribute to the 'stress' that is so often described as characteristic of modern times.[6]

Additionally, everyday social life has become considerably more complex, involving most individuals in a large variety of social settings, all of which make different demands on appropriate behaviour. Thus modern conditions make unusually strong demands on people's capacity to tolerate differences. Particularly in middle-class circles (where the pacifying effect of the civilising process is, perhaps, at its most extreme), there is much talk of tolerance as a desirable social value, and eruptions of tribal enmity (for example, between rival football fans) are frequently characterised as 'primitive'. Psychotherapy exists, in part, to deal with the difficulties people have in managing the demanding pressures of tolerance.

---

[5] Defined in Chapter 1 of this book.

[6] An analysis of 'role conflict' in producing stress appears in *Birth to Old Age: Health in Transition* (Open University Press, 2nd edn 1995; colour-enhanced 2nd edn 2001) Chapter 8, and is also relevant here.

Without the security provided by grand narratives, people are prone to project their difficulties onto others. At the same time, it is not always clear who these others should be. Grand narratives in traditional societies often serve to channel hostility towards 'safe' enemies — non-believers, people who believe in the 'wrong' things, the unhygienic, or simply strangers — who either live at a safe distance, or can be killed with impunity. Nowadays there are few enemies who are in this sense 'safe' for people to hate. The modern individual lives the life of a diplomat, whereas the traditional individual may be better characterised as a warrior.

This is not to say that opportunities for tribal enmity are entirely absent in modern society, or that grand narratives are unavailable to sustain them. The genocidal conflicts in Bosnia and Rwanda during the 1990s, and the violent politics of racial differences that occasionally erupt in the UK, are sufficient to remind us of the potential of grand narrative to identify 'safe' enemies to hate. However, in the usual run of everyday life in the UK diplomacy is better rewarded. On the one hand, because of the great variety of different social groups that continually present themselves, modern social conditions offer plentiful opportunities for categories of stigma to arise (Figure 2.2). On the other hand, these categories are also likely to be challenged. This may be followed by the negotiation of new categories of stigmatised identity.

Figure 2.2   *All societies contain groups that have a strong 'tribal' identity, reinforcing the sense of solidarity among their members, but frequently attracting stigmatising labels from outsiders. These 'travellers' at the Appleby Horse Fair are 'gypsies' to most householders. (Photo: Ian Simpson/Photofusion)*

The very fact that stigma can itself be a 'topic' for discussion and debate is a feature of modern social conditions which encourage us constantly to reflect on our attitudes. Indeed we gain university degrees for doing so! Because norms are not fixed matters but are constantly negotiated, those that define stigmatised individuals can at times be successfully challenged and overthrown. Sometimes such challenges come from the people who are stigmatised themselves, spurred on by the vicissitudes of managing this stigma — a trial to which we now turn our attention.

2.3 Managing stigma

The following was written by Paul Hunt, who lived and died with muscular dystrophy:

> … we are representatives of many of the things that they [the able-bodied] most fear — tragedy, loss, dark and the unknown. Involuntarily we walk, or more often we sit, in the valley of the shadow of death. Contact with us throws up in people's faces the fact of sickness and death in the world, which in themselves are an affront to all our aspirations and hopes. A deformed and paralysed body attacks everyone's sense of well-being and invincibility. People do not want to acknowledge what disability affirms — that life is tragic and we shall all soon be dead. So they are inclined to avoid those who are sick or old, shying from the disturbing reminders of unwelcome reality. (Hunt, 1966, quoted by Shearer, 1981, in Black *et al.*, 1984, p. 276)

Individuals with stigmatising conditions face particular problems in managing their self-identities in social interaction. In *Stigma: Notes on the Management of Spoiled Identity*, the sociologist Erving Goffman (1968) presented an illuminating set of ideas that summarise these problems, and these have been elaborated by subsequent writers, examples of whose work will be used here. Goffman describes encounters between people with stigmas and 'normals' as 'one of the primal scenes in sociology' (Goffman, 1968, p. 24); he believed that the management of boundaries between normality and abnormality is central to the organisation of social life (Figure 2.3).

Figure 2.3 *According to Goffman, managing the boundaries between 'normality' and 'abnormality' is central to the organisation of social life. Is this meeting between a visually impaired person and a sighted person a 'primal scene'? (Photo: Gideon Mendel/Network Photographers)*

The major ceremonial moments referred to previously, such as religious events, are large-scale and dramatic enactments of group solidarity. Goffman's insight lies in his perception that the mundane events of everyday social interaction also constitute *rituals*. Showing deference to one's social superiors by an appropriate use of words or body language, greeting friends in the manner you and they expect, serve to affirm membership by demonstrating common understandings. Encounters with stigmatised individuals provide a series of threats to membership and ontological security, which are routinely patched up.

2.3.1 Strategies to minimise stigmatisation

A summary of the main terms and distinctions used by Goffman and others in analysing the strategies used to manage and thereby to minimise the threat of stigmatisation is given in Box 2.2. Most of these terms will be used again later in this book.

Box 2.2 Strategies to manage stigmatisation

Virtual social identity and **actual social identity**: A *virtual social identity* is the character and attributes that 'normals' expect a person will possess. *Actual social identity* is what is discovered about the attributes a person truly possesses. Stigma arises from a discrepancy between the two that is discrediting. Thus a person whose history of admissions to mental hospitals is revealed may experience rejection for causing such a discrepancy in the eyes of those who expected something else.

Discreditable stigmas and **discredited stigmas**: Some stigmatised attributes are hidden from observers, such as being HIV-positive, and so the person is potentially *discreditable* if the attribute should eventually be revealed. Discreditable stigmas pose problems of managing the disclosure of information. Others, for example the deformities associated with advanced stages of rheumatoid arthritis, are obvious at first sight, and the person is immediately *discredited* in the eyes of disapproving others.

Passing and **covering**: These are strategies of information control relevant to discreditable and discredited stigmas. *Passing* involves the concealment of a 'discreditable' stigma (for example, a person concealing on an insurance form the fact of having had an HIV test); such behaviour is sometimes referred to pejoratively as 'passing oneself off' as normal. *Covering* involves preventing a visible, 'discredited' stigma from looming large, as when a person with visual impairment wears dark glasses.

Enacted stigma and **felt stigma**: Stigma may be experienced in acts of persecution or discrimination by others, in which case it is *enacted*. Alternatively, this enactment may be so feared by the stigmatised individual that he or she acts to avoid potential difficulties; this is known as *felt* stigma. Thus a person with epilepsy may avoid trying for job interviews, or proposing marriage, because he or she fears discrimination.

Master status: This refers to the 'spoiling' effect that a stigma has on other aspects of a person's identity. Once a stigma becomes known, many aspects of a person's behaviour come to be interpreted in that light. For example, if someone with a history of mental illness becomes angry, this is seen as a manifestation of the illness, which in another person might be interpreted as justified anger. Thus 'mentally ill' has become the person's *master status*. 'Secondary deviance' may then occur, whereby the person reacts to others' imputation of stigma by behaving in further deviant ways.

The own and **the wise**: These are two sets of sympathetic others, the *own* being the group of fellow sufferers (e.g. other HIV-positive people), and the *wise* being 'normals' who by virtue of their special knowledge and sympathy for the condition become 'courtesy' members of the stigmatised group (for example, 'buddies' for people with AIDS).

2.3.2 Classifying stigmatising conditions

Additionally, stigmatising conditions can be broadly divided into three classes:

1 blemishes of the body, including physical deformities like leprosy, scars or birthmarks, body-piercing and tattoos;

2 blemishes of the character or behaviour, like alcoholism or 'bad manners';

3 **tribal stigma**, gained by virtue of belonging to a particular social group which is already stigmatised, such as a religious, ethnic or racial group; other stigmatised 'tribes' include gay men and lesbians, 'the elderly', drug addicts, people with mental health problems or a criminal record.

● From your general knowledge, how does the stigmatisation of HIV and AIDS combine all the three classes listed above?

■ People with HIV or AIDS may: (i) exhibit visible signs of the disease such as severe weight loss or dark patches on the skin (Kaposi's sarcoma) which can be disfiguring; (ii) be blamed for bringing the virus upon themselves by sexual behaviour others consider to be wrong; and (iii) suffer prejudice (*enacted stigma*) because of the association of HIV with already-stigmatised 'tribes', such as gay men, drug users or prostitutes.

Other conditions may be restricted to only one of these classes of stigma.

● Which stigmas are sometimes applied to blindness or to mental illness?

■ Blindness attracts the first class of stigma — a blemish of the body. Mental illness attracts the second — a blemish of the character or behaviour.

2.3.3 Being in public

Gerhard Nijhof, a sociologist from the Netherlands, interviewed people with Parkinson's disease, gathering stories of how they felt when in public places. This disease, which involves gradually increasing signs of stiffness, trembling and shaking, illustrates how a stigmatising condition can progress from one that is *discreditable* to one that is obvious to all, and therefore *discredited*.

> I feel ashamed about the way I'm sitting here talking, totally different … Well, I don't talk any more when I am in a large group, because of the fact that the words come out so awkwardly, don't you think? … I stopped walking in the streets during the day, I found it very awkward to be so visibly in a bad condition … But it's specially with speaking that I have difficulties. I keep my mouth shut. When there are visitors, then my wife speaks. Yes, because I can't speak so well. I have the feeling that people notice. Isn't it? Don't you notice it?
>
> You can take me to a restaurant. If not too difficult things are being served, then I can have dinner with you as usual, without people thinking: what is that old man there, sopping and messing around.
>
> I was very good at disguising it. But one day I went to the hairdresser and he says, you must have a terrible back pain. I said, no, why? He said, you are walking very slowly. I said, I cannot walk fast at all.

So then, yes, I was disguising it for myself. I found it terrible. Of course, you cannot hide anything. Whatever you wear, I mean, everybody sees it. You start to walk with difficulty, you start to act more crazily. I found that very hard. And, well, yes, the hanging over while walking, too. So it is definitely something you cannot disguise. Everybody sees it. You cannot say, as if it is a bad scar, I'm going to wear a dress. Everybody sees it.

Sometimes I have to sign my cheque. Then I think, these people must … think I have stolen the cheque … It's embarrassing.

(Nijhof, 1995, pp. 196–8, 198, 200)

These four examples illustrate the complex strategies of information control that some stigmatised individuals adopt to *pass* as 'normals'. Because they *felt* the stigma of their disease these people did all they could to prevent it being *enacted*. With such a progressive illness, however, strategies for passing as normal may become difficult. A degree of *covering* is only possible at the expense of forgoing things that others take for granted, such as appearing in the street, in restaurants, or even speaking.

Apart from the strain of passing as normal, once disclosed, a stigma can evoke reactions in others which indicate that disability has become an overwhelming *master status*, spreading beyond the confines of the original impairment:

> … the perceived failure to see may be generalised into a gestalt[7] of disability, so that the individual shouts at the blind as if they were deaf or attempts to lift them as if they were crippled. Those confronting the blind may have a whole range of belief that is anchored in the stereotype. (Gowman, quoted in Goffman, 1968, p. 16)

Sometimes, the reactions of others can cause great pain as stigma is *enacted*, as one person with epilepsy told sociologist Graham Scambler:

> This is what I've found, that whenever I tell anybody that I'm epileptic they don't want to know me at all. I've had friends here: as soon as they know I'm epileptic they don't want to know me at all. (Scambler and Hopkins, 1988, p. 166)

And another person with AIDS:

> The nurses are scared of me; the doctors wear masks and sometimes gloves. Even the priest doesn't seem too anxious to shake my hand. What the hell is this? I'm not a leper. Do they want to lock me up and shoot me? I've got no family, no friends. Where do I go? What do I do? God, this is horrible! Is He punishing me? The only thing I got going for me is that I'm not dying — at least, not yet. (Kleinman, 1988, p. 163)

The enactment of stigma can involve an exploitation of power over people whose stigma is such that they are defined as sub-human:

> A Dundee researcher has uncovered an American professor's proposals in the 1950s for radiation experiments on 'idiots and

---

[7] *Gestalt* is a German term referring to the perception of an organised whole that is more than the sum of its parts (for example, a melody as distinct from its separate notes).

feeble-minded children' ... In May 1958 Donald M Pillsbury, professor of dermatology at the University of Pennsylvania, wrote ... 'It would be our plan to give carefully calibrated ionising radiation in varying amounts to small areas of skin in human subjects ...' the principal subjects would be 'idiots and feeble-minded children permanently committed to a home in New Jersey. An excellent rapport with the institution has been established and a number of experimental studies have been carried out there without incident ...' [later he said] 'There would be no concern about the possible genetic effects; these individuals will never reproduce.' (*Times Higher Education Supplement*, 1995, p. 3)

2.3.4 Idealisation and segregation

Some conditions, however, attract *idealisation*, where people imagine that the affected person, by virtue of their experience, possesses special qualities of insight, or is unusually gifted.[8] These idealisations can feel to their recipient, almost as inappropriate as the projection of negative qualities. Thus blind people are sometimes assumed to have special musical gifts, on grounds that deprivation of one sense must produce unusual sensitivity in others. One woman reported that she 'was asked to endorse a perfume, presumably because being sightless my sense of smell was super-discriminating' (Keitlen and Lobsenz, quoted in Goffman, 1968, p. 16). A blind writer described how other people expected him to have an unusually perceptive philosophy of life by virtue of his blindness. As a result:

> You develop a 'philosophy'. People seem to insist that you have one and they think you're kidding when you say you haven't. So you do your best to please and to strangers you encounter on trains, in restaurants, or on the subway who want to know what keeps you going, you give your little piece. You're a man of unusual discernment if you can realise that your philosophy is seldom one of your own devising but a reflection of the world's notions about blindness. (Chevigny, quoted in Goffman, 1968, p. 147)

One strategy that is available to stigmatised individuals is to form a life among their *own*, people who share the same stigma. While such befriending can be immensely helpful, it can also be experienced as unwelcome segregation, as the following example of a newly blind woman being shown around a facility for blind and partially sighted people suggests:

> We visited the Braille library; the classrooms; the clubrooms where the blind members of the music and dramatic groups meet; the recreation hall where on festive occasions the blind dance with the blind; the cafeteria, where all the blind gather to eat together ... I was expected to join this world. To give up my profession and to earn my living making mops ... with other blind people ... I became nauseated with fear as the picture grew in my mind. Never had I come upon such destructive segregation. (Keitlen, quoted in Goffman, 1968, p. 51)

---

[8] Susan Sontag in an article called 'Illness as metaphor', reprinted in *Health and Disease: A Reader* (Open University Press, 3rd edn 2001) discusses how tuberculosis attracted such idealisations in the nineteenth century. Open University students could usefully read this optional article now.

The harmful effects of such segregation have been more widely recognised since Goffman wrote his book on stigma. Additionally, some conditions that attract stigma have, as Goffman puts it, gradually evolved 'softer social labels' as where the word 'blind' is less often used to describe people with this difficulty; words like 'partially sighted', 'unsighted' or 'visually impaired' have come into common usage. This trend reflects a growing awareness of the stigmatising, painful effect of labels such as 'blind'. Indeed, over-use of euphemisms to avoid bad feelings has now become a source of humour, as where short people are described as 'vertically challenged', fat people as 'circumferentially challenged'.

2.3.5 Political action and alliances with 'normals'

The desire to disavow stigmatising labels, or to ameliorate their stigmatising effects, can take the form of an assertive proclamation of human rights. Thus Mike Oliver, a sociologist involved in the promotion of the rights of people with disabilities, has argued against the view that disability constitutes a personal tragedy which, he says, is: 'one more attempt by the able-bodied to disable people with impairment' (when interviewed in 1985 for an audiotape associated with the first edition of this book). At the root of the disability-rights movement is a challenge to standards of normality in a bid to assert membership:

> Able-bodied professionals have tended to see these problems as stemming from the functional limitations of the impaired individual, whereas disabled people have argued that they stem from the failure of physical and social environments to take account of the needs of particular individuals or groups. Is the problem of access to buildings caused by people not being able to walk or by the widespread social practice of having steps in buildings? (Oliver, 1993, p. 61)

Oliver opposes the dominant model of disability as located in the individual with a physical or mental impairment, and points to the society that erects barriers which 'disable' people with impairments from functioning effectively (Figure 2.4).[9] This sort of argument has formed the basis of a vigorous political alliance, where the word 'disability' itself is regarded as a stigmatising label.

The position of 'normals' who regularly interact with stigmatised individuals is of some interest, and relevant to the consideration later in this chapter of the perspective of health-care workers. It is the case that certain individuals become involved in the lives of people who are

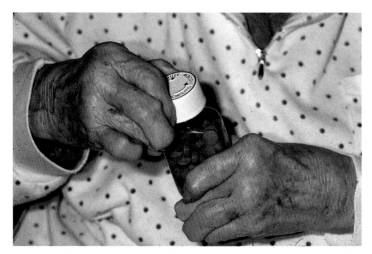

Figure 2.4 *Is physical disability caused by bodily impairments or by an environment that is geared to the needs of the able-bodied? (Photo: Dr P. Marazzi/Science Photo Library)*

[9] Definitions of disability and dependence in later life, and the consequences of adopting either the 'individual model' or the 'social model' of disability, are discussed further in *Birth to Old Age: Health in Transition* (Open University Press, 2nd edn 1995; colour-enhanced 2nd edn 2001), Chapter 11.

stigmatised, and come to identify strongly with their cause, sometimes taking part in the disputed politics of labelling, and achieving as a result what Goffman calls a *courtesy* membership of the group. This is not, however, always an easy position:

> ... a cult of the stigmatised can occur, the stigmaphobic response of the normal being countered by the stigmaphile response of the wise. The person with a courtesy stigma can in fact make both the stigmatised and the normal uncomfortable: by always being ready to carry a burden that is not 'really' theirs, they can confront everyone else with too much morality ... (Goffman, 1968, p. 44)

Relations between stigmatised individuals and others, then, involve a complex acting out of interacting rituals, with claims and counterclaims to membership being made, judged and policed in circumstances where standards are fluid and ever-changing. The ontological security of all parties is continually at stake, with subtle shifts in the negotiation of norms blocking old channels of projection and at the same time offering new opportunities for the negotiation of stigmatised identities.

Viewed from the present day, where 'softer social labels' (to use Goffman's term) have become the norm, the categories used in the past reflect a simpler, cruder world. Then, the 'blind', the 'deaf', the 'poor', the 'feeble minded', 'retarded', 'mad', 'cripples', 'idiots' or 'bastards' were defined quite clearly and, often, permanently. It is probably the case that fixed categories like this are psychologically more easy to maintain for people who are *not* stigmatised — Goffman's so-called 'normals'. But the potentially devastating effects of such labels on the self-esteem of people who *are* thus stigmatised is now more evident. On the other hand, virtues which may now appear outdated, such as compassion, charity, pity and gratitude, were also probably expressed with less inhibition than is now the case. These may have softened the impact of stigma, while at the same time accepting and sustaining the boundaries on which it rested.

2.4   The role of medicine

2.4.1   Medical labelling

If illness represents disorder in the body, medicine seeks to produce order. Medical knowledge, built up over centuries in the Western scientific tradition, categorises body parts, classifies diseases and seeks control over the disordered body through treatments designed to restore normal functioning. Medicine may have achieved its status as a grand narrative because it helps to give a sense of mastery and security in the face of apparently chaotic natural forces that otherwise threaten ontological security. Illness is a reminder of the temporary nature of bodily existence; medicine, in explaining and sometimes banishing disease, helps people 'forget' the limitations of their bodies.

A description of the normal body underlies scientific medicine,[10] and much medical research is devoted to establishing biological norms: blood pressure, temperature, blood sugar levels are some of the better known norms against which bodies are judged in investigations to establish disease.[11] People's experience of illness is inevitably permeated by medical ideas and practices, as Chapter 1 illustrated.

[10] See *Medical Knowledge: Doubt and Certainty* (Open University Press, 2nd edn 1994; colour-enhanced 2nd edn 2001), Chapter 3.

Diagnosis is a *dividing practice* in which the normal is separated from the abnormal, and the varieties of the abnormal are classified. Abnormal conditions are given **medical labels**, the delivery of which, if the label is considered stigmatising by the recipient, can cause shock, as revealed in this interview between Graham Scambler, a sociologist, and Mrs X:

> *GS*: How did you feel when he [the doctor] said it was epilepsy?
>
> *Mrs X*: I cried for two days. I think it was the word that frightened me more than anything.
>
> *GS*: Why was that?
>
> *Mrs X*: Oh, I just don't know. It was the way I felt I suppose. It's not a very nice word is it? I can't describe it really. I just can't describe how I felt.
>
> *GS*: It was something about this word 'epilepsy' that sparked that reaction off in you?
>
> *Mrs X*: Mm. Because, to me, when you tell people, they sort of shun you, that's the way I look at it. They, you know, they don't want to know; in fact my mother doesn't for one. If you go for a job and its on the form — and you've got to put down 'yes', more often than not — you don't get the job, you know.
>
> *GS*: Have you actually found this, or is this something you understood would happen?
>
> *Mrs X*: I understood it would happen, because those who I work with don't know I have them [fits] anyway.
>
> *GS*: What made you think this sort of thing does happen to people with epilepsy?
>
> *Mrs X*: I don't really know, to be truthful. I just don't really know.
>
> (Scambler, 1984, pp. 212–3)

Here, the force of the stigma comes not from the doctor delivering the diagnosis, but from the speaker's own beliefs about the stigmatisation of people with epilepsy.

● Refer back to the earlier summary (Box 2.2) of terms and distinctions used by Goffman and others in discussing stigma. Which concept describes the process outlined above?

■ The concept of *felt stigma* describes how people may fear being stigmatised without the stigma necessarily being enacted by others.

Health-care staff may, in fact, themselves be quite critical of the stigma attached to medical labels, even though they 'stick them on'. Indeed, health-care workers (and celebrities, Figure 2.5, overleaf) sometimes achieve the status of stigma champions, wise to the distress involved in particular illnesses, negotiating acceptance of stigmatised groups by the wider community. In later chapters of this book, for

[11] Biomedical research as a basis for establishing norms is described in *Studying Health and Disease* (Open University Press, 2nd edn 1994; colour-enhanced 2nd edn 2001), Chapter 9.

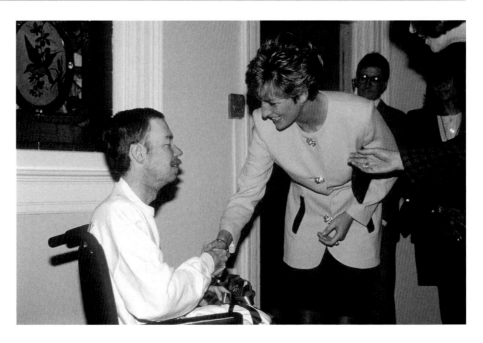

Figure 2.5   *Princess Diana in a well-publicised handshake with a person with AIDS. In modern societies tolerance is often promoted as a desirable social value and opinion leaders are often recruited as 'stigma champions'.*
(Photo: David Hartley/ Rex Features)

example, you will see how certain sections of the medical establishment have struggled to counter prejudice against people with schizophrenia (Chapter 6). In the case of mental illness, community care to reintegrate people previously separated in asylums has been championed by health workers.

Indeed, medical settings may be havens of security and acceptance for people who are stigmatised. The word 'asylum', though it now has connotations of segregation and exclusion, was once used to mean a place of refuge for the persecuted. Indeed, some critics of the failures of community care policies for people with mental illness have argued for the restitution of asylums for those unable to look after themselves in a hostile 'community'. In the 1980s it was well known among people with HIV or AIDS that certain health centres in London hospitals offered confidential and sympathetic treatment not always available from general practitioners.

One strategy used by those seeking to ameliorate the conditions of people who are stigmatised is to question the system of knowledge that underlies stigmatising categories. This has been done, with some success at times, in an area where diseases are inherently difficult to define objectively, that of mental illness. Thus, in the 1960s, a movement arose that was known as *anti-psychiatry* (described more fully in Chapter 6 on schizophrenia), headed by a variety of doctors and academics such as the dissident psychiatrists Thomas Szasz in the USA and Ronald Laing in the UK. Their chief proposition was that mental illness either did not really exist or, if it did, it was a normal reaction to abnormal circumstances.

●   Where have you seen this type of argument before in *this* chapter?

■   In the views expressed by groups campaigning against the stigmatisation of disability, where disability is conceived as the failure of others to provide an adequate environment for people with impairments.

An interesting and influential experiment took place in California in 1973, which demonstrated the arbitrary nature of psychiatric diagnosis. David Rosenhan and his colleagues conducted a study called 'On being sane in insane places', in which they sent eight sane research assistants to psychiatrists, faking mental illness. All were admitted to a mental hospital and, once there, behaved normally. Although other patients suspected they were frauds, none of the staff did, relying on the label given at admission to interpret their behaviour. Thus, the researchers' note-taking and their complaints of boredom were taken by staff to be signs of mental disturbance.

● What aspect of Goffman's analysis of stigma do these staff interpretations reflect?

■ Stigmatised individuals often attract a *master status* whereby actions that are considered normal in other people are interpreted as reflecting their stigmatised condition.

The history of psychiatry is littered with disease categories that were once popular medical labels, but that are now discarded in favour of new ones.[12] This apparent inconsistency is encouraging for those who wish to claim that the particular disease labels with which they are struggling are essentially arbitrary categories, of no lasting or objective importance. It is somewhat easier to mount such challenges in the arena of mental health than physical health, as the objective reality of mental conditions is harder to establish in the absence of physical pathology.

Additionally, some people may *seek* medical labels in order to disavow stigmatising labels emanating from non-medical sources. For example, the diagnosis of ME (myalgic encephalomyelitis, also known as post-viral fatigue syndrome), pre-menstrual tension and post-traumatic stress disorder may be helpful in countering imputations of malingering, irritability or weakness of character.

2.4.2 Typifications

At the same time, health-care work is done by people who are as subject to all the usual pressures of negotiating their way through social situations as are the rest of the population. They may themselves subscribe to stigmatising prejudices, and may incorporate these within their work. For example, medical practice is not simply the objective application of medical knowledge, but occurs in particular social settings that encourage particular ways of seeing patients. This leads to a variety of informal pressures to place people in non-medical categories, the force of which may be equally stigmatising as that of a medical label.

● Can you think of some non-medical categories that might be used by health-service workers when thinking about patients?

■ Here are a number of possible answers: elderly, stoical, complaining, hypochondriac, demanding, brave, tragic, caring, weak, patient, impatient, deserving, bed-blocker.

One of the means by which people manage their interactions with each other is through **typifications**, the use of which serve to simplify the demands made on individuals in otherwise complex situations. Typification operates at a very basic level, helping, for example, to categorise objects so that weapons are divided from tools, food from non-food, and so on. In relation to people, typifications help to construct broad categories of person, so that the young may be divided from the old, male from female, pleasant from unpleasant, and so on.

[12] An example is 'hysteria', discussed in *Medical Knowledge: Doubt and Certainty* (Open University Press, 2nd edn 1994; colour-enhanced 2nd edn 2001), Chapter 6.

When people are placed in demanding social settings, where they have to manage encounters with a large variety of people in short spaces of time — as is the case with much health work — the urge to typify people in order to simplify the mental difficulties of the task is strong. It is familiar, therefore, to hear of people in hospitals complaining of being treated 'like an object', or a 'number', envious comparisons being made with the more 'personal' service offered by private health care, where the demands on doctors' and nurses' time are not as pressing.

Informal models of 'typical' classes of patient very frequently emerge in health-care settings, and are shared by staff. These may be local in character, and attract official disapproval, yet nevertheless help staff to further the aim of their organisation to run smoothly. Roger Jeffery in his article 'Normal rubbish' (first published in 1979)[13] describes how typification operated in busy casualty departments in three hospitals in an English city. People who had attempted suicide, drunks, tramps and people presenting with 'trivia' were categorised by staff as 'rubbish'. 'Good' patients, on the other hand, were those with 'genuine' medical conditions, preferably ones that were interesting, allowing doctors to practise their medical skills at a high level. 'Rubbish' patients were treated in a hostile fashion, made to wait for a long time or threatened with the police. 'Good' patients obtained prompt and courteous treatment.

Such typifications are not exclusive to hospital work. Gerry Stimson, a sociologist, studied the typifications of general practitioners (GPs) in the UK. He asked 453 GPs to write brief descriptions of patients who were 'least trouble' compared to those who were 'most trouble'. His analysis of the content of their replies revealed that certain characteristics distinguished the two groups of patients, as in Box 2.3.

Box 2.3   Typifications of patients as 'trouble' by GPs

Patients who are *least trouble* are: men, healthy, with specific symptoms that are organic/physical, are easy to diagnose, can be treated, with medical problems, are easy to manage, get better, do not consult or can judge when to consult, are undemanding, do not take time, clearly present problems, have confidence in the doctor, accept limits to the doctor's skill, are grateful, want to get better or accept their illness, accept the judgement of the doctor, follow advice, are co-operative, intelligent, with common sense, can cope, are happy, settled, local, adequate, busy or working and have good homes and circumstances.

Patients who are *most trouble* are: women, ill, with vague symptoms which are psychiatric or psychological, hard to diagnose and treat, originate in social problems, are hard to manage, do not get better, consult or cannot judge when to consult, are demanding, take up time, vaguely present problems, do not trust the doctor, do not accept limits to the doctor's skill, are ungrateful, do not want to get better or deny their illness, are critical of the doctor, do not follow advice, unco-operative, with low IQ, lack common sense, unhappy, unsettled, lonely, insecure, from elsewhere, inadequate, are idle or malingerers, have poor social circumstances. Such individuals have been labelled 'heart-sink patients' by doctors describing their own reactions as the patient walks into the consulting room. (Adapted from Stimson, 1976)

---

[13] We recommend that Open University students should read this now if time is available. It is reprinted in *Health and Disease: A Reader* (Open University Press, 3rd edn 2001).

2.4.3 Defending the patient's moral reputation

It would be unfair to imply that all GPs subscribe to the stereotypes given in Box 2.3. In the last twenty years the *consumerist* approach in the health service in the UK and elsewhere has encouraged health-care workers to try harder not to stereotype patients in this way. However, if such a picture still underlies health work, it is hardly surprising that consultations with doctors can be important moments for the defence of the 'moral reputation' of the patient. In talking about medical encounters after the event, people may also seek to display 'moral behaviour' in order to avoid stigma. Consider the following extracts from interviews with two mothers of young children:

> I went to the baby clinic every week. She would gain one pound one week and lose it the next. They said I was fussing unnecessarily. They said there were skinny and fat babies and I was fussing too much. I went to a doctor and he gave me some stuff and he said 'You're a young mother. Are you sure you won't put it in her ear instead of her mouth?'. It made me feel a fool.
>
> When she was born they told me she was perfectly all right. And I accepted it. I worried about her, which most mothers do you know — worry about their first child … She wouldn't eat and different things. And so I kept taking her to the clinic. 'Nothing wrong with her my dear. You're just making yourself … worrying unnecessarily' you see.
>
> (Quoted by Silverman, 1993, p. 109)

● What typifications seem to be active here?

■ The first extract suggests that the doctor has a rather disparaging view of the 'typical young mother'. The second extract does not reveal a medical typification, but the mother describes what she believes to be a generally held stereotype about first-time mothers as worriers, fitting the doctor's reported speech.

Commenting on these interviews, the sociologist Geoffrey Baruch (who interviewed the second person) argues that the mothers were seeking to display to the interviewer an identity as responsible parents, reporting the patronising treatment given them by medical staff as 'atrocity stories' in order to contrast this with their own 'moral behaviour' in being concerned about their children's welfare (Baruch, 1982).

● How does the concept of *membership* help in understanding what is going on in the extracts above?

■ The women were claiming membership of the category of 'mothers who are concerned for their children's welfare', rejecting any imputation of a stigmatised identity as incompetent or obsessively anxious.

Medicine, then, may both sustain stigmatised identities and defend against stigma (as in the example given earlier of HIV clinics in London). By its most basic operation of diagnosis and classification, medical practice gives people illness labels that may attract stigma from a variety of sources. Health-care workers may be at the forefront of decrying such prejudice, providing a safe haven for people who are stigmatised and championing their cause. However, the conditions in which health-care work is conducted can lead to typifications (such as 'good' or 'bad' patients) that may themselves be stigmatising. Aware of the force of such informal medical labelling, patients often seek to negotiate non-stigmatised identities both during health care and afterwards in discussing their experiences with others.

2.5 Conclusion

This chapter has approached the topic of stigma by first exploring the roots of the desire to be 'normal', identifying this as a basic human need for security and membership that is fundamental to the organisation of social life. Illness is but one experience that threatens security, doing so because, ultimately, illness is a reminder of the limitations of bodily existence, and of eventual mortality. Claims to membership, which promote security, are based on agreed norms of behaviour. In both large-scale ritual events, and in small-scale interactions such as everyday conversation, claims to membership are made and judged between people. The exclusion of certain people in certain settings, if it is sustained and systematic, is called stigma, and is intimately linked to the attempts of the stigmatisers to maintain ontological security.

However, the effects upon those who are systematically stigmatised can be devastating, leading to a master status in which all actions are judged as emanating from a stigmatising condition. Covering up such conditions, trying to pass as if 'normal', angry protestations against the unfairness of the whole process, or collective action by stigma 'peers', are strategies available to people who are stigmatised. The damage done by stigma has become increasingly noticed in modern times as standards of 'civilised' conduct have developed, leading to a variety of attempts to negotiate and soften stigmatising labels. Permanently stigmatising categories are harder to maintain for any great length of time, as faith declines in the grand narratives that previously supported stigmatising categorisation, and as stigma champions arise to wage successful campaigns.

The final section dealt with the role of medicine and of health-care workers in managing stigma, pointing out that categorisation and labelling is an essential activity in diagnosis, with potentially stigmatising consequences. Although health-care settings can be a source of refuge and asylum for those stigmatised by the wider community, health-care work itself can impose conditions where stigmatising typifications are created. In these circumstances, the moral identities of those seeking health care can be a matter of concern, and represent an underlying agenda in both medical consultations and in discussions of consultations after the event.

You will find the concepts used in this chapter useful in understanding people's experience of the conditions described in the next five chapters, concerning rheumatoid arthritis, HIV and AIDS, asthma, schizophrenia and chronic pain. Some of these have attracted more stigma than others. All, to a greater or lesser extent, involve a search for a personal meaning for the disease, where you will find the concepts of *personal illness narrative, medical narrative* and *grand narrative* helpful.

OBJECTIVES FOR CHAPTER 2

When you have studied this chapter, you should be able to:

2.1 Define and use, or recognise definitions and applications of, each of the terms printed in **bold** in the text.

2.2 Discuss the psychosocial origins of the desire to be normal, and the part played by stigma and projection in maintaining the boundaries of membership of social groups.

2.3 Analyse the impact of stigmatising illnesses in modern social conditions, using key terms such as master status, passing, covering, discredited, discreditable, felt and enacted stigma, tribal stigma, the own and the wise.

2.4 Describe the role played by medicine and health-care workers in creating, defending against and managing stigma.

QUESTIONS FOR CHAPTER 2

1 (*Objective 2.2*)

In 1897 the sociologist Emile Durkheim wrote in his study of the causes of suicide:

> … great social disturbances and great popular wars rouse collective sentiments, stimulate partisan spirit and patriotism, political faith and national faith alike and, focusing activities on a single end, produce, at least for a time, a stronger integration of society … [As people] come together to face the common danger, the individual thinks less of himself and more of the common cause. (Durkheim, 1897, quoted in Lukes, 1973, p. 209)

Durkheim found that the suicide rate declines in times of war. How might the concepts of stigma, ontological security, membership and projection be used to explain this? How does this large-scale phenomenon relate to small-scale interactions, such as conversations between able-bodied and disabled people?

2 (*Objective 2.3*)

> Although I've been disabled since childhood, until the past few years I didn't know anyone else with a disability and in fact *avoided* knowing anyone with a disability. I had many of the same fears and anxieties which many of you who are currently able-bodied might feel about close association with anyone with a disability. I had … rebelled against the prescribed role of dependence … expected of disabled women. I became the 'exceptional' woman, the 'super-crip', noted for her independence. I refused to let my identity be shaped by my disability. I wanted to be known for *who* I am and not just by what I physically cannot do. (Galler, 1984, reprinted in Beattie *et al.*, 1993, pp. 152–3)

What aspects of this account, by Roberta Galler, a woman who was disabled by polio, illustrate the following concepts: master status, covering, discredited, the own, and enacted stigma?

3 (*Objective 2.4*)

Here is a report from a conference of American doctors discussing the management of patients with pain:

> At the conclusion of a presentation on the experimental usefulness of [a test] for gauging pain tolerance, a physician in the audience stood to make the following comment: 'All of these lab experiments you've been talking about [are] a lot of hogwash. All of our patients are on disability [benefits] or on litigation, and they scream at the littlest pressure you apply. It seems like they hurt when you look at them [audience laughter] ... There is no validity when the patient has no motivation not to be in pain ...' (Kotarba and Seidel, 1984, p. 1396)

These doctors were also found to refer to patients complaining of pains that had no identifiable physical cause as 'compensation neurotics' (that is, complaining of pain in order to increase the chances of financial compensation) or 'problem pain patients'. Are these medical diagnoses or stigmatising typifications? What is the difference?

C H A P T E R 3

Rheumatoid arthritis

Study notes for OU students

This chapter refers back to the role of antibodies and inflammation in the body's defence against infection, as discussed in *Human Biology and Health: An Evolutionary Approach* (Open University Press, third edition 2001), Chapter 6. The TV programme for Open University students, 'Why me? Why now?', associated with the first book in this series *Medical Knowledge: Doubt and Certainty* (Open University Press, second edition 1994; colour-enhanced second edition 2001), uses rheumatoid arthritis to illustrate the relationship between lay and biomedical perspectives on the causes of the disease. If you videotaped it, you will find it useful to watch it again now, but in any case you should re-read the relevant sections of the notes associated with this programme in the *Audiovisual Media Guide*.

This chapter was written by Gareth Williams, Professorial Fellow, School of Social Sciences, Cardiff University; Ray Fitzpatrick, Professor of Public Health and Primary Care, Nuffield College, University of Oxford; Alex J. MacGregor, Arthritis Research Campaign Senior Fellow and Honorary Consultant Rheumatologist, St Thomas' Hospital, London; and Alan S. Rigby, Senior Lecturer in Statistics and Epidemiology and Chartered Statistician, Sheffield Children's Hospital, University of Sheffield.

3.1   Introduction

> Of all the rheumatic disorders, rheumatoid arthritis is the condition that has been studied most extensively and over the longest period of time … It is frustrating, therefore, to have to acknowledge that all this effort has not led to commensurate enlightenment, and our appreciation of how and why this disease arises … remains rudimentary. (Wood and Badley, 1986, p. 63)

> I was really in a terrible state at that time, really was. I couldn't do anything. I wasn't working, couldn't work. I had a job to get a mug of tea, cup of tea, or even a fork to my mouth, it was so bad … It started in my arms. My arms and shoulders are the worst. It is very difficult to describe to anybody what the pain is like. (Middle-aged man with rheumatoid arthritis, quoted in Williams, 1984a, p. 242)

Rheumatoid arthritis — commonly abbreviated to RA — is a disease of considerable significance for clinical medicine, public health and, most of all, the people who have to live with it day to day. Between 0.8 and 1 per cent of the population of the UK are thought to have RA — at least half a million people, each with a detailed personal narrative of pain, uncertainty about the future and changes in their relationships and other features of everyday life.

Like many chronic diseases, RA has many aspects. There are a variety of different ways of knowing about this complex condition, and these may give rise to different accounts of the nature of the disease — its aetiology, pathology, and consequences. The two quotations above illustrate the contrasting narratives of epidemiologists and people living long-term with the disease. For the laboratory scientists studying this puzzling condition, the causes of which remain uncertain, the story they tell is about genes, cells and viruses. Physicians treating RA may focus on levels of antibodies in the blood, inflammation of the joints and the latest drug trials or surgical interventions. Social researchers may seek to unravel the impact of the disease on personal lives and the role of society in alleviating or exacerbating its effects. All of these stories have a place in this chapter.

3.1.1 What is rheumatoid arthritis?

First, we will define what we mean by **rheumatoid arthritis**. As you will see, the definition depends very much on whom you ask and where you cast your gaze.

To a rheumatologist — a doctor specialising in rheumatology, the medical treatment of arthritis and rheumatism,[1] who may also conduct research — RA is a chronic inflammatory disease mainly affecting the joints, although every organ system in the body can become involved in the disease process. We will return to the clinical picture of RA shortly, but it is important to emphasise at the outset that there is no single diagnostic test for the disease.

To the person affected by RA, the disease is not just the experience of pain or other common symptoms like fatigue and stiffness, nor is it simply a set of observable physical changes in the body. The illness reveals itself to the world over time in visibly swollen joints and loss of mobility as the disease process affects the soft tissue and bone. Other people can 'see' the RA, and it becomes, to a greater or lesser extent, part of the identity of the affected person, a chapter in his or her story. Moreover, RA is associated with considerable impairment in the functioning in the body's joints, and this interacts with the person's social and economic situation to create disability. The impairments produced by RA are often so severe and the provisions for affected people so meagre, that RA can be profoundly disabling.

3.1.2 Uncertainty and rheumatoid arthritis

Another defining feature of RA is also a central theme of this book: it is fraught with uncertainty at all stages in its development, progression and treatment. The onset of symptoms typically occurs slowly over months or even years, but there are individuals who describe going from 'normal' to bed-ridden over the space of a few days. Symptoms fluctuate day to day, week to week, and month to month. Prediction of the course of the disease is difficult both for the person with RA and the professionals who deal with it. It disrupts domestic and working lives unpredictably and undermines long-term planning. There is no easy systematic relationship between the 'objective' severity of the disease and the 'subjective' disruptiveness of the illness and disability. RA usually affects people in middle age, but can occur at any age, and it is roughly three times as common in women as in men — yet the reasons for this distribution and the precipitating causes are uncertain.

These uncertainties greatly increase the likelihood that people with RA and the health professionals with whom they make contact will have sharply different expectations, hopes, agendas and stories within which the experience and understanding of RA is given meaning. We start to unravel these differences by building up a clinical

---

[1] 'Arthritis' is the collective term for any disease or damage affecting the joints; 'rheumatism' has no precise definition but is widely used to describe any pain in and around bones, muscles and joints. There are about 200 different types of arthritis and rheumatism, which together are known as 'rheumatic diseases'.

description of the disease from the medical viewpoint, pointing to sources of diagnostic uncertainty. We describe the pathological processes occurring in the joints and organs of people affected by RA and the uncertain progression of the condition over a lifetime. Then we assess the consequences of this uncertainty from the patient's perspective, examining the difficulties that people experience in living with RA day to day. We explore its effects on activities, roles and relationships, and how these in turn are affected by public attitudes and social circumstances.

Next, we tackle another area of uncertainty: the question of what causes RA. In developing a greater understanding of this complex question, we draw on lay beliefs and personal illness narratives, and 'expert' knowledge from the disciplines of epidemiology and medical science. This leads to a discussion of how scientific knowledge about disease causation has influenced clinical strategies for disease management, and of the ways in which the patient's point of view has gradually become an increasingly regarded aspect of professional assessment of disability and of the outcome of medical and social interventions. Finally, as the backdrop to these personal and professional accounts, we refer to the history of RA as a disease category with attributes that have been 'socially constructed'.

3.2   The clinical picture of RA

3.2.1   Clinical features

RA is diagnosed on the basis of three groups of observations, which form part of the clinical method used by doctors to reach a diagnosis in all disease conditions.[2] A number of characteristic clinical features point the physician to a diagnosis of RA, which are best described by reference to normal joints (Figure 3.1 represents the structure of a normal knee joint).

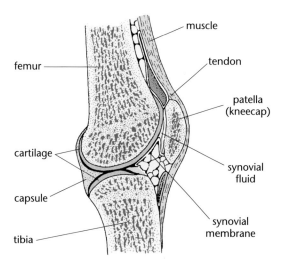

Figure 3.1   *Diagram of a 'side-on' section through a knee joint, showing normal anatomical features. Rheumatoid arthritis involves inflammation of the synovial membrane, leading to erosion of the cartilage covering the bones.*

[2] The clinical method is discussed in the first book in this series, *Medical Knowledge: Doubt and Certainty* (Open University Press, 2nd edn 1994; colour-enhanced 2nd edn 2001), Chapter 7.

The **clinical features** of a condition are the symptoms reported by the patient and the signs detected by the doctor during physical examination, or with X-rays or other scanning techniques. RA is characterised by symptoms such as stiffness and pain, physical signs such as symmetrical swelling in joints on both sides of the body, and X-rays showing erosion of the surface of the joints (Figure 3.2). Characteristically, the stiffness increases when the joint has been at rest and is eased by movement. Stiffness is often felt most intensely in the morning and may last for several hours.

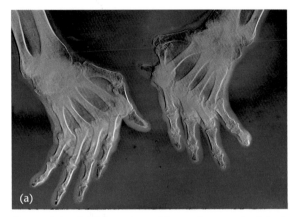 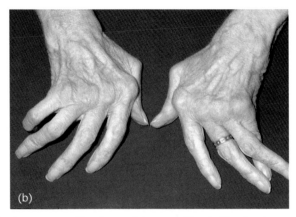

Figure 3.2   *(a) False-coloured X-ray photograph of the hands of a woman with advanced rheumatoid arthritis, showing erosion of the surfaces of the bones and loss of alignment of the finger joints and thumbs. (b) The hands of a person with advanced RA. (Photos: (a) CNRI/Science Photo Library; (b) Dr P. Marazzi/Science Photo Library)*

Histological features are findings on examination of involved tissues under the microscope (*histo* means tissue). In RA the synovial membrane lining the joints (Figure 3.1) is infiltrated by large numbers of white cells usually engaged in the body's immune defences against infection.[3] The inflammation resulting from the molecules they secrete causes the pain, stiffness and swelling recognised by the examining physician as a soft boggy feeling around affected joints, which are often warm. Excess fluid may be detected within the joint cavity.

Serological features are significant changes in the constituents of the blood (*sero*, in the serum, or liquid fraction of blood). In RA this refers principally to the detection of a specific type of antibody called **rheumatoid factor**, which is found in the blood of approximately 80 per cent of people with other signs of rheumatoid arthritis. The possible relevance of these antibodies to the progression of the disease is discussed in more detail later, but for the moment note that these antibodies are not present in 20 per cent of people who develop RA, and they are occasionally detected in people who do not develop the disease.

Although any joint may be involved in the inflammatory process in RA, the small joints of the hands (the knuckles) and the wrists are involved most commonly. Certain joints are characteristically spared, most notably the small joints at the ends of all the fingers. A remarkable feature in RA is the frequency with which there is symmetrical joint involvement with joint areas on both sides of the body involved simultaneously.

[3] Inflammation is discussed as a normal part of the defence against infection in another book in this series, *Human Biology and Health: An Evolutionary Approach* (Open University Press, 3rd edn 2001), Chapter 6. Chronic inflammation occurs when this process is so prolonged and intense that it damages healthy tissues. White cells and antibodies are central components of the immune system. We discuss chronic inflammation further in Section 3.6.4.

The consequence of inflammation in the lining of joints occurring continuously over a period of months to years can be profound disability and chronic pain. As the chronic inflammatory process continues in the tissue lining the joints, the cartilaginous layer that overlies the bones becomes roughened and eroded. On X-rays, punched out areas called 'erosions' become visible. Continuing erosion results in a loss of alignment of the bones in the joint as the normal direction of pull of the tendons is altered (Figure 3.2). The joints themselves may dislocate.

Although joint involvement is the cardinal feature of RA, the disease may affect any of the body's organs, and a chronic inflammatory response can become established in virtually any tissue. In up to 30 per cent of patients, lumps called rheumatoid nodules form when inflammation is localised, for example in the skin or lungs. Inflammation can also occur in the lining layers of the lungs, the heart and salivary glands, and more rarely in blood vessels, the eyes and peripheral nerves.

3.2.2 Case histories

The clinical picture described above cannot easily convey the variation between one patient and another. Boxes 3.1 and 3.2 present the first two (of several) case histories in this chapter illustrating the range of experience of rheumatoid arthritis. They have been constructed from medical experience in a rheumatology clinic; details have been altered only in order to protect confidentiality.

There are many interesting aspects to the case histories in Boxes 3.1 and 3.2, in addition to the fact that both involve women (RA is two to three times more common in women than in men). What is immediately striking, and highly typical, is that there is no characteristic pattern of onset of RA. The onset may be *acute*, coming on explosively over a matter of days (Mrs J), or it may be *insidious*, with transient joint symptoms appearing and disappearing over a number of years before the presence of RA is recognised (Mrs P). The disease progresses through relapse and remission, with no particular pattern to the timing and severity of episodes.

Box 3.1 Mrs J

At the age of 55 years, Mrs J suddenly developed pain and swelling in her knee. She was referred to an orthopaedic surgeon who drained fluid from the knee and injected steroids. She had no further problem with the joint. However, six months later she developed problems with her hands. Over a few days, the knuckles swelled and were acutely painful. She had to remove her rings. She noticed in particular that her hands were stiff in the morning and that they tended to seize up if she rested them. In the next few days, her left ankle also became swollen and painful and she was unable to put her foot to the ground. A blood test showed the presence of unusual antibodies, collectively known as rheumatoid factor. X-rays of her hands showed that the bone at the edges of the joints in her hand and ankles was eroded. Her GP made the diagnosis of rheumatoid arthritis.

Box 3.2 Mrs P

Mrs P, a 40-year-old woman who worked as a secretary, was referred to the rheumatology department of her local hospital with a history of a single episode of swelling of the hands and knuckles. When she was seen the swelling had virtually subsided and she could use her hands normally. The only abnormality found by the physician examining her joints was a mild swelling of the finger joints, producing a spindle-shaped appearance. Both hands were affected symmetrically. Her X-rays were normal. Blood tests were positive for rheumatoid factor. Thinking back, Mrs P remembered that she had had joint problems ten years earlier, shortly after the second of her two pregnancies, when her hands had been stiff. She had put this down to lifting her child. She also had 'tennis elbow' two years previously which her GP had told her had been due to typing.

3.2.3 Diagnostic uncertainty

The onset of RA is most often between the ages of 30 and 50 years, but it can occur at any age, including in childhood. In common with so many rheumatic diseases, it lacks a single uniquely identifying characteristic or biological hallmark that enables a doctor to diagnose the condition quickly and with absolute certainty — as the case history of Mrs P illustrates (Box 3.2). Rather, a process of **case ascertainment** goes on in which a range of features are investigated in combination in order to reach a definitive diagnosis. The most widely accepted basis for distinguishing RA as a clinical entity (illustrated in the case history of Mrs J, see Box 3.1) combines the detection of the characteristic clinical, histological and serological features described earlier.

One consequence of the lack of a single diagnostic test for RA is a degree of variation in methods of case ascertainment, which makes comparisons of epidemiological data from different sources somewhat problematic (a subject to which we return later in the chapter). Another, more pressing, consequence for the patient is the emotional effect of an often considerable delay in reaching a stable diagnosis of RA, which may be exacerbated by the tendency of signs and symptoms to 'wax and wane' over a prolonged period. Even when a diagnosis of RA has been reached, the uncertainties are not resolved. A number of the case histories given later in this chapter illustrate continuing uncertainty, both from the viewpoint of the clinician faced with deciding how best to treat individuals with such a variable condition, and for the patient trying to balance treatment benefits with possible adverse side effects.

3.2.4 Disease progression: the medical viewpoint

Like its onset, the course of RA is unpredictable and, although progression towards increasing disability fluctuates and periods of remission may occur, the affected joints often become intensely painful and their articulation can be profoundly impaired. Approximately half of patients with RA develop severe disability in a period of 15 years following its onset. The remainder have mild or moderate intermittent symptoms over a long period of time, sometimes with no apparent disability.

Not only is disruption of the joint architecture both painful and disabling, it may be life-threatening. In approximately one-third of patients with long-standing disease, the uppermost joint in the neck is involved in the inflammatory process. If instability and subsequent loss of alignment of the vertebrae occurs at this site, the bones themselves may press on the spinal cord within the spinal canal which, in 1 per cent of patients, leads to paralysis and possibly to death.

A review of death rates among people with RA by two American rheumatic disease epidemiologists, Theodore Pincus and Lea Callahan (1986), showed that mortality was 50 per cent higher than in unaffected people, when all causes of death were combined. The commonest cause of death in RA is through infection, a consequence of the fact that the body's immune defences are impaired through the continuing process of chronic inflammation.

Chronic inflammation in major organ systems in RA can also lead to impaired function; for example, inflammation in the lungs causes breathlessness and respiratory failure; inflammation of the heart may cause heart failure, and inflammation in nerves can result in numbness, weakness and paralysis. The majority of people with long-term RA are anaemic, as the chronic inflammatory process inhibits the bone marrow's ability to produce red blood cells.

If these are the potential long-term consequences of RA for the patient's morbidity and mortality, what effects does the illness and disability have on everyday activities, social roles and personal relationships? We turn now to the patients' experiences.

3.3 Lay perspectives on RA

3.3.1 The experience of uncertainty

In an early study of people with RA, Carolyn Wiener (1975) noted how the stock response of many doctors and nurses at that time — 'You're going to have to learn to live with it' — was of little help to someone confronting the personal experience of living with an unstable, unpredictable, chronic disease. She argued that people with RA are constrained by two conflicting imperatives: the physical reality of variable pain and disability, and the social reality of daily life with all its pressures of time-keeping, relationships and the expectation of 'normality'.

For someone who develops RA, the early stages of the illness are fraught with uncertainty, particularly where (as in the vast majority of cases) symptoms are present for months or even years before they are finally diagnosed. It is often very difficult for people with early RA to know whether something is 'really' going wrong; and even when they are sure, it is often difficult to convince others, both relatives and professionals, that this is the case.

The phase of pre-diagnostic uncertainty can last for a considerable period — Mrs P's symptoms could be traced back to a possible first episode ten years earlier. The prime source of uncertainty in the early stages lies in the disease itself. Symptoms such as pain, joint stiffness and discomfort and more generalised fatigue are common enough, and a vague awareness may grow that everyday tasks cannot be performed as easily as before. The process of coming to terms with these symptoms and making some sense of them is far from straightforward. For people who have previously only experienced acute illness episodes, where they are ill and then well again, symptoms that appear and disappear over a prolonged period are difficult to understand. For the person who develops RA, difficulties can arise in understanding normal bodily processes:

> It was just my knee ... [one man reported] ... it just blew up for no
> reason. It wasn't painful to start with, just swollen ... It was a
> funny shape and I thought 'what's going on here'? (Williams and
> Wood, 1988, p. 129)

The experience of uncertainty, however, does not exist in some kind of vacuum: the individual's response to bodily disorder and the way in which it is coped with depends to some extent on the person's background, understanding and experiences, as the case history in Box 3.3 illustrates.

The experience of being labelled a 'malingerer' or a 'hypochondriac' is not uncommon amongst people in the early stages of many chronic diseases (a point already made in Chapter 2). The threat posed by these often vague symptoms may be compounded by the sometimes disbelieving response of close friends and relatives, who may insist that it is 'all in the mind'. The quality of the uncertainty changes once a diagnosis has been made. People often respond to the diagnosis of a serious disease with relief rather than horror. It seems to bring to an end a long process of 'unknowing' and provides a hook on which to hang the many troubling and strange symptoms:

Box 3.3 Mrs A

Mrs A was in her early 30s and a registered nurse. She had a sister and an aunt who were severely disabled as a result of RA. When she began to experience joint symptoms, she was immediately disturbed by what they might mean and, in a state of great anxiety and uncertainty, she was taken into hospital for tests. The hospital doctors kept her in for a week, during which her symptoms went into remission. Blood tests were taken but, according to her account, nothing was found, and she was informed that there was nothing wrong with her. The doctor said: 'You're a nurse, your sister's got this disease, your auntie's got this disease, you're thinking about it too much. We all have aches and pains, you know'. Mrs A reported 'I felt terrible. I came out of there with my tail between my legs and I came home'. Six months later she had a further spell of severe joint pain and quickly became too ill to care for either herself or her young daughter. She was readmitted to a different hospital where a rheumatologist diagnosed RA.

> I thought I was going mental at the time … It came to the stage where I wasn't exactly glad that I had got arthritis, but at least there was really something that I was moaning about. (Williams, 1984a, p. 193)

Although the diagnosis of RA removes one dimension of uncertainty, there is then the problem of how to respond to a disease with symptoms that are literally there one day and gone the next. Some individuals come to doubt the original diagnosis when they experience a long remission, only to be knocked back again when the symptoms reappear. Moreover, not only is the disease unpredictable, it generates uncertainty in every aspect of a person's life. The person with RA is faced with having to accept the unpredictability of his or her body and its dictates, while continuing to respond to the demands and requirements of daily life.

Three major sources of uncertainty become part of life for the individual with RA and those close to them. The first can be summed up in the questions 'Why me?' and 'Why now?', which relate to the problem of cause (we return to this later). The second is raised by the question 'What should I do?' as the person addresses the problems of sustaining daily living, social roles and relationships. A third area of uncertainty is expressed as 'What will happen to me?', given the unpredictable outcome of RA. These uncertainties have a variety of implications for coping strategies and for the valued 'style of life' that someone is able to sustain in response to RA. These concerns are very similar to those of clinicians: 'What causes RA? What can we do for the patient? And what will influence the outcome?'.

As we pointed out earlier, following a diagnosis of RA, people commonly ask themselves the question: 'What should I do?'. Pain, stiffness and fatigue interfere in incalculable ways with everyday life, from relatively simple activities such as getting out of bed to more complex formal and informal relationships with others. Three aspects of everyday life are examined below: *activities of daily living*, the importance of *social roles*, and *dependency* in relationships. In reality, of course, these three aspects are closely interconnected, but for analytical purposes it helps to separate them.

3.3.2 Activities of daily living

In an in-depth study of living with RA, the sociologist David Locker (1983) interviewed 24 respondents who were severely disabled with RA and who had been affected for a number of years. Locker found that disability was often experienced as an accumulation of minor frustrations and difficulties — his respondents referred to the way in which it was the 'little things' that made life difficult and brought home the fact that they had disabilities. The everyday world becomes a world of obstacles (Figure 3.3).

Activities that for non-disabled people are more or less spontaneous, requiring no second thought, become matters of conscious deliberation for someone with RA:

> Last night I thought it's time to put that hot water bottle in. Well, I couldn't get the top out could I … so I thought there must be a way … so I put a screwdriver through the top and turned it round … Alright, it just needs a bit of thought and patience. (Williams, 1984a, p. 287)

The consequences of RA manifest themselves in relation to almost all areas of daily life: sleep and rest, walking and changing position, washing and bathing, dressing, mobility and housework. Locker's study established that it is only when it becomes difficult or impossible to do these things that people realise how significant the activities are. Moreover, both long-term planning and spontaneity are severely affected by the unpredictability of RA:

> Some days you feel ruddy marvellous and could jump over the moon, other days you're fit for nothing. (Locker, 1983, p. 18)

(a)

(b)

Figure 3.3   *The everyday world can become a world of obstacles to a person with active rheumatoid arthritis. See also Figure 2.4 in the previous chapter. (Photos: (a) Courtesy of the Arthritis Research Campaign; (b) Wellcome Trust Medical Photo Library)*

You can't make arrangements, you've got to do things when you can. I never plan ahead, I can't, there's no good in planning ahead 'cause I just don't know how I am going to be from one day to the other. (Locker, 1983, p. 21)

RA obliterates the taken-for-granted trust in one's body (a component of ontological security discussed in Chapter 2), which is necessary for a person to make plans about 'what to do'.

- What sort of strategies do you think someone with RA would have to adopt to deal with difficulties in the activities of everyday life?

- The strategies may involve getting others to help, doing tasks oneself but doing them differently, or finding a substitute for the activity that can no longer be done. (For example, David Locker found that people in his study started showering instead of bathing, or got adaptations to their bathroom which enabled them to go on bathing, or they had a wash instead and only bathed when visiting relatives who could help.)

However, it is not always easy to adapt: the impact of RA upon daily activities is mediated by a sense of what activities ought to be performed. Everyday life consists of moral imperatives that are difficult to resist, even where the experience of illness is severe and debilitating. People with RA sometimes define themselves as 'doers' who can no longer do things. The inability to open a tin of food is no problem if you have never wanted or needed to do this, or if there is somebody else there to do it for you. It is this wider aspect of the consequences of chronic illness that tends to be underplayed in most of the rehabilitation studies of activities of everyday life (Williams, 1987).

The impact of RA on individuals is seen particularly clearly in the context of paid work. Members of a specialist arthritis research centre in California (Yelin *et al.*, 1987) recruited a sample of individuals with RA and obtained data about their disease from their doctors. They interviewed the patients about their employment histories and showed that, of those individuals who were in work at the time of their diagnosis, 50 per cent stopped work within a decade. Such evidence is consistent with other studies in demonstrating how difficult it is to stay in employment following the onset of RA. However, the study also revealed how the specific circumstances of employment may determine whether or not the disease is associated with early retirement. The extent of the physical demands posed by the work, and the degree of control a worker could exert over the pace and content of the work, were better predictors of subsequent unemployment than were the person's disease characteristics. Such findings are powerful evidence of how the interaction between the disease and the social context ultimately shapes each individual's experiences of RA.

3.3.3   The importance of social roles

Tasks and activities are organised in terms of **social roles**.[4] While this is most clearly demonstrated in formal contexts such as paid work, social roles also structure activities and expectations in informal settings. Although the activities themselves

[4] The concept of social roles is an important one in sociology; you have already studied an extract from an article by Goffman which deals with the breakdown of social roles in mental illness (see Chapter 2 of this book and *Health and Disease: A Reader*, Open University Press, 3rd edn 2001).

may not seem particularly grand or important, their place within a role may accord them enormous significance. Where an activity is part of a caring role, the failure in this activity can have profound ramifications. For example, the tying of shoelaces involves a degree of manual dexterity that is a particular problem for many people with RA (Mason *et al.*, 1983). Sometimes it may be possible to make simple adaptations such as altering the type of footwear. However, when the person with RA is a parent, struggling alone to get children off to a school where they are required to wear lace-up shoes, the social effects run deep.

Other examples in which the meanings of activities vary with social role are provided by tasks associated with nurturing and homemaking, such as shopping and cooking. The importance of these tasks vary, among other things, with the position someone occupies in the domestic division of labour. In heterosexual couples in most industrialised countries, whereas a man may share in some domestic activities, the 'role responsibility' typically remains with the woman (Oakley, 1985), who — as we mentioned earlier — is two to three times more likely to develop RA. As one woman with RA put it:

> If I am trying to do something [in the kitchen] and I get frustrated, I'll be cursing and [my husband] says: 'why do you try to do it? I'll do it for you if you ask me'. And I say: 'well I shouldn't have to ask you'. (Williams, 1987, p. 99)

The inability to prepare a meal can be a profoundly unsettling experience if it is a basic activity through which a woman feels her social role is delineated. As one woman put it: 'You feel a bit incomplete, I suppose', while another explained:

> I've got a guilt complex. I don't feel the children and my husband should do so much of my work, I feel I should take a bigger part. He will cook a meal sometimes if I've been really bad and I feel really guilty. (Williams, 1987, p. 99)

Figure 3.4 *Difficulty in performing activities that are felt to be parts of the 'ceremony of daily life' may be experienced as a failure in the performance of a valued social role. (Photo: Courtesy of the Arthritis Research Campaign)*

The problem for someone with RA, therefore, is not just one of an inability to perform certain activities, it is the failure in the performance of social roles. Cutting and peeling vegetables, cooking, putting food on the table, and hanging out the washing (Figure 3.4) can be seen both as discrete activities with which the symptoms of RA interfere, but they are also common parts of the ceremony of daily life. People with RA develop techniques and adaptations for undertaking specific activities but, rather than struggling to find new ways of doing things, it is sometimes possible to alter the overall division of labour and the expectations about who does what in the household. One woman, for example, in a study by Williams, offered her children payment for cleaning windows, helping to prepare meals, and doing the shopping. By redefining her role as supervisory and managerial rather than operational, she managed to maintain a sense of competent involvement in spite of her disabilities.

The importance of social roles persists beyond the household. Although many people with RA have to give up work, others try to develop ways of adapting to the demands of their work:

> There were days when I couldn't really use a paintbrush in one hand. So I would get a piece of sandpaper and use the left hand and do a bit of sandpapering down for the next hour or so, ready for the next day … and I kept going. (Williams, 1984a, p. 344)

Compliance with sensible clinical recommendations (for example, to give up work) is often discussed as if it were an individual choice for patients, but it may simply not be practical for someone to comply:

> … it was necessity you see. My husband's only in a low wage bracket, and it did help pay the mortgage and keep things going properly here. (Williams and Wood, 1988, p. 130)

Failure to perform certain tasks is a major aspect of the experience of RA. These failures and the strategies used to offset them are often important in themselves, but they are particularly important in so far as they represent failures in the performance of social roles. It has been implicit in what has been said so far that this performance has implications for relationships of interdependence with others.

3.3.4 Dependence in relationships

The experience of disability is often described in terms of **dependence** — being dependent on others for help in meeting certain needs. Thus, dependence is generally but misleadingly defined as a property of *individuals* whose impairments prevent them from undertaking tasks and activities, such as washing and cooking, unaided. But individuals do not exist in isolation from society (however isolated they may sometimes feel). They are drawn into complex *social relationships* both with members of their informal networks and with agencies of the State — health services, social services and social security. However personal their experiences may be, those experiences are shaped by the features of economy, society and culture within which the person lives. Dependence is more accurately seen as a quality of relationships *in certain settings*.

The onset of RA disrupts the normal patterns of interdependence and reciprocity that are central to managing everyday life.[5] The severity of this disruption varies with the severity of the disease and the stability and robustness of the setting within which the person lives. One woman who had a severe and rapid onset of RA said:

> I just used to lie and shiver and couldn't move. Having got downstairs in the morning I used to spend most of the day wondering if my son and husband would get me back up there in the evening. (Williams, 1987, p. 100)

Studies of the experience of RA indicate that dependence gives rise to a great deal of anxiety and fear (Locker, 1983; Williams and Wood, 1988). Heavy dependency, such as that depicted by the woman above, is unusual and occasional. The experience of dependence is generally characterised by having to ask other people to do certain things, and having to wait for help. People with disabilities often

---

[5] Dependence and reciprocity in relationships among people who develop physical impairments in later life are discussed in more depth in *Birth to Old Age: Health in Transition* (Open University Press, 2nd edn 1995; colour-enhanced 2nd edn 2001), Chapter 11.

state that they do not want 'to be a burden' or 'to interfere with' the lives of others by making demands. Discomfort comes both from the sense of depersonalisation that can follow from having things done for you, and from the feeling that certain tacit moral rules about what can be expected of others are being infringed. Drawing too freely upon the time of other family members is seen, literally, 'as taking liberties'. Very often people with RA feel that they do not want help unless they ask for it, but they are also reluctant to ask. As one woman put it:

> It's alright me saying I've got relations — my sister will come and tidy up and everything for me — but they have their own lives to live, they have their own families to see to. (Williams, 1987, p. 101)

This problem of dependence is felt more in some relationships than others. For example, in a study by Williams, a 30-year-old woman and her baby daughter were both being looked after by her mother who was in her mid-60s. This caused a double burden of guilt and anxiety: failure to discharge her own duties to her baby and imposing unfair demands on her mother. The feeling of concern about dependence for people with RA is felt most acutely in relationships with their children:

> I don't want to be a burden to my family that's the main thing. I'd hate to think that, because I've seen so many people be a burden to their children and I think it's most unfair. (Newman *et al.*, 1995, p. 44)

RA is a process, not a state. For some people, having struggled to do everything for themselves, there comes a point where they accept a change in their relationships:

> It would be about the middle of when I was ill that I began to settle for them [the family] to do things for me. (Newman *et al.*, 1995, p. 45)

However, making a 'settlement' such as this is always provisional. Living with chronic illness involves continual adjustment to changing aspects of the disease, alterations in the domestic situation, the varying availability of benefits and services, and changes in the wider economic and social situation.

Although this discussion of dependence in relationships has centred on the domestic arena, people with RA will often turn to resources in the public sphere in order to prevent the occurrence of problems of dependence on close relatives. For example, one woman, although having two sons living nearby, was helped in her bathing by the district nursing service, until the provision of a bath-seat released her from any dependence on others for taking a bath. The provision of simple aids and adaptations can transform personal and social relationships. As Gareth Williams (1993) has shown in a detailed case study of an elderly widow with RA, although dependence upon aids and adaptations can be uncomfortable, it may have fewer negative connotations than direct dependence on other people, be they relatives or statutory services. It also circumvents the complications of reciprocity and indebtedness.

● Although RA is not generally thought of as a 'stigmatising' condition, in the sense in which we applied that term to schizophrenia or AIDS in the discussion in Chapter 2, how might a person with RA experience stigma?

■ The ramifications of feelings of incompetence, failure to fulfil social roles or 'moral imperatives' concerning normal daily activities such as taking a bath, dependency on others, and the visible disfigurement of joints, all constitute a considerable threat to personal self-esteem and 'moral reputation'. Some people with RA may experience *felt stigma*, in which they withdraw from certain activities or avoid situations in which they fear others will discriminate against them or judge them negatively.

So far in this chapter, we have described the diagnosis of RA and its longer-term consequences from the medical and the lay perspectives. The clinical signs and symptoms have been discussed in the context of the personal and social features of the condition. We can now delve into another area of importance to both doctors and patients, and one in which similar uncertainties abound: what causes RA.

3.4   Lay beliefs about the causes of RA

Lay beliefs about illness are shaped by the culture and society of which they are a part and, consequently, their content and structure exhibit considerable variation. However, in almost all studies of **lay illness beliefs**, the issue of the *cause* of the illness is prominent.

3.4.1   Arthritis and lay illness beliefs

Relatively little research has been done into lay beliefs about the causes of any form of arthritis. In one of the earliest studies, on osteoarthrosis (a degenerative form of arthritis that is particularly associated with ageing), an American social scientist, Ruth Elder, argued:

> The cause of arthritis symptoms ... is unknown or, at best, controversial, and as a consequence official communications concerning it are limited. Thus a fertile field exists for the development of ideas derived from empirical experience and non-scientific beliefs about bodily functioning. (Elder, 1973, p. 29)

Thirty years later the precipitating causes of arthritis remain obscure, and the 'fertile field' for the development of lay ideas persists. Some of these lay ideas are copies, elaborations, or corruptions of medical ideas, taken from direct encounters with doctors, nurses, and therapists, or gleaned from magazine articles or television programmes dealing with orthodox or alternative health care. Yet other ideas are based on everyday life, on observations of other people and conversations with friends.

The anthropologist Dennis Gray (1983) noted the wide variety of sources for beliefs about joint disease in his study of 104 'arthritis sufferers'. About three-quarters of their ideas about the cause of arthritis and rheumatism did not correspond with orthodox medical beliefs. Gareth Williams and his colleagues investigated lay beliefs about RA and also attempted to explain their logic and purpose (Williams, 1984a, b; 1986; Williams and Wood, 1986). This work was based upon in-depth interviews with a small number of people who had all had RA for at least five years since diagnosis. The wide variety of factors mentioned by respondents were grouped into 12 causal categories, displayed in rank order in Table 3.1 (overleaf).

The most significant aspect of lay beliefs in this study — invisible in a simple rank ordering like Table 3.1 — is the way in which these factors were accounted for and 'weighted'. For example, where factors relating to occupation and a virus were both given particular emphasis, the individual identified their occupation as having made them *vulnerable* to symptoms, and a virus was seen as playing a *triggering* role.

Table 3.1   Rank order of causal categories mentioned by 29 people who had all had rheumatoid arthritis for at least 5 years (respondents could choose more than one category).

Category	No. of respondents
stress/life crisis	12
heredity/genes	11
physical trauma	9
occupation	7
environment (including climate)	6
virus/germs	5
previous illness	3
ageing	3
personality type	3
wear and tear	2
divine influence	2
don't know	2

Source: Williams, G. (1986) Lay beliefs about the causes of rheumatoid arthritis: their implications for rehabilitation, *International Rehabilitation Medicine*, **8**(2), Table 3, p. 66.

In some cases these beliefs amounted to formal 'models' which drew together the impact of a large number of factors existing over a long period. For example, Figure 3.5 shows the complex model of cause and effect developed by Mr A, who was in his early 60s, to explain the origins of his RA. Although he had had RA for

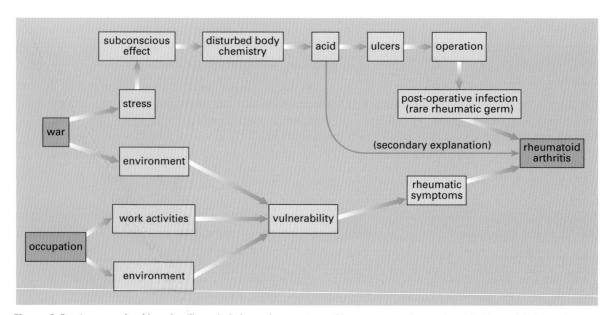

Figure 3.5   *An example of how lay illness beliefs can be constructed into a personal narrative: Mr A's model of how he came to develop rheumatoid arthritis. (Source: Williams, G. and Wood, P., 1986, Common-sense beliefs about illness: a mediating role for the doctor, Lancet, ii, un-numbered diagram, p. 1436)*

about ten years, he traced it to the time he was in the army 40 years earlier, working in harsh physical conditions and under considerable psychological stress, combined with many years in the building trade, and a post-operative infection following surgery for stomach ulcers.

3.4.2 Lay knowledge and narrative reconstruction

While medical explanations for diseases are related to a body of formal scientific knowledge, patients' views are woven out of the threads of their experiences, as Figure 3.5 illustrates. These experiences may include a strand of formal medical knowledge, but this is likely to be given no more weight than the information derived from friends, fellow-sufferers or the media.

The sociologist Mike Bury (1982) has described lay beliefs as a form of knowledge and understanding that enables people to re-establish some kind of meaning and cognitive order to cope with the 'biographical disruption' that chronic illness entails. (In Chapter 7 of this book you will learn about a related phenomenon — the ability of chronic pain to 'unmake the personal world' of the patient.)

Re-establishing meaning is not an event, but an ongoing endeavour. Gareth Williams (1984b) has analysed the process of *narrative reconstruction* (introduced in Chapter 1), which occurs as people with RA seek to build a relationship between their experience of the illness and the details of their own lives. Narrative reconstruction leads to a coherent set of beliefs that are simultaneously causal and *teleological* (that is, framed in terms of purposes): thus, the reconstructed narrative seeks to answer 'Why me?' and 'Why now?' not only in terms of 'What caused me to become ill?' but also 'To what end or purpose have I become ill?'.

Narrative reconstruction is apparent in the following extract from a long interview with a 68-year-old man, who had had RA for over 20 years. He remembered World War II:

> I went to North Africa, Italy, Austria, through and home. But we was getting drowned through the night, in Italy and Africa mostly, at Christmas time. We was going to make a big push at Christmas, but the weather was so bad that they cancelled it, and we was up to our knees in mud. In Italy there were weeks when I never wore a pair of socks, it was a waste of time. We was on this brow here and you couldn't stand up during the day. We dug little slits and you was in that slit all day lying in the sun, can't move, and at night its throwing it down on you ... and then they wonder why you're like this! (Williams and Wood, 1986, p. 1436)

Contained within this account is something much more than an explanation of what causes RA. He has reconstructed his narrative of wartime experience to explain 'why RA happened to me'. Other interviewees weave the cause of their RA into a narrative which emphasises the stresses of personal relationships and family life, as in this example from a middle-class woman in her 50s:

> I'm quite certain that it was stress that precipitated this. Not simply the stress of events that happened but the stress of suppressing myself while I was a mother and wife ... There comes a time in your life when you think, you know, 'where have I got to? There's nothing left of me'. (Williams, 1984b, pp. 188–9)

The teleological aspect of personal illness narratives can be seen most clearly when a religious concept is invoked to make sense of what has happened to an individual.

The Lord's so near and, you know, people say 'why you?' … and I [say] 'Look, I don't question the Lord, I don't ask … He knows why and that's good enough for me' … I've got the wonderful thing of having the Lord in my life. I've got such richness shall I say, such meaning. I've found the meaning of life, that's the way I look at it. My meaning is that I've found the joy in this life, and therefore for me to go through anything, it doesn't matter really, in one way, because I reckon that they are testing times. (Williams, 1984b, p. 193)

Lay beliefs such as those recounted here about RA can also be seen partly as attempts to understand the complexities of a disease that is inadequately understood within biomedicine. In the absence of a convincing medical explanation for 'Why me?' and 'Why now?', lay people are able to draw on a wide range of influences in constructing a narrative without direct contradiction from their doctors. Whether lay narratives are 'right' or 'wrong' in terms of biomedical knowledge, they clearly have a role in supporting someone attempting to live with RA. In the next two sections, we turn to the sources of 'expert knowledge' about the causes of rheumatoid arthritis, beginning with epidemiological studies.

3.5 Epidemiological knowledge

Arthritis and rheumatism as a whole are the biggest single source of disability in the United Kingdom and North American populations, and are among the main reasons for consultations with primary health care practitioners. A survey by the American epidemiologists L. S. Cunningham and Jennifer Kelsey (1984) of self-reported symptoms suggests that approximately 29 per cent of men and 32 per cent of women in the USA experience joint problems. This rises to 35 per cent and 51 per cent in people aged 55 or older. However, these estimates depend on individuals' own definitions of their symptoms and group together all forms of arthritis. Estimates of the prevalence of RA are much lower and vary considerably between populations. Caution must be exercised in interpreting apparent differences in the frequency of RA in different parts of the world.

● Can you suggest why?

■ The absence of a characterising diagnostic feature for RA leads to variations in methods of case ascertainment based on several features of the condition (as discussed earlier in this chapter). This in turn leads to variations in disease classification and makes comparisons of data from different populations problematic. (For example, a case of rheumatoid arthritis in one population may be classified as inflammatory polyarthritis in another.)

Attempts at standardising the reporting of the disease have been made by the development of disease classification criteria. For example the most widely used in epidemiological research was devised by the rheumatologist Frank Arnett and colleagues in the 1980s for the American Rheumatism Association and adopted by the American College of Rheumatology (ACR). Their classification (known as ACR 1987) is based on evidence from three sources: clinical assessments, such as whether a joint is swollen; standard laboratory assays, such as the level of rheumatoid factor in the blood; and X-rays of the hands and feet. A minimum score on these criteria must be reached before a person is labelled as having RA for study purposes. By using standardised classifications such as these, it is possible to estimate the prevalence and incidence of RA in different populations.

3.5.1 Prevalence and incidence estimates[6]

In 1986, Philip Wood and Elizabeth Badley published a comprehensive review of the epidemiology of rheumatic disorders. They noted that surveys using more rigorous definitions of RA show a remarkable degree of convergence in estimates of *prevalence* in most Caucasian groups across different geographical areas, varying between 0.8 and 1.0 per cent (i.e. about one case per 100 population surveyed at a single time point). All later surveys have confirmed this finding. However, the distribution of RA is not uniform: there is a marked excess in women, with estimates generally finding two to three times as many women as men are affected. In both sexes, the prevalence of the disease increases with age, approaching 5 per cent in women and 2 per cent in men aged above 55 years.

Epidemiological estimates of the annual *incidence* of RA (the number of new cases arising each year) pose even more problems than prevalence estimates, because of the long period that frequently elapses between the onset of symptoms and a confirmed diagnosis. A study conducted by Nicola Wiles and colleagues in the Norwich region, England, sought to overcome this problem by making annual assessments (using the ACR 1987 classification criteria for RA) of all patients who initially presented in 1990–91 with swelling of two or more joints. After 5 years of cumulative assessment, they were able to estimate the annual incidence of RA as 54 cases per 100 000 population for women and 24.5 cases per 100 000 for men, all ages combined (Wiles *et al.*, 1999). Table 3.2 shows that the incidence of RA increases with age in this study until 75 years, and then it declines. However, you should note that since RA is a relatively rare condition the numbers of new cases annually in each age group are small, so these data must be viewed cautiously.

Table 3.2 Age-specific incidence estimates for rheumatoid arthritis in males and females in the Norwich Health Authority, England, based on annual assessments for up to 5 years of patients presenting initially in 1990–91 with two or more swollen joints.

Age group/years	Incidence rate per 100 000 population (number of cases in brackets)	
	females	males
15–24	15.5 (5)	3.0 (1)
25–34	29.0 (10)	5.6 (2)
35–44	50.6 (17)	12.1 (4)
45–54	91.9 (29)	31.3 (10)
55–64	88.1 (24)	42.1 (11)
65–74	94.4 (26)	66.6 (16)
75+	29.8 (8)	57.0 (9)
all, age-adjusted	54.0 (119)	24.5 (53)

Age and sex were adjusted to the 1991 population of England and Wales. Rheumatoid arthritis was assessed cumulatively by applying the ACR 1987 classification criteria annually for up to 5 years. (Data from Wiles, N. *et al.*, 1999, Estimating the incidence of rheumatoid arthritis. Trying to hit a moving target? *Arthritis and Rheumatism*, **42**(7), Table 5, p. 1343)

● Why is the prevalence of RA so much greater than its incidence?

■ RA is a chronic disease lasting a long time, hence there are many more people with the disease at any one time than there are cases being newly diagnosed.

[6] Prevalence and incidence are defined and discussed in *Studying Health and Disease* (Open University Press, 2nd edn 1994; colour-enhanced 2nd edn 2001), Chapter 7.

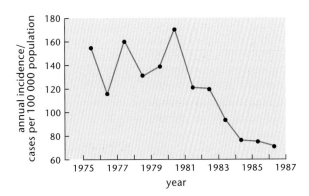

Figure 3.6 *Trends in annual incidence of RA among patients attending general practices in the United Kingdom in 1976–87 (all ages combined). (Source: Silman, A. J., 1988, Has the incidence of rheumatoid arthritis declined in the United Kingdom?* British Journal of Rheumatology, **27**, *pp. 77–8)*

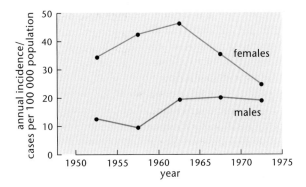

Figure 3.7 *Trends in annual incidence of rheumatoid arthritis in men and women in Olmstead County, Minnesota, USA, in 1950–74. (Source: Linos, A. et al., 1980, The epidemiology of rheumatoid arthritis in Rochester, Minnesota: a study of incidence, prevalence and mortality,* American Journal of Epidemiology, **111**, *pp. 87–98)*

Long-term trends in the incidence of RA have also been recorded within the same population. For example, Figure 3.6 shows the results of one of the few to be published on the trend in the UK, which was sharply downwards in the 1980s and approached 65 new cases per year per 100 000 population. Evidence from studies such as Table 3.2 indicate that it has fallen still further subsequently. A study in Finland revealed a trend in RA towards onset in the older age groups, with a rise in the median age at onset from 50.2 years to 57.8 years between 1975 and 1990 (Kaipiainen-Seppanen *et al.*, 1996). Incidence (like prevalence) increases with age in all studies, but it has also been suggested that the number of severe cases is declining.

● Figure 3.7 shows a much earlier trend in the annual incidence of RA in both men and women in a study in the USA. Describe the trend and suggest what insight this research gave into the biology of the disease. (*Hint*: What 'revolution' in the 1960s affected women but not men?)

■ The incidence of RA fell by almost a half in women in the 1960s and early 1970s, whereas it rose by a small amount in men. It may have occurred to you that this period coincided with the rapid and widespread uptake of the oral contraceptive pill in women, which has subsequently been shown to affect the occurrence of RA (discussed later in this chapter).

This example is an illustration of why, in the epidemiological study of any disease, it is difficult to disentangle 'real' changes in frequency from changes in the way in which the disease is defined and diagnosed over time. (You will meet this problem again in the epidemiology of AIDS, asthma and schizophrenia — the case studies in Chapters 4, 5 and 6 of this book.)

3.5.2 Risk factors for rheumatoid arthritis

Epidemiological data on prevalence and incidence, such as the studies reviewed above, can provide valuable information about the patterns of RA in populations and any associations with social and biological factors. These in turn suggest possible causal connections, but much more evidence is needed about the causes of RA.

Ethnicity

There are some interesting ethnic variations in the frequency of RA. For example, in urban Black African populations the prevalence of RA is about the same as that reported in Caucasians (Solomon *et al.*, 1975), but in rural Black African populations it is about one-tenth of that in Caucasians (Brighton *et al.*, 1988).

● What kinds of explanation do variations such as this suggest might be worth investigating?

■ In theory, reported ethnic variations in the prevalence of RA might be due to differences in susceptibility to RA arising from variations in genetic background, or to ethnic differences in the expression of symptoms, or to environmental effects associated with urbanisation.

The explanations are far from clear, but one of the authors of this chapter has attempted to investigate the role of urbanisation. Rheumatologist Alex MacGregor and his colleagues sent a postal questionnaire about the experience of RA to African-Caribbean and White respondents in a deprived, inner-city area of Manchester. MacGregor then examined those individuals who reported experiencing the disease. White respondents were found to have RA nearly three times more often than African-Caribbeans (MacGregor *et al.*, 1994). Such evidence makes urbanisation itself an unlikely causal factor in RA.

Social class

There have been occasional reports that the risk of developing RA is inversely related to income and occupational social class, but very few studies have examined the issue systematically. The majority of reports suggest that there is no overall relationship with social class (Lawrence, 1970; Jacob *et al.*, 1972), but interest was revived in 1994 by the work of Theodore Pincus and Lea Callahan in the USA (1994). They found an inverse relationship between 'educational level' — used as a 'proxy' for social class — and prevalence of RA in certain populations.

Age

The association of RA with age is twofold: as Table 3.2 demonstrated, the risk of onset increases with age, and the disability associated with the disease increases over time. Although 'wear and tear' damage to joints tends to increase with age, and repair processes become less efficient, simple mechanical explanations cannot account for the chronic inflammation in major organs of the body as well as in the joints, nor for the presence of rheumatoid factor in the blood, which are characteristic features of RA. Biological explanations for these phenomena must be sought, as you will see in Section 3.6.

Sex

Sex differences in the prevalence and incidence of RA are well established, but the underlying reasons are not well understood and represent an important challenge to research. The precise extent of the difference in prevalence is unclear but most studies estimate two to three times more RA in women. However, Fleming and co-workers (1976) could find no differences in rates between men and women when patients were examined within a year of disease onset.

● What does this finding suggest?

■ RA might have a similar *incidence* in men and women, but sex differences in *prevalence* appear over time. Perhaps there is more remission in men and the course of the disease is less severe.

Table 3.2 showed that there are much smaller sex differences in rates of onset of RA after 60 years of age and that the overall pattern of a much higher prevalence in women is due to an earlier age of onset in women, typically 45–64 years. Much of the evidence also supports the view that women experience RA in a more disabling form than men, but it is not consistent and there are variations depending on the measure of 'severity' used and which joints are studied.

Clearly, biological explanations for the observed sex differences in RA have been given great attention, and we will discuss them shortly, but the social and cultural influences of *gender* also need to be considered. Although these influences may not have a direct impact on the severity of the disease according to objective measures, there is evidence that gender does affect **illness behaviour** — the expression, perception and response to symptoms. However, findings from different studies are contradictory: Thompson and Pegley (1991) found that, at comparable levels of disease activity, disability for women was worse than for men, whereas another study by Deighton *et al.* (1992) found that sex differences in disability disappear after controlling for disease severity.

A related possibility is that aspects of *physical performance* that vary between men and women — for example, grip strength — result in greater disability for women after the onset of RA. Verbrugge and colleagues (1991) found that one of the biggest differences between men and women with arthritis is reported strength: similar tasks may thus pose greater challenges for women.

● Can you think of another explanation for sex differences in disability, based on the discussion of social roles earlier in this chapter?

■ It may be that traditional social and domestic roles are more revealing of disability in women than they are in men. For example, the finely controlled movements required in some domestic tasks, such as cooking and sewing, might reveal a woman's inability to perform them, whereas men with RA may not attempt them.

However, the most compelling explanations for sex differences in the prevalence of RA have come from biomedical research, which has also shed light on possible underlying causes of the condition and the pathological processes involved in its progression.

3.6 Biological knowledge

In this section we start by describing biological research suggesting that hormones, genes and infectious organisms may play a part in triggering the onset of RA or in increasing a person's susceptibility to other — perhaps still unidentified — precipitating factors. We then describe what is known about the underlying pathological processes in RA, and evaluate the strongly held view that the chronic inflammation in RA might be caused by inappropriate activity of the immune system against 'self', i.e. that it is an **autoimmune disease**.[7] Finally, we reflect on how

[7] Autoimmune diseases and the possible mechanisms by which they are mediated are discussed in more detail in *Human Biology and Health: an Evolutionary Approach* (Open University Press, 3rd edn 2001), Chapter 6.

more distant factors implicated by epidemiological studies of RA may be interacting with biological processes to cause the disease.

3.6.1 The role of hormones

The most obvious biological explanations for sex differences in the prevalence of RA relate to *sex hormones* such as testosterone and oestrogen. Hormonal influences could account for the common observation that women with RA experience temporary remission during pregnancy (Klipple and Cecere, 1989). Moreover, a study by Dutch epidemiologists provides evidence of a possible beneficial effect on RA of the oral contraceptive pill (Vandenbroucke *et al.*, 1982), as illustrated earlier in Figure 3.7. Two rheumatologists, Tim Spector and Marc Hochberg (1990) have suggested that oral contraceptives reduce the incidence of RA by postponing the onset of the disease, which occurs once the oral contraceptive has been stopped.

There are a variety of ways in which sex hormones might influence the causes or course of RA. There are, for example, many complex relationships between sex hormones and the immune system, which in turn is directly involved in the production of chronic inflammation. However, overall research evidence on sex hormones and RA is contradictory and inconclusive. For example, elevated levels of a sex hormone in patients with RA may turn out to be a *consequence* rather than a cause of the disease (Da Silva and Hall, 1992).

3.6.2 Genetic inheritance

It has long been known that RA has a 'family connection'. Women who have a sister or mother affected by RA are two to four times more likely to develop the disease than those without such a history. However, such close relatives commonly also share the same domestic environment, so this pattern does not prove that RA is an inherited disorder. The genetic link becomes clearer in studies of affected twin pairs. A nationwide study of twins in the UK, by Alan Silman, Alex MacGregor and colleagues, found the **concordance** (i.e. the probability that if one twin develops RA, so will the other) was 15 per cent in *identical* (monozygotic) twin pairs. However, concordance was only 4 per cent in *non-identical* (dizygotic) twin pairs (Silman *et al.*, 1994).

● What do these findings in twin pairs suggest about the importance of genetic inheritance in RA?

■ Concordance in identical twins is much higher than in non-identical twins, which indicates that a shared genetic component may be responsible for their increased susceptibility to RA. However, the fact that concordance even in identical twins is relatively low, despite their identical genes, indicates that environmental factors must have a major role in causing RA.

Although genetic susceptibility to RA is thought to be *polygenic* (that is, more than one gene is involved in disease predisposition), some strong associations with particular genes have been identified.[8] The most compelling evidence has come from studies of the association of RA with the presence of certain *HLA* genes, for example, in research by one of the authors of this chapter, Alan Rigby, and his

[8] The structures of genes and chromosomes, and the association of certain genes with disease susceptibility, are extensively discussed in *Human Biology and Health: an Evolutionary Approach* (Open University Press, 3rd edn 2001), Chapters 3, 4 and 9.

colleagues (Rigby *et al.*, 1991; Rigby, 1992). The *HLA* genes are concerned with regulation of the immune system. A breakdown in immunological regulation leading to an 'anti-self' (autoimmune) response in the joints is thought to be one of the precipitating factors in RA — a point we discuss further in a moment.

Several alternative forms (or *alleles*) of the *HLA* genes occur in humans, and one of them (known as *HLA-DR4*) occurs more frequently in people with RA than expected from its distribution in the population. New methods of genetic screening developed for the Human Genome Project[9] have enabled the complete mapping of variants of this and other genes associated with RA in 257 North American families containing at least one pair of siblings affected with the disease (Jawaheer *et al.*, 2001). 70 per cent of affected individuals in this study carried at least one *HLA-DR4* allele. Yet the variants of this gene cannot cause RA on their own because they are also found widely in non-affected people. Numerous other genes are also likely to be involved in the development of RA, each with a small effect, and involved in complex interactions with each other and with environmental factors. Different *HLA* alleles are also associated with a range of diseases that show perturbations of the immune system, ranging from thyroid disease to multiple sclerosis.

As new technology increases the speed at which genetic associations with diseases can be found, there is hope that the major genetic components of RA will be identified, leading to greater understanding of the disease processes and advances in treatment and perhaps even prevention. However, there are major scientific difficulties in applying such knowledge, and there are serious ethical concerns about the effects on individuals of genetic information about their disease susceptibility.[10] Finally, it is important to note that since RA is rare, the majority of relatives of an affected person will not actually develop the disease themselves.

3.6.3 A role for infection?

There is considerable uncertainty about the possible role of infectious organisms in RA (reviewed by Alan Silman, 1991). One of the most commonly studied viral agents is the *Epstein–Barr virus*, which is found in populations worldwide and has been implicated in many different diseases. Many studies have shown higher levels of antibodies to Epstein–Barr virus in RA patients, when compared to individuals without disease. Another viral candidate agent is *human parvovirus B19*, which has been isolated from the joints of individuals with an arthritis resembling RA. A bacterial agent, *Mycobacterium tuberculosis*, has been shown to produce a type of arthritis in laboratory animals that is similar to RA, and a bacterium *Proteus mirabilis*, which causes urinary tract infections, has also been identified as a possible cause (Wilson *et al.*, 2000). But the flaw in all theories concerning infectious agents is a lack of specificity for the disease — not everyone who has RA can be shown to be infected with one of these organisms, and many infected people do not have RA.

---

[9] The biological, ethical and social implications of the Human Genome Project, genetic screening and gene therapy are discussed extensively in *Human Biology and Health: An Evolutionary Approach* (Open University Press, 3rd edn 2001), Chapter 9, and in the associated TV programme and audiotape band for Open University students.

[10] This point is illustrated by an article in *Health and Disease: A Reader* (Open University Press, 3rd edn 2001), by Ruth McGowan, entitled 'One parent's reflection on genetic counselling'; it was set reading for Open University students during *Human Biology and Health: An Evolutionary Approach* (Open University Press, 3rd edn 2001), Chapter 9.

● What does this suggest about the role of infectious agents in RA? Can you suggest an alternative explanation, based on the discussion so far?

■ It seems highly unlikely that any infectious organism is the single precipitating factor. Perhaps the best bet for the aetiology of RA is an infectious organism triggering an autoimmune reaction in a genetically susceptible host.

3.6.4 Autoimmunity

Chronic inflammation is a central part of the disease process in RA. Microscopic examination of the synovial membrane of affected joints (refer back to Figure 3.1), reveals a thickened, swollen appearance. White cells of the types normally involved in producing inflammation at the site of an infection infiltrate the joint in huge numbers. Blood vessels become dilated and proliferate in the inflamed tissue, bringing more white cells to increase the inflammation.

This process is mediated by signalling molecules, known collectively as *cytokines*, which are released into the joint by white cells participating in the inflammatory response. They promote the proliferation and activity of cells in their local environment. One particular cytokine, called *TNF-alpha*, predominates and is the basis of a novel treatment for RA (described shortly).

The development of a chronic inflammatory response in normal tissue is the most compelling evidence that RA is an autoimmune disease. Autoimmunity means that the disease process involves the loss of the immune system's normal *tolerance* to 'self'. The pathology is at least partly due to the production of 'anti-self' *autoantibodies* and other components of an immune response directed inappropriately against the body's own tissues. As you already know, unusual antibodies, known collectively as rheumatoid factor, can be found in the blood of about 80 per cent of individuals with RA. However, the precise role of rheumatoid factor in RA remains controversial, and other autoantibodies have also been identified. Although autoantibodies are involved in the disease process, it is by no means certain that they are the primary *cause* of RA (Smolen and Steiner, 1998). Inflammation in the joints may be triggered by an infection or by some as yet unknown factor, producing tissue damage, which in turn provokes the immune system into an inappropriate attack.

Another possible mechanism is *antigenic mimicry*, in which parts of the structure of infectious organisms resemble components of 'self'. The Epstein–Barr virus, for example has proteins in its coat that resemble proteins in the cartilage that lines human joints. Hence, when the immune system sets up an attack on the infectious agent, it cannot avoid simultaneously attacking those similar components of the body's own tissues.

3.6.5 Multifactorial theories

As the previous discussion indicates, complex interactions between biological and environmental factors in the aetiology of RA are suggested by current research. In this respect, RA is similar to other chronic degenerative conditions, such as heart disease and cancers, in being *multifactorial* in origin. For example, it has been suggested that the decline in incidence and severity since the 1980s (Figure 3.6) may be due to changes in the biological nature of a viral agent, but it may also be related to the increased use of the oral contraceptive pill among women (Figure 3.7).

Other factors (mainly anecdotal) such as the weather, diet and stress, have been implicated in multifactorial theories. Many of these theories have not withstood rigorous scientific scrutiny, but they remain of interest — particularly to patients — and cannot be discounted. Although symptoms of RA may vary with the weather, biochemical indicators of disease inflammation do not show similar changes. The relationship between diet and disease has been reviewed by Mangge *et al.* (1999) and particular attention has been paid to the protective effect of diets high in fish oil.

The epidemiology of RA implicates both genetic and environmental factors in the cause of the condition. What we have tried to indicate here is that while much recent work in immunology and cellular biology has been helpful in illuminating disease processes, 'true causes' — the events that initiate RA — remain elusive. A number of studies have indicated that RA may eventually comprise several distinct subsets, each with particular distinguishing clinical features. Alternatively, the clinical picture that is currently recognised as RA may represent a final common pathway for several aetiologically distinct chronic inflammatory processes.

3.7 Putting knowledge into practice: therapeutic strategies

In view of the elusiveness of the cause or causes of RA, there is no adequate strategy for its prevention. The rationale for clinical management is based on the current understanding of the pathological processes involved. Chronic inflammation is established as the cause of joint destruction in RA, so suppression of inflammation by drugs remains the cornerstone of strategies aimed at treating the disease. We begin by briefly reviewing the major classes of drugs used in RA, their benefits, side effects and limitations.

3.7.1 Drug treatments

One of the earliest and most effective methods of suppressing inflammation in RA was the use of *steroids* (synthetic forms of naturally occurring steroid hormones), introduced with dramatic effect in the 1940s. They abolished inflammation in patients in whom apparently irreversible disease had been present for decades. But it soon became clear to both clinicians and patients that the doses required to control RA produced many unwanted effects, including diabetes, high blood pressure, damage to blood vessels, and thinning of bone leading to collapse of vertebrae in the spine. At the time of writing (2002), the precise place of steroids in the treatment of RA still remains controversial. The use of steroids is generally limited to short courses or to injections directly into joints, which produce few adverse effects on the rest of the body.

Another effective class of drugs was the *salicylates* (aspirin), and for many years the long-term use of high-dose aspirin formed the mainstay of drug treatment for RA. This was, however, also associated with serious adverse effects, in particular a high frequency of gastrointestinal complications including haemorrhage and perforation.

A number of drugs have since been developed which have similar properties to aspirin, with fewer adverse effects. These are broadly classed as *non-steroidal anti-inflammatory drugs* (or NSAIDs), and their use remains central in the day-to-day control of both pain and inflammation in the majority of patients with RA. They are not, however, believed to influence the long-term outcome of the disease. Despite their apparent superiority over aspirin, NSAIDs remain an important cause of morbidity from gastrointestinal haemorrhage and renal impairment. The risk is particularly high in elderly people.

A separate group of drugs, known collectively as *disease-modifying anti-rheumatic drugs* (or DMARDs), is used in RA to control the inflammatory process in the long term. They are believed to influence the rate of progression of disease, but the mechanisms of action of DMARDs are diverse and inadequately understood: most act directly on cells involved in the inflammatory process to suppress their activity. All DMARDs are associated with important and potentially serious toxicity, primarily affecting the bone marrow, liver and lungs, and their use necessitates careful monitoring.

Clearly, the benefits of drug treatments have to be weighed against the multiple risks of side effects, but there are several problems in evaluating outcomes.

● Can you suggest what they are? (Think back to the nature of the disease from the patient's perspective.)

■ Any benefit may take a considerable time to show; different measures of outcome will show different benefits; and what is a benefit in clinical terms may not be seen to be so by the patient. The relapsing and remitting course of the disease makes it difficult to be sure that an improvement is due to a given drug.

In addition, the most potent drugs available for use in RA are frequently associated with the most adverse effects and are reserved until late in the disease — which makes their usefulness in early disease hard to evaluate. Drugs in combination may be more effective than agents used singly, yet few data are available. Finally, in assessing published reports, it is important to consider bias toward the publication of drug trials that show a positive rather than a negative outcome.

Given these limitations, it is perhaps not surprising that the available data on RA show no clear long-term effectiveness of any of the available drug treatments, and initially effective regimens are frequently discontinued because of adverse reactions. The majority of patients with a disease lasting 15 years will have changed drugs on average three times.

3.7.2 New treatment strategies

Advances in drug design in recent years have seen the development of new, specifically targeted treatments for RA based on an understanding of the biology of the disease. Knowledge of the specific enzymes activated in the inflammatory process has resulted in a new class of non-steroidal anti-inflammatory drugs, collectively known as *selective Cox-II inhibitors* (the full name of the enzyme is cyclo-oxygenase II). These drugs are directed only at tissues affected by inflammation, so they have considerably fewer side effects on normal tissues such as the gastrointestinal tract, compared with predecessor drugs.

Synthetic antibodies directed against TNF-alpha, the central mediator of inflammation, have also been developed and initial experience suggests that they are highly effective in halting the progression of disease. (See Taylor *et al.* (2001) for a review of therapeutic strategies involving the immune system.) New approaches also under development include *gene therapy*, in which genes are inserted directly into joints to correct defects in the function of cells there.

One difficulty with the introduction of new treatments for RA is that patients' expectations of their value are often inappropriately raised. New treatments tend to be hailed in the popular press as 'cures'. This optimism is perhaps fuelled by those involved in the expensive and competitive process of research and development of new biological therapies, who understandably emphasise their short-term successes. However, as discussed earlier, it will take years before the true impact of these treatments on the course of RA can be adequately evaluated.

The high cost of the new treatments themselves has also introduced problems for health-care funding. In the UK, it is estimated that switching people with RA to selective Cox-II inhibitors would lead to an additional cost to the NHS of approximately £25 million per year. Guidelines have been introduced to direct their use to those patients considered to be at 'high risk' of developing serious gastrointestinal problems with conventional drugs. Anti-TNF therapies cost £8 000 per patient-year of treatment; prescription is advised only in those with severe disease, which has not responded to other forms of therapy. At present (2002), the availability of anti-TNF drugs is dictated by local health-care policy and shows variation from region to region.

3.7.3 Other medical and surgical interventions

Medical management of RA must include treating the 'whole body' manifestations of the disease, such as anaemia, and the involvement of major organs, such as the heart, lungs and kidneys. The consequences of persisting joint damage — joint destruction, muscle wasting and problems with locomotion — also have to be addressed. An important liaison in the management of RA is between rheumatologists, physiotherapists and orthopaedic surgeons who specialise in joint surgery and have a crucial role in maintaining function and managing pain — as the case history in Box 3.4 illustrates.

> **Box 3.4   Mr K**
>
> Mr K, who has had RA for 40 years, has had numerous joint operations in that time, including replacements of both hips and knees, artificial joints in the small joints of his hands, and an artificial elbow and shoulder joint. His early operations relieved the pain in his joints, but they did not improve his joint function to any significant extent. However, the surgery performed on his hip in the last five years and on his shoulder two years ago has transformed his life and has enabled him to function at a level that he would not have previously imagined. Given the levels of disability he had previously experienced, he now leads a remarkably independent existence and manages his life by himself.

Mr K's experience illustrates the advances in joint surgery and in the technological development of artificial joints in recent years. Physiotherapy also has a crucial role, in particular in preserving joint stability and muscle strength to prevent joint deformity and maintain function. Physiotherapists have an important part to play in the management of chronic pain through the use of techniques such as ultrasonic massage and weak electrical stimulation of affected areas. (Chapter 7 of this book discusses pain-control techniques.)

However, the use of surgery and physiotherapy is not routinely accepted everywhere. For example, the frequency and timing of surgical intervention show marked variation between hospitals, and the long-term value of physiotherapy is also debated and is used considerably less in the UK than in other European countries.

3.7.4 Unorthodox treatment strategies

As we described earlier, several theories about the causes of RA exist at the fringes of medical orthodoxy, and these have led to considerable uncertainty about the place of alternative treatments in the management of RA. The value of dietary modification is one such area of controversy, as the review by Mangge *et al.* (1999) confirms. The widespread public perception that diet influences RA is not well supported by scientific data. There is an indication that dietary fat content may influence disease activity, and some rheumatologists believe that allergy to foods such as cheese has a role in RA and prescribe exclusion diets.

Many people with RA turn to a variety of complementary therapies, and most interest has focused on *homeopathy*. It is not clear whether the search for alternative treatments reflects the inefficacy of conventional medical management or the therapeutic potency of the alternatives. There are currently no adequate data suggesting the value of homeopathic remedies in RA but, given the difficulty in assessing the outcome of orthodox anti-inflammatory agents, it is unlikely that such data will become available unless new forms of evaluation and outcome assessment are devised.

3.7.5 Keeping the patient in view

RA affects all aspects of patients' lives. Doctors should take account of the patient's knowledge, circumstances, hopes and fears in order to arrive at strategies for medical management that are appropriate to the patient's present and future needs. Hip pain, for example, may not only impair walking but may affect sexual function, and this is an important consideration in planning hip surgery. A detailed occupational history is needed in planning and staging surgical procedures, which may require long periods off work to convalesce. Future hopes of pregnancy must be known when planning drug treatment in RA because it may impair fertility and may have to be stopped prior to conception.

The individual's response to his or her symptoms is another important component of the problem which the clinician has to consider when planning management strategies. Failure to understand the patient's experience can lead to situations like the one in Box 3.5.

Box 3.5   Mrs L

When Mrs L was referred as a new patient to the rheumatology clinic, she showed features of well-established RA with inflammation affecting her hands, wrists and elbows, and deformities of both wrists. During the consultation, she said she had attended hospital two years earlier when the symptoms had first developed. She remembered being told at that time that she had a chronic disease of the joints which would not get better without treatment. She was recommended to take a drug which she was told might affect the back of her eyes and could impair her eyesight. She did not take the drug or keep her follow-up appointment. She put up with the symptoms until increasing pain in her hands made her ask to be seen in the clinic again.

In order to manage the uncertainties being experienced by someone such as Mrs L, it is important to understand her point of view, to provide information in a manner and in a context that facilitates dialogue about the risks and benefits of different treatments, and to shape advice to her actual circumstances. There may be many months of trying various strategies before an adequate treatment regime is found, and this compounds the uncertainty of living with the symptoms of RA.

The unpredictable benefits of treatment, along with the psychological effects of having RA (such as depression and anxiety), may have important consequences for a patient's willingness to comply with lengthy spells of out-patient treatment, which place enormous demands on an individual's time and resources. Compliance is important from the doctor's viewpoint in order to make a realistic evaluation of the effectiveness of particular drug regimens, as measured in clinical or biochemical terms. However, what is 'effective' to a doctor will not necessarily be so for the patient. The doctor treating the person with RA has the difficult task of combining his or her abstract scientific understanding of the disease with the way in which it makes itself known in the body and the life of the individual patient.

Patients and their doctors have different expectations, hopes, agendas and stories within which the experience and understanding of RA are framed. As we indicated at the start of this chapter, the scientific story of RA — by epidemiologists, laboratory scientists and doctors — is only one of the stories to be told. The problems of treatment outcome and disease impact are central to the management of everyday life with RA, and are of growing importance within health services seeking to make their interventions more effective and more appropriate to patients' needs. In the next section of this chapter, we look at attempts to develop measures for evaluating the outcome of treatment and other interventions that do justice to the everyday experience of the person with RA.

3.8 Patient-provided measures of outcome

3.8.1 The patient-centred approach

We have already discussed a variety of biological and clinical methods of assessing the severity and course of disease in RA, including blood tests and X-rays. Considerable efforts have also been made to assess the personal and social impact of RA. Standardised, precise and quantifiable questionnaires and interview-based assessments have been developed, which attempt to elicit the patient's own report of his or her disease and its personal consequences. This **patient-centred approach**[11] to measuring the course of RA is beginning to be used in basic research on the effectiveness of different therapies, as well as in the more routine provision and monitoring of care.

It is interesting to consider why efforts have been made to obtain and use assessments provided by patients — given that medicine is reputed to have strong 'reductionist' tendencies, i.e. a greater readiness to trust and be concerned with biologically measured parameters of disease rather than with subjective evidence such as patients' reports. Whereas the patients' own perspectives are beginning to be regarded as of increasing interest in their own right, moves within health care

---

[11] Patient-centred approaches to health care in medical settings — particularly the clinical consultation — and the more traditional doctor-centred approaches, are discussed in *Medical Knowledge: Doubt and Certainty* (Open University Press, 2nd edn 1994; colour-enhanced 2nd edn 2001), Chapter 9.

since the 1990s to make it more sensitive to 'consumers' have opened up discussion and research on ways of using assessments provided by patients.

Health services are increasingly being required to evaluate cost-effectiveness by devising and using **outcome measures** — systematic measures of the benefits of specific health-care interventions.[12] Since the primary objectives of health care for RA are to reduce pain, disability and disadvantages arising from the disease, so outcome measures should relate to these objectives. In turn, the objectives of health care have to relate to and derive from the main concerns of patients. It will already be clear to you that such apparently desirable reciprocity does not necessarily occur.

Another factor in the development of patient-provided outcome measures stems from the growing acceptance that the patient is uniquely placed to know the impact of disease upon him or her, and is also capable of providing reports with the same accuracy as is sought from conventional measures such as blood tests. If patients' personal experiences can be as reliably captured as biological processes, then they offer potentially powerful evidence of the benefits or side effects of interventions.

The drive to find relevant as well as accurate measures of outcome ultimately stems from one crucial feature of all forms of intervention for RA. Beneficial effects — whether from drugs, surgery, psychological or complementary therapies — are invariably modest and therefore difficult to detect. This factor alone leads pharmaceutical companies, clinical researchers and indeed any agency interested in improving the care of individuals with RA, to search for more sensitive, appropriate and ultimately convincing measures of the outcomes of interventions. If such measures could be obtained directly from the patient via reliable, useful and practical methods, then traditional reservations about the weaknesses and 'softness' of subjective data will erode.

3.8.2 Questionnaires and the assessment of arthritis

A number of questionnaires have been developed that are completed by patients and intended to assess, with adequate accuracy, the personal and social consequences of RA. This kind of research has developed more extensively in rheumatology than almost any other area of medicine. Questionnaires on the impact of RA have been put to a wide variety of uses:

- In a diverse range of clinical trials to assess the benefits to patients with RA of drugs, surgery, psychological therapies and alternative methods of providing care (e.g. in-patient versus out-patient care);
- To track the natural history of the disease in cohorts of patients with RA so that more precise statements can be provided about the usual range of progression of pain and disability over time;
- In clinical audit and quality assurance in health care;[13]
- By clinicians in individual patient-care to detect and monitor problems in patients over time and to evaluate the impact of therapy.

[12] Difficulties in the evaluation of cost-effectiveness in health-care interventions are discussed in *Dilemmas in UK Health Care* (Open University Press, 3rd edn 2001), Chapter 2.

[13] Clinical audit is a method of 'peer-review' among doctors of the outcomes of medical interventions; the factors that led to its incorporation into NHS procedures are discussed in *Caring for Health: History and Diversity* (Open University Press, 3rd edn 2001), Chapter 7, and in the context of other methods of health-care evaluation, in *Dilemmas in UK Health Care* (Open University Press, 3rd edn 2001), Chapter 2.

To serve a useful and convincing role in such diverse contexts, health-evaluation questionnaires need to produce answers that match a clear set of requirements, summarised in Box 3.6.

> **Box 3.6   Criteria for health-evaluation questionnaires**
>
> They should produce answers that are:
>
> - *reliable* (that is, answers that are consistent on repeated administration, provided no real change has occurred in the subject matter);
> - *valid* (that is, the information provided does actually provide a measure of what the questionnaire purports to measure):
> - *sensitive* to changes of importance to the patient over time;
> - *acceptable* to the patient; and
> - *feasible* for use in the context intended.[14]

3.8.3   Assessing disability and pain

The most widely used questionnaire in the assessment of RA is the *Health Assessment Questionnaire* (HAQ), devised by Fries *et al.* (1982). The core of the HAQ consists of 20 simple questionnaire items asking individuals to assess their degree of difficulty with various tasks (for example, 'Are you able to cut your meat?'). The answers produce scores for an individual in eight aspects of daily life: dressing and grooming, rising from a chair or bed, eating, walking (Figure 3.8), hygiene, reach, grip and activities (for example, getting in and out of a car). The average of the eight scores is used as a summary **Disability Index**. The questionnaire performs very well against the criteria outlined in Box 3.6: respondents give consistent answers and find it easy and quick to complete, and it also has substantial validity.

● How would you test the validity of a questionnaire such as this one?

■ By direct observation of patients to corroborate their questionnaire responses.[15]

A group of general practitioners in Glasgow directly observed a sample of patients with RA perform the eight areas assessed by the HAQ, and scored what they estimated to be the patients' degree of difficulty (Sullivan *et al.*, 1987). The patients then also completed the HAQ themselves. There was a very high level of agreement between the two sets of evaluations.

The HAQ is also a very practical tool for tracking the natural history of the disease. Two rheumatologists (Wolfe and Cathey, 1991) followed up a series of people with RA in a Kansas clinic over a twelve-year period. They showed a steady progressive deterioration in HAQ Disability Index scores over the period of the study. Moreover the best predictor of the extent of deterioration in disability was the patients' own answers to the HAQ at the beginning of the study.

[14] The design of questionnaires and issues of reliability and validity are discussed in more detail *Studying Health and Disease* (Open University Press, 2nd edn 1994; colour-enhanced 2nd edn 2001), Chapter 5.

[15] The use of observation studies to corroborate data obtained from questionnaires or interviews is discussed in *Studying Health and Disease* (Open University Press, 2nd edn 1994; colour-enhanced 2nd edn 2001), Chapter 5.

As you have seen, pain is also a central feature of RA. Pain is a more obviously personal and, in measurement terms, subjective phenomenon. (It is the subject of Chapter 7 of this book.) The HAQ uses a simple technique to assess pain, inviting individuals to mark a position that represents their degree of pain on a linear scale. Simple measures such as this have proved just as useful as more sophisticated methods in which, for example, detailed account is taken of the vocabulary patients select to describe their pain (an example of the latter appears as Table 7.1 in Chapter 7). Another widely used questionnaire in RA — the *Arthritis Impact Measurement Scales* (AIMS) (Meenan *et al.*, 1980) — asks about the frequency and severity of pain, summing the answers to a single scale.

Consistency between different outcome measures is essential, if results from different studies are to be compared. Ray Fitzpatrick (another of the authors of this chapter) and his colleagues asked patients with RA to complete the AIMS and several other similar questionnaires on a single occasion. There was less consistency between different questionnaires in scoring pain than there was in scoring disability (Fitzpatrick *et al.*, 1992). It is essential to include measures of pain despite such measurement problems, because it is not possible to predict from a knowledge of the severity of the disease, the degree of pain that someone with RA experiences. Indeed, when a group of rheumatologists from Missouri assessed their patients with RA for pain, they found that older age, lower income and various psychological measures of distress and helplessness were all better predictors of pain than conventional laboratory and clinical measures of disease severity (Parker *et al.*, 1988).

Figure 3.8 *Assessing the degree of disability of a person with rheumatoid arthritis is complicated by variations in the restriction or pain involved in different tasks (e.g. walking up a slope, using a key to open a door), and variations over time as the condition remits and relapses. (Photo: John Callan/Shout)*

3.8.4 Assessing social aspects

Many questionnaires given to patients with RA also attempt to provide standardised assessment of its social aspects. As you already know, RA can have wide-ranging effects on the individual's social world, including problems of employment, loss of contact and diminished quality of relationships. However, it may be difficult within the confines of a short set of simple items in a questionnaire to capture all relevant aspects of individuals' social lives. The AIMS questionnaire emphasises the impact of RA in reducing the ability to maintain contact with friends and relatives, whether by visits or telephone. Other questionnaires focus on the individual's sense of being isolated and a burden to others.

● Why might two different questionnaires produce somewhat different impressions of the impact of RA, even if completed by a single group of patients?

■ The questionnaires may differ in which aspects of daily life they emphasise. Thus, the social dimension may be defined in one questionnaire as activities like maintaining contact with friends, and in another questionnaire as anxieties like feeling a burden to others.

It has been shown that if patients with RA complete several different questionnaires, there is little agreement in the picture portrayed by the various social assessments (Fitzpatrick *et al.*, 1992).

Another problem has been identified by a group working in a specialist arthritis research unit in Connecticut (Reisine *et al.*, 1987). They claim that a fundamental bias exists in all questionnaires on social aspects, which tend to assess the impact of RA on household activities such as cooking and washing, but neglect what the authors term 'nurturant functions'. These functions include childcare, caring for other household members who are sick, and maintaining the family's social relations with the outside world.

●   Think back to Section 3.3.2 on 'Activities of daily living'. What do you think might be the result of the questionnaire bias that Reisine *et al.* identified?

■   It is argued that 'nurturant functions' are more relevant to the lives of many women. Thus, existing questionnaires may have a gender bias that systematically *underestimates* the degree of impact of RA on women.

Problems of definition and emphasis also arise in attempting to assess the psychological consequences of RA systematically. There is evidence that individuals with RA have increased levels of serious psychological symptoms such as anxiety and depression and, for this reason, questionnaires such as the AIMS give most attention to such experiences. However, others would argue that the most important psychological problems for patients with RA are far more common, if less severe, symptoms such as feeling out of control and losing autonomy.

3.8.5 Personalised assessments

It should be clear to you from the previous discussion that it is very difficult to identify a standard list of questionnaire items that is suitable for assessing the impact of RA on everyone with the disorder. Not only does RA have a very diverse range of possible consequences for everyday life, individuals will vary enormously in their concerns and priorities.

A group of rheumatologists in Ontario tackled this problem by devising a personalised method of assessing the impact of RA, which attempts to be sensitive to variations between individuals (Tugwell *et al.*, 1987). Instead of asking patients a standard set of questions, they are invited to identify for themselves the areas and activities in their lives that are most affected, and that they would regard as the highest priority for improvement by means of therapy. Patients would therefore identify a list of personal priorities and then rate the degree of improvement or deterioration that occurred in relation to this list in subsequent assessments. The priorities most commonly selected by patients are not surprising: walking and housework. However, some patients selected activities that are rarely if ever assessed in conventionally formatted questionnaires: for example, getting to church or the pub or playing golf.

This method was subsequently used by the group in a double-blind randomised trial of the benefits of methotrexate, a slow-acting DMARD (disease-modifying anti-rheumatic drug), (Tugwell *et al.*, 1990). Eliciting and measuring patients' personal priorities proved more sensitive to the therapeutic benefits of the drug than either the doctors' traditional clinical measures, or a patient-completed questionnaire about disability with conventional standard questions asked of all respondents.

● Can you foresee a drawback of employing this personalised approach to evaluating the outcome for each patient?

■ It requires an interview which, for the large-scale studies usually required for trials of new therapies, is not as feasible as a self-completed questionnaire.

There is still no consensus about the most sensitive and useful method of assessing the broader consequences for individuals of having chronic diseases like RA. Although it may be argued that attempts to simplify the diversity of individuals' personal experiences into quantitative forms are inevitably flawed, the purposes of such efforts should be kept in mind — to go beyond narrow measures of outcome to identify broader benefits. The use of questionnaires of the kind described here is becoming widespread in assessing the advantages and disadvantages of the many drugs now in use for patients with RA.

Research is still needed to discover what aspects of health care or social interventions can most improve the well-being of patients with RA, but a multidisciplinary approach has emerged as more beneficial than management by a hospital doctor alone. A number of trials have demonstrated significant improvement in patients following short programmes of intensive intervention by a team including a rheumatologist, physiotherapist and other professionals (for example, Jacobsson *et al.*, 1998). It is generally accepted that the benefits of all forms of care — social as well as medical — must be examined by methods that reflect patients' perceptions as much as possible. You should now be aware of the potential as well as the pitfalls of current methods of including the patient in such assessments.

In the final section of this chapter, we stand back from the personal and professional narratives of RA, and briefly consider the impact on those narratives of the social history of arthritis in the twentieth century.

3.9 An historical footnote

There is little literature on public attitudes or societal reactions to arthritis, beyond Badley and Wood's study in 1979. This is in sharp contrast to AIDS, schizophrenia, or even asthma — as you will see in the case studies in later chapters of this book. Sex, drugs, madness, and children 'gasping for breath' have greater cultural resonance than middle-aged or elderly women and men living quietly alone in chronic pain. Nonetheless, all forms of arthritis, including RA, do have a **social history**. The historian, David Cantor, has done some important work in unpicking the threads of that history by looking at the wider social context in which the diagnosis and treatment of arthritis developed (Cantor, 1991, 1992, 1993).

Many times in earlier books in this series, it has been demonstrated that diseases are not stable and timeless entities. At least some aspects of every disease are not so much revealed as 'produced' by the social and cultural processes of analysis and interpretation.[16] The history of RA illustrates this rather well. In common with many other diseases, progress towards discovering the distinct nature of RA is often portrayed as a difficult but fundamentally unproblematic 'discovery of the facts'.

[16] The main discussion of health, disease, disability and health-related behaviours as 'socially constructed' can be found in *Medical Knowledge: Doubt and Certainty* (Open University Press, 2nd edn 1994; colour-enhanced 2nd edn 2001), Chapter 7; but see also *Birth to Old Age: Health in Transition* (Open University Press, 2nd edn 1995; colour-enhanced 2nd edn 2001), Chapters 1, 9 and 10.

But the history of RA has in fact been much more complex, and reveals something about attitudes to arthritic disorders in general. In particular, as David Cantor has shown, images of arthritis were bound up with the politics of industry and empire in Britain in the early twentieth century.

The history of professional and public attitudes to arthritis and rheumatism in general, and RA in particular, cannot be understood without analysing the factors influencing two developments. The first is the gradual emergence of a medical speciality — *rheumatology* — dealing with the treatment of arthritis and rheumatism, and the second is the establishment of research into these conditions. Both these developments affected the perceived importance of arthritis and rheumatism in society, and their status in relation to other organised interests such as the government, medical charities and the pharmaceutical industry. For example, public interest in arthritis and rheumatism clearly took off in the inter-war period in Britain as a result of concern about a number of social factors: the costs of these diseases to the National Health Insurance scheme set up by Lloyd George in 1911; their effects on 'national efficiency'; concern about infant and child welfare (particularly the impact of rheumatic heart disease); the revival of spa economies during World War I, and the inter-war growth of medical hydrology (medicinal use of spa and other waters).[17]

Many of these concerns were given a further push by the socio-economic problems of the 1930s. With government reluctance to increase spending on health care, doctors turned to philanthropy for support. It was during this period that the major rheumatological research charity, the Empire Rheumatism Council, was set up. The early donations to this charity came predominantly from industrialists and businessmen concerned about the impact of rheumatic diseases on the efficiency and productivity of the workforce.

These developments had a significant impact on the development of rheumatology, and thus upon the development of knowledge about — and therapeutic intervention for — rheumatic diseases. At the time of the instigation of the NHS in 1948, rheumatology was a small and insignificant specialty. The Empire Rheumatism Council (later the Arthritis and Rheumatism Council, or ARC) now the Arthritis Research Campaign, played an important role in encouraging research, and engaging in negotiations with the government over the position of rheumatology in the health service. Rheumatology is now a medical specialty, with its own hierarchies of prestige, its conference circuit and its journals and newsletters. Although it cannot call forth public beneficence on the scale of cancer or heart disease, charities representing arthritis and rheumatism are consistently in the income 'top twenty'.

The present-day Arthritis Research Campaign exists to finance and organise research into the causes and means of treatment of rheumatic diseases, to encourage teaching about the diseases, and to stimulate public bodies to provide treatment. In the financial year 1999/2000, ARC spent almost £22 million on these objectives, providing the major source of support for rheumatology research through institutes, research units, research grants and fellowships. It supports university appointments and has endowed a number of Chairs of Rheumatology. Its income is made up of donations and legacies and the work of more than 1 000 fund-raising branches throughout the country. The ARC thus plays a crucial role in the management of public attitudes to RA and other related diseases. It lies at the heart of a network of national and regional structures, which link the general public, business, the medical

[17] All of these topics are discussed in *Caring for Health: History and Diversity* (Open University Press, 3rd edn 2001), Chapters 5 and 6.

profession and the government. At times of economic and political uncertainty over the direction of health services, and when many worthy causes are competing for public attention, the intelligent construction and representation of the impact of a disease like RA play an important role in influencing public attitudes and hence funding.

In concluding the chapter with this historical footnote, we seek to remind you that RA — like all diseases — has a social history, which can have a profound impact on the way a disease is perceived in society. In turn, the 'public image' of arthritis and rheumatism affects the experience of people who have these conditions, both directly through the availability of specialist medical help and research funding, and indirectly through the attitudes of others. For example, arthritis and rheumatism have not received much attention from the media and, in consequence, the personal narratives of people who have RA have been neglected and individual lives are rendered invisible. RA often leads to physical impairments, which can become severely disabling in a society that offers inadequate support. Partly through the activity of charities such as ARC, the 'public profile' of RA is beginning to rise and the patient's viewpoint is gradually being incorporated in the evaluation of treatment and social services.

People with RA often feel distressed about becoming a burden on their families or failing to fulfil their social roles, but their 'moral reputation' in society is preserved and they are seen as genuinely in pain and disabled through no fault of their own, once the diagnosis has been confirmed. They are not overtly stigmatised or actively discriminated against, except inasmuch as they experience the disadvantages in employment, housing and social security that are a common feature of the lives of all disabled people. As you will see at the start of the next chapter in this book, people with HIV infection or AIDS have a different experience of stigmatisation and discrimination, which flows from the social history of these conditions.

OBJECTIVES FOR CHAPTER 3

When you have studied this chapter, you should be able to:

3.1 Define and use, or recognise definitions and applications of, each of the terms printed in **bold** in the text.

3.2 Discuss the social and personal consequences of RA in terms of: the effects of uncertainty; difficulties in the performance of the activities of daily living and the fulfilment of social roles; and loss of autonomy and increasing dependence on others.

3.3 Review current biomedical knowledge of the pathological processes involved in RA, and the main strategies for its medical management, pointing to potential sources of difficulty for doctor and patient.

3.4 Discuss a range of theories about the causes of RA, drawing on epidemiological and biomedical research, and pointing to areas of continuing uncertainty.

3.5 Illustrate the complexity and significance of lay knowledge about RA and the ways in which it differs from professional knowledge.

3.6 Discuss the strengths and limitations of using patient-provided measures of outcome for assessing the impact of RA and the costs and benefits of treatment.

QUESTIONS FOR CHAPTER 3

1   (*Objective 3.2*)

Explain why it is important to include the performance of social roles in any assessment of the experience of RA.

2   (*Objective 3.3*)

Why is it so difficult to decide whether a drug treatment for RA is having a beneficial effect on the patient?

3   (*Objective 3.4*)

What do you see as the major problems in identifying causes in RA?

4   (*Objective 3.5*)

Read the following extract from an interview with a woman in her 50s. She was asked what she thought had caused her RA. What characteristic features of lay illness beliefs can you identify in this account?

> Well, if you live in your own body for a long time, you're a fool if you don't take note of what is happening to it. I think that you can make naive diagnoses which are quite wrong. But I think that at the back of your head, certainly at the back of my head, I have feelings that this is so, and I'm quite certain that it was stress that precipitated this … Not simply the stress of events that happened but the stress perhaps of suppressing myself while I was a mother and wife — not 'women's libby' but there comes a time in your life when you think, you know, 'where have I got to? There's nothing left of me.' … And then on top of that feeling of … not really discontent, but rather confusion about identity … to have various physical things happen like, you know, my daughter … I'm quite certain that the last straw was my husband's illness. So, I'm sure it was stress induced. I think that while my head kept going my body stopped. (Williams, 1986, pp. 188–9)

5   (*Objective 3.6*)

There are two quite distinct approaches to assessing the personal consequences of health problems such as RA:

(a) ask a standard set of questions of everyone, and

(b) ask individuals to identify their own personal priorities and concerns.

Give one strength and one weakness of each of these contrasting approaches.

C H A P T E R   4

HIV and AIDS

Study notes for OU students

This chapter builds on material in earlier books in this series, most notably: the epidemiology of HIV/AIDS, in *World Health and Disease*, Chapters 8 and 9; the immune response to infection, in *Human Biology and Health: An Evolutionary Approach*, Chapter 6; and the HIV/AIDS epidemic as a force in health sector reform, in *Caring for Health: History and Diversity*, Chapters 8 and 9 (all titles from Open University Press, third edition 2001). Three articles in *Health and Disease: A Reader* (Open University Press, third edition 2001) are set reading for this chapter: two linked articles by David Finkel and Thomas Garrett under the joint title 'Costs of treating AIDS in Malawi and America' (in Section 4.5), and 'Global AIDS epidemic: time to turn the tide' by Peter Piot (in Section 4.6). We suggest that you replay the video, 'South Africa: Health at the Crossroads' during Section 4.4, to remind yourself of the impact of HIV and AIDS on that country. A TV programme, 'A Future with AIDS' relates to Section 4.6. The authors of this chapter are Basiro Davey, Senior Lecturer in Health Studies, Department of Biological Sciences at The Open University, and Graham J. Hart, Professor and Associate Director, MRC Social and Public Health Sciences Unit, University of Glasgow.

4.1 From individual experiences to international responses

> AIDS has become the most devastating disease humankind has ever faced … In countries often already burdened by huge socioeconomic challenges, AIDS threatens human welfare, developmental progress and social stability on an unprecedented scale. (UNAIDS/WHO, 2001, pp. 2 and 7)

Of all the diseases affecting human populations in the twentieth century, none has had so great an impact as AIDS (acquired immune deficiency syndrome). From the early 1980s, the rapid increase in suffering and loss of life associated with the AIDS epidemic, first in the developed and then in the developing world, and the inability of medical science to control it, gave this hitherto unknown infectious disease an unprecedented media and public profile.

Governments around the world floundered in their attempts to reduce the spread of the causative agent, HIV (the human immunodeficiency virus), amid growing accusations that too little was being done to protect their citizens. Self-help groups and campaigning organisations sprang up to fill the void in national and international action. The medical and pharmaceutical research industry redirected its resources on a massive scale to identifying and then dismantling the structure of HIV, in the hope of developing a vaccine to protect the uninfected and drugs that would destroy it in the body. For individuals in the Western industrial democracies, the perception of sexual safety inherited from the 1960s was shattered, and the most private of behaviours was brought into the public domain for analysis and comment in numerous TV documentaries and newspaper articles.

As HIV infection spread around the world, countries in Africa and Asia saw their already fragile economies devastated by AIDS as millions of young adults fell sick and the orphanages overflowed. By the start of the twenty-first century, the World Health Organisation (WHO) estimated that AIDS had already killed over 18 million people worldwide in less than 20 years, and another 34.3 million were living with HIV infection or AIDS. As each year passes, the numbers climb at an accelerating rate: in 2001, 40 million people were living with HIV or AIDS, there were 3.4 million new HIV infections that year in Sub-Saharan Africa alone, and globally AIDS had become the fourth largest cause of death.

Like the other case studies in this book, this chapter takes a multidisciplinary approach to the discussion of HIV and AIDS, which brings together biological, epidemiological, historical, psychological and sociological perspectives. In the course of this analysis, you will see how profoundly the individual experiences of the disease are influenced by the prevailing social, scientific, ethical and political context within different countries, and how these interact with international responses to this global health problem. One consequence of these complex interactions is that the meanings attached to HIV and AIDS vary between families, communities and cultures, and these colour the ways in which the lives affected by the disease are celebrated or mourned (Figure 4.1).

People at risk of HIV infection or who have already developed HIV-related disease, and the political groupings and self-help movements that support them, have strong views on the national and international responses to the AIDS epidemic. But the experience of HIV and AIDS is not limited to those who are directly affected by the virus. The providers

Figure 4.1 *Panels from the AIDS Memorial Quilt, made to commemorate people who have died from AIDS in the UK. (Reproduced by kind permission of the NAMES Project (UK). Photo: Patsy Wilson)*

of health and social services, the media and political organisations, medical research establishments, pharmaceutical companies, national governments and international bodies such as the WHO and the World Bank all have something to say about the subject. These contrasting narratives are reflected in this chapter. We begin with a brief history of the emergence of AIDS as a recognised medical condition, which touches on all the themes that will be discussed in more detail in later sections.

4.2 A brief history of HIV and AIDS

4.2.1 Socio-medical history

The identification of AIDS began in the USA in 1981 at the Centers for Disease Control in Atlanta, which receive morbidity and mortality reports from throughout the country. Reports came in of unexplained weight loss and a growing number of deaths among previously healthy gay and bisexual men who had developed an uncommon pneumonia caused by a single-celled fungus-like organism (*Pneumocystis carinii*), commonly found in healthy people from childhood onwards, but rarely causing symptoms. At about the same time, deaths were reported in other gay men from *Kaposi's sarcoma* — a generally benign tumour associated with a type of herpes virus, which is rarely developed by people under 60 years; in these young men, it began as painless purple-black patches growing in the skin or inside the mouth.

Other deaths from usually innocuous infections were recorded in gay men. Symptoms tended to begin with a series of skin, chest, mouth or stomach problems, many of which were caused by common infectious organisms that the immune system normally keeps in check. The list of these **opportunistic infections** (which only have the 'opportunity' to progress if the immune system is suppressed) got longer as more cases were identified. Episodes of more serious and debilitating illnesses occurred, indicating increasing **immunodeficiency**, a collapse of the cellular and biochemical mechanisms of the normal immune response to infection.[1] Mental confusion and deficits in coordinating movement were often apparent. Persistent digestive problems and diarrhoea led to weight loss and muscle weakness, until the person became unable to fend off any further infection and died.

The initial association of the condition with gay men was so powerful that it was termed *gay-related immunodeficiency disease* (*GRID*), more colloquially known as 'gay cancer'. Medical researchers in the early 1980s even proposed a mechanism to explain it: they suggested it was an *autoimmune* disorder,[2] caused when the immune system of 'promiscuous' gay men self-destructed as a consequence of repeated exposure to sexual infections and/or drug misuse. As we discuss later, the fact that the disease was inextricably linked with gay men in the early years of the epidemic in the USA has had major consequences for social and public perceptions of HIV transmission, which have persisted long after it became clear that globally the virus was overwhelmingly being transmitted between heterosexuals.

As time passed, epidemiologists identified groups outside the gay community in the USA and then in populations around the world, who were dying from opportunistic infections as a consequence of immunodeficiency. The syndrome was found first in people with *haemophilia* (a genetically determined inability to form blood clots), who had received injections of Factor VIII, a clotting agent prepared from donated blood. Then it was detected in recipients of blood transfusions and donated organs, and also among injecting drug users who shared needles and syringes. Later it was found that the male and female sexual partners of people in these groups, and the babies of women with the syndrome, could also be affected, and high rates were identified in sex workers in various parts of the world.

● What did this epidemiological evidence suggest about the cause of the condition?

■ The emergence of the disease in these groups strongly suggested that the breakdown in immune function was caused by a single infectious agent, transmitted by blood-to-blood contact, for example via Factor VIII, transfusions and organ transplants, or from mother to unborn baby, or during unprotected penetrative sex.

The condition was renamed **AIDS — acquired immune deficiency syndrome**: *acquired* because it is not inherited by genetic transmission, but requires contact with an infectious agent; *immune deficiency* because this is the consequence of

---

[1] The immune response to infection is described in detail in *Human Biology and Health: An Evolutionary Approach* (Open University Press, 3rd edn 2001), Chapter 6.

[2] The status of rheumatoid arthritis as an autoimmune disease has already been discussed in Chapter 3 of this book; the immunological basis of autoimmune diseases is described in more detail in *Human Biology and Health: An Evolutionary Approach* (Open University Press, 3rd edn 2001), Chapter 6.

infection; and *syndrome* because the cluster of symptoms that indicate AIDS shows some variation from person to person, although certain features such as opportunistic infections are always present (Section 4.3 explains why).

The race to identify the cause of AIDS began in laboratories around the world. In 1983, when many thousands of people had already been diagnosed with AIDS worldwide, Luc Montagnier of the Pasteur Institute in France and Robert Gallo of the National Institutes of Health in the USA claimed, independently of each other, to have identified the virus that causes AIDS. Each gave their virus a different name, and it was not until 1986 that an international committee of eminent virologists renamed it **HIV** — the **human immunodeficiency virus**. Subsequently, it was recognised that there are two types of HIV: the strain originally identified in 1983 (HIV-1, see Figure 4.2), which has the most extensive worldwide distribution, and a related but less prolific strain (HIV-2).

The identification of HIV is a striking reminder that science is a social activity beset with just as many dramas as any other branch of human endeavour. Gallo and his colleagues in the USA developed and patented a blood-testing kit, designed to detect **anti-HIV antibodies**.[3] Antibodies are specialised proteins made by the immune system in response to an infection; those made in response to HIV infection can only bind to HIV. The test kit contains molecules taken from HIV with which some serum (liquid fraction of the blood) is mixed. If antibodies in a person's serum are able to bind to HIV molecules in the test kit, this is taken as evidence of HIV infection and the person is said to be 'HIV-positive'.

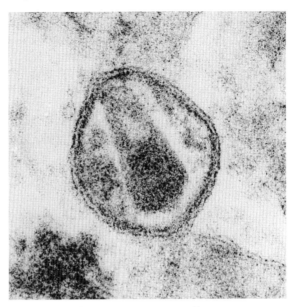

Figure 4.2 *The most common type of human immunodeficiency virus (HIV-1), magnified 200 000 times by an electron microscope. The outer envelope appears 'knobbly' because it carries about 100 molecules of a protein called GP120, any of which can bind to the human cells that HIV infects. The protein core is thimble-shaped and contains the viral genes encoded in RNA. (Photo: Courtesy of the National Institute for Biological Standards and Control)*

Initially Gallo claimed that his team had used the virus isolated in their own laboratory to develop the kit, and not the French virus that Montagnier had sent him as part of a collaborative exchange of scientific knowledge. Montagnier accused Gallo of using the French virus to develop the American test kit, and a heated debate ensued. Subsequent genetic analysis confirmed that the French virus had indeed been used, although Gallo maintained the two virus samples had been confused accidentally. The Pasteur Institute began legal proceedings claiming compensation for US$20 million in lost income from sales of the blood-testing kits. The outcome was eventually settled out of court, with the two research institutes sharing the profits from the test kits, and Montagnier and Gallo agreeing to be referred to as the 'co-discoverers' of HIV.

The personal and legal battle over the discovery of HIV is an early instance of what Cindy Patton, an American activist and academic, has termed the 'AIDS industry', in which scientific discovery tends to be characterised as much by the quest for personal or financial gain as for health gain (Patton, 1990).

---

[3] Antibodies are discussed in greater detail in *Human Biology and Health: An Evolutionary Approach* (Open University Press, 3rd edn 2001), Chapter 6.

In the years that followed, the initial confidence that a vaccine would be developed to protect the world's population from HIV evaporated. Unlike other viruses, for example those causing polio, rubella and smallpox, which had been brought under control or even eradicated by vaccination programmes, HIV proved a much more difficult target. In the late 1990s, hope gradually transferred to the generation of new anti-viral drugs to delay the progression to AIDS in people already infected with HIV, but optimism has gradually been tempered by new realisations. These drugs are not curative, they have many side effects, they are unaffordable by the majority of countries with high rates of HIV infection, and they drive the evolution of drug-resistant strains of virus. Biological reasons why an effective medical response to HIV remains so elusive are discussed in later sections of this chapter.

4.2.2 Socio-political history

A consistent feature of the history of HIV and AIDS is the stigmatisation of people who are infected with the virus, and the extension of this social marginalisation to everyone identified with what was originally called a 'high risk' group. In Chapter 2, we discussed Erving Goffman's concept of *tribal stigma*, where membership of a group seen as threatening to the stability of dominant social norms attracts hostility and discrimination from the majority in a population. Most of the groups in which HIV was originally identified in Western countries — gay men, injecting-drug users, sex workers — were already highly stigmatised. The advent of AIDS reinforced and 'legitimised' attacks against them. As tabloid newspaper reporting in the UK at the time strongly indicates, being a gay man or an injecting-drug user was evidence of moral corruption and HIV was its 'just rewards'.

> The message to be learned — that the Department of Health should now be urgently propagating — is that active homosexuals are potentially murderers and that the act of buggery kills. (*Daily Mail*, 21 July, 1989)

> AIDS is a homosexual, drug-related disease. They and they alone are responsible for people dying of AIDS. (*Sun*, January, 1990)

Initial medical and societal responses to HIV and AIDS represented homosexuality itself — rather than infection — as the source and cause of a fatal illness, and homosexual behaviour was once again articulated as a 'criminal act'. AIDS resurrected a potent socio-political history common to other sexually associated diseases or 'evils' of the past, such as syphilis and prostitution. The social historian, Jeffrey Weeks was an influential voice in the early years of the epidemic, arguing that most Western countries in past times have associated homosexuality with sin, sickness and disease. Past epidemics or 'plagues', particularly where sexual transmission is a factor, were viewed as signs of decay in moral standards and a threat to the 'public good'.

> AIDS has a medico-moral history already partly written for it: a history of civilisation-threatening plagues, offering a repertoire of responses and remedies, from mass hysteria to moral panic to prejudice and the threat of compulsory quarantine. (Weeks, 1990, p. 134)

Responses to homosexuality, illicit drug use, sexually transmitted disease and prostitution have all been characterised by largely punitive measures of containment, designed to protect the 'innocent' from 'pollution' by members of these marginalised groups. The writer and activist Simon Watney has documented how initial UK government responses to HIV and AIDS emphasised the threat of 'promiscuity' and 'otherness' to the stability of the family and 'normality' (Watney, 1989). There was effectively no AIDS-related policy in the UK until 1984, despite warnings made by gay men's organisations that an epidemic was imminent. Government policy at this time was to contain the virus by recommending that gay men should not donate blood. The emphasis was on preventing the further 'leakage' of HIV from gay men (who were by implication 'guilty'), to stop the creation of any more 'innocent victims' — the term routinely used to describe people whose infection had been acquired from blood products, transfusions or organ transplants. Demands that all gay men should be compulsorily screened for HIV were hotly debated in the media.

> It is more important to protect the lives of those who might innocently or accidentally catch the disease than to protect the reputation of those who have caught the disease through their own self-indulgence. (*Daily Express*, 30 August, 1985)

Policies initiated by the Thatcher governments of the 1980s emphasised the protection of the 'ideal' family unit of a heterosexual couple and their children. Same-sex relationships came under further pressure when Section 28 of the *Local Government Act 1988* made the 'promotion' of homosexuality in schools illegal. As a result teachers were uncertain as to whether, and to what extent, sex education was legally able to refer to homosexuality, and feared disciplinary action if they confronted homophobic bullying.

Central allocations of funds to primary HIV prevention in the UK did not occur until 1986. These funds were directed almost exclusively to government-sponsored mass media advertising about AIDS, which emphasised warnings to the uninfected 'general public' against the dangers of sexual promiscuity ('The more partners, the greater the risk'), and individual responsibility for protecting oneself ('Don't die of ignorance'). Mass health education initiatives have been politically constrained in their ability to present sexual activity as healthy and pleasurable or to offer *practical* safer sex advice. Government policies promoting the sanctity of monogamy and the family over 'sexual promiscuity' or sexual diversity have tended to generate campaigns associating sex with danger, death and disease.

> The linking of sex and health is in itself problematic in a cultural context that endows sex with meanings which are far from healthy. (Holland *et al.*, 1991, p. 129)

Campaigns to promote safer sexual practices (e.g. non-penetrative sex and condom use) were left to HIV and AIDS charities and support organisations such as the Terrence Higgins Trust in the UK, and the San Francisco AIDS Foundation (SFAF) in the USA, which successfully mobilised gay men to protect themselves and each other from spreading the virus. Public funding of a national survey of sexual lifestyles in the UK was withdrawn in 1989 because the survey was thought to be unnecessarily intrusive,[4] while an advertising campaign targeting heterosexuals was halted for being too sexually explicit (Figure 4.3 overleaf).

---

[4] This survey was subsequently conducted with funding from the Wellcome Trust; the organisation derives some of its income from the pharmaceutical company which manufactures Zidovudine (also known as AZT), a drug used in the treatment of HIV infection. Some of the survey results are discussed in *Birth to Old Age: Health in Transition* (Open University Press, 2nd edn 1995; colour-enhanced 2nd edn 2001), Chapter 7.

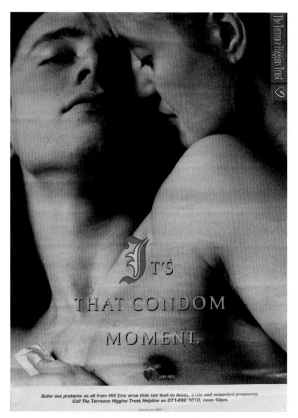

Figure 4.3   *In the late 1980s, the success of the Terrence Higgins Trust's 'Love Sexy, Love Safe' campaign to promote safer sexual practices among gay men encouraged the British government to give them a grant for a similar campaign aimed at heterosexuals. Their posters showed erotic images of loving sex made safer by the use of condoms or alternatives to penetration. The grant was cancelled in 1993. (Poster by kind permission of the Terrence Higgins Trust)*

Even when government-sponsored advertisements were targeted at some of the population groups most affected, they often carried stigmatising messages (as in the UK example in Figure 4.4). Government-initiated AIDS policies thus have as much to say about the ideological and political climate of the time as they do about the practical imperatives of preventing HIV disease.

The representation of AIDS as a 'punishment for wrong-doing' has not been confined to Western industrialised countries. As the pandemic spread to Africa and then to Asia and Latin America, the perception that an AIDS diagnosis was irrefutable evidence of sexual promiscuity reinforced its power to destroy the social worlds of people infected with HIV.[5] Particular emphasis has been placed on the spread of HIV by the male clients of female sex workers, and the difficulties faced by women in affording condoms or persuading men to use them.[6] In Eastern European countries, as the Soviet Union collapsed in the 1990s, news began to emerge of the spread of HIV largely as a consequence of injecting drug-use, further confirming the belief among Western heterosexuals that AIDS was a disease of stigmatised 'others'.

In 2001, when the number of new cases of heterosexually acquired HIV in the UK first exceeded the number acquired from sex between men, a new stigmatised group could be seen emerging as the latest target for blame. It was widely reported that most heterosexuals with HIV had been infected outside the UK and 'imported' the virus, primarily from African countries. The 'ethnicisation' of AIDS in the UK had thus begun, just as it did in the USA in the early 1980s, when Haitians were accused of bringing the virus into the country. In Section 4.4 we return to these themes, when we discuss problems in initiating and sustaining effective health protection measures, against a background of discrimination against already stigmatised groups, whose marginalisation has been increased by beliefs about HIV infection.

Alongside this socio-political history, the 1990s saw biological knowledge about HIV and AIDS advancing rapidly, largely due to unprecedented levels of research funding. We turn now to a review of the central findings of this research effort, and the explanations it provided for the slow progress in developing medical treatments or anti-HIV vaccines.

[5] A video for Open University students, entitled 'South Africa: Health at the Crossroads', includes interviews with people at an HIV support group who explain why they have not told their families about their HIV status.

[6] The TV programme associated with this chapter, 'A Future with AIDS', examines projects to promote condom use in Zambia, Brazil and India.

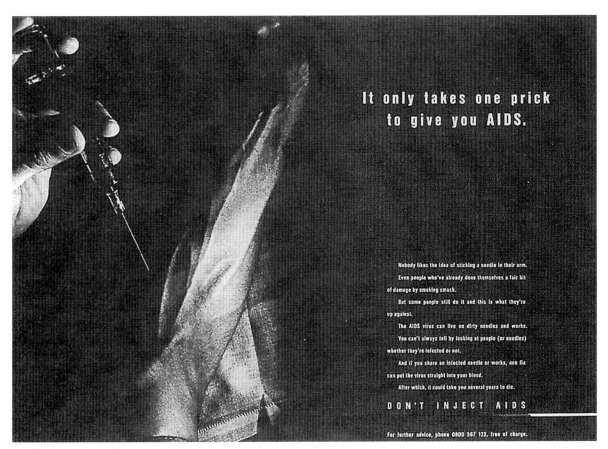

Figure 4.4 *In 1987 this poster broke new ground in UK government health campaigns by using the vernacular of drug users ('smack' is heroin and 'works' are syringes and other paraphernalia). But the image of a dirty arm with needle poised over it, and the use of innuendo in the slogan 'It only takes one prick to give you AIDS', reinforced the association of AIDS with a stigmatised group. (Reproduced by permission of the Controller of Her Majesty's Stationery Office; Crown Copyright)*

4.3 The biology of HIV and AIDS

Although the biological description of the physical and molecular structure of HIV rapidly followed the identification of the virus, it was not until the mid-1990s that a reasonably clear picture emerged of the 'natural history' of a viral infection as it progresses in the human body. As you will see, at the time of writing (2002) there are still some unanswered questions. We begin with some controversies that illustrate the potential for scientific research to have different interpretations and to serve different agendas. Scientific knowledge is not 'value neutral' and its presentation affects how HIV and AIDS are viewed in societies and experienced by individuals.

4.3.1 Controversies about the virus

Two biological controversies about HIV have generated the most heated arguments in the scientific community, in the popular media and at the level of national governments and international agencies. Does HIV really cause AIDS and how did the virus originate? The arguments put forward on both these questions have contributed significantly to the stigmatisation of people with HIV-related disease.

The association of HIV with AIDS was originally disputed in 1987 by an American professor of molecular biology, Peter Duesberg. He claimed that HIV could not be the cause of AIDS because, with the technology available at the time, the virus could not be isolated from a substantial minority of people with a clinical diagnosis of AIDS, and the viral load in the majority of cases was too small (in his view) to cause such devastating effects on the body. Both these assumptions were shown to be false when new methods for detecting the virus were developed, but until well into the 1990s Duesberg continued to assert that HIV infection was just another opportunistic infection commonly found in people with AIDS, and not the cause of the underlying immune deficiency. In the early years of the epidemic he gave spurious scientific credibility to certain media accounts of AIDS as a 'self-destructive' illness, caused when the immune system collapsed through overload in people who had contracted multiple sexually transmitted infections over a long period, and/or routinely used illegal drugs.

When individuals who did not fit the stereotypical risk profile began developing AIDS in the USA and other Western economies, Duesberg and his supporters suggested that their 'apparent' absence of 'sex and drugs' risk factors could not be verified. Such stigmatising insinuations forced people with AIDS into defending their moral reputation against the charge that they were to blame for their own illness. This additional burden came at a time when HIV infection inevitably presaged a decline into illness and death, even with the most advanced medical care.

The 'Duesberg hypothesis' had all but disappeared under the weight of scientific evidence until, at the end of the 1990s, the controversy was reactivated by the president of South Africa, Thabo Mbeki. He has repeatedly expressed doubts about whether HIV is the direct cause of AIDS or only a contributory factor in a proportion of cases. He also questioned data on the extent of HIV infection in his country and on the death rates from AIDS. A consequence of president Mbeki's views has been a significant delay in drug-therapy programmes in South Africa to reduce the transmission of HIV from pregnant women to their babies — a subject we return to in Section 4.5.

The second controversy is about the origins of HIV and has proved even more difficult to resolve. It began in the 1980s with speculation in tabloid newspapers that the Soviet Union had deliberately infected Americans with a virus developed in its germ warfare laboratories. Then a less powerful 'foreign' target presented itself.

Structural similarities were noted between HIV and a virus found in sooty mangabey monkeys and chimpanzees, termed SIV (simian immunodeficiency virus). In these primates, SIV causes at worst a mild transient illness and many individuals harbour it without apparent harm. Since it was known that HIV could be sexually transmitted, articles appeared hinting at the possibility of a sexual route by which SIV could have been transferred to Africans in tribal communities. This is an early example of what we referred to at the end of Section 4.2 as the 'ethnicisation' of HIV and AIDS, characterised by stigmatising accusations about 'foreigners', particularly those from black ethnic groups.

By 2000, comparisons of the genes of HIV and SIV pointed to a common ancestral virus in chimpanzees at least a hundred years ago. At some point in the early decades of the twentieth century, this virus is believed to have infected people in central Africa, and transformed into HIV as it adapted to its new host. The transfer from primate to human most probably occurred as hunters cut up primate carcasses, and open sores or cuts on their hands were contaminated by infected blood.

● The virus is likely to have passed from primates to humans by this route on many occasions in rural African communities over several decades. Why do you think it took until the early 1980s to identify the illness syndrome it caused in infected people?

■ Each time the virus entered a small, isolated community, it could have remained confined to the original 'case' and his or her sexual partners, and then died out along with the people it infected. Only when these communities were disrupted and population movements began to occur on a wider scale, did HIV spread outwards from its rural origins. In Africa, the significance of a syndrome characterised by multiple infections and wasting was missed against the background of many other infectious diseases. But when it reached the USA, the disease surveillance system rapidly detected the arrival of a very unusual syndrome in Western medical experience.

However, the genetic association between HIV and SIV led to another hypothesis about the circumstances in which the virus 'jumped' from primates to humans. In the 1950s, the Wistar Institute in Philadelphia had developed a vaccine against another viral disease, polio. They 'grew' stocks of the vaccine in macaques, a species of monkey that does not harbour SIV, and over a million people in what is now known as the Democratic Republic of Congo in central Africa were immunised with it. In 1999 it was suggested that some batches of the vaccine had instead been grown in chimpanzees infected with SIV, and that the virus had transformed into HIV in immunised people. The Wistar Institute denied the accusation, but a damaging shadow had been cast over immunisation campaigns in Africa, which continues to have an impact on the uptake of vaccinations (a point we return to in Section 4.6). Evidence to support the purity of the Wistar polio vaccine came in 2001, when batches kept in storage since 1958 were found to contain traces of macaque DNA but not chimp DNA, and to be free from contamination with either SIV or HIV.

These controversies also serve as a reminder that the rapid development of scientific knowledge about HIV and AIDS continues to take place in an often hostile and politically charged atmosphere, where the reputations of individual scientists and research institutes have repeatedly been in the firing line. We turn now to the current understanding of how HIV infection leads to the immune deficiency that characterises AIDS.

4.3.2 Genetic variability of HIV

There are two major types of HIV, distinguished on the basis of major differences in their genes, their global distribution and their clinical manifestations: HIV-1 (shown in Figure 4.2), first identified in 1983 and the cause of the worldwide AIDS epidemic, and HIV-2, isolated in 1986 in West Africa, where all known infections have originated. Although both viruses cause immunodeficiency, the condition develops more slowly and with a milder course in people infected with HIV-2. An important difference is that transfer of HIV-2 from mother to baby, either in the womb, during labour or via breast milk, is extremely rare. By contrast, unless preventive treatment is given, over 40 per cent of pregnant women who are infected with HIV-1 pass on the virus to their babies. In the rest of this chapter, all references to 'HIV' refer to HIV-1.

HIV is an *RNA virus*, one of a large number of viruses in which the genetic code for making new virus particles is contained in molecules of RNA.[7] HIV has only nine genes, compared with up to 40 000 in humans, and it turned out to be highly variable in its genetic structure. It has been distinguished into at least 10 distinct subtypes (the technical term is 'clades'), with different geographical distributions.

---

[7] Many viruses use DNA as their genetic material, but RNA viruses are very common. The encoding of genetic information in the sequence of bases in RNA follows exactly the same principles as described for DNA in *Human Biology and Health: An Evolutionary Approach* (Open University Press, 3rd edn 2001), Chapter 3.

AIDS in North America, Western Europe and Australasia is almost exclusively due to HIV subtype B, whereas eight different subtypes have been identified in Africa and three in South America. Subtype C predominates in the Indian subcontinent, subtype E in South-East Asia, and subtype F in Eastern Europe.

● What challenge does this genetic variability present in terms of medical strategies to attack the virus or vaccinate people against HIV infection?

■ It means that even if anti-viral drugs or vaccines are developed for use in one part of the world, they may not be effective against HIV subtypes elsewhere. (In Sections 4.5 and 4.6 we discuss problems associated with anti-viral therapies and the development of vaccines.)

The genetic variability of HIV does not end there. All viruses reproduce by infecting a host cell and redirecting its biochemical functions to make thousands of new virus particles, each with a complete set of viral genes. When HIV infects a cell and thousands of copies of its nine genes are made, numerous tiny changes (mutations) occur in the RNA sequences, each generating a slightly different variant of the original virus. Thus, as an HIV infection progresses in a single individual, new variants of HIV are continually appearing, and different variants can be isolated from different parts of the body of the same individual. A comparison of the variants isolated from different individuals can help to 'map' the transmission of infection from person to person; the greater the similarities between variants isolated from two people, the greater the likelihood that HIV has been transmitted between them.

The additional problems for medical intervention arising from such extreme variability are obvious, but the high mutation rate is also the key to how HIV survives in the person it infects.

4.3.3 How HIV evades immune destruction

HIV is a relatively fragile virus, which cannot survive for more than a few days outside the body (except in laboratory cultures). It is killed by the temperatures reached in the hot-wash cycle of an ordinary washing machine, and infected blood spills can be safely dealt with by mopping up with weak domestic bleach. It is vulnerable to attack by the immune system within the body of a healthy person, which destroys virus particles and infected host cells. How then does HIV evade complete destruction by the host's immune response and ultimately 'turn the tables' by overwhelming the immune system itself?

● Part of the answer lies in the ability of HIV to generate variant strains within the lifetime of its host. Explain why this is an important 'escape' mechanism.

■ The human immune response to a novel infectious agent (i.e. one not previously encountered) is relatively weak at first, but it rapidly adapts and becomes increasingly effective at attacking that source of infection.[8] If all new HIV particles were identical to the original infective virus, the host's immune response would soon become so effective at recognising and attacking them that they would be eradicated. But HIV continually mutates, generating new strains that the

[8] The mechanisms by which the human immune system adapts from a weak primary response to a more effective secondary response are discussed in *Human Biology and Health: An Evolutionary Approach* (Open University Press, 3rd edn 2001), Chapter 6.

immune system has not 'seen' before. Although the older strains gradually succumb to immune attack, they are replaced by successive waves of new variants.

The ability of HIV to mutate in this way is known as **antigenic drift**. The host's immune system recognises the virus as an antigen (i.e. a legitimate target for attack), because it has unique viral molecules in its structure, but new variants have slightly different molecules so the immune system has to adapt all over again.

The second reason why HIV is eventually so successful at overwhelming the immune system is because the cells it infects and destroys are central to the immune response itself. HIV appears to 'select' certain white cells in the immune system as its target, but in reality it can bind to and subsequently enter only those cells that carry specific molecules on their surface membrane. The most important cells that HIV infects are the *helper T cells* and various phagocytic cells, particularly the *macrophages* (phagocytes engulf foreign material and break it down). These cells have a crucial similarity — they all carry a unique molecule known as CD4 on their surface membrane, closely associated with a co-receptor. In helper T cells the co-receptor is called CXCR4; macrophages have a different co-receptor called CCR5. (The reason for specifying the names of these molecules will become apparent in Section 4.3.5, when we discuss why some individuals can resist HIV infection.)

HIV can bind to CD4 in association with either of these co-receptors because it has on its surface about 100 copies of a molecule called GP120 (look back at Figure 4.2), which exactly 'fits' their shape, much as a key fits into a lock. Figure 4.5 (overleaf) shows the replication cycle of HIV, beginning with the initial binding event (stage 1 at the top of the diagram). Study Figure 4.5 and its caption carefully, following stages 1 to 6 clockwise around the diagram.

- ● HIV belongs to a small group of RNA viruses, known as **retroviruses** (retro means 'backwards'). Look at stage 3 in Figure 4.5 and explain why HIV is termed a retrovirus.

- ■ The normal sequence of transcription of genes in all living cells is from DNA into RNA.[9] Retroviruses reverse this sequence; they transcribe viral RNA into viral DNA (a process called reverse transcription).

In Section 4.5, we will refer to Figure 4.5 again when we discuss the mechanisms of action of anti-retroviral drugs.

The third reason for HIV's success is that the activation of viral genes and the construction of new virus particles occur soon after infection, and the replication cycle continues relentlessly thereafter (Figure 4.5 stages 4–6, and Figure 4.6 overleaf). It has been estimated that in a person with an active HIV infection, at least *ten billion* new virus particles are produced each day. New methods of directly detecting virus particles (rather than detecting anti-HIV antibodies with the original blood-testing kits) have shown that replication primarily occurs hidden away in the host's lymph glands. For most of the natural history of an HIV infection, relatively few virus particles get into the bloodstream, but a significant sign of the progression towards AIDS is when the virus concentration in the blood rapidly increases.

---

[9] The transcription of the coded instructions contained in DNA into a corresponding code in messenger RNA (mRNA) is described in detail in *Human Biology and Health: An Evolutionary Approach* (Open University Press, 3rd edn 2001), Chapter 3. The chapter also deals with mutation, the principal process by which the code can change its sequence.

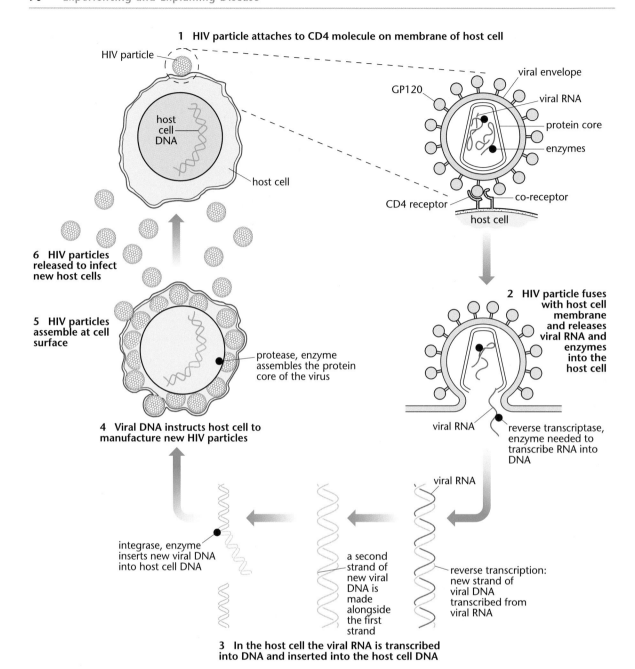

Figure 4.5   *The cycle of infection and replication of the human immunodeficiency virus (HIV) in cells of the human immune system. Stage 1: HIV has molecules of GP120 on its surface, which selectively bind to CD4 molecules in association with a co-receptor on the surface of white cells in the hosts' immune system. Stage 2: this binding event allows the viral RNA genes and the enzyme reverse transcriptase to enter the host cell. Stage 3: reverse transcriptase enables the viral genes to be transcribed into a new molecule of viral DNA; this replicates to form a double helix, which is incorporated into the host cell's own DNA, with the help of an enzyme, integrase. A variable period of dormancy may then occur. Stage 4: when the viral DNA is re-activated, a protease enzyme helps to assemble the proteins to make new HIV particles, each containing a copy of the viral RNA genes. Stages 5 and 6: thousands of new HIV particles 'bud' from the surface of the host cell, killing it as they shower into the circulation, where they infect more CD4-positive host cells.*

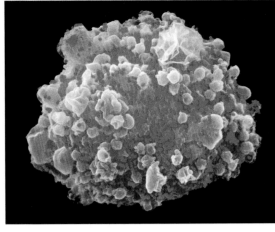

(a)   (b)

Figure 4.6   *(a) Electron micrograph (magnified 96 000 times) of new HIV particles 'budding' from the surface of a human white cell. (b) A scanning electron micrograph (magnified 5 600 times) of a virus 'shower' on the point of erupting from a white cell, an event that destroys the cell. (Photos: (a) and (b) NIBSC/Science Photo Library. The colours have been artificially added.)*

Successive waves of new virus particles are attacked by the host's immune system, which continually adapts to detect HIV as each variant strain emerges, wherever they are located. This immune response is sufficient to keep the viral load in check for a period usually lasting for several years. Although anti-HIV antibodies that bind to virus particles make a contribution to the attack, the most effective response is from 'killer' white cells, which destroy host cells that have become infected with HIV. However, the presence of HIV in a host cell is only revealed when new particles start to bud from its surface.

It is now known that there is a fourth reason why HIV can evade complete destruction by the immune system. After the initial wave of infection, a proportion of infected host cells become dormant 'carriers' of the viral genes hidden in their own DNA (Figure 4.5, stage 3). They can remain in this dormant state for years, without making new virus particles, undetected by the host's immune system because they are indistinguishable from normal cells. Research to discover what triggers the viral genes to reactivate, and begin the manufacture of new virus particles, is being pursued in the hope that some way can be found to suppress them permanently.

4.3.4 Effect of HIV on the body

Within a few weeks of the initial infection with HIV, some people develop a 'flu or glandular fever-like illness as the virus begins an initial acute phase of unchecked proliferation. Most people experience no symptoms at all before the immune response gets underway and causes the viral load in the bloodstream to fall to the low level it maintains for the next few years. Antibodies against HIV appear in the blood, usually within three months of infection. This event that is termed **seroconversion**, because the serum (liquid fraction of the blood) converts from being negative for anti-HIV antibodies to being antibody-positive. When a person is diagnosed as 'HIV-positive', it is usually based on the presence of these antibodies in their blood, rather than on the presence of virus particles. Tests that detect the virus itself are expensive and take longer to perform, but are increasingly used in wealthier countries to guide treatment decisions (as Section 4.5 describes).

● After the initial infection, there typically follows a **latent period** of several years in which the virus replicates without causing symptoms. How does this contribute to the speed with which HIV spread around the world?

■ In the first few years of the epidemic, the vast majority of people who became infected with HIV in the USA were unaware that they were *infectious*, i.e. capable of transmitting the virus to others through certain behaviours. This is still the case in most developing countries. The fact that the latent period lasts for years vastly increases the number of people to whom HIV can be unwittingly transmitted, who in turn pass it on before symptoms develop.

The latent period is highly variable between individuals, and between populations in different parts of the world. Symptoms of HIV disease first appear on average 8–10 years after the initial infection in otherwise healthy, well-nourished people. But it can be as short as 2–3 years, particularly where the person's health is already compromised by other infections, malnutrition, illegal drug use, or where the initial viral 'dose' was very high, as in recipients of infected blood transfusions.

As we noted earlier (Figure 4.6), when a shower of HIV particles erupts from an infected cell, it dies in the process. A significant feature of the progression to AIDS is that HIV infection leads to a steady decline in helper T cell numbers, as the personal case history in Figure 4.7 illustrates. It comes from the early years of the AIDS epidemic, before new anti-retroviral drug treatments were developed.

● How does the host's own immune response against the virus contribute to the increasing immunodeficiency?

■ The infected host cells that the immune response destroys are helper T cells and macrophages — essential components of the immune system itself. Thus, the immune response against HIV accelerates the collapse of the person's immune defence against other infections.

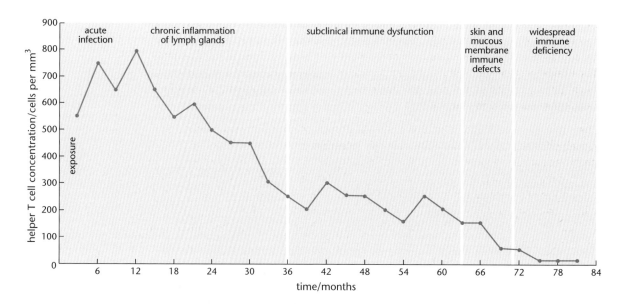

Figure 4.7   *Decline in helper T cells (identified by the presence of surface CD4 molecules) in the blood of a person infected with HIV during progression through various stages of HIV disease to widespread immune deficiency (AIDS) and death 83 months after infection. 'Subclinical immune dysfunction' refers to defects in the immune system that did not lead to overt symptoms. (Source: Scientific American, 1988, **259**(4), October, p. 74)*

Other mechanisms in the immune system, as yet imperfectly understood, appear to induce *apoptosis* (programmed cell death) in many *un*infected helper T cells. New T cells are being produced in the bone marrow and thymus all the time to replace those that die, but at some point the balance tips, and (as Figure 4.7 shows), an inexorable decline in the number of helper T cells follows unless drug treatment is commenced. The ability to fight off other infections collapses with the fall in helper T cells because they secrete over 20 different signalling molecules (cytokines), which activate and direct virtually every aspect of the immune system.

Without T cell 'help', the immune response becomes ineffective against normally innocuous infectious agents. Over 100 different opportunistic infections have been identified as AIDS-defining illnesses, including respiratory infections such as PCP (*Pneumocystis carinii* pneumonia), diarrhoeal diseases caused by a range of infectious agents including *Salmonella* bacteria and *Cryptosporidium* parasites, skin rashes and blisters caused by herpes viruses, and fungal infections of the mouth and genitals. Some infections lead to tumours, such as Kaposi's sarcoma; others cause anaemia. In developing countries, by far the most important opportunistic infection is *tuberculosis* (TB), which has increased to epidemic proportions in Sub-Saharan Africa and reappeared in Western industrialised countries as a direct result of the spread of HIV.

Macrophages infected by HIV are responsible for other disorders, in particular the *AIDS dementia syndrome* which occurs in 10–20 per cent of people. Infected macrophages can migrate into brain tissue, carrying the virus with them. The resultant damage can lead to impairment of thought processes (cognition), memory loss, fits, behavioural change and movement disorders. Opportunistic infections in the brain are also common, including bacterial meningitis and lesions caused by *Toxoplasma* parasites, usually acquired from domestic cats.

4.3.5 Resistance to HIV

The variety of clinical manifestations of AIDS, and the variation in time of progression from initial infection to HIV disease, may be due to differences in the variants of HIV that have been generated in each individual. Some HIV variants may be more prone to multiply than others, and some may cause more damage to host cells. The likelihood that the host response also makes some contribution to susceptibility or resistance to HIV was greatly strengthened in 1996 by the identification of the first **HIV-resistance mutation**.

The mutation was found in several different groups of long-term sex workers who remained well and without detectable HIV infection, even though they must have been repeatedly exposed to it. The mutation was in the CCR5 co-receptor on macrophages, which we mentioned earlier. (Figure 4.5, stage 1 shows the initial binding event between HIV and the CD4 molecule on a host cell, in association with a co-receptor.) The mutation was termed CCR5-delta32 because it results in the loss of 32 amino acids from the coiled protein chain that gives the co-receptor its unique shape.

● How could this deletion prevent HIV from infecting macrophages?

■ The loss of 32 amino acids alters the shape of CCR5, so HIV can no longer bind to it, because the GP120 molecule will not 'fit' the altered shape. Binding is essential for HIV to insert its genes into the macrophage, and if it cannot do this, then new virus particles cannot be made, and the original 'dose' of virus is left exposed outside the macrophage where the person's immune response can destroy it.

Individuals who inherit two copies of the mutated *CCR5* gene (one from each parent) are far less susceptible to HIV infection than the rest of the population, and inheritance of only one copy results in a significant delay in the progression from HIV infection to AIDS. It is not yet certain how a resistance mutation in the macrophage co-receptor leads to a generalised resistance to HIV, since the virus should still be able to infect helper T cells. One possibility is that helper T cells can only acquire the virus from infected macrophages, or that resistance mutations in the helper T cell co-receptor must also exist.

The distribution of the CCR5-delta32 mutation has been mapped in populations around the world. It occurs with a frequency between 2–14 per cent in Caucasians, with the highest occurrence in Swedish, Russian, Estonian and Polish peoples, but it has not been found in native African, American Indian and East Asian ethnic groups (Stephens *et al.*, 1998). Genetic modelling techniques suggest that the CCR5-delta32 mutation arose in Europe about 700 years ago, in populations that suffered a high death toll during the Middle Ages from epidemics such as plague, syphilis, smallpox and TB. It is speculated that individuals with the CCR5-delta32 mutation were better able to resist these infections, which explains its relatively high frequency in Caucasians. Other HIV-resistance mutations have been identified in African populations, which do not give protection from infection with HIV, but appear to delay the progression to AIDS by 2 to 4 years.

- ● What does the theory of natural selection predict should happen to the frequency of HIV-resistance mutations in human populations in the future?

- ■ The prevalence of these mutations in the population should rise, because HIV resistance — even if only partial — increases the survival chances of individuals who have the mutation. This in turn means they are likely to have more children, and some of these will inherit the mutation and be at an advantage themselves in resisting the effects of HIV.

However, it is sobering to reflect on the time it will take for HIV-resistance mutations to spread through a population. A research group at the University of California have calculated that in the next 100 years the frequency of one AIDS-delaying mutation in African populations will rise from 0.4 per cent of the population to 0.53 per cent (Schliekelman *et al.*, 2001).

4.3.6 HIV transmission and risk behaviours

Using modern detection methods, HIV particles can be found in the body less than three months after the initial infection. A person who is HIV-positive can transmit the virus to others by certain **risk behaviours** even when symptom-free. It is notable that the focus of discussion about HIV transmission shifted from 'high risk *groups*' in the 1980s to risk *behaviours* by the 1990s. The change of emphasis followed the recognition that within the groups in whom infection was highest there were many individuals whose behaviour put them at low risk (for example, monogamous gay men, sex workers who always use condoms). Moreover, the identification of HIV with certain stigmatised groups in the population also created the false impression that everyone else was not 'at risk'.

The prevalence of HIV particles in blood and semen explains why it is primarily a *sexually transmitted infection* (STI). The penis and vagina are in close abrasive contact during penetrative heterosexual sex, and the rectum can suffer abrasions to its delicate lining by penetration during anal sex. Tiny 'breaks' in blood vessels in these organs can allow transmission of the virus from person to person if a condom is not used.

It is not known to what extent the low concentrations of HIV particles in the saliva, urine and vaginal secretions of an infected person constitute a possible source of transmission during unprotected oral sex. Guidelines on oral sex strongly advise that condoms are used if the infection status of the participants is uncertain, and it should be avoided if there are lesions in the mouth.

However, there may be a 'threshold dose' of HIV required to initiate an infection. Evidence for this comes from the low infection rate after *needle-stick injuries*. Since the epidemic began, thousands of health-care workers have accidentally spiked themselves with a hypodermic needle containing HIV-infected blood, while caring for people with AIDS. Less than 0.1 per cent have been infected with HIV as a result. Health workers have also been splashed in the eyes, nose and mouth with infected blood or other body fluids, and even in these circumstances their infection rate is under 3 per cent.

By contrast, HIV is readily transferred between injecting-drug users who share needles and syringes. The risk is greatly increased by the common practice of drawing blood back into the syringe after injecting the drug, to flush out the residue. Whereas needle-stick injuries tend to be superficial wounds to the skin, people who inject illegal drugs insert the needle directly into a vein, so any virus particles are rapidly circulated around the body.

So far, we have been discussing **horizontal transmission** of HIV, when infection is passed between individuals during certain risk behaviours. **Vertical transmission** relates to infection passing from one generation to the next, from parent to offspring. Mother-to-baby transmission of HIV can occur in the womb, when infected maternal cells carry the virus across the placenta, or during labour and delivery when a baby is exposed to its mother's blood, and from infected breast milk. The combined total risk from all these routes results in the infection of up to 48 per cent of babies born to women infected with HIV-1 (see Figure 4.8). Breastfeeding may speed up the progression to AIDS in HIV-positive women, and it approximately doubles the risk of transmission of HIV from mother to baby.

Figure 4.8   *These boys from just outside Durban, South Africa, are members of the same extended family and were all infected with HIV as a result of transmission from their mothers; their life expectancy is under 10 years. HIV infection rates among women of childbearing age reached 25 per cent in 2001; half the child deaths before the age of five in South Africa are due to AIDS. (Photo: Elizabeth Rivers)*

● What dilemma for child-health agencies in developing countries is posed by breastfeeding as a source of HIV infection in newborn babies?

■ Advising women not to breastfeed will reduce the number of babies infected with HIV by this route, and hence the continuation of AIDS in the next generation. But it will inevitably also increase illness and deaths from gastro-intestinal infections associated with unsterile formula feeding, and reduce the 'passive protection' of babies acquired from maternal antibodies in breast milk. The nutritional benefits of breast milk are undisputed, and the expense of formula milk may result in it being diluted, further compromising infant growth and development.

Health agencies in developing countries with high female HIV-infection have generally promoted breastfeeding as the 'least worst' option in the absence of safe substitutes.

Another risk that is very difficult for individuals to avoid is medical exposure to HIV. Since the mid-1980s, the blood transfusion services in high-income countries have screened for HIV in donated blood, clotting factors extracted from human blood, and in organs and tissues for transplantation. In the UK and the USA, men who acknowledge that they have sex with men are not allowed to donate blood — a ban that has rankled with HIV-negative gay men. Although new cases of HIV infection from contaminated blood have fallen to a very low level in developed countries, 80 per cent of the world's population do not have access to a safe blood supply. Blood screening is not routinely or effectively performed in more than 120 countries, and the WHO estimates that 10–20 per cent of all new HIV transmissions come from this source (WHO, 2000). In 2001, the Chinese health ministry acknowledged that between 30 000 and 50 000 people had been infected with HIV from contaminated equipment when they sold blood to the transfusion service, raising fears that the next decade will see a huge rise in deaths from AIDS in its vast population.

Before we move on to discuss the global epidemiology of HIV and AIDS, a final point about transmission of the virus has to be emphasised. It has been known from the earliest days of the epidemic that due to its fragility outside the body, HIV is not *contagious* — it cannot be transmitted by ordinary social contact such as shaking hands or hugging, nor by handling plates, cups and cutlery used by an infected person. However, the fear of contagion continues to fuel the ostracisation of people with HIV. Some parents still refuse to accept HIV-positive children in local schools, workers may shun HIV-positive colleagues, and health-service personnel who are found to be HIV-positive cause uproar even when their occupation places no one at risk. In Section 4.7 we conclude this chapter by considering the stigmatisation associated with HIV and AIDS in more detail.

4.4 The epidemiology of HIV and AIDS

Epidemiological surveys of the prevalence of HIV and AIDS, and of the annual incidence of new infections, have mapped the course of the epidemic and enabled trends to be projected into the future for all regions of the world. Estimating the geographical and population distribution of HIV are of pivotal importance in planning health care and social resources for affected people, and in targeting health-promotion initiatives to prevent further HIV spread. However, it is important to recognise the limitations of even the best epidemiological estimates of HIV and AIDS, and to acknowledge that the speed of change is so great that the figures we cite in this chapter will be overtaken before it is printed. (Most of the data relate to

2001; you can update them by visiting the websites given in Further Sources at the end of this book.)

4.4.1 Accuracy of 'case' estimates

Epidemiological data on HIV and AIDS are based on two main sources of information: counts of medically confirmed 'cases' of AIDS and HIV reported to regional or national disease surveillance centres, and estimates for whole populations based on the prevalence of infection in a defined sample.

An important source of data on HIV prevalence in high-income countries is the **unlinked anonymous survey** (UA survey), in which blood samples taken from a defined population group are tested for HIV, but without linking the identity of the donor to the outcome of the test. In the UK, for example, repeated UA surveys are conducted on routine blood samples from people attending genito-urinary medicine clinics (which specialise in the detection and treatment of STIs, sexually transmitted infections), injecting-drug users, pregnant women and their newborn babies, and women undergoing termination of pregnancy. UA surveys increase the accuracy of information about HIV prevalence in a population because they avoid the distorting effect of asking people to come forward for testing. They have no therapeutic value because individuals who test positive cannot be identified.

In most low-income countries, UA surveys are uncommon and resources for HIV testing are generally directed towards 'named' screening of individuals who are deemed to be at highest risk, or whose symptoms suggest they may be infected. Many individuals who are eventually given an AIDS diagnosis (on clinical criteria described below) have never been HIV tested and, as a result, the accuracy of data for developing countries has been questioned. In the 1980s, it was even suggested in one British newspaper that developing countries were deliberately inflating their HIV and AIDS figures to attract international aid.

- ● Suggest some reasons why HIV and AIDS estimates might be inaccurate, particularly in developing countries. Are these inaccuracies more likely to result in under- or over-reporting of cases?

- ■ Low-income countries lack the infrastructure and resources for systematic disease surveillance and routine HIV testing, so a substantial proportion of cases go undetected. Nor do they have adequate resources to care for people with HIV-related illnesses, so there is little incentive to come forward for testing or treatment. And since HIV and AIDS carry a high stigma in all countries, fear of discrimination may deter people from consulting a doctor or seeking an HIV test; (e.g. a study in Tanzania found that 50 per cent of adult women knew where to get an HIV test, but only 6 per cent had done so; UNAIDS/WHO, 2001, p. 17). All of these reasons lead to *under*estimates of the numbers of people affected.

Estimates for developing countries have had to be revised *upwards* as detection methods became more reliable and large surveys were conducted by research teams funded by international agencies like the WHO. A striking example occurred in 2000, when the Indian government agency responsible for collecting HIV data admitted that its published figures for the previous three years were gross underestimates. Only 98 000 people with HIV had been officially reported by surveillance centres around India, compared with an estimated 3.5 million cases based on the screening of blood samples. Even in the USA, where disease surveillance is well organised and well resourced, confirmed reports of HIV infection are thought to underestimate the true figure by 10–20 per cent.

● Which groups in a population are likely to be most affected by under-reporting?

■ Data collection problems are particularly acute in 'hard-to-reach' groups, where HIV transmission is associated with an illegal or stigmatised activity, such as injecting-drug users, sex workers and men who have sex with men.

Some countries have attempted to conceal the extent of HIV infection in their populations for political reasons, or downplayed the statistics. In 1999, the South African president, Thabo Mbeki, began challenging his own health ministry's data, refusing to accept that on average 24.5 per cent of pregnant women attending antenatal clinics had tested HIV-positive. Figure 4.9 shows the increase in adult HIV infection rates in the continent of Africa between 1984 and 1999, based on estimates made by the WHO and UNAIDS, the United Nations Programme on HIV/AIDS. Even if some allowance is made for inaccuracies in case reports, the rapidly rising trend is not in doubt.

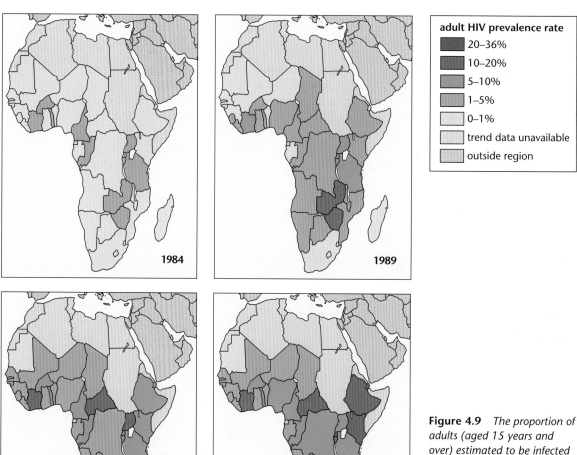

Figure 4.9 *The proportion of adults (aged 15 years and over) estimated to be infected with HIV in most regions of Africa, 1984, 1989, 1994 and 1999. (Maps adapted from UNAIDS/WHO poster 'A global view of HIV infection at the end of 1999', published 2000 by UNAIDS/WHO, Geneva)*

Changes over time in the **case definition** for AIDS have also affected estimates of how many people have passed the threshold at which AIDS is diagnosed. When TB was added to the list of AIDS-defining opportunistic infections in 1993, the number of cases of AIDS in developing countries leapt upwards. Variation also arises because the spectrum of HIV-related illnesses differs between individuals and between different parts of the world, and access to tests to confirm the presence of HIV is highly variable. The world's poorest countries cannot afford routine HIV tests for everyone suspected of having AIDS, so the WHO case definition in these circumstances rests on clinical observations: weight loss greater than 10 per cent of body weight, with chronic diarrhoea and/or fever for more than one month, and at least one other sign such as an opportunistic infection or Kaposi's sarcoma.

The case definition used in the USA is unusual in recording an AIDS diagnosis when an HIV-positive person's helper T cells fall below 200 per mm^3 of blood, regardless of other symptoms. (If you look back at Figure 4.7, you can see that on this basis an AIDS diagnosis would have been given somewhere between 39 and 60 months after the initial infection.) In the early years of the epidemic, conditions such as vaginal warts, recurrent candidiasis (thrush) and cervical cancer were excluded as AIDS-defining diseases, resulting in significant underestimates of AIDS among women, which were not rectified until the late 1990s.

In considering the epidemiological data that follow, you should bear these caveats in mind. It is also worth remembering that data aggregated from an entire country conceal higher and lower rates in certain sectors of the population, and that estimates from global regions disguise significant variations between constituent countries.

4.4.2 A global view: from epidemic to pandemic

The scale of HIV and AIDS is unprecedented in the history of human disease. No other epidemic has claimed so many lives, nor affected every region of the world in what became a global *pandemic* in less than a decade after it was first identified. For this reason, we have chosen to describe the global epidemiology in greater detail than you will find in the other case studies in this book.

UNAIDS and the WHO estimated that by the end of 2001 more than 60 million people had been infected with HIV since the epidemic began and at least 20 million had died. Figure 4.10 (overleaf) shows the global distribution of the 40 million who were estimated to be living with HIV infection or AIDS at the end of 2001. UNAIDS/WHO also estimated that there were 5 million new infections with HIV during that year — an incidence of 16 000 a day — and 3 million deaths from HIV-related illnesses, including 580 000 children aged under 15. AIDS had become the fourth largest cause of death worldwide.

Africa

It is immediately apparent from Figure 4.10 that in 2001, Africa (with 28.1 million people living with HIV or AIDS) was the worst affected region. Over two-thirds of all new HIV infections (3.4 million) occurred in Sub-Saharan Africa that year, the majority during unprotected sex between men and women, or transmitted by HIV-positive mothers to their babies. In 2001, 2.3 million Africans died and almost 2 million children had lost either their mother or both parents to AIDS.

The worst affected countries include Botswana, Lesotho, Namibia, South Africa, Swaziland, Zambia and Zimbabwe, where at least 20 per cent of the adult population

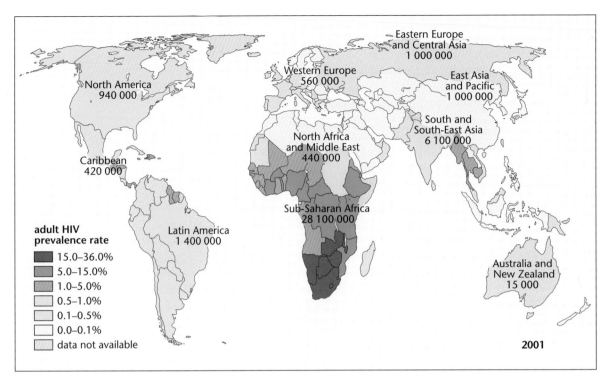

Figure 4.10   *Numbers of people of all ages living with HIV infection or AIDS at the end of 2001, by world region (total = 40 million). The colours indicate the prevalence of HIV infection in the adult population aged over 15 years, but note that the prevalence bands in the key differ from those used in Figure 4.9. (Map adapted from UNAIDS/WHO, 2000, poster 'A global view of HIV infection at the end of 1999'; data from UNAIDS/WHO, 2001,* AIDS Epidemic Update, *UNAIDS, Geneva, p. 27)*

is believed to be infected with HIV. In some provinces, for example KwaZulu-Natal, the figure is over 36 per cent (UNAIDS/WHO, 2001, p. 16).[10]

The effect on life expectancy in Botswana is illustrated in Figure 4.11, but similar population projections apply in other Sub-Saharan countries. The loss of so many adults in their most productive working years is expected to reduce the Gross Domestic Product (GDP) in one of the poorest regions of the world by 20 per cent by the year 2020. Educational progress has been all but halted in some places as teachers die from AIDS; for example, in 1998 Zambia lost over 1 300 teachers — a number equivalent to two-thirds of the new teachers trained that year.

However, one East African country, Uganda, has led the way in reversing the trend. HIV prevalence among pregnant women has fallen steadily since 1992, when it peaked at almost 30 per cent — by 2000, the rate was down to just over 11 per cent. In Section 4.6 we consider how vigorous programmes to increase access to condoms and their acceptance by Ugandans have achieved this remarkable turnaround. Similar programmes have begun to produce some reduction in HIV transmission in Senegal, but it should be kept in mind that an infection rate of 11 per cent is still catastrophically high.

HIV infection in North Africa and the Middle East is believed to affect under 1 per cent of the population, but surveillance systems are generally poor and there is much uncertainty about the true figure.

[10] 'South Africa: Health at the Crossroads' (a video for Open University students) considers the impact of HIV and AIDS in the Cape Town district of South Africa. It was originally studied with *World Health and Disease* (Open University Press, 3rd edn 2001); we suggest that you watch it again at around this point in the chapter.

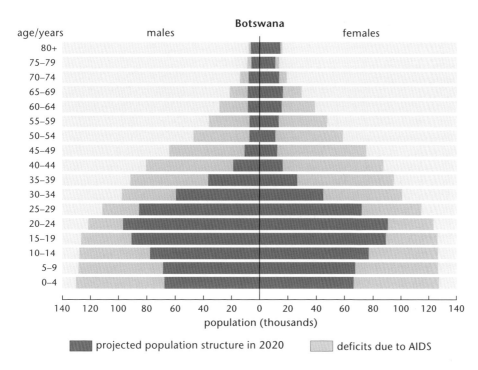

Figure 4.11   *Projected population structure in Botswana in the year 2020, with and without the AIDS epidemic. The population 'pyramid' which is typical of a country with a high birth rate is expected to become a 'chimney' in which dwindling proportions of adults survive their mid-twenties. Average life expectancy at birth in 2000 is estimated at 39 years, compared with 71 years without AIDS. (MAP Network, 2000,* Durban MAP Symposium Report: The Status and Trends of HIV/AIDS in the World, *MAP Network Co-ordinating Office, Harvard University, Boston, p. 31, based on data from the US Bureau of the Census)*

Latin America and the Caribbean

HIV in Latin America and the Caribbean is also primarily a heterosexually transmitted infection, but there are many variations between countries. In Argentina, Brazil, Chile and Uruguay injecting-drug use is a significant additional route. Caribbean countries such as Haiti and the Bahamas have the highest prevalence of HIV outside Sub-Saharan Africa, exceeding 5 per cent of the adult population. In 2001, there were 60 000 new HIV infections in the Caribbean and 130 000 in Latin America; altogether, 110 000 people died in these regions from AIDS that year.

Asia and the Pacific

In 1998, three South-East Asian countries — Cambodia, Myanmar (formerly Burma) and Thailand — contained the majority of the region's 6.7 million affected people. By the end of 2001, containment measures particularly in Cambodia and Thailand had succeeded in reducing the regional total to 6.1 million (Figure 4.10), but HIV was on a steep upward curve elsewhere — most obviously in China, India and Indonesia.

● Why will rising rates of HIV infection in these countries have a huge impact on the global total of people living with HIV and AIDS?

■ China is the world's most populous country, India has the second largest population and Indonesia the fourth largest. HIV-prevalence rates that appear relatively low in comparison with those in Africa result in huge numbers of affected people. (For example, at the end of 2001, adult HIV prevalence in India was just under 1 per cent, but this translates into almost 4 million people.)

Over 1 million new cases of HIV infection occurred in the Asian and Pacific regions in 2001, and the incidence trend suggests that the epidemic had reached a critical point where acceleration to the levels seen in Sub-Saharan Africa is likely. A feature of the Asian epidemic is the greater range of transmission routes compared with the predominantly heterosexual pattern in Africa. Injecting-drug users (IDUs), men who have sex with men (MSMs),[11] and contamination of the blood supply are major additional sources of HIV infection. This diversity and the complex interactions between risk behaviours in a significant proportion of individuals (for example, men who have sex with both men and women, injecting-drug users who are also sex workers), multiply the challenges for HIV-prevention programmes in the region, as elsewhere.

Eastern Europe and Central Asia

Transmission of HIV through injecting-drug use is the dominant feature of the fastest growing AIDS epidemic in the world, in the former communist economies of the Soviet Block, the Central Asian republics and the Baltic states. New infections in the region reached a quarter of a million in 2001 — a rise of 270 per cent since 1998. Although three-quarters of this increase is believed to be IDU-related, sexually transmitted infections also began to rise very quickly, suggesting that a new phase of the epidemic was about to begin.

The majority of the 1 million people living with HIV or AIDS at the end of 2001 were in the Russian Federation, the Ukraine and Estonia. After the collapse of the Soviet Union, injecting-drug use trebled in these countries in less than five years to over 3 million individuals, and there were few programmes aimed at halting the spread of HIV from shared needles and syringes. By contrast, Poland acted swiftly to stop HIV spreading from its IDU population, and the rates were low in 2001 in several other states including the Czech Republic, Hungary and Slovenia.

High-income countries

A combined total of 1.5 million people were estimated to be living with HIV or AIDS at the end of 2001 in all of North America and Western Europe. Almost 27 000 people in these regions died from HIV-related diseases that year, over half of them in one country — the USA. Large differences are evident in the prevalence of HIV infection in the adult populations of high-income countries, as Figure 4.12 shows.

● How do the HIV-infection rates in the countries shown in Figure 4.12 compare with those discussed earlier for the most heavily affected regions of the world?

■ Even in the most affected European country — Portugal (where HIV transmissions have primarily been IDU-related) — less than 0.8 per cent of the adult population are infected with HIV. In the UK, the rate is about 0.1 per cent, or 1 person per 1 000 in the age group. This is in stark contrast to the estimated 25 per cent population prevalence in most of Sub-Saharan Africa.

---

[11] The acronyms IDU (injecting-drug user) and MSM (men who have sex with men) are frequently used in discussion of HIV transmission characteristics. MSM has tended to replace terms such as homosexual, bisexual or gay men, since it can be applied to all men who have sex with men, regardless of whether they identify themselves as 'gay' or also have sex with women.

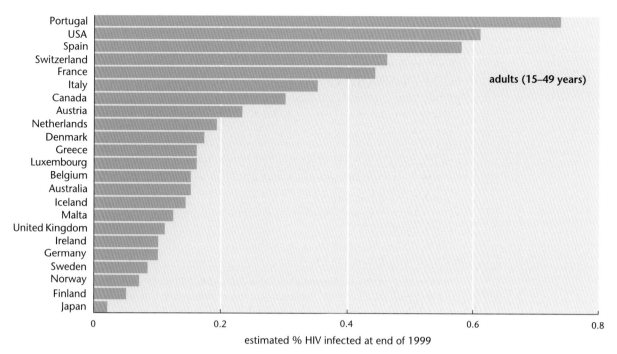

Figure 4.12 *Estimated national prevalences of HIV infection in adults aged 15–49 years in major industrialised countries in Western Europe and North America, with Australia and Japan, at the end of 1999. (PHLS, 2002,* HIV and AIDS Reporting Section (HARS) Slide Set, *Public Health Laboratory Service: Communicable Disease Surveillance Centre, London, slide 17, based on data from UNAIDS)*

However, the fact that HIV prevalence in advanced industrial nations is low *relative* to the most affected parts of the world may obscure public understanding that a prevalence of 1 in a thousand (as in the UK) represents a significant problem in *absolute* terms. In the late 1990s, surveys of young heterosexuals and gay men revealed that sexual contacts with new partners were more likely to be without a condom than had been the case 5 years earlier, and the number of partners in the previous year was also increasing. Health agencies concluded that young, sexually active people were becoming 'complacent' about their risk of HIV infection and failing to protect themselves adequately.

> … more widespread risk-taking is eclipsing the safer sex ethic promoted so effectively for much of the 1980s and 1990s … wide access to anti-retroviral therapy has encouraged misperceptions that there is now a cure for AIDS and that unprotected sex poses a less daunting risk. (UNAIDS/WHO, 2001, p. 20)

The anti-retroviral drugs referred to became widely available in high-income countries from 1996; (we consider their impact in Section 4.5). The assumption that complacency underlies the gradual increase in risk behaviours since that time is contentious, and will be referred to again at the end of the chapter. But whatever the reason, the relatively stable rates of new HIV infections (incidence) that characterised most of the 1990s were replaced by a rising trend from about 1998. The first column of Table 4.1 (overleaf) shows the trend in new HIV infections in the USA from 1993–2000, a pattern that has been described as the **HIV rebound**. Similar increases have also been recorded in other sexually transmitted infections, such as syphilis and gonorrhoea, which are seen as indicators of the rates of unprotected sex outside monogamous relationships.

Table 4.1   Annual number of new cases (incidence) of HIV infection and new AIDS diagnoses, total living with AIDS and deaths, USA, 1993 to 2000 (all ages combined).

year	new HIV infections	new AIDS diagnoses	total living with AIDS	deaths from AIDS
1993	15 313	79 752	173 984	45 598
1994	18 602	72 684	196 559	50 418
1995	15 210	69 172	215 252	51 117
1996	12 538	60 747	238 420	38 025
1997	14 515	49 407	266 086	21 999
1998	19 393	42 508	290 403	18 397
1999	21 419	40 671	314 054	17 172
2000	21 704	40 106	338 978	15 245

Data for new HIV infections and new AIDS diagnoses derived from CDC *HIV/AIDS Surveillance Reports* (various years); all other AIDS data from CDC (2001) *HIV/AIDS Surveillance Report*, **13**(1), Tables 23, 25 and 28, pp. 30, 32 and 34, Centers for Disease Control and Prevention, Atlanta, Georgia.

● Describe the trends in Table 4.1 in relation to AIDS in the USA. To what extent do they support the conclusion quoted above from the UNAIDS/WHO report?

■ The number of new AIDS diagnoses halved and the number living with AIDS almost doubled during the 8 years covered by Table 4.1; deaths from AIDS fell by two-thirds. These trends reflect a decrease in the progression to AIDS in people with HIV and an increase in life expectancy for people with AIDS due to advances in medical treatment, which had a major impact on deaths from 1996. The upward trend in new HIV infections from 1998 may be connected to a greater confidence in treatments for AIDS, as the UNAIDS/WHO report concluded. But the number living with AIDS is growing so quickly that people who are not HIV infected are increasingly likely to know someone with AIDS, and this might deter them from taking risks.

At the time of writing (Spring, 2002), it is unclear what psychosocial and cultural forces are driving the HIV rebound, but there is real concern that the epidemic could return with the force that marked its first decade. In the USA, the cumulative total of deaths from AIDS to the end of June 2001 was 457 667. As doubts grow about the long-term efficacy of the new drug treatments, an upturn in new HIV diagnoses may cause death rates to rise once more.

However, the risk of HIV infection in one group in the USA population has been transformed by anti-retroviral drugs. Figure 4.13 shows the annual number of children diagnosed with AIDS as a result of vertical transmission of HIV from their mothers. The supply of these drugs to pregnant HIV-positive women in developing countries has been a source of bitter controversy, as Section 4.5 describes.

In the UK, the long-term trends in HIV and AIDS diagnoses (i.e. new cases diagnosed that year), and in deaths from AIDS (Figure 4.14), have mirrored the patterns already discussed for the USA, although the numbers involved are much smaller. Figure 4.15 shows how the new HIV diagnoses in the same period were distributed between different transmission routes. The first two years of the epidemic were characterised by a huge increase in HIV transmitted during sex between men, and a smaller peak in cases due to infected blood and clotting factors (the source of infection for 1 255 people before 1986).

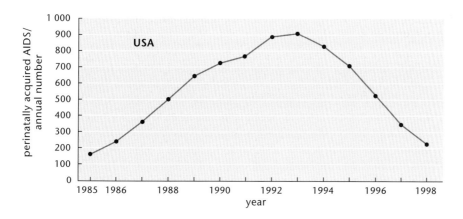

Figure 4.13 *Annual number of cases of AIDS among children born in the USA to HIV-positive mothers, 1985 to 1998. (MAP Network, 2000,* Durban MAP Symposium Report: The Status and Trends of HIV/AIDS in the World, *MAP Network Co-ordinating Office, Harvard University, Boston, p. 20)*

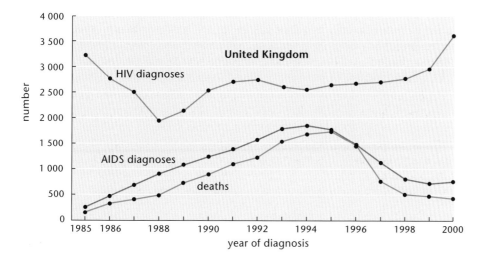

Figure 4.14 *Number of reported HIV diagnoses, case reports of AIDS and deaths from HIV-related disease, in the year in which the diagnosis was made or the death occurred, UK, 1985 to 2000. Numbers for the most recent years may rise as further reports are received. (PHLS, 2002,* HIV and AIDS Reporting Section (HARS) Slide Set, Public Health Laboratory Service: Communicable Disease Surveillance Centre, London, slide 7)

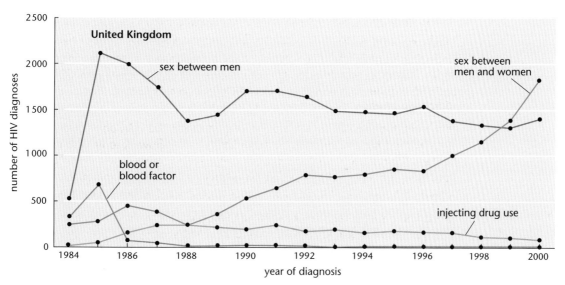

Figure 4.15 *Number of HIV infections resulting from the major transmission routes, by year of diagnosis, UK, 1984 to 2000. Numbers for the most recent years may rise as further reports are received. (PHLS, 2002,* HIV and AIDS Reporting Section (HARS) Slide Set, Public Health Laboratory Service: Communicable Disease Surveillance Centre, London, slide 5)

● According to Figure 4.15, how did UK transmission characteristics develop after 1986?

■ New HIV infections in MSMs rapidly declined until 1988, when they rebounded somewhat and then stabilised on a very gradual downward trend until 1999, when a slight increase occurred. Heterosexual transmission rose steadily from 1988 and the upward trend accelerated about 1996. In 1999, for the first time, the number of heterosexually acquired cases of HIV exceeded the number in MSMs. New HIV infections in IDUs remained at a relatively low level in the 1980s and declined further throughout the 1990s. After 1987, effective blood screening reduced medically related HIV infections to under 20 a year.

In Section 4.6, we will look at the initiatives that helped to bring about the falling incidence of HIV infection among MSMs and IDUs in the 1990s, and the evidence that this trend may have reversed in the UK since 2000.

The rise in heterosexually acquired HIV in the UK is primarily occurring in people who are already HIV-positive at the time they enter the country. In 2000, there were 1 746 new diagnoses of heterosexually acquired HIV, 68 per cent of which occurred in Africa, and a further 11 per cent occurred elsewhere outside the UK; the country of infection could not be established in 11 per cent of cases, and in 10 per cent HIV was acquired within the UK. The detection of HIV in immigrant people generally only happens when they begin to develop an AIDS-defining condition, in contrast to most incidences of HIV acquired within the UK, which tend to be identified much earlier in the course of the infection. Britain's colonial history partly explains the inward migration of people from Commonwealth countries where HIV prevalence is particularly high, and this trend has increased since the mid-1990s.

Not shown in Figure 4.15 is the trend for babies who acquired HIV from their mothers. In contrast to the USA (Figure 4.13), numbers in the UK began rising in the mid-1990s, primarily as a result of immigration by women whose HIV status was not determined until after their babies were born. By 2000, close to 100 children with HIV were being born each year in the UK.

4.4.3 Gender, ethnicity and disadvantage

Throughout the preceding review of the global pattern and regional trends in HIV and AIDS, we have talked about their unequal distribution in populations according to the routes of transmission. In one country they are more prevalent among heterosexuals or MSMs and in another IDUs are most affected. However, HIV and AIDS are also unequally distributed *within* populations along lines of gender, ethnicity and disadvantage. There is not space here for a detailed analysis of the evidence, but certain features stand out and represent a summary of the epidemiology of HIV and AIDS.

First, although the epidemic developed originally in white males in the gay communities of Western high-income countries, by the start of the twenty-first century HIV and AIDS had become a predominantly heterosexually transmitted infection among Black and Asian people of both sexes in low- and middle-income countries.

Second, HIV and AIDS among women is now increasing faster than among men in almost all parts of the world. At the end of 2001, women made up 47 per cent of the adults living with HIV or AIDS globally, and 46 per cent of the deaths from AIDS in that year. Women tend to become infected with HIV at younger ages than men, particularly in cultures where a large age difference between heterosexual partners is common. Thus, infection in women is more likely to occur before or during their main reproductive years, when they are least able to afford condoms or persuade men to use them.

Third, the premature death of women from AIDS is creating a new generation of orphans and children without mothers — over 12 million of them in Africa alone by the end of 2000. Many of these children are themselves HIV-positive and destitute, without any means of support.

Fourth, in all countries where there is a minority ethnic group that suffers material disadvantage and unequal access to services, HIV and AIDS are found in greater proportions than in the majority ethnic group. For example, in the USA, 73 per cent of all new HIV cases in the year to June 2001 were among Black, Hispanic, Asian and Native American people. In the UK, the majority of heterosexually acquired HIV in the 1990s occurred among people arriving from Africa.

Fifth, even within majority ethnic groups, HIV and AIDS is inversely associated with income and other indicators of material disadvantage. The middle-class professional male who typified the epidemic in 1982 is now vastly outnumbered by people who live in relative poverty.

Sixth, the demographic characteristics of gender, ethnicity and disadvantage interact with and compound some of the main behavioural risks. Thus, poverty may lead to illegal drug use and vice versa; the majority of sex workers are women on low incomes.

One disadvantage that people who are HIV-positive and poor within rich countries nevertheless share with those whose country is poor, is unequal access to drugs that can prolong their lives. It is to treatment for HIV and AIDS that we now turn.

4.5 Treating HIV and AIDS

4.5.1 The challenge for medical care

HIV infection poses unique problems for medical care for several reasons. Most obviously, drugs are needed to attack the virus itself and eradicate it from the body. But the virus is continually mutating, which greatly increases the likelihood that new **drug-resistant strains** will be generated that have less susceptibility to whatever drugs are available. We discuss anti-retroviral drugs in Section 4.5.2.

● What challenges does HIV present in terms of the medical management of people who become ill? (Think back to Section 4.3.4, on the effects of HIV on the body.)

■ The immunodeficiency caused by HIV can lead to infection with any of over 100 different opportunistic agents, ranging across many kinds of bacteria, viruses, fungi and parasites, which vary hugely in their biology and hence in the treatment required to control them. Other AIDS-defining conditions also need medical intervention, such as Kaposi's sarcoma, and neurological and psychological problems frequently develop as the disease progresses. Each person develops an individual spectrum of disorders in a complex syndrome that differs from that seen in other patients, requiring individualised medical management.

Difficult decisions have to be made about which drugs to use, in which combinations and at what times. In high-income countries, some drugs are widely prescribed in **prophylatic regimens** aimed at preventing opportunistic infections from developing, but these drugs are unaffordable in most developing countries. The long-term prescription of antibiotics and other prophylactic drugs runs the risk of driving the evolution of drug-resistant strains of bacteria and other infectious agents in the future, but at present the benefits outweigh this potential hazard.[12] Another problem is that many of the drugs used to treat active opportunistic infections are associated with unpleasant and sometimes life-threatening side effects, including nausea, vomiting, diarrhoea, skin rashes, ulceration, anaemia and damage to the kidneys, liver and bone marrow. Physicians must continually negotiate a fine line between using drugs that alleviate one set of symptoms but cause or exacerbate others.

4.5.2 Anti-retroviral therapies: new hope or false dawn?

Viruses are particularly difficult to attack with drugs, as the dearth of remedies for common viral diseases testifies. They are not living cells and their biology is completely different to that of infectious organisms. Retroviruses present medical science with the added problem that they transcribe (copy) their genes into a double strand of DNA and then incorporate it into the DNA of the cells they have infected. It is difficult to conceive of a drug that could destroy HIV particles before they get into human cells, and also eliminate host cells that have HIV genes hidden in their own DNA. The approach has been to design drugs that stop HIV from replicating, with the expectation that the host's immune system would gradually eradicate the small number of viruses that might 'escape' the control of the drug.

The first **anti-retroviral drug** to show some activity against HIV was Zidovudine (also known as AZT), which was first used in clinical treatments in 1987 and for several years was the only drug approved to treat HIV directly. It belongs to a class of drugs known as *reverse transcriptase inhibitors* because they interfere with the transcription of viral RNA genes into DNA inside infected human cells. If you look back at Figure 4.5, stages 2 and 3, you can see why drugs that inhibit the action of the enzyme reverse transcriptase prevent HIV from replicating.

The structure of Zidovudine resembles one of the chemical building blocks (nucleosides) that make up DNA. Other *nucleoside analogues* were developed in the early 1990s. Reverse transcriptase cannot distinguish nucleoside analogues from genuine nucleosides, so it incorporates them into new copies of the viral genome. The mistake halts the replication process at that point, so the viral genome is incomplete and cannot instruct the manufacture of new virus particles.

Several non-nucleoside reverse transcriptase inhibitors have also been developed, which work by binding directly to the enzyme and inhibiting its action.

● What other targets for anti-retroviral drug design are suggested by Figure 4.5?

■ Drugs that block GP120 from binding to host cells (stage 1), or that interfere with either of the enzymes integrase or protease (stages 3 and 4), would prevent HIV from replicating. Blocking integrase would stop the viral genome from being incorporated into the DNA of the host cell, and inhibitors of protease would stop new viral particles from being assembled.

---

[12] Antibiotic resistance is discussed in the case study on tuberculosis in *Medical Knowledge: Doubt and Certainty* (Open University Press, 2nd edn 1994; colour-enhanced 2nd edn 2001), Chapter 4, and in *Human Biology and Health: An Evolutionary Approach* (Open University Press, 3rd edn 2001), Chapters 5 and 11.

At the time of writing (2002), only the *protease inhibitors* had joined the reverse transcriptase inhibitors in widespread clinical use. Before 1996, single-drug trials in high-income countries of nucleoside analogues, such as Zidovudine, had disappointing results in treating HIV-positive individuals. Small improvements occurred in the life expectancy of some who had already developed AIDS, but the latent period between HIV infection and symptoms of HIV disease was not extended.

However, the nucleoside analogues proved spectacularly successful in reducing the transmission of HIV from mother to baby, first in the USA (see Figure 4.13) and later in trials in Thailand and Uganda. In women who do not breastfeed, the number of HIV-infected babies can be reduced by over 90 per cent, even in developing countries, when two injections of a nucleoside analogue are given to the mother shortly before the birth and during labour, and another is given to the baby soon after birth.

Then, in 1996, another breakthrough occurred. Trials began in people with advanced HIV disease of certain combinations of anti-retroviral drugs. Those who were prescribed two different nucleoside analogues, plus a non-nucleoside inhibitor of reverse transcriptase or a protease inhibitor, experienced rapid remission of their symptoms. To support this outcome, some patients were also prescribed drugs to boost the immune system. Blood tests showed that the number of helper T cells in their circulation rose steadily, and at the same time the HIV load in their bloodstream fell to barely detectable concentrations. The effective drug combinations became known as HAART, or **highly active anti-retroviral therapy**.

The impact of HAART on deaths from AIDS in the USA since 1996 was noted when we discussed Table 4.1 earlier. For some people with AIDS in what became known as the 'treatment era', HAART restored health to near-normal levels. Average survival time from the date of an AIDS diagnosis had previously been less than a year, but with the new combined treatments it extended to over four years. Hopes were expressed that the remission might have no upper limit and that the drugs could 'cure' AIDS altogether by eradicating all traces of HIV from the body.

But the early optimism about HAART was short-lived. As Table 4.1 shows, the rate of decline in deaths slowed as time passed: the number of AIDS-related deaths fell 42 per cent between 1996 and 1997, but 11 per cent between 1999 and 2000. Three problems with HAART have emerged that cast doubt on how much longer the currently available drugs will remain effective. The first, and most serious, is the evolution of HIV strains that are resistant to some or all of the HAART drugs.

- People on HAART regimens have to take up to 15 different pills a day at set times, some with food and others on an empty stomach. How might the practical difficulties in following such a regimen strictly over several years contribute to the emergence of drug resistant strains of HIV?

- HIV is mutating all the time, producing large variations in the susceptibility of different virus particles to inhibition by the drugs. If the drugs are not taken in strict accordance with the prescribed regimen, their effectiveness is reduced and the virus particles with the greatest natural resistance survive and replicate, increasing their prevalence in the body. Adherence to the HAART regimens is difficult to maintain, so, over time, increasingly drug-resistant viruses evolve and HIV-related diseases gradually return.

In order to try to prevent drug resistance from taking hold, clinicians generally alter the combination of drugs in the HAART cocktail at the first sign that the viral load is increasing again. But HIV mutates so rapidly that it may not take long for resistance to emerge to the new combination. By 2002, 40 to 50 per cent of patients in the USA had withdrawn from treatment within a year of commencing HAART, and a major reason was drug resistance.

● What are the wider implications for the HIV epidemic when HAART regimens are stopped because drug resistance has developed?

■ The risk of passing on an already drug-resistant strain of HIV increases; people who acquire these viruses have fewer drugs available that might have some effect on the progress of the infection.

Studies in Europe and the USA revealed that from about 1999 onwards up to 14 per cent of new HIV infections were with a drug-resistant strain; for example, this rate was reported by the UK Collaborative Group on Monitoring the Transmission of Drug Resistance (2001). At that date, only 16 HAART drugs were licensed for use in combinations of three or four per patient, so the options for treatment can dwindle rapidly as drug resistance spreads.

The second problem with HAART is also thought to be a major reason for withdrawing from treatment programmes: the side effects are too distressing for a proportion of patients. Diarrhoea, nausea, vomiting and severe headaches are common. Anaemia tends to develop because the nucleoside analogues interfere with the replication of new DNA all over the body, and this damages the production of new blood cells in the bone marrow. The drugs also disrupt the metabolism of fats, leading to a condition called *lipodystrophy syndrome*, which develops slowly in about a third of people on HAART regimens for over three years. Fats are redistributed in the body, causing wasting of the face and limbs, but extra deposits develop on the abdomen and particularly in a 'hump' on the upper back. The metabolic disturbances also increase the occurrence of diabetes and heart disease.

The third reason why early optimism has not been confirmed is that when people in whom HAART has had the most success stop taking the drugs, HIV rebounds in abundance from hidden reservoirs in the body. A research team in the USA tracked the resurgence of HIV in volunteers who had previously had no detectable viruses in their blood for more than two years while on HAART regimens. Within three weeks of stopping the HAART drugs, their viral loads soared to high levels and drug-resistant strains also rapidly emerged. Analysis of the genetic profile of the emergent viruses suggested that at least some had arisen from the pool of 'resting' helper T cells with viral genes in their DNA, but the majority appeared to have come from reservoirs in other sites, perhaps in the bone marrow, lymph nodes or brain (Chun *et al.*, 2000).

● A vigorous debate has arisen about whether HAART should be started as soon as possible during the latent period when HIV-positive people are still in good health, or if it should be delayed as long as possible until symptoms of HIV disease first appear. Explain the reasons for this dilemma.

■ Starting therapy 'early' may have more effect against reservoirs of HIV because the viral load is at its lowest, and it may support a more effective immune response by protecting helper T cells from slow destruction. However, it increases by several years the period in which the drugs are being taken, and this greatly enhances the risk of drug-resistant strains of HIV evolving, and also of serious damage occurring to the person's metabolism as a side effect of the drugs.

In 2001, new clinical guidelines were issued by the US government health department advising that HAART should be delayed longer than previously recommended. By 2002, HAART had been recast as a temporary 'holding' device for keeping HIV replication in check, rather than a potential cure.

4.5.3 Experiences of anti-retroviral therapy

Open University students should now read the two short articles in *Health and Disease: A Reader* (Open University Press, 3rd edn 2001), under the joint heading 'Costs of treating AIDS in Malawi and America'. They illuminate the contrasting experiences of HAART in high- and low-income countries.[13] When you have done so, answer the following question:

● What are the main similarities and the main differences in the accounts by Thomas Garrett about his experience of HAART in the USA, and the description of what happened when Yasaya needed drug therapy for AIDS in Malawi?

■ Both men are middle-aged successful business people in their own countries and both acquired HIV sexually; their descriptions of the symptoms they experienced are similar, and they were both 'in denial' for a long time (Garrett that his HIV infection would progress to AIDS, and Yasaya that his illness was due to HIV). The most obvious difference is that Garrett has found a way to afford the combination drugs he has been taking for the past year (he does not tell us how he managed this without medical insurance), whereas Yasaya's medical insurance will not cover the cost of anti-retroviral treatment. A month's supply of just one of the drugs (a protease inhibitor) costs US$500, the same as his monthly salary. Garrett's health has greatly improved since he began HAART a year earlier and he is determined to 'beat' the disease, whereas Yasaya is resigned to dying soon.

4.5.4 Controversy over access to HAART

The high cost of drugs to treat HIV and AIDS has been one of the most bitterly contested issues in the twenty years of the epidemic. The HAART regimen alone costs over £5 000 (US$7 000) per patient per year; drugs to treat the commonest opportunistic infections can add over £50 per day; tests to measure helper-T-cell counts and viral loads in order to time drug interventions effectively cost over £100 each. The implications for access to treatment in low-income countries are obvious, where even £50 to provide the short course of anti-retroviral treatment to prevent mother-to-baby transmission of HIV is unaffordable.

The arguments put forward by the major pharmaceutical companies to protect their patents on 'brand named' anti-HIV medications have been discussed elsewhere in this series.[14] In 1999, law suits were brought by 36 drug companies with headquarters in the developed economies to prevent the government of South Africa from importing cheaper generic versions of these drugs from factories in Brazil, India and Thailand. The international furore provoked by this action led to

[13] The articles are 'In impoverished Malawi, one man faces the odds' by David Finkel (2000), and 'America: one year on therapy and counting' by Thomas Garrett (1998).

[14] See *Caring for Health: History and Diversity* (Open University Press, 3rd edn 2001), Chapters 8 and 9.

an out-of-court settlement, in which it was agreed that some cheaper generic drugs could be imported into poor countries, and others would be sold to them at reduced prices. For example, in 2001 GlaxoSmithKline agreed to sell Trizivir (which combines three reverse transcriptase inhibitors) to South Africa at a cost of £4.47 per treatment-day, compared with £19.26 for the same drug in the USA. Other drug companies agreed to cut their prices even more and for a short time there was some competition between them for the moral high ground. By 2002, prices had stabilised at levels that international aid organisations such as Oxfam recognised were probably the lowest they could expect to achieve.

● What difficulties do you foresee in providing drug treatment for people with HIV even under the new pricing agreements?

■ In low-income countries the *annual* spending on health care is generally under £5 per person, so even the reduced-price anti-HIV drugs are out of reach; although South Africa is a middle-income country, HIV infection rates are so high (25 per cent of the adult Black population) that the cost of treating everyone would be astronomical.

The major pharmaceutical companies have argued that even if the drugs were provided free, the delivery systems are not in place to manage their prescription effectively. Concerns have been raised that if HAART in particular is inadequately monitored (and the cost of repeated viral load tests are just one stumbling block), then the evolution of drug resistance will explode with catastrophic consequences. Critics of this viewpoint have argued that drug companies are protecting their lucrative first-world markets, which would collapse if drug-resistant HIV spread from low-profit developing countries. Nonetheless, it is difficult to see how HAART regimens could be managed effectively in poor countries without a huge international effort to set up and maintain long-term delivery services and monitoring for people with HIV-related disease.

However, these arguments do not apply to the provision of short-course therapy and counselling to reduce mother-to-baby HIV transmission, particularly after some pharmaceutical companies agreed to donate drugs free for this use. Yet the introduction of even this apparently straightforward intervention was delayed in South Africa by the continued reluctance of the president, Thabo Mbeki, to accept that HIV causes AIDS or that HIV infection was a major health problem in his country. In 2001, he questioned health ministry spending on HIV treatment and research, and expressed the view that inflated figures on HIV prevalence in South Africa were being 'peddled' by drug companies eager to sell their products. But by 2002, the health authorities in several provinces of South Africa had begun treating pregnant HIV-positive women in defiance of the government's recommendations. Tacit agreement seemed to have been reached for all provinces to make this treatment available after former president Nelson Mandela made a speech stating that the importance of preventing mother-to-baby transmission was 'beyond argument or doubt'.

The difficulties in designing effective treatments for HIV and AIDS, even with all the resources of wealthy economies, underline the overwhelming importance of establishing strategies to prevent the spread of infection. In the next section, we review some of the issues involved, beginning with the continuing lack of progress in producing a vaccine to protect people from HIV.

4.6 Preventing the spread of HIV

4.6.1 Vaccines: why so little success?

A **vaccine** works by exposing the immune system to inactivated or harmless samples of an infectious agent (pathogen), 'provoking' the immune response to adapt so that it will attack the active pathogen more effectively if it subsequently gets into the body. If the priming effect of the vaccination is so potent that subsequent infections with that pathogen are completely eradicated, then the vaccine is said to induce **sterilising immunity** in the recipient.

In the case of HIV, sterilising immunity is an essential attribute of any vaccine that aims to protect people from infection. No other vaccine has to achieve 100 per cent protection because the immune system remains intact during other infections and can 'mop up' any pathogens that escape. But HIV infects the immune system itself, so if even a few virus particles escape, they can replicate at a rate of billions per day and ensure the gradual collapse of the immune response that might otherwise eradicate them.

●   Why is a vaccine that produces sterilising immunity against HIV particularly difficult to envisage?

■   HIV genes are constantly mutating and changing the structure of the surface molecules that the immune system recognises (antigenic drift was described in Section 4.3.3). In order to 'prime' a completely effective immune response against all possible variant strains, a vaccine would have to contain samples of all known HIV variants. Even if such a vaccine could be produced, it would still not offer protection against any new variants that might evolve in the future.

Given these difficulties, the research community is cautious about predicting when (or if) a genuinely *protective* vaccine might be developed, and estimates generally place this goal far into the future. However, there is some hope that *therapeutic* vaccines may become available more quickly, to slow down disease progression in people who are already HIV-positive.

There are many other scientific, ethical and political problems in developing an anti-HIV vaccine. For example, unlike most other pathogens, there are no laboratory animals in which to test candidate vaccines, and HIV cannot be grown for very long in tissue culture. Although it can be grown in chimpanzees, they do not develop diseases that mirror AIDS in humans. Therefore, trials of potential vaccines have to be carried out in human volunteers. At the time of writing, in 2002, a total of 70 candidate vaccines were being tested.

There is no shortage of people who are already HIV-*positive* who are willing to take a chance that a therapeutic vaccine might have some beneficial effect, and almost all the candidate vaccines are in small-scale trials in these groups. But there is considerable reluctance among people who are HIV-*negative* to participate in trials of potentially protective vaccines.

●   What are the two most pressing concerns about volunteering for such trials?

■   Vaccines must contain fragments of HIV or inactivated virus particles. So the first concern is that there may be a few intact viruses contaminating the vaccine. If so, they could cause active HIV infection for which there is currently no cure.

How could infected volunteers and their families be compensated? Second, if a vaccine succeeds in eliciting anti-HIV antibodies in trial participants, how can these individuals be distinguished from people who are HIV-positive because they are infected with HIV? Many forms of discrimination are directed at people who have anti-HIV antibodies in their blood, and vaccine trials will add to their number.

A further difficulty has arisen about the geographical locations of vaccine trials. In Section 4.3.2 we described how different subtypes (clades) of HIV were distributed around the world. Vaccines that aim to protect people from the subtypes that prevail in Africa or Asia for example, must be tested locally to ensure that they give protection against local HIV subtypes. However, when the first vaccine trials occurred in developing countries, there were accusations that their populations were being exploited as 'research subjects' by first-world scientists and pharmaceutical companies. For example, during the first African trial of a candidate vaccine, the Ugandan research team reported that

> Ugandans were concerned about reports in the foreign media that manufacturers might choose to trial vaccines in poor countries to reduce product liability in case of injury or to exploit weaker legal, ethical or regulatory mechanisms for conducting biomedical research. (Mugerwa *et al.*, 2002, p. 227)

Conversely, some campaigning organisations in developing countries have demanded that more vaccine trials should be conducted there rather than in Europe and North America, because the need is far greater. Regardless of which population is involved, achieving genuinely **informed consent** among volunteers for vaccine trials is another difficulty, because the biology of HIV and its effects on the body are so complex to explain and understand. Misunderstandings may occur among trial participants about the possible effects of the vaccination, and what risks are involved. This was the experience at the outset of the Ugandan trial cited above:

> Most of the confusion was due to widespread rumours and conflicting media reports about the vaccine … some journalists confused the vaccine with the newly-introduced combination of anti-HIV drugs. [This] error led to false hopes of treatment and to demands that [the vaccine] be given to as many people as possible. Meanwhile, an ongoing campaign by the Ministry of Health to increase vaccination of children against polio was disrupted by allegations that the polio vaccine was contaminated with HIV. (Mugerwa *et al.*, 2002, p. 226)

Difficulties in organising the large-scale testing of promising candidate vaccines are illustrated by the AIDSVAX trial, which began in 1998 on HIV-negative volunteers. The participants were 1 600 people in North America and the Netherlands who were considered to be at high risk of contracting HIV, and 2 500 injecting-drug users in Thailand. Each person was randomly assigned to receive either the candidate vaccine or placebo injections. However, some AIDS activists demanded that the placebo 'wing' of the trial be abandoned as unethical, because individuals in the placebo group are 'denied' any protection that might arise from the vaccine.

● Can you explain why the placebo group is a necessary part of a vaccine trial in participants who are at high risk of becoming infected with HIV?

■   Trials in high-risk participants are based on the expectation that some will inevitably be exposed to HIV during the trial period. If the vaccine *is* providing some protection from HIV, then there should be fewer cases of infection in the vaccine group than in the placebo group. Without a placebo group, it is impossible to judge whether the vaccine is having any effect.

Another problem is that some participants may change their behaviour as a result of the trial, exposing themselves to greater risks than they might otherwise have taken, in the belief that the vaccine will afford some protection.

The problems in developing and testing potential anti-HIV vaccines reinforces the ongoing need to provide effective support for behavioural change as the *central* strategy in reducing the spread of HIV. The world's population cannot afford to wait another decade or more for an effective vaccine to come into production. And even if this goal is achieved, the problems of distribution and access already discussed for anti-HIV drugs will still have to be solved before a vaccine has a significant impact on the growth of the HIV epidemic.

4.6.2 Local action to achieve behavioural change

The history of HIV and AIDS is marked by people taking collective action, independently of governments or health organisations, to prevent the spread of HIV through behavioural change and to resist stigmatisation or discrimination. Here we discuss community responses to HIV prevention among two of the populations most affected by HIV and AIDS in developed countries: men who have sex with men, and injecting-drug users; and a third group — sex workers and their clients — taking a global view.

Men who have sex with men

In the absence of a cure or vaccine, the only way in which people can prevent HIV infection is to minimise their risk behaviour. Gay men — the first identified group affected by AIDS in developed countries — responded rapidly with **community action** initiatives. They set up organisations such as the Terrence Higgins Trust in the UK and the San Francisco AIDS Foundation (SFAF) in the USA, to distribute what little information was available to help gay men protect themselves and each other from HIV infection. They also put pressure on governments, the medical establishment and pharmaceutical companies to take the epidemic seriously. In major American and European cities this happened within the first two years of the recognition of AIDS and preceded any organised governmental response.

Volunteers distributed health education information to men in gay bars and clubs, warning of the dangers of unprotected penetrative sex. Initially doctors had simply told gay men to stop having sex altogether, but gay communities pioneered the concept of 'safer sex', which advocated, among other things, the use of condoms when having penetrative sex. Gay men were able to mobilise rapidly because of the progress they had achieved in community and civil rights action associated with the 'gay liberation' movement during the 1970s.

A feature of local initiatives that brought about behavioural change was the commitment to involve participants in **peer-education programmes** that encourage mutual responsibility and support for sexual safety and HIV-risk reduction. They promoted a *collective* response within gay communities, rather than attempting to change the beliefs and opinions of individuals. Evaluations of these projects (by Kelly *et al.*, 1992; and by Prout and Deverell, 1995) showed that the most effective advocates for change in the gay community were gay men themselves. In using peers as educators and employing 'opinion leaders' within specific networks or groups of gay men, these projects were significantly more successful than conventional health education approaches at the time, which tended to rely on information-giving alone as the basis for behaviour change.[15]

● What effect did these local campaigning initiatives have on the rate of HIV infection among gay men?

■ The sharp reduction in HIV transmission among gay men in the UK in the first decade of the epidemic is evident if you look back at Figure 4.15. Similar outcomes occurred elsewhere in Western Europe and in the USA.

By the start of the new millennium, some of the original campaigning organisations had developed from local collectives to national institutions; for example, the SFAF had an annual budget for 2001 of over US$24 million.

However, new diagnoses of HIV and other sexually transmitted infections in men who have sex with men (MSMs) began to increase from about 1995 in the UK, Western Europe and North America. (The pattern in England up to 1999 is reviewed by Nicoll *et al.*, 2001.) Researchers, particularly in the USA, have attempted to explain the increase by suggesting that MSMs were 'relapsing', that is returning (even if only occasionally) to risky sexual behaviour in the belief that they were no longer at risk, or because the new combined drug treatments made the risk of HIV infection seem less threatening. The **relapse thesis** has become prominent in HIV-prevention programmes in the USA and is the focus of much recent research, but it suffers from a number of problems.

● Can you suggest reasons why an increase in new cases of HIV may not be due to MSMs returning to risky sexual behaviour they gave up during the 1980s?

■ Some new HIV diagnoses are among men who are not relapsing but actually *beginning* their sexual lives by having unsafe sex, perhaps because they are young and consider AIDS to be a disease of older men. Men who never changed their behaviour and continued to have unsafe sex may have delayed coming forward for testing until they were encouraged to do so by improvements in drug treatment.

The concept of 'relapse' has also been criticised for its negative association with disease progression and 'moral back-sliding' (for a review of the issues, see Flowers, 2001). It rests on an assumption that all MSMs have multiple sex partners throughout their lives, and measures 'relapse' into unsafe sex by asking about the number of unprotected sex acts in a defined period. Such counts fail to acknowledge that unprotected sex is not 'unsafe' within relationships between HIV-negative partners. But whatever the underlying reasons, the increase in HIV infection among MSMs is a consistent finding in many countries around the world. New approaches to achieving behaviour change have been attempted with mixed success, including counselling sessions focused on changing the way MSMs think about sexual safety and risk-taking (for example, Imrie *et al.*, 2001).[16]

---

[15] The problems of health education campaigns as a means of achieving behavioural change to reduce the risks of coronary heart disease are discussed in *Dilemmas in UK Health Care* (Open University Press, 3rd edn 2001), Chapter 8.

[16] Some programmes have used cognitive behavioural therapy (CBT), a technique which is discussed in Chapter 6 under interventions in schizophrenia.

Injecting-drug users

It has been less common for injecting-drug users (IDUs) to organise themselves on a community basis to prevent HIV infection than has been the case with gay men. This is for two related reasons. First, in the 1980s there was already an infrastructure for community action and organisation among gay men. In contrast there is little evidence of a collective or community identity among populations of drug injectors. Second, IDUs have less collective power, in part because of a lack of cohesiveness and the absence of external support for an illegal activity, but also because of the everyday demands of drug-using lifestyles and the generally low economic and social status associated with drug use.

Despite these obstacles, drug injectors also made significant changes in behaviour to prevent HIV transmission in the first decade of the epidemic. Research in the UK by Tim Rhodes (1994) showed that the proportions of drug injectors who reported sharing used needles and syringes declined over time. HIV prevalence among injecting populations in the UK stabilised in the early 1990s, but there are some signs that it began to rise again from about 1998, prompting concern that the 'relapse' dynamic already discussed for gay men was having an effect among IDUs.

Syringe-exchange programmes (also called needle-exchange programmes), where used and possibly infected injecting equipment can be exchanged for sterile supplies, are the cornerstone of HIV-prevention initiatives targeted at drug injectors. One of the earliest was established in 1984 in Amsterdam by the *Junkiebonden* (Junkies' Union), founded initially as a civil-rights action group.

● What do you think are the main problems for community action approaches among IDUs?

■ The lack of a community identity among drug-injecting populations means there is little infrastructure for raising resources and organisational support for such initiatives. Drug injectors may avoid participation for fear of criminal prosecution. Syringe and needle exchanges have been opposed by people who see them as encouraging drug use.

Evaluations of local programmes worldwide have confirmed that syringe exchanges have cut the rate of new HIV infections without increasing the number of new drug injectors, or the frequency of drug use among current injectors. Among the most successful programmes are those in Thailand. Conversely, studies in the USA showed higher rates of HIV prevalence among drug injectors in states where syringe exchange schemes were prohibited (Watters, 1996). In many other countries with large drug-injecting populations, religious and moral objections have prevented the setting up of syringe exchanges.

An important development in HIV-prevention initiatives aimed at drug injectors has been the use of **outreach projects**, which employ peer educators (in this case drug users themselves) to get in touch with individuals who would otherwise remain out of contact with treatment and support services. In the USA, the *National Institute of Drug Abuse* (*NIDA*) commissioned outreach projects in over 50 cities, and such projects have become an established feature of prevention work among drug injectors in the UK.

Sex workers and their clients

Female sex workers in developing countries are rarely able to insist that their clients use condoms because of their financial dependence on prostitution: many send earnings back to families engaged in subsistence farming.[17] As in developed countries, unprotected sex often carries a higher fee, as well as a higher health risk. Condoms may also be unaffordable or unobtainable. Exactly the same issues affect the sexual safety of women who are not sex workers, but whose power to influence their male partners to use condoms is very limited.

In both developing and developed countries a number of exceptional female sex workers have organised collective action to protect the health of their co-workers by promoting the use of condoms. Women sex workers have engaged in political lobbying in an attempt to legalise prostitution, increase their access to health services and improve the 'occupational safety' of sex work. Self-help and peer initiatives, such as *Red Thread* in Amsterdam and *Call Off Your Old Tired Ethics* in California (*COYOTE*), argue that sex workers themselves are only marginally able to create safer working conditions and to promote safer sex within these conditions.

● What do you think is the biggest obstacle to reducing the risk of HIV among sex workers?

■ The behaviour of men who purchase sexual services and insist on unprotected sex.

There have been relatively few attempts to research or educate the clients of sex workers. Two exceptions are shown in the TV programme for Open University students mentioned earlier — one in India, where long-distance lorry drivers have been targeted, and another in Zambia, employing peer educators in rural villages where male migrant workers often return after having sex with prostitutes in the cities. Both of these initiatives are examples of outreach projects.

However, outreach projects such as free condom distribution to sex workers are less successful where commercial sex interacts with illegal drug use. This combination represents a particularly difficult challenge for HIV-prevention programmes, because sex workers who need money for drugs are even less likely to insist that their clients use condoms if they can command a higher price for unprotected sex.

Despite research evidence that sex workers are at greater risk of infection from their clients than clients are from them, the general tendency has been to view sex workers as major vectors of disease. A possible reflection of this bias is the slow pace of research into anti-viral gels that could reduce HIV infection rates if used in the vagina, and the provision of female condoms. Although such products could help protect women in general during penetrative sex, their use among female sex workers could have a significant impact on their risk of acquiring or passing on HIV and other sexually transmitted infections.

4.6.3 Social norms and sexual safety

A commonly criticised feature of strategies to reduce HIV through behaviour change has been their focus on risk-taking by *individuals* and their neglect of the *social norms* (Chapter 2) that influence individual actions. For example, a review by Graham Hart and Paul Flowers (1996), showed that perceptions of HIV risk and risk behaviour in a wide range of groups, including gay men and injecting-drug users, are not simply dependent on individual knowledge, beliefs and attitudes.

[17] The TV programme associated with this chapter for Open University students, 'A Future with AIDS', illustrates this dilemma among women sex workers in India, and among children living rough on the streets of Rio de Janeiro, some of whom earn money from sexual services.

They are also influenced by the opinions of others and the situational and social contexts in which risk behaviour occurs.

For example, social norms have been shown to affect individual attempts to reduce the risk of HIV infection during sexual encounters. Condom use is more likely within heterosexual and gay relationships when they are endorsed by partners, close friends and peers (Kippax *et al.*, 1992). Conversely, a combination of love, trust and intimacy are all associated with the non-use of condoms in gay relationships, and this social norm appears to have greater importance than sexual safety (McLean *et al.*, 1994).

The influence of social norms can also be demonstrated in community-wide changes among networks of injecting-drug users. For example, Jill Burt and Gerry Stimson (1993) showed that as safer injecting behaviour became the norm, it was increasingly difficult for individual drug users to borrow or lend used syringes, even in situations where availability of equipment was scarce. However, in certain social situations or relationships, different norms may exist. Neil McKeganey and Marina Barnard (1992) discovered that needle sharing in Glasgow was still occurring because a social value was placed on reciprocity and 'sharing'. Drug users are in great part no different from the people around them in being willing to share what they own.

Thus, if community interventions are to change individual risk behaviours, they may also need to bring about changes in the social contexts that influence why and how people behave in a certain way. But there is usually fierce resistance among influential sectors in a population who are against the changing of social norms. The controversy about whether techniques to increase sexual safety could be taught in sex education programmes in schools is one illustration of this point (Figure 4.16).

In some developing countries, for example where social norms endorse polygamy or where fertility is highly prized, far-reaching socio-cultural changes may need to occur before HIV-prevention initiatives are successful. The undoubted difficulties in achieving such changes can, nonetheless, be overcome, as the experience in certain countries, including Uganda, Senegal and Thailand, testifies. In the next section we briefly consider the characteristics of successful national strategies to reduce the spread of HIV, and some of the main factors that interfere with their implementation.

Figure 4.16 *'Safer sex' posters on display at a Brook Advisory Centre. Safer sex education for children in primary schools in the UK has been controversial; advocates argue that it will protect them from sexually transmitted infections when they become sexually active, but critics claim it encourages children to start having sex at a younger age. (Photo: Tony Woodcock)*

4.6.4 National strategies to reduce HIV

Students of the Open University should begin by reading the article by the Executive Director of UNAIDS, Peter Piot, entitled 'Global AIDS epidemic: time to turn the tide' (in *Health and Disease: A Reader*, Open University Press, 3rd edn 2001). Then answer the following question.

● According to Piot, what are the key features of the most successful national programmes to prevent the spread of HIV in developing countries, such as those in Uganda, Senegal and Thailand?

■ Compare your answers with the list in Box 4.1.

Box 4.1   Characteristics of successful national HIV-prevention programmes

- All agencies and organisations who can make a contribution coming together under one strategic national plan;
- Visibility and openness about the epidemic, including involving people with AIDS, as a way of reducing stigma and shame;
- Addressing core issues of vulnerability to HIV by introducing new social policies;
- Targeting efforts on those who are most vulnerable to infection;
- Focusing on young people, for example in terms of sex education;
- Recognising the synergy between prevention and care;
- Encouraging and supporting strong community participation.

(adapted from Piot, 2000, p. 2178)

Government commitment to mass education campaigns, community participation in outreach projects targeted at the most vulnerable groups, and widespread condom promotion and distribution programmes have seen some notable successes. For example, they have reduced new cases of HIV year-by-year since 1992 in Uganda. Senegal's success in keeping HIV at low levels has partly been due to the licensing and HIV testing of sex workers, and the support of the imams in this predominantly Muslim country for condom distribution schemes. In Thailand, a vigorous '100 per cent condom use' programme among sex workers is thought to have been the main factor in reducing the incidence of new HIV infections from 143 000 in 1991 to 20 000 in the year 2000.

An essential feature of successful HIV-prevention programmes not mentioned in Box 4.1 is the assurance of **confidentiality**. Unless individual identity can be safeguarded, people will not come forward for HIV testing, or attend health protection schemes such as syringe exchanges and condom distribution centres. The threat of discrimination, intimidation and in some cases violence against those whose identity is disclosed as being 'at risk' of HIV, still acts as a powerful deterrent against participation in prevention programmes.

The need for confidentiality is illustrated by countries where HIV has been reduced by identifying and treating individuals with *other* sexually transmitted infections (STIs), such as syphilis, gonorrhoea and chlamydia. The stigmatisation of people with STIs often prevents them from seeking treatment, even though they can be cured with short courses of antibiotics. The lesions caused by untreated STIs increase the risk that exposure to HIV will result in active infection, and also that HIV will be passed on during unprotected sex. In Mwanza, a rural district of Tanzania, the incidence of new diagnoses of HIV was reduced by 40 per cent during a concentrated effort to identify and treat other STIs; (for a review of this and other interventions to reduce heterosexually transmitted HIV in low-income countries, see Lamptey, 2002).

However, there are so many barriers to effective national HIV-prevention programmes in developing countries that there are relatively few examples of significant success. Here we highlight some of the most difficult problems that must be overcome if the AIDS epidemic is ever to be brought under control.

Factors leading to increased **vulnerability** to HIV risk have become a central concern of prevention policies since the mid-1990s. We have already referred to the greater vulnerability of women to demands for unprotected sex from economically or physically more powerful men. But the vulnerability model also applies at the level of whole countries. International trade barriers, slow economic development, crippling levels of national debt, civil wars, famines, inadequate infrastructure and lack of political commitment increase the vulnerability of low-income countries to HIV. The population sectors most affected are those who are disadvantaged by, for example, poverty, unemployment, illiteracy, homelessness, lack of access to services, and human rights abuses. Piot argues that action to alleviate these structural problems is critical to success in reducing HIV:

> Whether we conceptualise AIDS as a health issue only or as a development and human security issue is not just an academic exercise. It defines how we respond to the epidemic, how much money is allocated to combating it, and what sectors of government are involved in the response. (Piot, 2000, p. 2177)

Piot emphasises that the response to the HIV epidemic cannot just be about the export of 'best practice' — it also requires the continual search for new locally relevant social policies to prevent HIV from spreading. Achieving the multisectoral community participation that he advocates is fraught with difficulties. Different stakeholders in a community often have conflicting motivations: for example, religious leaders may advocate sexual abstinence and oppose sex educators who are trying to promote greater use of condoms; biomedical scientists may attempt to steer funding towards medical interventions at the expense of social initiatives involving peer educators.

Straightforward practical problems can also restrict the success of national HIV-prevention initiatives. One that tends to be disregarded in debates about how to achieve behaviour change is the provision of condoms.

● In countries with a high prevalence of heterosexually transmitted HIV, what practical problem is likely to undermine national programmes to encourage condom use?

■ The very large populations of these countries means that a huge number of condoms would be required to give protection during all acts of penetrative sex. (For example, in 1999, the availability of condoms in Sub-Saharan Africa totalled 4.6 per man in the age group 15–59 years (Shelton and Johnston, 2001); the annual unmet need for condoms in this region has been estimated at 13 billion (Myer *et al.*, 2001).)

The emphasis on condom provision in developing countries has, in the view of some biomedical experts, deflected attention from non-sexual sources of infection.

In high-income countries, the screening of blood, organs and blood products, and adequate infection control measures in health-care settings (for example, in the handling and disposal of 'sharps'), have reduced new HIV infections from medical sources to a very low level. But national blood banks with effective screening policies are expensive to set up and maintain, and the cost of sterile disposable syringes and intravenous lines is too great for the health systems of poor countries. As a result, very little progress has been made and contaminated blood and medical equipment remain a significant source of HIV infection in many parts of the world.

The need to develop and maintain health systems that are not themselves a source of HIV transmission, and which deliver adequate treatment and care to the millions of people with HIV-related disease, will require a huge international effort — way beyond anything envisaged before the AIDS epidemic became a global crisis. In the final section of this chapter, we discuss some of the major issues for the future, beginning with the international cost of tackling HIV and AIDS.

4.7   Issues for the future of the AIDS epidemic

In concluding this chapter, we highlight three issues for the future:

- the lack of adequate funding and organisation for a global strategic plan to tackle the epidemic;

- the need to resolve profound dilemmas about equity and justice in access to resources, particularly for treatment;

- and the challenge to develop inclusive communities that value people with HIV and AIDS.

4.7.1 How much will it cost?

In 1998, a total of US$300 million was contributed by the richer nations of the world to aid organisations involved in tackling the AIDS epidemic in developing countries. That year over 33 million people were living with HIV and AIDS — over 90 per cent of them outside the wealthy industrial economies — so the available funding for 1998 amounted to less than US$10 per person. By 2001, donations to international HIV/AIDS programmes had accelerated to US$1 billion, but the gap between this sum and the estimated requirement remained immense. For example, treating even 25 per cent of the HIV-positive population of Botswana with HAART drugs, bought at the lowest price on offer, would still cost twice the country's annual budget for all forms of health spending.

In May 2001, the United Nations secretary general, Kofi Annan, called for annual donations to what he called the AIDS 'war chest' to rise to US$7–10 billion (£5–7 billion), to be spent on five priority areas (summarised in Box 4.2). This sum is the equivalent of a donation of US$10 (£7) a year from each person living in the world's high-income economies. A UN special assembly met in June 2001 to debate how the goals summarised in Box 4.2 could be achieved, and to set targets and a timetable for action. The resolution passed by the UN committed all member countries (among other agreements):

- to attempt to reduce the incidence of HIV by 25 per cent by the year 2005;

- develop care and support strategies;

- improve the legal protection of human rights;

- and support the empowerment of women to reduce their vulnerability to HIV.

Box 4.2   UN priority areas for HIV/AIDS funding (2001)

- *Preventing further horizontal transmission of HIV*, through mass awareness campaigns, peer education, voluntary counselling, HIV testing, and (where appropriate) condom distribution and syringe-exchange schemes.

- *Reducing vertical transmission of HIV from mothers to babies*, through HIV testing, provision of short-course anti-retroviral therapy, voluntary counselling, and support to find alternatives to breastfeeding.

- *Ensuring that care and treatment is available to all*, including access to affordable anti-retroviral drugs, treatment for opportunistic and sexually transmitted infections and HIV-related cancers, voluntary counselling, and community and home-based support.

- *Protecting those made vulnerable by the epidemic*, especially the 13 million children orphaned by AIDS, and women in developing countries.

- *Delivering scientific progress* in research to develop a vaccine, effective treatments and ultimately a cure.

However, resolutions are not a substitute for a globally coordinated strategic plan, which — according to Jeffrey Sachs, chair of the WHO's Commission on Macroeconomics and Health — had still not emerged after two decades of the AIDS epidemic. In the absence of such a plan, only US$1.7 billion of the funding requested by the UN has been promised for 2002. An editorial in the *British Medical Journal* offered this explanation for the shortfall:

> ... there is still almost no public knowledge about exactly what the fund will pay for (perhaps treatments, perhaps health system support, or both), and how [the UN board] will make its funding decisions. This is worrying. We need reassurance that the fund will avoid the major pitfalls — lack of governance and poor accountability — that have plagued other public-private health initiatives ... Donor money is not flowing into the fund because donors currently see no guarantee from their investment. (Yamey and Rankin, 2002, p. 181)

Yet what are the costs of *not* funding a comprehensive global strategy to tackle HIV and AIDS? The economic impact is already immense in the countries of Sub-Saharan Africa. In South Africa, for example, the economy is heavily dependent on mining, but miners have among the highest rates of HIV infection, so productivity is falling and labour costs are rising. The loss of skilled workers is particularly devastating in some occupational sectors, including health care; 20 per cent of student nurses in South Africa are reported to be HIV-positive (cited in Dixon *et al.*, 2002). The most conservative economic models estimate that growth in GDP in Africa as a whole has already been reduced by 2–4 per cent per annum due to lost productivity and declining exports, as a consequence of HIV and AIDS. By 2010, South Africa's GDP per capita is predicted to be 8 per cent lower than it would have been without the epidemic (Arndt and Lewis, 2001).

- In the article by Peter Piot (quoted in Section 4.6.4), he referred to HIV and AIDS not as a health problem but as a global development and human security issue. How does the global epidemiology of HIV (Section 4.3) explain the basis for this statement?

■ The speed at which HIV is spreading throughout Asia, Latin America and the Caribbean means that economic disruption will overtake these countries, just as it is already doing in Africa, unless HIV is brought under control. Put simply, the epidemic threatens global productivity and trade — the basis of prosperity and security in the world's richest nations.

Self-interest could therefore be one motivation for spending the US$10 billion requested by the UN — a tiny fraction of the joint GDP of Western Europe, the USA, Canada, Australia, New Zealand and Japan, which was estimated at US$20 000 billion in 1998 (Maddison, 2001, pp. 173 and 206). An alternative rationale is on moral grounds — that wealthy countries should support developing nations to combat HIV and AIDS as an act of social justice. But in the absence of adequate funding to ensure equitable access to resources, how can justice be delivered? And how will priorities be decided when there are insufficient resources to meet all needs?

4.7.2 Should prevention take priority over treatment?

Strategies aimed at preventing new cases of HIV infection are self-evidently a vital component in national responses to the AIDS epidemic. However, the prevention agenda has tended to dominate discussion of how to deal with HIV in developing countries. When the HAART drugs became available in wealthier nations in the mid-1990s, it seemed that most governments and aid organisations had tacitly agreed that providing such costly treatment to 90 per cent of the people living with HIV and AIDS was simply out of the question. In 2002, a director of Médecins Sans Frontières noted that

> … because donors and some in the international health community traditionally favour prevention at the expense of treatment, patients already infected will be written off as not sufficiently cost effective to treat. (Quoted in Yamey and Rankin, 2002, p. 181)

Without substantial international funding for treatment programmes, poor countries cannot afford to do otherwise. In the article by David Finkel referred to earlier (Section 4.5.3), he asks Wesley Sangala, the government coordinator of Malawi's HIV/AIDS plan, what provision has been made for the 16 per cent of the adult population who are already infected with HIV.[18] Sangala replies:

> In reality we cannot entertain it … It is just too expensive to contemplate. So all we are saying, unfortunately, is that they have to die. (Quoted in Finkel, 2000, p. A01)

This bleak verdict lies at the heart of the case for social justice as the guiding principle in tackling HIV and AIDS. While the drugs to treat even curable sexually transmitted and opportunistic infections are beyond the reach of all but the well-off in poor countries, how can anti-retroviral therapies be afforded for all who need them?

Campaigners such as Donald Berwick (2001), president of the Institute for Healthcare Improvement in the USA, have argued that pharmaceutical companies should supply these drugs to poor countries at zero cost. The industry could (according to Berwick) easily forego the modest profits it can expect to make from supplying HAART drugs to developing countries at the reduced prices already offered.

[18] This article is set reading for Open University students and is reprinted in *Health and Disease: A Reader* (Open University Press, 3rd edn 2001).

● What arguments could be put forward to counter this claim?[19]

■ Drug companies spend over US$40 billion annually on research and development and, without a guaranteed return on their investment, new products could take longer to deliver. Significant problems with the first generation of HAART drugs (Section 4.5) mean that innovation in drug design is urgently needed to achieve better outcomes, and this cannot be done cheaply. Some would argue that it is only the potential for huge profits that drives on the research that will, one day, deliver therapeutic breakthroughs and vaccines to prevent HIV infection.

In the absence of affordable health care for everyone with HIV, priorities have to be set about what kinds of treatment will be provided. In July 2000, the MAP Network (Monitoring the AIDS Pandemic) held a symposium in Durban attended by experts from all regions of the world affected by the epidemic. Among other recommendations, they set targets for the proportion of people who should be receiving treatment for HIV and AIDS in developing countries by 2005. They aimed to treat:

• 40 per cent of those needing palliative care

• 25 per cent of those needing treatment for opportunistic infections

• 20 per cent of those needing prophylaxis for opportunistic infections

• 12 per cent of those needing HAART (adapted from MAP Network, 2000, p. 31)

With so few scheduled to receive anti-retroviral drugs even on the most ambitious targets, a question arises as to who will be selected for this treatment and on what basis? Some commentators have voiced the most divisive dilemma in the AIDS debate. As long as anti-retroviral drugs are in short supply in developing countries, should priority be given to individuals who add most economic 'value' to the community?

> ... to maintain economic stability, it may be necessary to target expensive anti-retroviral drugs at highly productive socioeconomic groups in specific industries on the basis of their contribution to economic output rather than their healthcare needs. Such a strategy would generate greater economic prosperity and government funds, allow time for replacement labour to be trained, and thereby reduce the overall impact of the epidemic. (Dixon *et al.*, 2002, p. 234)

Thus, as the AIDS epidemic begins its third decade, new forms of discrimination are being considered that will reinforce existing social stratifications along lines of education, skills, status and income. If this road is travelled, then the most vulnerable groups in poor countries — who are already at greatest risk from HIV — will be last in the queue for treatment. As always, women and children will be disproportionately represented among them, and members of highly stigmatised groups (sex workers, injecting-drug users, illegal immigrants, prisoners and gay men) may find themselves excluded altogether. Even in the UK it is estimated that over 11 000 people are infected with HIV but remain undiagnosed (CDSC, 2001), and discrimination is the most important factor in maintaining their disadvantage.

---

[19] Issues concerning the role of the pharmaceutical industry in health care are discussed in *Caring for Health: History and Diversity* (Open University Press, 3rd edn 2001), Chapter 9.

4.7.3 Is discrimination still a serious problem?

From the beginning of the AIDS epidemic in the 1980s, a positive HIV test has had major financial and social implications. In Western countries, many workers lost their jobs when their HIV status became known as a result of pressure from colleagues or employers. The Disability Discrimination Act, 1995, made it illegal for employers in the UK to discriminate against a worker who becomes ill with HIV-related disease, but people with HIV still experience difficulties in finding work, or face stigma and prejudice in the workplace even when they are in good health (Terrence Higgins Trust, 2000).

Legal constraints are one method for reducing direct discrimination, but they cannot outlaw stigmatising attitudes towards people with HIV. Paradoxically, the negative impact of such attitudes may be increasing in certain areas as a result of the greater integration of HIV-positive people into 'mainstream' society.

In the UK in the 1980s, there was an unusual degree of involvement of those affected by HIV disease in the running and organisation of health services directed towards their care. But as health-sector responses to HIV became increasingly professionalised, so participation by service-users declined, and the direction and organisation of services for people with HIV became less influenced by their own ideas and suggestions. Resources were increasingly targeted towards HIV prevention in the 'general population', at the expense of stigmatised groups (such as gay men), where the need for care and support was greatest. The disempowerment of people with HIV in their dealings with the health service may have contributed to the slow pace of change in what Gill Green and Stephen Platt (1997) have termed the 'fear and loathing' they have often encountered in health-care settings.

● Another area in which people with HIV have found themselves disempowered is in access to financial services. What form of discrimination became routine in the financial services industry in the UK in the 1990s?

■ It became virtually impossible for people who knew they were HIV-positive to buy life insurance, obtain a mortgage or negotiate other long-term loans. Just having an HIV *test* (even if the result is negative), or being advised to have one by a doctor, has been sufficient for certain insurance companies to refuse to supply a policy, or to add substantial penalty clauses and increased premiums.

Policy in relation to HIV screening has varied around the world. Although never considered a viable option by governments in the UK, some commentators in the early years of the epidemic demanded *compulsory* screening of the whole population to protect the 'innocent' from the 'guilty'. Screening for HIV has most often been advocated in relation to health workers, despite the outcomes of 22 'look-back' exercises in the UK since 1988, in which thousands of patients of HIV-positive practitioners have been reviewed without a single case of transmission being identified.

Compulsory screening has been applied at various times to specified groups (for example, army recruits, illegal immigrants, prison inmates) in several countries in Western and Eastern Europe, North America, Cuba, the Caribbean and the Middle East. In most of Africa and Asia the emphasis has always been to encourage voluntary testing. However, part of Thailand and Senegal's success in reducing the rate of new HIV infections is attributed to the licensing and compulsory testing of sex workers.

● The medical profession in the UK has consistently argued against compulsory HIV testing — in part because it may lead to an *increase* in the spread of HIV infection. How might this come about?

■ Compulsory testing could result in HIV being 'driven underground' because those most at risk of infection might seek to avoid the adverse social and economic consequences of a positive test result. They would then be denied access to medical and counselling services, which could have reduced their risk behaviour. In the absence of this support, they are more likely to transmit HIV to others.

In the view of some experts in the field, this outcome was made more likely in Scotland as a result of the Glenochil judgement, which criminalised the 'reckless' transmission of HIV (Bird and Leigh Brown, 2001). An HIV-positive man who had acquired HIV from shared drug-injecting equipment while at Glenochil prison, was sentenced to five years imprisonment for 'culpably and recklessly transmitting HIV to a female sexual partner' (ibid, p. 1174) to whom he had not disclosed his HIV status. Evidence that the man had been the source of the infection was provided by molecular comparison of the viral strains in his body and those taken from his sexual partner.

● Why might the Glenochil judgement deter people in Scotland from coming forward for HIV testing in future?

■ It is now legal to perform viral-strain analysis on blood samples taken for HIV testing, and use the results as evidence in criminal prosecutions of people accused of transmitting HIV to others.

There are many reasons why people with HIV avoid telling even their family and friends about their HIV status. Among the most common is that they do not want to be treated as 'different'. In short, concealment is a strategy to ensure that you are 'treated like anyone else'. (Strategies for avoiding the adverse consequences of stigma were termed *passing* in the typography devised by Erving Goffman; Chapter 2, Box 2.2.)

> I don't want the others to look at me differently. I don't want any condescension, and even less, pity. I want to have the same relations with people, especially since, for now, there's no need to talk about it. (Carricaburu and Pierret, 1995, p. 73)

In communities in many developing countries, the fear of stigmatisation, discrimination and possible violence against people with HIV have been so widespread that the majority who know that they are HIV-positive have kept their infection status hidden.[20] Studies in several countries, including India, Jamaica and Papua New Guinea, found that women were afraid to ask their male partners to use a condom because they feared a violent reaction (Gupta, 2002). A peer-education project in a mining town in South Africa uncovered physical and emotional abuse of female sex workers by their male clients, the ridicule of young men by their peers if they admitted to using condoms, and attitudes that young women who carry condoms must have 'loose morals' (Campbell and Mzaidume, 2002).

---

[20] For example, in a self-help group for people with HIV filmed for 'South Africa: Health at the Crossroads' (a video for Open University students), only one person had told family members that she is HIV-positive.

It is important to recognise that people are not merely passive recipients of imposed meanings and practices, against which they cannot argue. Representations of HIV disease in the media reflect wider social responses to HIV and AIDS, and these have often characterised affected people either as 'innocent victims' (whose infection came from medical procedures, or from mother to baby), or as 'guilty and blameworthy' (because they were 'promiscuous' or drug-injectors). These distinctions were rampant in the 1980s, but they remain easy to find even in the twenty-first century. For example, a headline in the British newspaper, the *Mail on Sunday* (17 December, 2000) asked 'Why do we treat gays as heroes?' and began 'If homosexual acts were as common as smoking, we would have to bury the victims in mass graves.' An opinion poll in the UK in 2000 showed that most respondents thought anyone whose HIV was acquired through sex or drugs 'only had themselves to blame' (National AIDS Trust, 2000; cited in Terrence Higgins Trust, 2001, p. 9).

Attitudes of this kind contribute to the psychological burden of being HIV-positive. A report by the Terrence Higgins Trust (2001) pointed out that in recent surveys of people with HIV in the UK, under 20 per cent had experienced some form of direct discrimination; however:

> … because of a combination of media reports, personal witnessing and anecdotal evidence of discrimination against others, many people with HIV fear discrimination and the prejudices they will encounter should their status become known. This fear can deter them from active involvement in everyday life, discourage them from employment, from new activities and from finding a partner. For many people, this fear of discrimination may be causing more harm than the reality. (Terrence Higgins Trust, 2001, p. 13)

● What term did Erving Goffman use to describe this process?

■ He called it *felt stigma* (Box 2.2), in which the distress caused by living in a society that is perceived as rejecting is itself a significant health burden and acts as a cause of social exclusion.

Although working to reduce the stigmatisation of people with HIV is undoubtedly a means of combating social exclusion, greater (and quicker) benefits are more likely to flow from tackling the practical causes of social exclusion directly. Many schemes have been set up in developing countries to increase the opportunities for people with HIV to participate fully in society. They often encompass literacy programmes and the development of other skills, and practical support to create new employment. 'Jennifer' from Uganda illustrates the success of this approach:

> I had five babies — three died and two are still alive. My husband divorced me. I was diagnosed HIV-positive when I had my fifth baby. I started attending the day centre for comfort because my baby had died. I learned tailoring, handicrafts, sharing experiences with existing clients and helping where needed. The whole sense of death from AIDS disappeared. I made up my mind to plan for the future of my children … Through counselling, the AIDS organisation discovered that we HIV-positive mothers have a common financial problem. A club was formed to meet our needs and from discussions, income-generating activities were suggested. These are handicrafts, poultry farming and breadmaking. (Quoted in Richardson and Bolle, 1992, p. 83)

People with HIV disease are generally represented as 'suffering' or 'dying' from AIDS, rather than as individuals who are living with an illness, earning a living and looking after their families. They are often described as the 'victims' of HIV, despite the prominence of local opinion leaders, peer educators and mutual-support organisations in HIV-prevention programmes and information sharing, and in campaigning for national and international strategies to combat the epidemic. All over the world, people with HIV have supported each other through voluntary and self-help groups, providing food parcels, respite care, practical training, and helping to find jobs and accommodation. Particularly in English-speaking countries, people with HIV have volunteered as 'buddies' giving practical and emotional support when their peers progressed to AIDS.

But the long-term commitment of people with HIV and AIDS to help each other has not succeeded in changing their status from 'outsiders' to valued members of the wider community. It is interesting to note that when new cases of HIV began to rise slowly in the USA and Europe towards the end of the 1990s, the explanatory rhetoric drew on notions of 'complacency' and 'back-sliding' among people who 'ought' to have protected themselves against exposure. Paul Flowers (2001) has pointed out that when resistant strains of HIV emerged after HAART regimens were introduced, health professionals spoke of the 'failure' of individuals to comply with complex treatment protocols. People with HIV were blamed for 'allowing' the new strains to evolve, rather than placing the fault in the inadequacy of the drugs themselves. Thus, new ways are being found to locate the 'risks' associated with HIV in the behaviour of stigmatised individuals — where they have remained throughout the past two decades.

In concluding this case study, two over-arching themes emerge. First, the epidemic of HIV and AIDS cannot be seen simply as a 'health' problem for individuals, communities, or nations – but must be understood from a multidisciplinary standpoint, which combines (at the very least) inputs from the biomedical and social sciences, epidemiology and health economics, political and legal theory, and the organisation of trade, scientific research and international aid. Second, the 'othering' of people with HIV and AIDS in societies around the world can be identified as the most powerful barrier to achieving social justice for them and their families. Adequate international funding to support equity in access to resources is unlikely to flow unless people with HIV and AIDS are valued as members of inclusive communities.

OBJECTIVES FOR CHAPTER 4

When you have studied this chapter, you should be able to:

4.1 Define and use, or recognise definitions and applications of, each of the terms printed in **bold** in the text.

4.2 Summarise the main contributions that (a) biomedical research and (b) epidemiological surveys have made to the understanding of HIV and AIDS.

4.3 Discuss the advantages and limitations associated with a range of (a) HIV-prevention initiatives and (b) treatment strategies, in rich and poor countries and give examples of the outcomes.

4.4 Discuss some major social, ethical, economic and political issues raised by national and international responses to the HIV and AIDS epidemic; summarise the limitations of tackling the epidemic as a global health problem rather than as a problem of global development and social justice.

4.5 Illustrate how social and political responses to HIV and AIDS, and media representations of the epidemic, can influence the experience of HIV-positive people.

QUESTIONS FOR CHAPTER 4

1 (*Objective 4.2*)

Describe how the viral load in the bloodstream of a person changes over time from the initial infection with HIV to the point when symptoms of HIV-related illness develop, and explain why it has this pattern. What happened when people on HAART regimens with no detectable HIV in their blood stopped taking the drugs, and what did this indicate about the natural history of HIV infection?

2 (*Objectives 4.2 and 4.4*)

What features of the biology of HIV have contributed to the absence of an effective vaccine? What ethical difficulties have arisen in the organisation of trials of candidate vaccines?

3 (*Objective 4.3*)

Explain why information-giving strategies (for example, based on leaflets or mass advertising campaigns) have achieved relatively little success in changing HIV-risk behaviours in most communities where this method has been the main approach to HIV prevention.

4 (*Objective 4.4*)

What arguments have been put forward against distributing HAART drugs free to people with HIV in developing countries? On what grounds have campaigners argued that this treatment should be provided?

5 (*Objective 4.5*)

Chapter 2 referred to the philosophical concept of 'ontological security' and the psychoanalytic concept of 'projection'. How might these concepts help to explain why people with HIV and AIDS have persistently experienced stigmatisation and discrimination? What historical and political forces may also be at work?

CHAPTER 5

Asthma

Study notes for OU students

At the start of this chapter, you should listen to the audiotape band entitled 'Reflections on asthma'. Near the end of the chapter, we suggest that you listen to it again and then attempt the questions in the associated notes in the *Audiovisual Media Guide*. During Section 5.6.2 you will be asked to read an article by Andrew Nocon and Tim Booth, entitled 'The social impact of childhood asthma', in *Health and Disease: A Reader* (Open University Press, 3rd edn 2001). An optional Reader article by Sally Macintyre and David Oldman, 'Coping with migraine', is also recommended in Section 5.6.1 if you have time. This chapter extends the discussion of hypersensitivity (which used asthma as one example) in Chapter 6 of *Human Biology and Health: An Evolutionary Approach* (Open University Press, 3rd edn 2001). The chapter was written by Bill Bytheway, Senior Research Fellow, School of Health and Social Welfare, and Basiro Davey, Senior Lecturer in Health Studies, Department of Biological Sciences, both at the Open University. We gratefully acknowledge the contribution to the previous edition of this chapter by Anna Furth, formerly Lecturer in Biology at the Open University.

5.1   Asthma: a public concern

One of the reasons why asthma has been selected as a case study for this book is that in recent years it has been the subject of considerable public concern. During the last half of the twentieth century, it increased significantly in all countries studied around the world, but particularly in the UK, Ireland and English-speaking industrial economies including Australia and New Zealand. The asthma 'epidemic' contributed to a wider anxiety about atmospheric pollution and climate change. During the 1990s it was generally felt that polluted air must have damaging effects upon lungs, particularly the lungs of young children. Air quality continues to be a major political issue involving international policies on power generation and transport, so it is important that the arguments are examined critically.

However, there is considerable uncertainty about whether poor air quality *causes* asthma to develop in people who would not otherwise have suffered from it. Scientific and medical opinion now generally favours the view that asthma is an *allergic* condition, which is *aggravated* by inhaled pollutants, not caused by them. This is in marked contrast to much media publicity which has presented vehicle emissions and atmospheric pollution from industrial processes as 'the' cause of asthma, rather than engage with the complex story of a multifactorial disorder. In this chapter, we have brought together a range of contributions to an understanding of asthma as a focus for international research, a major public health issue worldwide, and a chronic source of personal difficulty for affected individuals and their families.

Before beginning the chapter, Open University students should listen to the audiotape band entitled 'Reflections on asthma'.[1] A number of people describe their experiences of asthma and its treatment, and discuss the factors which — in

[1] The audiotape 'Reflections on asthma' has been recorded for students studying this book as part of an Open University course. You should consult the relevant notes in the *Audiovisual Media Guide* before listening to the tape, and then play it straight through. We suggest that you do not attempt the questions at the end of the audiotape notes until you have completed the chapter.

their view — may have contributed to causing their asthma or triggering an asthma attack. This audiotape provides an overview and some personal illustrations of the issues to be presented later in this chapter.

5.2   What is asthma?

5.2.1   Peter's story

Four-year-old Peter has just started school. His asthma began two years ago, two months after his father left home. Symptoms now often follow the onset of a cold but other factors also trigger them off, especially pollen, smoke and the smell of pigs or paints. They are also sparked off if he becomes upset or excited.

During the past year his asthma has been under better control and the amount of drugs he takes has been reduced. His hospital has provided a home nebuliser, which helps to avoid hospital admissions.

Peter's asthma means that he cannot have the pets he would like. He does sometimes have problems when out walking or in sport at school — but his asthma does not prevent him from joining in. However, he has to avoid bonfires and has to stay indoors on bonfire night. Even the smoke from candles on a birthday cake can trigger him off.

Peter's mother previously had to take time off work to look after him and lost money as a result. She now has a part-time job but still has to accompany him and take along his nebuliser when he goes on school trips. Peter's asthma means more housework for her, mainly in the form of regular wet-dusting.

The asthma now only tends to worry her when Peter has a bad attack. Nevertheless, she continues to feel angry with her ex-husband for having contributed, however unwittingly, to its onset, with all the resultant suffering that it has caused her and her son.

While Peter's asthma is no longer severe, it still places some restrictions on what he is able to do. It continues to have a mild social impact on his own life and that of his family. (Nocon and Booth, 1990, pp. 60–1)

This account is taken from a research study carried out by Andrew Nocon and Tim Booth. (A longer extract from their report appears in *Health and Disease: A Reader*, Open University Press, 3rd edn 2001; Open University students will be directed to read it in Section 5.6.2 of this chapter.) Nocon and Booth investigated a sample of 50 patients who had all been admitted to a Sheffield hospital with a primary diagnosis of asthma. Nearly two-thirds of the sample were school-age children or younger; parents were interviewed where the child was under 10 years old. The aim of the research was to illuminate the social impact of asthma on the lives of the patients and other members of their families. Inevitably, it also shed light on *lay beliefs* about what causes asthmatic attacks.

● What clues about the possible causes of Peter's asthmatic attacks can you distinguish in the account above?

■ Five groups of causes can be identified.

(a) *Emotional upset*: his mother believes that the asthma is partly a response to Peter's father leaving home, and notes that it can be sparked off if Peter gets upset or excited.

(b) *Chemicals*: smoke provokes a particularly strong reaction, and paints are also mentioned.

(c) *Animal and plant material*: the smell of pigs, and pollen cause problems. (The reference to 'wet-dusting' implies that house-dust mites are seen as a trigger; these mites are microscopic animals that inhabit bedding and carpets, feeding on dead organic matter such as shed skin fragments.)

(d) *Exercise*: walking and sports occasionally cause problems.

(e) *Infection*: Peter often gets an asthma attack with the onset of a cold.

All of these factors (and many others) have been implicated in asthma at various times in its history.

Asthma is a disease that most people know something about, but one that is still poorly understood and difficult to diagnose consistently. In medical terms, **asthma** can be described as a constriction of the airways (*bronchoconstriction*), causing shortness of breath or laboured breathing (*dyspnoea*), the underlying causes of which are inflammation and the build-up of mucus in the lungs. In addition to breathlessness, the typical symptoms are audible 'wheezing' sounds as the chest expands and contracts, coughing (especially at night), and tightness in the chest (especially on waking up). Most children with asthma, and a much lower proportion of asthmatic adults, are also **atopic**, that is, prone to develop allergies to various environmental triggers (for example, the droppings of house-dust mites, pollens, cat fur and skin flakes), which are collectively known as **allergens**. When contact with an allergen causes an increase in breathing difficulties (as it does in Peter's case), the person is said to have *atopic asthma*. In Section 5.3 we discuss the biological mechanisms underlying this process.

Doctors also distinguish between *chronic* asthma, a primarily self-managed condition requiring long-term 'maintenance' treatment, and the potentially life-threatening exacerbation of breathing difficulties seen in an *acute* asthma attack. In acute asthma, the respiratory constriction can become so severe that it causes great distress and requires immediate medical intervention (Figure 5.1).

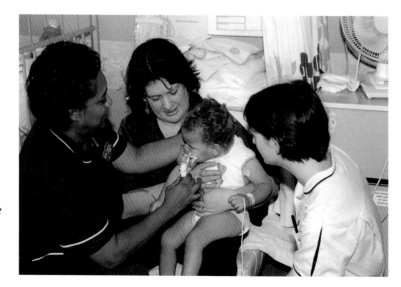

Figure 5.1 *A child having emergency treatment for an acute episode of asthma; a fine spray of anti-asthmatic drugs is inhaled through a face-mask.*
(Photo: Mike Levers)

A fundamental question about Peter's asthma is whether or not it is an inherent part of his biological make-up: was he *born* asthmatic? Or is it something that has developed in response to *external* causes, and could any of these have been prevented? Did his asthma really begin two years ago when his father left home, and are these events causally related? We address these and other questions about asthma in this chapter, and you will see that, like rheumatoid arthritis and schizophrenia (Chapters 3 and 6), asthma is associated with considerable uncertainty about its medical definition and its underlying causes.

Although we tend to think of asthma as a 'modern' condition, it has a long history in which doctors and society at large have held widely varying views about its nature. In this respect it is typical of many other diseases.

5.2.2 The history of scientific explanations for asthma

In ancient Greece, the physician Galen taught that asthma was not an entity in itself: it was no more than a symptom of disordered bodily *humours*.[2] This view was dominant up until the sixteenth century, when the idea developed that asthma was an *attack* upon the body, and hence one that was subject to cure. Initially, medical attention centred upon the abdomen as the source of asthma, and it was only in the eighteenth century that attention shifted to the chest. In the course of most of the nineteenth century the idea that asthma was due to *nervous spasm* of the airways was popular. The theory that it was due to peculiarities in the bronchial mucus began to gain ground, but the growing debate was then overtaken by early research on the immune system, which suggested that asthma was closely related to *allergies*. In the 1930s, the connection with emotion was proposed and the idea that asthma was perhaps primarily a *psychosomatic* condition became fashionable.

By the 1990s, psychosomatic theories of asthma had largely been discounted in medical thought, but they remain powerful in lay beliefs — as Peter's case history illustrates. The trend of scientific opinion is towards an explanation of asthma as a muscle spasm in the airways, accompanied by inflammation, and triggered by (among other possibilities) allergic reactions to material in the atmosphere. Air quality became a major issue in the *social history* of asthma at the end of the twentieth century. Before we examine the features of present-day scientific understanding of asthma, however, it is worth reflecting for a moment on the assertion that it is (in common with other disorders, see Chapter 1), at least partly a *socially constructed* phenomenon.[3] This is most readily demonstrated by examining scientific and public views of asthma in the past.

John Gabbay, a professor of public health with an interest in medial history, undertook a study of the history of asthma (Gabbay, 1982). His analysis centred on *A Treatise of the Asthma* — the classic work of Sir John Floyer (1649–1734), published in 1698. For Gabbay, a critical feature of Floyer's work and that of several other early scientists, is that they had personal experience of asthma. Floyer focused upon abdominal symptoms as much as those in the chest, and ascribed pain in his gut to his asthma. He tried to make full use of 'sensible' (or sensory) observation, a growing priority in medical research at that time, but he was also anxious to confirm

[2] Humoral theory and its continuing influence on medical thought and practice, even in the twenty-first century, is discussed in *Medical Knowledge: Doubt and Certainty* (Open University Press, 2nd edn 1994; colour-enhanced 2nd edn 2001), Chapters 2 and 3.

[3] The idea that diseases are 'constructed' rather than 'revealed' by medical science is discussed extensively in *Medical Knowledge: Doubt and Certainty* (Open University Press, 2nd edn 1994; colour-enhanced 2nd edn 2001), Chapters 7 and 8.

the truth of the ancient doctrines he had been taught. As a result, he interpreted what he observed in terms of traditional theories involving, for example, *defluxion* (the deposit of humours on selected organs) and *inciding* (medicines cutting through the humours). Floyer's commitment to humoral theory, roughly 1 500 years after it had been developed, was consistent with prevailing religious and political beliefs in the seventeenth century.

This glimpse into the past alerts us to the need for caution in accepting current scientific knowledge about asthma as necessarily the last word on the subject.

> Far from medical knowledge about asthma having consisted of proven, timeless, objective facts, it has appeared under scrutiny to be composed of limited interpretations of the complex phenomena of illness. (Gabbay, 1982, p. 43)

The essence of Gabbay's argument is that medical knowledge has to be viewed in its *social context*. He argues that researchers such as Floyer change, and continue to change, the meaning of asthma. To a social constructionist, it is an illusion to assume that medical research has simply led to an accumulation of knowledge about the inherent nature of any disease. According to this argument, diseases cannot exist independently of the social context that constantly shapes the direction and interpretation of medical knowledge.

Extending this hypothesis to the twentieth century, one can note the decline in the importance of *anatomy* in modern medicine and the rise of *pharmacology* (the use of medical drugs). This was reflected in the growing significance of medication in the 1990s in the process leading up to the diagnosis of asthma: at the extreme, asthma became the diagnosis given to people whose symptoms were relieved by anti-asthmatic medication. When the manufacturers of inhalers and nebulisers provide diagnostic aids to doctors, they are shaping the way in which doctors think about and diagnose asthma. In the twenty-first century, the construction of asthma may change once again, if genetic technologies can be developed to intervene in this condition.

5.2.3 Personal and professional narratives of asthma

When you read an account of asthma such as Peter's, it is easy to assume that everyone knows what the word itself represents. It is part of the common vocabulary. Lay knowledge of asthma — in common with that of all diseases and disorders — is based partly on medical narratives acquired through direct contact with health professionals, and from the educational, popular and news media. However, it also draws heavily upon the personal illness narratives of family and friends who have experienced it, and who then develop their own complex explanations for its occurrence. Thus, asthma is both an *illness* with a distinct social identity, and a medically defined *disease* category. Peter's mother obtains a medical label for his experience of illness, which legitimates it as a recognised disease.[4]

- ● Can you identify clues that a medical narrative of asthma has been incorporated into the account of Peter's asthma, which you read earlier?

- ■ His asthma is described as having *symptoms* and occasionally these lead to *attacks*. It is being *controlled* through the use of *drugs* and a *nebuliser*.

---

[4] The power of medical 'labels' to legitimise a disease is also discussed in *Medical Knowledge: Doubt and Certainty* (Open University Press, 2nd edn 1994; colour-enhanced 2nd edn 2001), Chapter 2.

The doctor's diagnosis that Peter has asthma provides a link between his mother's personal experience of her son's illness (including the way those concerned for him talk about it), and the expert scientific knowledge of the doctor about this disease entity and the interventions presently available to treat it. Despite having received relatively successful treatment, Peter's asthma continues to have an impact on the life of his family. So, in addition to its medical meaning, asthma also has a personal and social meaning. People with asthma and their families often make strenuous efforts to cope with its effects and strive to live normal lives — not always with support from others. The restrictions that asthma can impose may be met with intolerance, and there may sometimes be doubt about its recognition as a 'legitimate' illness, as you will see later in this chapter.

● What different meanings do you think 'asthma' might have for Peter, his mother and his doctor?

■ Peter is only four. He will be learning the meaning of all sorts of words. 'Asthma' may mean that he feels special, different from other children. To his mother, the word might mean the anxiety of seeing Peter struggling for breath, or giving him his medication and getting him to use his nebuliser. It also means vigilance: no bonfires, and no candles on his birthday cake. His asthma is no longer a constant worry, but it still poses a threat to her son's life. It also means a loss of income, extra housework and a restriction upon her own lifestyle. For the doctor, Peter's asthma is a disease experienced by many other patients. It has been diagnosed through standard procedures, has involved referral to hospital, and it requires treatment based on drugs, nebulisers and effective preventive action.

Thus, even in Peter's four-year-old world, his asthma can have several meanings. Similarly, in the world of medicine and academic research, the concept of 'asthma' is understood differently by the various disciplines. To the clinician, asthma is a distressed patient with potentially serious respiratory problems; to the epidemiologist it is a disease represented by a complex array of statistics, which are difficult to interpret; and to a biologist it is abnormalities in the function of the lungs and the immune system. All of these different meanings of asthma are represented in this chapter. First, we describe what is known about the state of Peter's lungs.

5.3 The biology of asthma

5.3.1 The lungs in health

In normal breathing, the lungs are like a pair of bellows, drawing fresh air into the chest and pumping stale air out. Fresh air is needed to replenish the body's supply of oxygen — vital for the production of energy.[5] Air enters through the nose and mouth, and passes down the windpipe or *trachea* into the chest (see Figure 5.2 overleaf). Here the trachea splits into two *bronchi*, one to each lung, and the bronchi subdivide into smaller and smaller tubes like the branches of a tree (it is often referred to as the 'respiratory tree'). The narrowest tubes are less than 1 mm in diameter and end in a cluster of tiny airsacs or **alveoli**.

---

[5] The role of oxygen in energy production in living processes is discussed in *Human Biology and Health: An Evolutionary Approach* (Open University Press, 3rd edn 2001), Chapters 3 and 7.

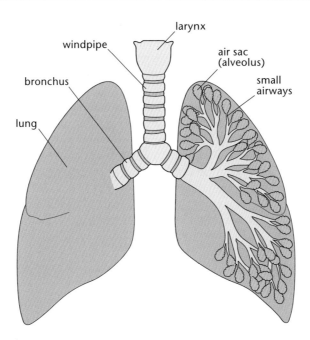

Figure 5.2 *Diagram to show basic structure of human airways: at the surface of the alveoli, oxygen and carbon dioxide are exchanged between the inhaled air and the bloodstream.*

The inside of the human lung resembles a sponge formed from millions of alveoli; if they were all laid out flat, they would cover a tennis court. The alveoli are bounded by a thin membrane surrounded by blood vessels. The membrane and blood-vessel wall are all that separate the inhaled air from the bloodstream. Oxygen molecules can diffuse easily from the oxygen-rich air to the blood, which has a lower oxygen concentration; molecules of the waste gas, carbon dioxide, diffuse in the opposite direction and are expelled as the stale air is breathed out.[6]

The trachea and bronchi are large-diameter tubes and are supported by rings of cartilage to prevent them collapsing (you can feel the larger tracheal rings through the skin below your voicebox). However, the smallest airways have no rigid support, and are very easily constricted if the layer of smooth muscle that surrounds them goes into spasm. They are also easily blocked by mucus. Both these processes contribute to asthma, as you will see below.

Figure 5.3 shows the three most important layers of the airway lining: the innermost layer or *epithelium*; the thick 'spongy' layer of connective tissue; and the outer layer of smooth muscle. The epithelium is a single sheet of closely packed cylindrical cells, and has two features vital for lung function: cilia and mucus-secreting cells. *Cilia* are the tiny hairs that protrude into the cavity of the airway. By beating in unison they drive fluid up the airway lining towards the mouth (where it can be coughed up and spat out). Much of this fluid is the mucus secreted by specialised epithelial cells; it serves to protect the airway lining, and traps dust and other unwanted particles breathed in with the air.

---

[6] The passive diffusion of biological molecules (e.g. the dissolved gases, oxygen and carbon dioxide) along 'concentration gradients' is described in *Biology and Health: An Evolutionary Approach* (Open University Press, 3rd edn 2001), Chapter 3.

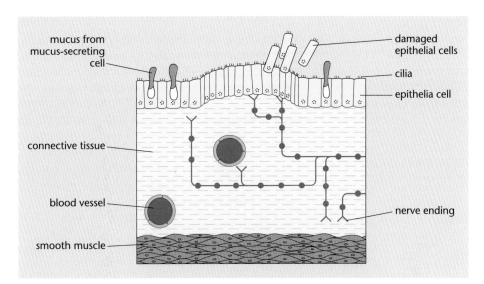

Figure 5.3 *Diagram to show the basic structure of the airway lining. (The functions of the three layers are described in the text.)*

5.3.2 The lungs in asthma

The connective tissue layer between the epithelium and smooth muscle (Figure 5.3) contains very few cells, being composed mainly of water loosely held by a mesh of fibres. In asthma, this layer swells as fluid leaks out from blood vessels, and many different types of white cells are drawn out of the circulation and into the connective tissue. They include white cells involved in generating and sustaining an *inflammatory response*, which in many respects resembles the inflammation seen at infection sites and the inflammation in joints already described in Chapter 3 in rheumatoid arthritis.[7]

Even in mild asthma, the airway lining is permanently inflamed. There is an accumulation of inflammatory white cells, particularly the *eosinophils* and *mast cells*, which secrete a variety of inflammatory chemicals. These include *bradykinin* (which stimulates nerve endings), *histamine* (which stimulates smooth muscle contraction and leakage of plasma from blood vessels) and several different *leukotrienes*, which may be the most potent mediators of asthma symptoms.

As asthma progresses, patches of damaged epithelial cells are sloughed off, exposing some of the underlying nerve endings; this makes the lining excessively sensitive to stimulation. The outer layer of the airways is a continuous sheet of smooth muscle fibres, surrounding all the airway tubes, including the smallest ones. In people with asthma, it is prone to contract when the lungs are stimulated by an inhaled irritant or allergen.

● What symptoms might a person feel if the smooth muscle layer contracted throughout the airways?

■ Breathlessness. Smooth muscle contraction tends to squeeze the airways shut (bronchoconstriction), narrowing the passage so that air flows in and out only with difficulty.

Over time, the thin protective layer of mucus lining the airways tends to thicken, because the epithelial cells are over-stimulated and secrete too much, and the cilia beat less vigorously, failing to push the mucus towards the mouth. The combination

---

[7] Note that the inflammation seen in lung tissue in asthma is not thought to be 'autoimmune' (i.e. an immune response inappropriately directed against the body's own tissues), in contrast to the inflammation in rheumatoid arthritis.

of bronchoconstriction and obstruction by mucus (see Figure 5.4) also accounts for the wheezy 'squeak' that characterises asthmatic breathing. The walls of the airways themselves thicken and become **hyper-responsive** — excessively 'twitchy' and prone to contract in response to environmental triggers that would have little impact on normal lungs. For example, chemicals and small particles in the atmosphere can trigger an asthma attack in susceptible people, particularly if their airways have already been damaged by chronic inflammation. In Section 5.5.2 we look at the effects of traffic pollution on asthma episodes.

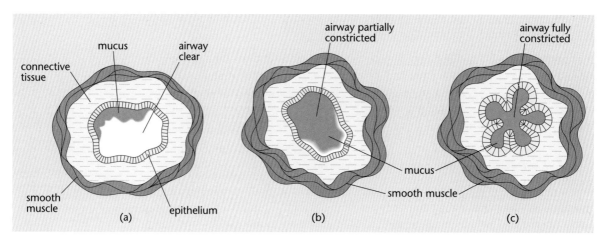

Figure 5.4 *Diagram to show airway constriction during an asthma attack: (a) normal airway; (b) mild asthma attack; (c) severe asthma attack, in which the air passage fills with mucus.*

5.3.3 Exercise-induced asthma

The asthma brought on by physical exercise is known as **exercise-induced asthma (EIA)**. It is seen particularly in children — who do a lot of running about in short bursts — and young adults engaged in vigorous sport. Airway hyper-responsiveness is thought to be triggered by the increased ventilation. Faster, deeper breathing can make the airway lining dry out, and in susceptible people this can stimulate the underlying nerve endings and cause white cells to release inflammatory chemicals.

Typically, a person who is prone to EIA feels fine for the first few minutes of exercise (Figure 5.5), with the worst symptoms beginning only after about six minutes. However, the consequences of this acute response may still be felt several hours later. EIA can usually be avoided by inhaling preventive drugs *before* starting to exercise.

Figure 5.5 *Exercise-induced asthma (EIA). Lung function in terms of 'peak flow' in the same person at rest, and during and after a 6-minute exercise period. Note how lung function continues to fall beyond the end of the exercise period, and does not return to baseline for well over 20 minutes.*

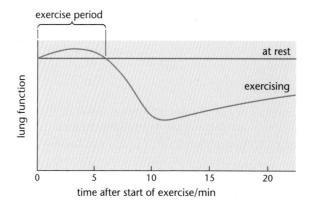

5.3.4 Atopic asthma

Susceptibility to asthma is strongly associated with atopy — a tendency to develop acute inflammatory responses to harmless substances (allergens) inhaled from the atmosphere, and to develop allergic skin conditions such as eczema. The range of materials that can behave as allergens in a susceptible person is large. It includes airborne particles of naturally occurring substances such as animal 'dander' (fragments of fur and skin cells, most commonly from domestic pets), house-dust mite and cockroach droppings, plant pollens and the spores of moulds and fungi. Once an individual is sensitised to a particular allergen, exposure even to very small quantities will invoke an allergic inflammation.

Less common chemical allergens primarily affect adults who encounter them at work. A person may gradually become sensitised to a range of materials including glues, dyes and sterilising agents, which eventually provoke *occupational asthma*. Avoiding exposure usually means leaving that form of work and perhaps losing one's livelihood, if no alternative occupation can be found.

A defining feature of atopic asthma is the over-production of a type of antibody known as *IgE* (pronounced 'eye-gee-ee'). IgE has a particular role in the body's normal immune response to parasites, by binding to the parasite and triggering inflammation around it. In allergic people, molecules of IgE are produced in response to harmless allergens. These IgE antibodies coat the outside of the mast cells (Figure 5.6), which are particularly abundant in the lining of the respiratory system and around the eyes. When the allergen is next inhaled, it binds tightly to these IgE molecules, which then trigger the mast cells into releasing inflammatory chemicals and setting off an allergic reaction.

In the majority of sensitised individuals the allergic reaction is characterised by the streaming nose, red puffy eyes and slight breathlessness popularly known as 'hay fever'. In people with atopic asthma, the reaction can be severe enough to trigger significant constriction of the airways. It is probable that allergic reactions of this type are involved in most (perhaps all) cases of chronic asthma, but the biological

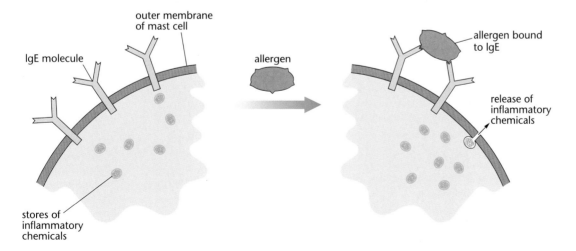

Figure 5.6 *Release of inflammatory chemicals by mast cells is mediated by molecules of the antibody, IgE. When IgE molecules bind to a mast cell and to an allergen, they influence events inside the cell. Inflammatory chemicals are stored in packets of membrane (vesicles) inside mast cells, which fuse with the outer cell membrane, thus releasing inflammatory chemicals to the outside. (This diagram is not to scale; IgE molecules are actually much smaller than vesicles.)*

basis of the condition is far from understood. It is not known why some people produce IgE to the allergens we all inhale, nor why the majority of people who do so suffer from hay fever without ever developing asthma. And it should not be forgotten that atopic asthma is also mediated by chemicals released from other white cells (particularly eosinophils), which are not dependent on IgE.

Atopic asthma is most frequently associated with sources of 'indoor' allergens such as domestic pets, house-dust mites and cockroaches. There continues to be major differences of view as to whether these allergens can be tackled by strategies such as daily vacuum cleaning, washing bedding regularly and freezing teddy bears and pillows (thought to kill house-dust mites), replacing fitted carpets by wooden floors or linoleum, and exclusion of all pets. Advice remains confused about whether pillows and duvets stuffed with feathers are more or less likely to harbour mites than those with synthetic fillings. Outdoor allergens like pollen and fungal spores are seasonal, and can sometimes be avoided by staying indoors, for example on days when the pollen count is high. All these actions have social implications by placing severe restrictions on lifestyle, and there are often financial costs in carrying them out.

However, the description of what happens in the lungs of a person with asthma brings us no closer to resolving why some people develop it and others do not, despite being exposed to the same environmental triggers.

5.3.5 Genes and asthma

The extent to which asthma occurs in members of the same family, and the fact that it is more common in identical-twin pairs than in non-identical twins, strongly suggests that there must be genetic components in its development. However, proving that the inheritance of certain genes is involved in asthma is fraught with difficulties, for two reasons. First, the naturally occurring inflammatory response is dependent on the expression of, and interactions between, many different genes.

● Why must this be the case?

■ The inflammatory response is a complex process, involving the coordinated action of many different cell types, signalling molecules and inflammatory chemicals such as histamine, each of which is dependent on the action of multiple genes. Collectively, the number of genes potentially involved is huge.

Trying to find out if any of these genes (many of which have not yet been identified) might be altered in people with asthma is like hunting for a needle in a very large haystack. And there is no reason to believe that everyone with asthma develops it in the same way, so different genes may be involved in different individuals.

Second, asthma does not have a definitive and reliable diagnostic 'marker' (unlike HIV for example, which can be detected in blood tests), and the range of symptoms is highly variable between individuals. Moreover, everyone experiences an 'asthmatic' symptom sometimes; for example, wheezing and coughing are common during a chest infection or among heavy smokers. This makes it impossible to identify a homogeneous group of 'asthmatics' whose genes can be studied in comparison with a homogeneous group of 'controls' who never experience anything resembling asthma. (In Chapter 6, we discuss the same problem in comparing the brains of people diagnosed with schizophrenia, and so-called 'normal' brains.)

Nevertheless, the identification of genetic associations in asthma is a growing area of international research. A major focus has been on genes that may be involved in the excessive production of IgE in people with atopic asthma, but no conclusive linkage has been found. Areas of at least nine different chromosomes have been proposed as possible contributors to the asthma syndrome, some of which are also implicated in other allergic disorders (reviewed by Anderson and Cookson, 1999).

The difficulty in reliably locating genetic components in asthma, despite its obvious family associations, illustrates both the complex aetiology of multifactorial diseases and the huge challenge they will continue to pose for genetic intervention strategies in the future.[8]

5.4   The epidemiology of asthma

5.4.1   Asthma mortality

An important element in the experience of asthma is the fear of death. A serious asthmatic attack would be distressing enough if recovery were guaranteed, but the thought that it could be life-threatening makes it all the more stressful for the affected person and anyone else who is present. Although the greatest public concern about asthma is often focused on the risk to children, Table 5.1 shows that older age groups are far more likely to suffer a fatal attack. In 2000 in England and Wales, 1 272 deaths were attributed to asthma, less than 10 per cent of which were in people aged under 40 years and less than 2 per cent among children under 15 (ONS, 2001).

Table 5.1   Percentage of deaths due to asthma in different age groups, England and Wales, cumulative total, 1983–1995.

age group/years	% of deaths*
0–4	0.5
5–14	1.0
15–44	12.0
45–64	27.0
65–74	26.0
75–84	24.0
85+	10.0
total deaths in the period	23 3111

* Percentages have been rounded to the nearest whole number. Data derived from Campbell, M. J., Cogman, G. R., Holgate, S. T. and Johnston, S. L. (1997) Age specific trends in asthma mortality in England and Wales, 1983–95: results of an observational study, *British Medical Journal*, **314**, pp. 1439–41.

The study of trends in England and Wales from which Table 5.1 is derived, concluded that although death rates in people aged 5–64 years had risen through most of the 1980s, they had peaked by 1989 and have fallen at about 6 per cent a year thereafter. The improvement is attributed to earlier and more effective use of medication. However, the mortality decline in people over 65 has been slower. (The number of deaths in the under fives were too few to allow trends to be estimated.)

A feature of asthma mortality rates is that different long-term patterns have been observed in countries with apparently similar environments and health care. But generally where a trend has been detected, it is towards stable or declining death rates in industrialised countries, despite the increasing prevalence of asthma as a health problem. But before we examine trends in morbidity, we must unpack the reasons for interpreting all population data on asthma cautiously.

● Why should caution be applied even to data on asthma mortality?

[8] The medical potential of new genetic technologies such as gene therapy, and the ethical dilemmas raised by these methods, are discussed in *Biology and Health: An Evolutionary Approach* (Open University Press, 3rd edn 2001), Chapter 9.

■ Variations in the cause of death recorded on death certificates, and inaccuracies in the coding of data taken from death certificates, have been detected in many studies.[9] Such variations are likely to be even more significant when comparisons of asthma mortality are made between countries where the definitions of what constitutes 'asthma' may vary.

5.4.2 Problems in measuring asthma morbidity

The difficulties outlined above are even greater in epidemiological studies of asthma morbidity. Without a definitive diagnostic marker for asthma it is impossible to count 'cases' reliably, and this uncertainty produces unpredictable variations in estimates of asthma incidence and prevalence, and hence in the measurement of trends over time. A similar problem occurs in trying to measure the 'severity' of asthma symptoms as a means of estimating the disease burden in a population. Comparisons of estimates of asthma morbidity from around the world (and from different studies in the same country) have, until recently, been flawed because they often used different diagnostic criteria. This situation is not unique to asthma and the discussion that follows has its counterparts in the epidemiology of many other chronic conditions.

The majority of large-scale estimates have been based on **self-reported asthma**, using questionnaires completed by adults or older children, or **parent-reported asthma** for estimates in younger children.

● What problems might confound the outcomes of such studies?

■ As discussed in Section 5.2, the understanding of what constitutes 'asthma' varies between cultures and individuals and it changes over time. For example, rising concern about atmospheric pollution may increase the likelihood that people will describe themselves or their children as 'having asthma'. Some may no longer think of themselves as 'asthmatic' because they have kept it under control for several years, whereas others may say they have asthma even though they have not experienced symptoms since childhood. Some parents will avoid attaching an asthma 'label' to a child, whereas others may use the term very loosely.

A study in London investigated what the parents of children attending a chest clinic understood by the term 'wheeze', and found that they used it differently to the definition employed by clinicians and epidemiologists in diagnosing and counting asthma (Cane *et al.*, 2000). Another example of the pitfalls in basing estimates on self-reports was revealed by an Italian study, which obtained self-reported symptoms of asthma from 13–14-year-olds and separately from their parents. There were significant differences, which varied according to the sex of the child and the nature of the symptom (Renzoni *et al.*, 1999).

Prevalence is usually expressed as the number of people in a defined population who have a certain disease or disability at a certain *point* in time (e.g. on a chosen day), divided by the total number of people in that population at that point.

● Suggest why this method of calculating the prevalence of asthma is unsatisfactory and how this problem might be overcome.

---

[9] Discrepancies in data derived from death certificates are discussed in *Studying Health and Disease* (Open University Press, 2nd edn 1994; colour-enhanced 2nd edn 2001), Chapter 7.

■ A substantial proportion of asthmatic people will not be experiencing symptoms at the designated time point, so estimates of *point prevalence* could underestimate the burden of asthma in the population. It is more accurate to estimate *period prevalence*, i.e. the number of people experiencing symptoms of asthma or receiving treatment for it in a given period (e.g. a year), divided by the number of people in the population at risk during that period.

A further complication is that people may associate 'having asthma' with having an acute attack, rather than with chronic but generally mild symptoms. Thus, studies of self-reported asthma generate different estimates when respondents are asked (for example) 'Have you had an asthma attack in the last 12 months?' or 'Have you had wheezing or whistling in the chest in the last 12 months?'

The *clinical* approach to defining asthma leads to estimates of **doctor-diagnosed asthma**, for example based on surveys of medical records. But, as in the diagnosis of rheumatoid arthritis (Chapter 3), clinical judgement is an important variable. Different doctors in the same country will employ slightly different criteria when deciding whether to assign an asthma diagnosis and they, like other members of the population, can be influenced by social factors such as media reports of an asthma 'epidemic' or pharmaceutical advertising for new medications. A further problem is that the *severity* of asthma is classified differently by doctors in different countries. For example, doctors in the USA use a scale based on the frequency of asthma *symptoms* combined with the extent of airflow obstruction, whereas doctors in the UK use a scale based on the frequency of asthma *medication* and the type and dosage of drugs required to relieve breathing difficulties (Cates, 2001).

Increasingly, a *scientific* approach to defining asthma based on standard measurements of lung function is used both in medical diagnosis and in population studies. The simplest property to measure is **peak flow** — the fastest rate at which air can be pushed out of the lungs during a forced outbreath. Peak flow is usually expressed in litres per minute (written as $l\,min^{-1}$ in scientific notation), and is measured with a peak-flow meter like the one in Figure 5.7. Readings are compared

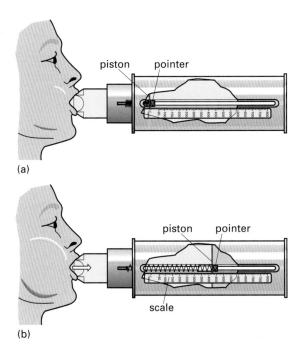

(a)

(b)

(c)

Figure 5.7 *Diagram to show the operation of a peak-flow meter at (a) the beginning, and (b) the end, of a forced outbreath. The outbreath forces the piston towards the end of the cylinder, pushing the pointer in front of it. When the person stops blowing, the piston falls back (pulled by the spring), leaving the pointer where its new position can be read from a scale calibrated in litres per minute. (c) A young person blowing into a peak-flow meter. (Photo: Mike Levers)*

with standard charts showing the 'normal' range of peak flow for men and women of different ages, and children of different heights. A peak flow that fails to reach a certain threshold is one of the indicators of **scientifically defined asthma**.

●   Identify the main strength and a potential weakness in the scientific approach to measuring asthma morbidity, compared with assessments based on clinical judgement.

■   The scientific approach relies on standardised tests, which generate reproducible results, in contrast with the individual variations that influence doctor-diagnosed asthma. However, the strength of a medical diagnosis is that it takes account of the person's medical history and the effects of the condition on their daily lives, whereas the scientific approach ignores the extent of morbidity due to the asthma. (Another way of representing this comparison is to suggest that doctor-diagnosed measures of asthma morbidity are likely to be less *reliable* but more *valid* than scientifically defined asthma.[10])

5.4.3   International variations in asthma prevalence

In the 1990s, a concerted international effort began to address the problems in measuring asthma by developing and validating questionnaires and applying them systematically to very large population samples in many different countries. The International Study of Asthma and Allergies in Childhood (ISAAC) collected responses to the same questionnaire in a survey of almost three-quarters of a million children worldwide in two age groups. The outcomes were expressed as self-reported asthma symptoms in 13–14-year-olds in 56 countries, and parent-reported asthma symptoms in 6–7-year-olds in 38 countries (ISAAC Steering Committee, 1998).

In a comparable study of 140 000 adults aged 20–44 years in 22 countries, the European Community Respiratory Health Survey (ECRHS) correlated self-reported questionnaire responses with scientific measurements of lung function and the presence of allergic reactions to skin-prick testing with known allergens (Janson *et al.*, 2001). A red 'flare' appears around the test site if an inflammatory response develops. Despite its name, the ECRHS also included four non-European countries: India, USA, Australia and New Zealand.

The results of these studies show the extent of asthma as a global health problem. The ISAAC estimates revealed that 'wheezing in the last 12 months' affected around 12 per cent of the world's 6–7-year-olds and around 14 per cent of 13–14-year-olds. The ECRHS estimated that 20 per cent of adults in the survey countries suffered this symptom. However, these global averages conceal large geographical variations in asthma morbidity, with up to 15-fold differences between countries. The highest rates were found in English-speaking countries and parts of Latin America, and the lowest rates were in the Mediterranean region and Eastern Europe. The UK was among the worst in the world, with over 30 per cent of 13–14-year-olds affected in Scotland, Wales and mainland sites in England, the Channel Islands and the Isle of Man. (Northern Ireland was not surveyed; the rate in the Republic of Ireland was 29 per cent in this age group.)

---

[10] Reliability and validity are technical terms in experimental research, which are discussed in *Studying Health and Disease* (Open University Press, 2nd edn 1994; colour-enhanced 2nd edn 2001), Chapter 5. Reliability refers to the reproducibility of the results in repeat tests or surveys; validity refers to evidence that the tests or surveys actually measured what they claimed to measure.

The prevalence of treated asthma determined from General Practice statistics in England and Wales in 1998 is shown in Table 5.2. These rates are based on 'periods of sickness' during which the patient was both experiencing the symptoms of asthma and consulting a GP.

Table 5.2 Prevalence rates of treated asthma per 1 000 patients by age and sex, determined from General Practice statistics, England and Wales, 1998.

Age/years	0–4	5–15	16–24	25–34	35–44	45–54	55–64	65–74	75–84	85+
male	97	132	73	55	47	45	59	81	89	62
female	63	104	85	65	62	65	80	88	80	52

Rates have been rounded to the nearest whole number. Data from ONS, 2000, *Key Health Statistics from General Practice 1998*, Series MB6, No. 2, Dataset 5A11, Office for National Statistics, The Stationery Office, London.

● Compare the data in Table 5.2 (on prevalence of treated asthma) with that in Table 5.1 (on asthma mortality). What differences can you see in the patterns?

■ In children and young people aged under 15/16, asthma morbidity is at its highest, whereas asthma mortality is at its lowest. Middle-aged people suffer the lowest rates of asthma symptoms, but contribute the largest proportion of asthma deaths.

● What explanations occur to you for these apparently contradictory patterns?

■ There are two main possibilities (which are not mutually exclusive). First, childhood asthma may be a less severe condition than asthma in adults, as well as genuinely more common. Second, doctors may be more willing to diagnose asthma in children than in adults, and under-diagnosis of adult asthma may contribute to treatment delays and higher mortality rates.

Evidence that untreated asthma is a common problem in older adults was found in a study of 6 000 men and women aged 65 years and over in Bristol, South West England (Dow *et al.*, 2001).

5.4.4 Has the asthma 'epidemic' peaked?

The ISAAC and ECRHS studies are cross-sectional, that is they estimate the extent of asthma at a single time point. Until they are repeated, they cannot answer the key question about whether — and if so, where and to what extent — asthma rates are increasing around the world. The greatest concern relates to those English-speaking countries in which many studies during the 1980s and 1990s reported that the prevalence of asthma was rising sharply, particularly among children.

One of the longest running studies has been conducted by Jennifer Peat and colleagues in Wagga Wagga, a small inland town in New South Wales, Australia, where almost two-thirds of the 8–11-year-olds have been surveyed at three time points. Table 5.3 (overleaf) shows some of the results from parent-completed questionnaires (Downs *et al.*, 2001), which revealed that the prevalence of hay fever and nasal allergies had increased even faster than symptoms of asthma. This study is particularly interesting because the climate in Wagga Wagga is dry and warm, with low levels of atmospheric pollution, yet the prevalence of 'wheeze in the past 12 months' in 1997 was very similar to the levels recorded by ISAAC among children in four major Australian cities.

Table 5.3 Prevalence of indicators of asthma and atopy among 8–11-year-olds (both sexes combined) in Wagga Wagga, New South Wales, Australia, in 1982, 1992 and 1997.

Asthma or atopy indicator	1982 (%)	1992 (%)	1997 (%)
Parent-reported indicators			
ever wheezed	23.9	36.9	42.3
recent wheezing (in past 12 months)	15.5	22.1	27.2
4 or more wheezing episodes in past 12 months	5.2	13.7	16.9
ever had asthma medicines	8.5	35.0	46.0
ever had hay fever or nasal allergies	22.5	43.7	44.0
Doctor-diagnosed asthma	12.9	30.5	38.6
total number of children (= 100%)	769	850	1016

Data from Downs, S.H., Marks, G. B., Sporik, R., Belosouva, E. G., Car, N. G. and Peat, J. K. (2001) Continued increase in the prevalence of asthma and atopy, *Archives of Disease in Childhood*, **84**, Table 1, p. 20.

Trends in some other English-speaking countries have shown similar patterns to those in Australia. Figure 5.8 shows the incidence of new asthma episodes in England and Wales from 1976–2000, based on data from a large sample of General Practitioners' weekly records (National Asthma Campaign, 2001a). (*Incidence* refers to the rate of symptoms occurring for the *first time* in a given period, in this case a year.) A detailed analysis of these data revealed that the trend shown in Figure 5.8 not only occurred in both sexes, but also in all regions of England and Wales, including rural and urban locations (Fleming *et al.*, 2000). The authors concluded that a genuine increase in the presentation of asthma to GPs occurred up to 1993/94, particularly in the youngest age groups, followed by a genuine decrease. No explanation for either the UK asthma 'epidemic' or its subsequent decline could be inferred from these data.

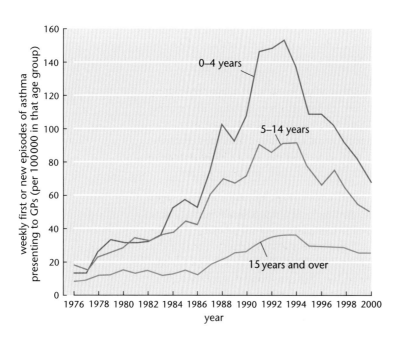

Figure 5.8 *New episodes of asthma, incidence rate per 100 000 population by age group (sexes combined) as notified by a sample of General Practitioners in England and Wales, 1976–2000. (Data derived from the Weekly Returns Service of the Royal College of General Practitioners, by the Lung and Asthma Information Agency, for the National Asthma Campaign; diagram based on National Asthma Campaign (2001a) Out in the Open,* The Asthma Journal, *Special Supplement, 6(3), Figure 1, p. 4)*

In Section 5.5, we review the vexed arguments about what may be causing asthma rates to rise or fall. First, we conclude this discussion of asthma morbidity by considering its impact on individuals in the UK, the health and social services, and the national ecomony.

5.4.5 The costs of asthma

[handwritten margin note: Treating @ home reduces Hosp admis.]

The cost of asthma should not be measured simply in terms of the threat to life. Around 5 million people in the UK are estimated to suffer from asthma requiring medical treatment. A number of studies have investigated the effects of asthma morbidity on the activities of daily living.

For example, Kevin Jones, a GP, coordinated a small-scale study covering three general practices in the Southampton area (Jones *et al.*, 1992), which focused on the restrictions that asthma places upon people's lives. A random sample of 296 patients with an asthma diagnosis were surveyed (5.8 per cent of everyone registered with the three practices). Some of the results are shown in Table 5.4. Just over half of the patients surveyed suffered attacks of wheezing during the night, and just under half had a 'wheezy or asthmatic condition' at least once a week. Nearly one in three had stayed off work or school at least once in the past year as a result of asthma.

Table 5.4 The morbidity of asthma in 296 patients in three general practices in the Southampton area, England, in 1990.

	Percentage of all asthmatic patients
attacks of wheezing during the night	51
a wheezy or asthmatic condition at least once a week	49
stayed off work or school at least once in past year	31
avoids at least some activities between attacks	23
asthma interrupts daily life at least monthly	11
everyday activities affected at least 'quite a lot' in past year	10

Source: Jones, K. P., Bain, D. J. G., Middleton, M. and Mullee, M. A. (1992) Correlates of asthma morbidity in primary care, *British Medical Journal*, **304**, Table II, p. 362.

An analysis of asthma in 12–14-year-old children in Great Britain, using the ISAAC questionnaire, found that nearly 10 per cent had experienced four or more attacks in the past 12 months, almost 9 per cent had wheezing severe enough to limit speech to only one or two words between breaths, and just over 5 per cent reported that wheezing interfered with their daily activities to a moderate or greater degree (Kaur *et al.*, 1998).

The National Asthma Campaign (a charity involved in research, advice to patients and campaigning for better services), published a study in 2000 on the needs of people with asthma. 28 per cent of those who attempted jogging, running or similar exercise were unable to sustain this, or were very constrained by their asthma. Over 10 per cent of those attempting to walk upstairs, to garden, or to go to the pub also reported that they were unable to do so, or were subject to severe limitations.

Another cost is the financial impact of asthma. The National Asthma Campaign (2001a) estimated that £850 million of the NHS budget is spent on asthma annually, and a further £161 million is incurred in social services costs. It reported that over

18 million working days are lost in the UK every year due to asthma, costing the national economy over £1.2 billion. Individuals and families can also pay substantial sums in prescription charges, for medical equipment (such as a nebuliser), or for household expenses such as new bedding or steam cleaning their carpets.

5.5   Controversies over the causes of asthma

The fact that asthma rates, particularly among children, rose during the 1980s and 1990s in many parts of the developed world, has sparked heated debates in the scientific community as well as in the popular media about the possible causes. The fact that rates in England and Wales have been falling since 1994 is equally mysterious, since other English-speaking countries have not (by 2002) detected a similar downturn, nor has it occurred in near neighbours such as France. Explanations, for the global rise in asthma can be distinguished into three main categories: changes in diagnostic criteria and consultation rates; a rise in atmospheric pollution; or the effect of wide-ranging social changes on the development of the immune system in infancy.

5.5.1   Diagnostic changes and consultation rates

The problems with defining asthma outlined in Section 5.4.2 could partly explain changes over time in the extent to which asthma is diagnosed within a population. In other words, increases and decreases could be an artefact produced by diagnostic changes. For example, a German study carried out in 1989–92 by Erika von Mutius and her colleagues compared respiratory disorders and allergies in over 3 000 children aged 9–10 years in the cities of Leipzig and Halle in former East Germany, with over 7 000 similar children in the West German city of Munich (von Mutius *et al.*, 1994). The authors concluded:

> Differences [in asthma rates] may reflect differences in medical practice and diagnostic labelling in the formerly separated states. One could argue that some of the children with bronchitis in East Germany would have been labelled as having asthma if they had lived in West Germany. Similarly, the higher prevalence of wheezing and cough could point towards an underdiagnosis of asthma in East Germany. (von Mutius *et al.*, 1994, p. 362)

After German reunification, as diagnostic practices merged over time, some of the reported increase in asthma in former East Germany could be attributed to a **diagnostic transfer** to 'asthma' from what was once called 'bronchitis'. Thus, without any change in respiratory symptoms, the medical label they attract can shift over time.

● Look back at Table 5.3, and see if you can find further evidence of changes in medical labelling among doctors in Wagga Wagga, Australia.

■ In 1982, doctors diagnosed asthma *less* often than parents reported wheeze in their children in the past 12 months. But in 1992 and 1997 the prevalence of doctor-diagnosed asthma was substantially *higher* than parent-reports of recent wheezing. This suggests that some children who were diagnosed by doctors as asthmatic in the 1990s had *not* been suffering from recent wheezing according to their parents. So part of the increase in asthma diagnoses over time may be due to changes in diagnostic criteria (an interpretation that Peat and her colleagues acknowledge).

There may also have been changes in *consultation rates* which brought more previously undiagnosed cases of asthma to medical attention. The lay perception of asthma, both in terms of what constitutes the condition and when doctors should be consulted, may have changed during the 1980s. Three factors may have contributed both to increased consultation rates and to diagnostic changes among health professionals:

1   Media coverage has ensured that both doctors and parents have become more aware and concerned about the possibility that environmental pollution is contributing to a rise in asthma, and the anxiety this generates may have increased consultation rates and the likelihood that an asthma diagnosis would result.

2   The availability and marketing of nebulisers, inhalers and other aids are making treatment for asthma more visible to the wider public. These interventions appear to relieve distressing symptoms in many patients, raising awareness of the availability of effective treatment, and hence increasing consultation and prescription rates.

3   With the trend away from long-term hospitalisation for children in the UK, GPs and community nurses are becoming more actively involved in the management of asthma in the community, increasing their awareness of the condition and their readiness to diagnose and treat it.

It is reasonable to suggest that these factors in combination could have led to a rise in the 1980s and early 1990s in the number of 'border-line' children who emerge from a medical consultation equipped with an inhaler and an asthma diagnosis. But if this hypothesis is correct, you would also have to postulate that doctors in England and Wales changed their practice around 1994, and became *less* likely to label respiratory problems as asthma, thus producing the downward trend in Figure 5.8. There is no evidence that this occurred.

Epidemiologists around the world have concluded that despite the contribution to asthma rates of diagnostic changes and rising consultation rates, there *has* been a genuine increase in the condition since the 1980s in all countries in which surveys have taken place. England and Wales is unusual in showing a subsequent decline. Before we review the main hypotheses to explain the general upward trend, you should bear in mind that although all the evidence points towards *environmental* factors, at the time of writing (2002) there is no consensus on which aspects of the environment are to blame.

5.5.2 Atmospheric pollution

The rising trend in asthma prevalence — until at least the mid-1990s — has coincided with significant changes in atmospheric pollution at 'street-level' in developed industrial nations. The two have frequently been linked in media reporting of asthma, but the evidence for health-damaging effects from traffic pollution is stronger for other respiratory conditions such as chronic obstructive airways disease (COAD), and for cardiovascular diseases including heart attacks and strokes, than it is for asthma. The vexed question is not about whether inhaling chemicals and smoke particles is bad for health, but whether it *causes* asthma.

As part of the APHEA project (Air Pollution and Health: a European Approach), studies in 29 European cities have correlated health outcome measures with the

Figure 5.9 *The evidence is far from convincing that traffic pollution causes asthma to develop in people who would not otherwise have suffered from it, but other health-damaging effects include exacerbating breathing problems in people who already have respiratory disorders. (Photo: Marcus Enoch)*

daily concentrations of four pollutants emitted in vehicle exhausts: *sulphur dioxide* (SO_2), *nitrogen dioxide* (NO_2), *ozone* (O_3), and *black smoke* — measured as **PM_{10}** (*Particulate Matter less than 10* micrometres in diameter).[11] The significance of black smoke is that the minute airborne particles are so small that they can remain suspended in the atmosphere indefinitely, and can penetrate deep into the narrowest branches of the airways.

Although sulphur dioxide and black smoke levels fell very sharply in the UK after the Clean Air Act of 1956, which restricted the burning of coal fires and abolished the infamous post-war 'smogs', they remain a serious cause for concern in cities.[12] Urban atmospheric concentrations of nitrogen dioxide and ozone have increased with the rise in traffic (Figure 5.9). The association of NO_2 levels with major cities and trunk roads in the UK is evident from Figure 5.10.

The APHEA project has established that short-term fluctuations in atmospheric pollution are statistically associated with fluctuations in death rates from 'all causes' combined, and for all cardiovascular and all respiratory diseases combined (Katsouyanni *et al.*, 2001). However, evidence specifically on asthma has generally been less convincing, and sometimes contradictory. For example, a study of daily fluctuations in air pollution and cases of asthma presenting to 12 London Accident and Emergency (A&E) departments during 1992–1994 found a statistically significant association between asthma consultations and nitrogen dioxide, sulphur dioxide and PM_{10} levels (Atkinson *et al.*, 1999). However, there were exceptions to this pattern. In the summer of 1994, exceptionally high numbers of asthma cases presented in A&E departments, but without any associated rise in atmospheric pollution. Moreover, members of the same research team showed that admissions to hospital for asthma did *not* rise in the winter of 1991, when nitrogen dioxide levels in London reached five times the seasonal average in mid-December — an historically high level (Anderson *et al.*, 1996).

[11] One micrometre (abbreviated as 1 μm) is one-millionth of a metre.

[12] The campaign to reduce urban air pollution in the 1950s is described in *Caring for Health: History and Diversity* (Open University Press, 3rd edn 2001), Chapter 6.

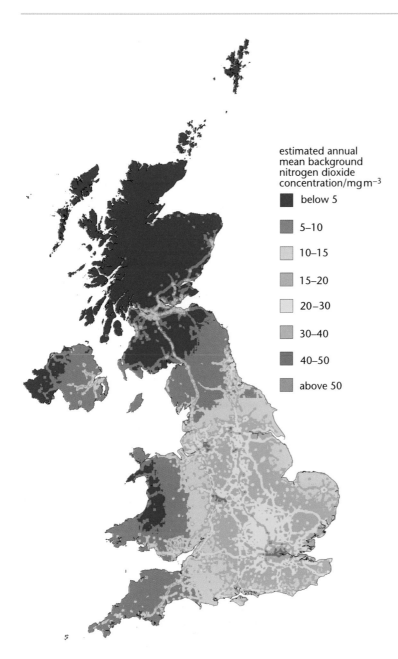

estimated annual
mean background
nitrogen dioxide
concentration/$mg\,m^{-3}$

■ below 5

■ 5–10

□ 10–15

■ 15–20

□ 20–30

■ 30–40

■ 40–50

■ above 50

Figure 5.10 *Estimated mean background nitrogen dioxide concentration, UK, 1999, produced for the Department of the Environment, Transport and the Regions and other government departments in response to a European Directive on Ambient Air Quality Assessment and Management. (From Stedman, J. R. and Bush, T. (2000) Mapping of Nitrogen Dioxide and PM_{10} in the UK for Article 5 Assessment, AEA Technology Environment, Harwell, Figure 1, p. 8)*

In general, studies have tended to show that people who *already* have a respiratory disorder are most at risk from poor air quality, even at modest pollution levels. In Manchester, Higgins and co-workers (1995) showed that levels of sulphur dioxide or ozone well *below* the limits recommended by the World Health Organisation's Air Quality Guidelines, could trigger respiratory problems in people with a history of asthma or COAD. In the USA, Pope and Dockery (1992) established a link between respiratory problems in asthmatic children and PM_{10} emissions from a local steelmill in Utah. Figure 5.11 (overleaf) illustrates the link between coughing in asthmatic children and two violations of permitted PM_{10} levels. The authors of the Utah study point out that *averaging* data from a large number of people may conceal *individual* cases of considerable distress, where children with particularly sensitive airways take a long time to recover from a pollution episode. Even small changes in lung function, when averaged over large populations, can add up to a considerable amount of illness.

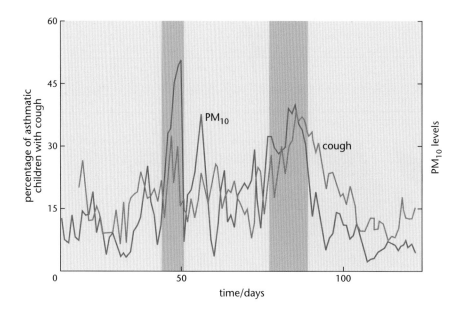

Figure 5.11   *Link between PM$_{10}$ emission and cough in asthmatic children in Utah, USA between December 1990 and March 1991. Tone bars indicate two periods when emissions from a local steelmill violated regulations and PM$_{10}$ levels rose above 'standard' concentrations. (Data from Pope, C. A. and Dockery, W., 1992, Acute health effects of PM$_{10}$ pollution on symptomatic and asymptomatic children,* American Review of Respiratory Diseases, **145,** *Figure 1, p. 1124)*

The APHEA project results suggest that on average an increase in PM$_{10}$ air pollution of 10 micrograms per cubic metre of air (10 μg m^{-3}) above background levels is associated with an increase in emergency hospital admissions for asthma of just over 1 per cent (Atkinson *et al.*, 2001). In 1999, the background PM$_{10}$ concentration in the centre of major British cities was estimated at around 25 μg m^{-3}. However, there are significant variations in health outcomes between cities with the same levels of pollution, for example pollution has worse health effects in warmer climates, and in cities where smoking prevalence is high.

The consensus in European governments is represented by the UK's Committee on the Medical Effects of Air Pollutants, an expert panel set up by the Department of Health, which reported in 1995:

> There is clear evidence of associations between concentrations of particles, similar to those encountered currently in the UK, and changes in a number of indicators of damage to health. These range from changes in lung function through increased symptoms and days of restricted activity, to hospital admissions and mortality … It is well established from the reported studies that people with pre-existing respiratory … disorders are at most risk of acute effects from exposure to particles … There is no evidence that healthy individuals are likely to experience acute effects on health as a result of exposure to concentrations of particles found in ambient air in the UK. (Committee on the Medical Effects of Air Pollutants, 1995, pp. 1, 2)

People with asthma are now routinely advised to take preventive action during periods of poor air quality, for example by increasing the dosage of their medication and avoiding vigorous outdoor exercise (e.g. not running for a bus). Such restrictions on lifestyle extend the adverse experiences associated with asthma far beyond the immediate threat of an attack. The needs of society for transport and industry, which pollute the atmosphere, may be at odds with the needs of individuals to optimise their health and quality of life. However, it is worth noting that, for at least some individuals with lifelong asthma, urban atmospheric pollution seems to make no difference to their symptoms (as in the case of one of the speakers on the audiotape band for Open University students associated with this chapter).

Another problem that casts some doubt on how much of the rise in asthma can be attributed to traffic pollution is that asthma has also risen in *rural* locations in English-speaking countries, and in small towns with low pollution levels (like Wagga Wagga, Table 5.3). In rural areas most of the PM_{10} load consists of fragments of pollens and spores, which leads us into another controversial hypothesis about what causes asthma to develop.

5.5.3 Allergies, infections and the 'hygiene hypothesis'

Considerable research interest has been directed towards determining whether a rise in exposures to naturally occurring allergens in Western industrialised countries might be contributing to the increase in asthma prevalence.

The most influential research in this field has been conducted by Erika von Mutius and colleagues, whose comparison of asthma in children in former East and West Germany was mentioned earlier (von Mutius *et al.*, 1994). They also tested children for sensitisation to common allergens and airway hyper-responsiveness to a blast of cold air. The West German children had a significantly higher prevalence of asthma *and* allergic reactions to domestic allergens than the East German children. Significantly, the atmospheric pollution with sulphur dioxide and black smoke particles was substantially higher in the East than in the West German cities.

●   Can you suggest possible reasons for the higher asthma rates among West German children, even though they experienced less atmospheric pollution?

■   Before unification, most families in West Germany had a higher living standard than those in East Germany and could afford to install central heating and fitted carpets, or keep domestic pets which can increase the exposure to allergens, particularly among children.

These observations led to the proposition that changes in the concentration of allergens in the domestic environment associated with rising living standards were the underlying cause of the asthma epidemic among children. Another piece of the puzzle was already waiting be fitted into the jigsaw. In what has become a landmark study, the epidemiologist David Strachan analysed data from a national sample of 17 414 children in England who were all born in the same week in March 1958, and who have been followed up ever since.[13] In 1989, he reported an *inverse* association between the number of children in a household and the prevalence of hay fever (i.e. hay fever was *less* common in households with more children). The effect was also consistent with birth order, so second children were less likely to develop hay fever than their first-born siblings, and third children were still less likely to be affected.

---

[13] This birth cohort is the basis of the National Child Development Study — one of several longitudinal cohort studies discussed in *Birth to Old Age: Health in Transition* (Open University Press, 2nd edn 1995; colour-enhanced 2nd edn 2001), Chapter 14.

Strachan speculated that early exposure to infection was greater in households with more children, and that infection might, in some way, 'train' the juvenile immune system to recognise appropriate targets. As a consequence, children raised with older siblings might be less likely to react to inappropriate targets — allergens — as they grew up, and so be less susceptible to hay fever and perhaps also to asthma. Strachan's application of this reasoning to explain the increase in asthma has become known as the **hygiene hypothesis**, which he summed up as follows:

> Over the past century declining family size, improved household amenities and higher standards of personal cleanliness have reduced opportunities for cross-infection in young families. This may have resulted in more widespread clinical expression of atopic disease. (Strachan, 1989, p. 1260)

Erika von Mutius and colleagues (1994) found indirect support for Strachan's hypothesis in the very different patterns of day-care in East and West Germany. In the 1980s, around 70 per cent of East German children aged 1–3 years mixed with other children at some form of day-care, whereas only around 7 per cent of West German children in this age group attended day-care facilities. The East German children also had higher rates of respiratory infections, including bronchitis, than their West German counterparts, as well as lower rates of asthma and allergies — just as the hygiene hypothesis predicted.

Initially, the reaction among immunologists to these ideas was sceptical, since infection had hitherto been seen as a threat to be avoided in young children. It took a major shift in thinking to consider the possibility that, over millions of years of coevolution between humans and the pathogenic organisms that infect us, our immune system has adapted to 'home in on' whatever it encounters early in life. If the early environment has a high concentration of allergens and low exposure to respiratory-tract infections, the immune system may be 'programmed' towards allergies and atopic asthma. This outcome may be more likely in individuals with certain patterns of genes.

Research in laboratory animals has since discovered a biologically plausible mechanism for this process. The white cells known as *helper T cells* (described in Chapter 4 as the principal target for HIV infection) produce chemical signals that stimulate and direct the action of the immune system as a whole. It is now known that they occur in two populations, distinguished as Th1 and Th2 cells. Early in life, the balance between these two populations can be altered by exposure to infection, which promotes the development of Th1 cells and suppresses Th2 numbers. Mild respiratory-tract infections and exposure to the 'friendly bacteria' that rapidly colonise the gut after birth may both be important triggers for this process (for a review, see Holt *et al.*, 1997). Significantly, Th2 cells are involved in the production of allergies and, moreover, early exposure to allergens can tilt the balance in favour of the Th2 population. Patrick Holt, a leading Australian immunologist involved in this research, sums up the modern version of the hygiene hypothesis as follows:

> The measures in question, which have come to represent the norm in first world countries over the last 20–30 years, include the introduction of effective public health and hygiene programs targeted at water supplies and foodstuffs; vaccination programs which limit the impact of infectious diseases during childhood; widespread use of antibiotics in paediatrics; increasingly stringent infant feeding (and associated hygiene) practices; and reduction in family and school class sizes which limit sharing of infections.

Collectively, these measures have markedly reduced mortality and morbidity during early childhood, but (we speculate) at the expense of the efficient early education of the immune system, resulting in increasingly frequent 'errors' in T-cell memory development against non-pathogenic environmental antigens, which can be translated in later life into atopic disease. (Holt *et al.*, 1997, p. 56)

The construction of a new medical narrative for asthma as a disease of sheltered Western children raised in homes full of allergens remains controversial because (as its originator, David Strachan, acknowledged in his 2000 review) there is some contradictory evidence. But at the turn of the twenty-first century it came closest to a unifying theory about why asthma rates have risen, although it does not explain why they have fallen so quickly in England and Wales since 1994. Could a reduction in the age at which children enter pre-school classes, or an increase in nursery places, be protective? Have fears about over-prescription of antibiotics to children played a part? These and other speculative explanations cannot yet be resolved.

5.5.4 A multifactorial approach to causation

The foregoing discussion points to an aetiology for asthma in which a number of different factors interact. There is agreement that a genetically determined tendency to over-produce IgE antibodies which bind to allergens is a key factor. Additionally, persistent exposure to domestic allergens coupled with low exposure to infections in early life may direct the immune system towards a lifelong hypersensitivity to allergens — particularly those in the atmosphere. Atmospheric pollution undoubtedly exacerbates existing respiratory hyper-responsiveness. But this is not the whole story.

● Can you suggest any other factors that have been implicated in the development of asthma, or the triggering of an asthma attack?

■ You may have come across some of the following, all of which have at least some support from large-scale research studies: passive inhalation of cigarette smoke (asthma is more common in the children of parents who smoke); exposure to fumes from bottled gas, paraffin and other unusual fuels used in domestic heating and cooking; summer thunderstorms, which stir up pollens and other 'outdoor' allergens; diet (children who are breastfed or raised in communities with a high intake of cereals, vegetables and polyunsaturated fats have lower asthma and allergy rates); frequent paracetamol use (the highest average doses occur in English-speaking countries); and the 'epidemic' of obesity among children.

Asthma, then, can be seen as a classic example of a multifactorial disorder, in which many highly varied factors interact in complex ways. The pattern of contributory causes is likely to differ between individuals, between places and over time, making it particularly difficult to devise strategies for asthma prevention.

5.6 The experience of asthma

In this section of the chapter, we ask what it is like to *experience* asthma. In approaching this question, we focus on two aspects: the experience of *symptoms* described by people who are asthmatic, and the *social impact* that asthma has on them and their families. (The audiotape band for Open University students 'Reflections on asthma' is particularly relevant to this discussion.) Disease experience has been the subject of much research by medical sociologists using qualitative methods. Typically they have interviewed relatively small samples of people in depth, in contrast to the large-scale epidemiological surveys described in previous sections of this chapter. The basic objective has been either to describe the common experience of all those with the disease, or to identify groups who have contrasting experiences.

5.6.1 Gaining control

Mike Bury has provided a basic sociological model regarding the experience of chronic illness (1991). He refers to an **illness career** in which the affected person passes through three stages: onset, explanation and legitimization, and adaptation.

A similar conceptual model of the experience of asthma from first diagnosis onward has been developed by David Snadden and Judith Belle Brown (1992). They identify two key transitions: from the asthma 'being in control' to the asthma 'being controlled', and from fear of the disease to its acceptance. Snadden and Belle Brown claim that this process is greatly helped by a 'mentoring relationship', where the mentor is someone experienced in coping with asthma, with whom patient or parent can discuss their worries. In this way, the asthmatic person gains experience, knowledge and self-awareness, all of which contribute to a growing sense of control.

The process described by Snadden and Belle Brown extends over several years and, as the authors point out, may never be completed. Thus the experience of coming to terms with asthma is a *dynamic* process.[14] It begins with symptoms and confusion. The diagnosis of 'asthma' may bring a temporary period of relief for the person in knowing what is wrong, that it isn't 'nothing', and in believing that something can be done about it:

> *JK*[15]: It's nice to know that what I have is something. I don't like the idea of 'wait a minute, I'm having trouble breathing' and not knowing why. It's fine I can say it's asthma, that I'm asthmatic now. It's not all up in my head, I'm not dreaming this. (Snadden and Belle Brown, 1992, p. 1354)

This comment demonstrates the importance of there being a name, a medical label, that can be put to the condition. (This experience has already been discussed in Chapter 3 in relation to rheumatoid arthritis — another 'hard-to-diagnose' condition; we will return to it in Chapter 7, where failure to identify the cause of chronic pain poses similar problems of 'legitimacy' for patients.) The GP and anthropologist Cecil Helman (1990) has argued that doctors need to be able to organise their health work around a set of identifiable and largely familiar diseases and problems, procedures and treatments, which fit within accepted *medical narratives*. In the same way, people who have chronic health problems need to organise their own 'health work' and develop *personal narratives* of their illness.

[14] It is helpful to compare the psychosocial model developed by Snadden and Belle Brown with the stages described by Sally Macintyre and David Oldman in 'Coping with migraine' (originally published 1977). Open University students will study an edited extract in *Health and Disease: A Reader* (Open University Press, 3rd edn 2001) with Chapter 7 of this book, but could usefully read it now. Macintyre and Oldman suggest that people faced with migraine acquire knowledge of the disease in a series of discrete stages: experiencing the complaint, identifying it as migraine, and then acquiring a repertoire of methods of coping.

[15] This is the first of several extracts from interviews conducted by Snadden and Bell Brown with adults who suffer from asthma; respondents are identified by their initials.

If individuals accept that they are asthmatic it generally makes it easier to collaborate with health professionals in treating the illness and in routinely monitoring changes in their state of health. However, in accepting a medical label, the person also has to address the uncomfortable question of 'Why me?'

> *ND*: There was a lot of panic and anger about why me, because I have two sisters and neither one of them are affected. It's just me and I'm going like 'why me, why do I have to get dumped on with this?' and things like 'why can't it just be divided out between all three of us or whatever, like why does it have to be me, that I have to get all these problems'. (Snadden and Belle Brown, 1992, p. 1355)

In the following extract, KM conveys something of the fear that asthmatic people have to cope with as they attempt to control an attack, and also how they gain useful knowledge from experience of attacks in the past.

> *KM*: You start to get tight and then all of a sudden you get thinking 'Gee, I can't breathe' and you're pumping on the puffers and it's not working, and then you start to hyperventilate, you start to get really excited, and then you see that's a bad thing if you get excited with asthma, you'll bring an attack on … Well I've been able to stop them myself, but the big thing is you've got to stay cool. (Snadden and Belle Brown, 1992, p. 1354)

JK also indicates the importance of knowledge as the source of her power to control her asthma, and the benefits of a mentoring relationship when she was trained to cope with asthmatic children. Both she and AJ show how important self-awareness is, in experiencing and accepting the disease.

> *JK*: What has helped me adjust? Understanding it more I guess, understanding that what I have can be controlled, not cured. It can be controlled so you can live a normal life. I worked as a counsellor at a day camp and we had asthmatic children. We had to go on a special course, the counsellors did, and they taught us things to do with the children. In the back of my head I've remembered them. It was just real simple exercises and I try doing them now. (Snadden and Belle Brown, 1992, p. 1355)

> *AJ*: I tend to keep it always in the back of my head. I am always conscious of what's going on in myself. I am always listening to my own breathing to see if I am whistling or wheezing or whatever. I guess it's subconscious but I know I do it a lot. (Snadden and Belle Brown, 1992, p. 1356)

Different individuals have been shown to use different coping strategies in managing their reactions to an asthma diagnosis and the need for medication. Adams *et al.* (1997) interviewed 30 adults with asthma in South Wales, and distinguished several groups. The first group of 15 included 'deniers' (all they have, they claim, is 'just a bit of chest trouble') and 'distancers' who admitted only that they may have 'slight' asthma. Medicines to relieve their symptoms were used by all these patients, but only in private. They had chosen to present themselves as leading a normal life and saw 'asthmatics' as a stigmatised group with which they did not wish to be associated:

> *Interviewee 1:* Well people would be very shocked if they knew I had asthma. That's why I've never told them though the doctor suggested that I did. Though I haven't of course. It's just not the

way people see me. It's not the way I see myself come to that.
I don't know if I could cope if I really had it. (Adams *et al.*, 1997,
p. 194)

A second group of nine respondents were classed by the researchers as 'accepters' who had accepted asthma as being 'part of their lives'. They took their medicines 'properly', including the prophylactic drugs that had become part of their daily routine, 'just like putting my watch on' according to one. As a result they felt they were able to lead a normal life. They believed that 'if only other asthmatics controlled and coped the way they themselves did, asthma need present little problem to anyone' (Adams *et al.*, 1997, p. 195). Like the deniers and the distancers, the accepters rejected what they saw as the stereotyped image of 'the asthmatic', but they differed in being prepared to include asthma in their identity and routine way of life. The third group were six 'pragmatists'. The themes of normalisation, self-presentation and medication were equally relevant to them, but they were distinctive in displaying a conflict between the social identity of 'asthma sufferer' and their other identities. One man, for example, was concerned about his job:

> *Interviewee 28:* You have to be careful who you tell. I don't mind certain mates knowing but not those who might tell people I work with. Mind, I was surprised ... I was out with a friend of mine ... and he got out his pump. He had asthma! I hadn't known ... we work in the same place but we hadn't told each other ... I was shocked. I told him then. I wouldn't have minded him knowing if I'd known he had it. Because I explained what type I'd got. The type that just bothers you sometimes.. ... Mind, I wouldn't take the inhaler in front of management ... If he sees I've got a bad chest ... he doesn't know I'm asthmatic, and he might say, 'No way can I have you working here, you are a risk to me'. (Adams *et al.*, 1997, p. 198)

Adams and co-workers concluded that the management of social identity was critical to understanding the experience of asthma. They referred to a concept developed by an American sociologist, Kathy Charmaz (1987)[16], that chronic illness results in 'the diminished self'. Adams *et al.* argued that this only applied when an individual could not reconcile the social identity of 'asthmatic' with their other social identities. Failure to achieve this reconciliation resulted in a diminished sense of self. Experiential accounts such as these provide important insights into the personal worlds of people who are coping with chronic illness.

5.6.2 The social impact of childhood asthma

The account of Peter's asthma at the beginning of this chapter is taken from a research report on the *social* impact of the condition. For this reason it concentrates on the ways in which Peter's asthma complicates his life, for example by restricting what he is able to do at school and by imposing extra routine chores upon his mother. It also indicates something of the changing history of Peter's condition: the onset of asthma, the steps taken to control it, the acquisition of his nebuliser, the reduction in severity, and so on.

[16] This concept is also discussed in a more recent article by Kathy Charmaz (1997), entitled 'Identity dilemmas of chronically ill men'; an edited extract appears in *Health and Disease: A Reader* (Open University Press, 3rd edn 2001).

● In order to obtain a broader view of the social dimension, Open University students should now read the article in *Health and Disease: A Reader* (Open University Press, 3rd edn 2001) by Andrew Nocon and Tim Booth, entitled 'The social impact of childhood asthma'. As you do so, make out three lists of things that are mentioned:

(a) the *apparent causes* of asthma or asthmatic attacks;

(b) the *negative outcomes* of asthma;

(c) the *positive outcomes* of asthma.

■ Compare your lists with ours in Table 5.5.

Table 5.5 Apparent causes and social impact of asthma in a sample of 32 children who had all been admitted to a Sheffield hospital in the previous year.

(a) Apparent causes of asthma or asthmatic attacks	(b) Negative outcomes of asthma	(c) Positive outcomes of asthma
exercise	difficulty keeping up with friends, walking uphill, running, sports	a more health-conscious approach to food
allergies to animals, foods, plants	restrictions on certain trips, visits, activities, public transport, etc.	household members gave up smoking
smoke in atmosphere, especially from cigarettes	withdrawal from some activities (e.g. riding, parties, keeping pets, cancelled holidays)	families brought closer together, everyone 'helps out', parents share worries
feather bedding, carpeting	child absent from school, loses friends, gets 'picked on'	greater appreciation of the asthmatic child
cold air, cold water	parent takes time off work, loses or changes job, delays finding job	appreciation of siblings' help and concern
excitement, getting over-tired	family loses income, incurs extra expenses	inhaler makes asthmatic child feel special
	family suffers sleep loss, worry, exhaustion, tension, anger	
	parents have to do extra cleaning	
	parents feel guilty about causing/failing to prevent asthma	
	behavioural problems in asthmatic child or jealous sibling	
	dispute with school about supervision of medication	

Derived from Nocon, A. and Booth, T. (1990) *The Social Impact of Asthma*, University of Sheffield; an edited extract entitled 'The social impact of childhood asthma' appears in Davey, B., Gray, A. and Seale, C. (eds) (2001) *Health and Disease: A Reader*, 3rd edn, Open University Press, Buckingham.

It is clear from Nocon and Booth's research that, overall, childhood asthma places considerable strains upon the family. The parents of asthmatic children, like adult asthmatic patients, were fearful, anxious and angry, particularly in the period immediately following the onset of the condition or subsequent attacks. But some positive outcomes were also mentioned. Many parents felt they were gaining experience and knowledge in the treatment of their child's asthma. A few said they 'had now learned to live with it'. Most were making changes in their lives by studying the circumstances in which attacks occurred, and by following the advice of their doctors on bedding, pets, smoking, food, etc. A few, in the light of experience, were making their own decisions *not* to implement suggested changes: retaining normal carpeting and bedding, and keeping the family cat, for example. Their response reflects the concerns of the adults in the South Wales study described earlier (Adams *et al.*, 1997) to retain what they perceived to be 'a normal lifestyle'.

The parents of an asthmatic child, however, are constantly taxed by the problem of deciding whether or not to call the doctor. The doctor may say: 'Call me if you're in any doubt', but the parents know that doctors too live under pressure and they fear being criticised for 'wasting the doctor's time'. As one of the speakers in the audiotape band for Open University students associated with this chapter says:

> … you obviously don't want to turn up at casualty with a fairly healthy baby and say 'Well, we thought he was a bit wheezy' when there's obviously nothing wrong with him. So you leave it as long as you dare, and then suddenly it seems to get worse and you can't do anything about it. (David Riley, interviewed for the audiotape band 'Reflections on asthma')

Most of the children interviewed by Nocon and Booth were not seriously affected by their asthma, and seemed less concerned about the condition than their parents. A problem that three of them faced was sustaining their parents' trust; these children were said to 'use' their asthma to their own advantage. This raises questions about the legitimacy of the illness and the degree of tolerance that others show towards it.

5.6.3 Legitimacy, tolerance and stigmatisation

People with uncontrolled asthma often feel anxious or depressed about it. Emotional stress can make the symptoms worse, as is the case for many illnesses, even though the current medical view is that asthma is *not* a psychosomatic condition. However, the notion that it may be psychosomatic surfaces in personal narratives, for example when Peter's mother suspects that his asthma was brought on by his father leaving home. This raises a more general anxiety about how should people with asthma behave if their illness is to be considered *legitimate* and therefore *tolerated* by others? The quote from David Riley (above) illustrates this very well.

Judgements about legitimacy involve a wide range of others in several overlapping social circles: for example, in the case of asthmatic children, their parents, siblings, relatives, friends, teachers, nurses and doctors may all have a say in the matter. These 'others' may play an important part in the process of accepting and controlling the condition but, conversely, their reaction can aggravate the negative impact of the illness on the child and the family. Nocon and Booth's report refers to a teacher who is sympathetic but doesn't have time to supervise medication, and an aunt who refuses to look after the child because she fears she couldn't cope with an attack. References to parents dealing with the Benefits Agency and trying to claim allowances for taking time off work also reveal the need to 'manage' the presentation of the child's asthma as legitimate.

● The Canadian and South Wales studies described in Section 5.6.1 revealed something of the challenge facing adults with asthma in managing the appearance and presentation of their attacks to others. What clues can be discerned about this in the interview extracts from those studies?

■ In the Canadian study, JK prefers to say that her problem is asthma rather than 'having trouble breathing'. She implies that people will be more understanding if her condition is legitimised by a medical label. However, the label itself may attract intolerance, if the experience of interviewee 28 in the South Wales study is typical: he felt that his job was at risk if management knew of his asthma.

Problems in inter-personal trust, legitimacy and tolerance are discussed by the sociologist Simon Williams (1993), in his study of adults with COAD (chronic obstructive airways disease). What is critical, he argues, is the perception by others of the 'limits of tolerance' — the extent to which others can tolerate the failure of the person with the chronic disease to do what is required of them. The illness will be tolerated only if it does not impose 'unreasonable' burdens upon others. Perceptions of this limit may vary greatly between individuals and over time. For example, in one workplace, a person who is sometimes unable to work through chronic breathlessness may feel enormously indebted to the tolerance and help of colleagues; whereas, in another, given the same level of breathlessness, there may be a strong sense of grievance if employment was terminated after only a brief absence through sickness. It is not difficult to think of parallel situations regarding the limits of tolerance in the home, at school and in the use of health services.

Gay Becker and her colleagues studied how 95 adults with asthma, living in California, coped with the need for urgent care (Becker *et al.*, 1993). The majority indicated that they wanted to manage their asthma unassisted; they wanted to be self-reliant and to be in control of their illness. When this was no longer possible, they then had to *negotiate* access to appropriate medical treatment. The researchers concluded:

> Individuals who have asthma are caught in a bind created by extremely narrow definitions of appropriate symptoms in the delivery of health care in the emergency department: they must not delay too long or seek help too soon. ... the fear that health professionals might create additional danger through their ignorance of the complexities of the medical treatment of asthma, thereby endangering the individual's life, creates sustained efforts to avoid such interactions. Yet resistance to using the health care system puts individuals at increased risk of death, should efforts to manage an episode alone fail. The juxtaposition of these concerns creates a constant push-pull dynamic, as individuals struggle to make decisions about emergency department use that will provide relief, ensure autonomy, deter the experience of stigma, and diminish the threat of death. (Becker *et al.*, 1993, p. 311)

This dilemma is echoed by David Riley, the parent of an asthmatic child, interviewed for the audiotape band for Open University students associated with this chapter, when he says: 'Even though we know what the condition's like, I think we've left it too late on all occasions'.

The problem of legitimacy is experienced most acutely by those who are on the borderline of being asthmatic. There is a cultural assumption that one either does or does not have a disease. If a doctor says you have asthma, then (as JK from the Canadian study recognised) it is difficult for anyone else (other than another doctor) to dispute that you do indeed have it. The implications of this diagnosis are fairly straightforward in the case of acute illness. As the sociologist Talcott Parsons (1951) argued in his theory of the *sick role*, people are normally expected to cooperate fully in efforts to get them 'better' again and, as a consequence, they acquire certain temporary rights as being legitimately sick.[17]

● What difficulties do you foresee in applying this reciprocal agreement to a chronic episodic illness such as asthma?

■ Asthma intermittently 'attacks' and only marginally disables most of the time, so a question mark often hangs over the asthmatic person's right to present themselves as 'ill', to be excused from normal duties and to expect support from others.

Much of the potential *stigma* of asthma stems from the need to be ever-conscious of the importance of treatment and the need to avoid unnecessary risks. Asthmatic children have, in the past, sometimes been misunderstood at school by teachers and classmates. The stigma of being 'no good' at sport, frequently 'excused' from games, or absent altogether, can be made worse by people in authority over the child who do not understand the biological rationale of asthma treatment, nor the legitimacy of exercise-induced asthma. An instruction to 'see how long you can do without your inhaler' may mean that the asthmatic child suffers a build-up of otherwise avoidable symptoms, which can then take days to disappear. Teachers may get exasperated when seemingly fit adolescents start gasping for breath after only ten minutes' exercise. Being excused from games, but labelled as a 'neurotic who doesn't really like sport anyway', is hardly helpful. Parents have sometimes faced a struggle to persuade sceptical teachers and others of the legitimacy of the asthmatic child's needs, despite the evidence of medically prescribed treatment for asthma.

● Comparing Becker's study with that of Nocon and Booth, what do you think is the main *similarity* in the way in which the management of asthma attacks is negotiated by asthmatic adults and by the parents of asthmatic children?

■ They face a common dilemma in deciding when to deal with an attack themselves and when to seek medical help; wait too long and the consequences could be life-threatening, but seek help too soon or too often and risk being stigmatised as someone who 'over-reacts' and wastes precious medical time.

What is apparent from this review is that research on the experience of asthma has shown the importance that parents and patients place upon maintaining a normal way of life, on managing their social identity and having the condition accepted as legitimate, on obtaining appropriate treatment, and developing and implementing strategies for minimising the threat of asthma attacks. It is to a discussion of treatment and prevention that this chapter now turns.

5.7   Treating and preventing asthma

5.7.1   Medical management of chronic asthma

An initial difficulty for the clinician in deciding how to treat chronic asthma is that it can be confused with bronchitis or other recurring respiratory infections, particularly in children. In older people, mild heart failure and emphysema

[17] Talcott Parsons, sick role 'politics' and negotiations about the legitimacy of an illness are all discussed in *Medical Knowledge: Doubt and Certainty* (Open University Press, 2nd edn 1994; colour-enhanced 2nd edn 2001), Chapter 8.

(inflammation of the lining of the chest wall) can also give similar symptoms. To obscure diagnosis further, the lungs may be behaving normally at the time of investigation, so the case history becomes particularly important.

As you already know, the typical symptoms of asthma are breathlessness, wheezing, coughing (especially at night), and tightness in the chest (especially on waking up). These symptoms are not relieved by antibiotics because the underlying cause of the hyper-responsiveness and constriction of the airways is inflammation, not infection. The medical treatment of asthma has improved steadily as the underlying pathology became better understood, as the falling mortality rates testify. Drugs have improved in effectiveness and selectivity, and delivery systems in the form of inhalers and nebulisers are more widely available. Asthma medication involves two groups of drugs, known respectively as *relievers* and *preventers*. They offer two very different approaches to long-term asthma management.

Use of relievers

The relievers are a group of drugs that usually give instant relief from asthmatic symptoms by acting as *bronchodilators*.

● Why should a bronchodilator relieve the feeling of breathlessness?

■ Bronchodilation is the opposite of bronchoconstriction; it reverses the narrowing of airway tubes brought about by contraction of the underlying smooth muscle (shown earlier in Figure 5.7b).

Figure 5.12 shows peak flow, as a measure of lung function, in an asthmatic person before and after inhaling a bronchodilator; the benefits can last up to six hours. Even with good medication, the peak flow in someone with asthma may not be more than 80 per cent of normal. Relievers are used 'as needed' and not as a prophylactic against possible future attacks.

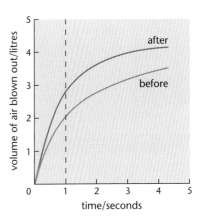

Figure 5.12 *Effect of inhaling a bronchodilator on the lung function of an asthmatic person. The dashed line indicates the response after 1 second.*

The most widely prescribed relievers belong to a group of drugs called the *β_2-agonists* ('β_2' is pronounced 'beta-two') developed in the 1960s. As 'agonists' they mimic the effect of a natural hormone — in this case, adrenalin — which stimulates relaxation of smooth muscle. The drug binds to special receptor molecules in smooth muscle, stimulating the muscle fibres to relax. The term 'β_2' indicates that binding is only to the β_2-receptors of smooth muscle in the airways, and not to the rather similar receptors of heart muscle. The early bronchodilators were less specific, and could cause heart palpitations as a side effect. Large doses of β_2-agonists may still give mild palpitations.

The most effective way to administer these short-acting bronchodilators is by *inhaler* (Figure 5.13a overleaf), preferably with a spacer between the mouth and the drug canister (Figure 5.13b and c). When the canister is pushed down into the inhaler, a measured quantity of drug solution spurts out of the sidearm in a fine spray, which is inhaled directly into the lungs. Having a spacer increases the proportion of active drug reaching the lungs; less falls at the back of the throat, to be lost by swallowing. An asthmatic person will feel instant relief on inhaling the reliever drug, provided the asthmatic state is not so advanced that mucus and bronchial constriction together prevent the drug from reaching the site of action.

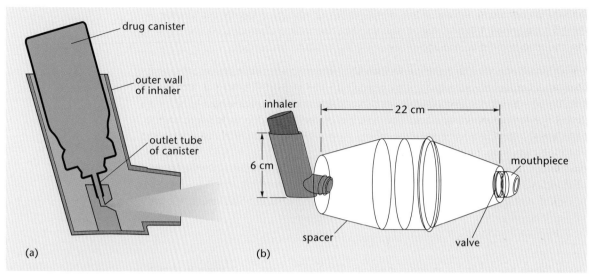

Figure 5.13 *Devices for inhaling bronchodilating drugs directly into the lungs. (a) Diagram of an inhaler (often colloquially called a 'puffer'), showing outlet tube of drug canister resting on the valve inside the inhaler, and (b) an inhaler connected to a spacer. (c) Children with asthma may find a spacer bulky to carry around, but it improves drug delivery. (Photo: National Asthma Campaign)*

Longer-acting bronchodilators were developed in the 1980s and are taken by mouth in tablet form. The 'oldest' of these is theophylline (also found in tea), which was first prescribed in the 1930s and is still the most popular drug for treating asthma in developing countries because it is cheap. However, side effects including headaches and nausea are quite common.

Bronchodilators may have other useful effects, such as speeding up the movement of cilia (the fine 'hairs' that sweep mucus through the airways, see Figure 5.3), and reducing the leakage of fluid from blood vessels in the connective-tissue layer of the lungs. But it is important to stress that they do not reduce the inflammatory reaction underlying the symptoms of asthma. Since chronic inflammation is characteristic of all asthma, many people are advised to use preventers as well as relievers.

Use of preventers

Preventers are drugs that prevent, or at least suppress, the inflammatory reaction in asthmatic lungs. Since the symptoms are attacked at source, there is less need for bronchodilators. People with asthma who use a reliever drug more than once a day are generally advised to take a regular course of a preventer. This requires forward planning, since the effects of most preventers are barely noticeable for several hours, and it may then be many days before the inflamed airways improve and the true benefit of therapy is felt.

The most effective and widely used preventer drugs are inhaled *corticosteroids* (steroids and their side effects were discussed in Chapter 3 in the treatment of rheumatoid arthritis). Just how they work is still not fully understood, but they inhibit the formation of inflammatory chemicals, and reduce the leakage of fluid from blood vessels and the build-up of mucus in the lungs. Overall, inflammation is reduced and the airways are less twitchy. Some people with asthma have been reluctant to use steroids because of their side effects, but problems associated with asthma treatment are much less than in some other conditions because inhaled steroids are effective at much lower doses than those taken by mouth.

●   Can you explain why?

■   Drugs given by mouth have to be at a high-enough concentration to overcome the diluting effect of being dissolved and absorbed into the bloodstream and carried round the body. Only a small proportion of the oral dose reaches the site of action. Inhaled drugs are delivered direct to the lungs, so a much lower initial dose can achieve the same effect.

However, some people experience greater vulnerability to respiratory infections and sores in the mouth if inhaled steroid treatment is prolonged. Oral steroids can be used to provide higher and sustained treatment after a severe asthma attack. Taken as a short 'crash' course of seven to ten days, these doses cause few adverse effects as long as the drug is then reduced gradually.

In the 1990s, a new class of preventer became available which can be taken orally, usually in conjunction with inhaled steroids. These *leukotriene antagonists* block receptors in the lungs, which would otherwise be triggered by leukotrienes released from white cells during an allergic inflammatory response. As well as being anti-inflammatory, they also have a mild bronchodilating action and may be particularly useful in controlling exercise-induced asthma, and in people who have not responded well to steroids.

Preventing fatal asthma attacks

In the most acute asthma attack, the airways may become completely constricted, so the person is no longer even wheezing. 'Blueing' of the lips occurs as the oxygen content of the bloodstream falls, and immediate emergency treatment — usually in hospital — is essential. Oxygen and large doses of bronchodilator may be given through a mask, as well as steroids to reduce the inflammation.

The routine use of preventers in accordance with medical instructions has reduced the probability of suffering such a major asthma attack. Except for the comparatively few people with 'brittle' asthma (characterised by sudden deterioration interspersed with symptom-free periods), emergency treatment can usually be avoided. People with chronic asthma are generally advised to increase their normal dose of preventer drug at the first sign of wheezing, or even in anticipation that it might be triggered, for example by the start of a cold or 'flu. Treatment is always more effective if given *before* the inflammation builds up.

Educated use of a peak-flow meter is also advised, as lung function may fall so gradually that people who have learned to 'live with' their asthma sometimes do not realise how low their lung capacity has become. Self-management procedures worked out with medical advice often include instructions on what to do if peak-flow readings fall below normal; for example, a drop of 30 per cent might lead to a doubling of the preventer dose, whereas a drop of 60 per cent might be the signal to seek emergency treatment in hospital. People with even moderate asthma are usually advised to travel with a peak-flow meter and oral steroids in their luggage.

Treatment and prevention of acute asthma are closely linked, illustrating the old saying 'prevention is better than cure'. At the individual level, this means sensible planning and self-monitoring. Prevention at the national level, for example by tackling the sources of potent triggers such as airborne particles, might be even more beneficial, but the difficulties in achieving significant improvements are obvious.

5.7.2 Organising routine treatment and providing support

The person with prime responsibility for the management and administration of treatment for asthma, on a day-to-day basis, is the patient, parent or other adult caregiver. He or she has to take or give medication in accordance with medical instructions, and decide when to consult a doctor and when emergency action is appropriate. This is not unusual in itself, since most illness conditions are self-treated.

● A particularly high level of responsibility for asthma treatment is carried by lay people. Can you explain why this is the case?

■ Asthmatic symptoms fluctuate in response to environmental triggers, which are themselves highly variable. Thus, the patient or parent has to judge whether to use a reliever or a prophylactic preventer drug sporadically or routinely, how much medication to give and how soon, whether to increase the dose in anticipation of a certain trigger, what significance to place on self-administered peak-flow measurements, and finally when to seek medical help and with what degree of urgency.

The Canadian study described earlier (Snadden and Belle Brown, 1992) demonstrated that patients with asthma can develop a sophisticated expertise in the management of their illness. They consult the doctor not just because they feel ill, but for more specific reasons, expressing particular concerns and having particular expectations of the action the doctor will take. Treatment is often based on an on-going collaboration between doctor and patient. This is consistent with a trend in Western medicine towards viewing the 'patient as an expert' who shares responsibility for treatment in partnership with health professionals.[18] The need for a more equitable relationship between prescriber and patient underpins the decision in 1997 of the Royal Pharmaceutical Society of Great Britain to advocate that the concept of 'concordance' should replace that of 'compliance':

> Concordance is a new approach to the prescribing and taking of medicines. It is an agreement reached after negotiation between a patient and a health care professional that respects the beliefs and wishes of the patient in determining whether, when and how medicines are to be taken. Although reciprocal, this is an alliance in which the health care professionals recognise the primacy of the patient's decisions about taking the recommended

[18] The 'patient-centred' approach to medical consultations is illustrated in *Medical Knowledge: Doubt and Certainty* (Open University Press, 2nd edn 1994; colour-enhanced 2nd edn 2001), Chapter 9; and in an audiotape for OU students entitled 'The consultation'.

medications. (Royal Pharmaceutical Society of Great Britain and Department of Health, 1997)

Whilst respecting the wishes of patients, this strategy can place a heavy responsibility on them. When asthma symptoms become acute, for example, patients can be faced with a difficult dilemma, as illustrated in several of the research studies discussed earlier and in the audiotape band for Open University students associated with this chapter. Anxieties about what to do for the best can affect a person's judgement. When Bonnie Sibbald (1988) studied 211 adults with asthma in Surrey, she found that those who suffered most morbidity were also the most likely to delay using their inhalers or summoning medical help. She argued that — rather than attempting to increase the patient's 'general knowledge' about asthma — education should be directed more to helping individuals to cope with the day-to-day demands of their illness. In particular, people with more severe asthma should be taught the importance of speedy action in the event of an attack.

Routine medication is just one element of a wide range of adjustments that follow an asthma diagnosis. Often a system of support develops that is intended to ensure that the condition is well controlled and that the patient has as normal a life as possible. To this end, the advice and experience of other people with asthma have a particular value. Snadden and Belle Brown stressed the importance of a mentor — someone to whom the patient or parent can turn, who has direct experience of asthma. It is clear from the comments of interviewee 28 in the South Wales study (by Adams *et al.*, 1997) that he was pleased to discover that his mate had asthma too, opening the possibility that they might help and support each other in the future. Nocon and Booth's respondents expressed a similar need, but with the emphasis on professional rather than lay help:

> When they were at their wits' end, parents wanted someone to talk to, someone who could sit and listen while they aired their grievances or anxieties … this should be a professional person: they felt that other parents, for all their understanding and helpfulness, might not preserve the same degree of confidentiality. (Nocon and Booth, 1990, p. 52)

In the conclusion of their report, Nocon and Booth list eight areas in which people with asthma and/or their carers would value assistance (Box 5.1).

Box 5.1 Areas where assistance with asthma management would be valued by patients and carers

- more information about their own asthma;
- more information about the practical implications of asthma;
- counselling;
- practical help, including financial help;
- information about where to obtain help;
- increased awareness on the part of medical and nursing staff about the social impact of asthma;
- increased awareness in schools and workplaces about the nature of asthma and its management;
- increased public awareness.

(derived from Nocon and Booth, 1990, pp. 65–6)

Nocon and Booth argue that much of the social organisation of support mechanisms, such as those in Box 5.1, can be developed by the members of local asthma societies. People who have asthma share many everyday challenges, and questions about 'treatment' can extend to many areas of social life. By obtaining specialist advice, not just from doctors but also from experts in welfare rights, social services, etc., and by helping each other, people with asthma can do much to reduce the negative impact that the disease can have on the quality of life.

At this point in the chapter, Open University students should play the audiotape band 'Reflections on asthma' for a second time, and then answer the questions in the associated notes in the *Audiovisual Media Guide*.

5.7.3 Asthma — a neglected condition?

Throughout this chapter, we have presented asthma as a condition that arouses major public concern, and from the evidence reviewed earlier you can see that it has been the subject of huge and costly international research endeavours. It may therefore seem strange to end by drawing attention to the 'neglect' of asthma in the UK, where the prevalence is among the highest in the world.

The National Asthma Campaign has persistently (and by 2002 unsuccessfully) lobbied the UK government to waive prescription charges for adults with asthma, which represent a substantial lifelong drain on their finances.

> The current prescription charges system runs the risk of undermining the Government's commitment, contained in last year's NHS Plan, to empower people to actively manage and control long term chronic conditions and improve quality of life. We welcome the Government's excellent work in this area and urge them to consider the effect of prescription charges on people living with asthma and other long term conditions. Patients are sacrificing their health because of their inability to pay. Eradicating unnecessary financial barriers will give people the opportunity to effectively control their asthma in the long term. This will not only improve the quality of life for people with asthma but also save NHS resources by reducing A&E visits, hospitalisations and readmissions to hospital. (National Asthma Campaign, 2001b)

Backing up these claims is research drawing upon the UK-wide National Asthma Management Study of a panel of over 12 000 patients (Hoskins *et al.*, 2000). The estimated annual health-service cost per patient of the 2 653 who had an acute attack over a 12 month period was £381, compared with £108 per patient for those whose asthma was kept under control. The authors conclude that:

> Increased expenditure in, and correct use of, preventive treatment may help to reduce asthma attack rates with a subsequent improvement in patient lifestyle and a potential financial benefit to the health service. (Hoskins *et al.*, 2000, p. 23)

Some members of the medical profession also point to the neglect of respiratory medicine. An editorial in *Thorax*, a leading academic journal notes that:

> The UK government has launched admirable initiatives on cancer, coronary heart diseases, mental health and diabetes ... While lung diseases will feature within some of these other national programmes, the lack of a specific programme devoted to lung diseases is a worrying omission. (Partridge, 2001, pp. 744–5)

And what of local health services? The same editorial notes that the All Party Parliamentary Group on Asthma had recently surveyed all primary care organisations in the UK and found that 39 per cent 'said they needed the government to develop a national programme for asthma before they could make asthma a local priority'.

5.8 Conclusion

In this chapter we have reviewed some of the current literature on asthma. It seems to us that a full understanding of asthma is frustrated by one important paradox. In short, whereas there is no ambiguity for the person who regularly suffers from asthmatic attacks, the disease itself becomes enigmatic when you try to study its occurrence within a population. Asthma has proved to be an elusive phenomenon to identify and define, for a number of reasons.

First, asthma takes time to diagnose and then is often totally controlled by treatment. Many people who could be described as 'asthmatic' because they routinely take anti-asthma medication, rarely or never suffer an asthma attack. As a result, the numbers of people recorded as 'having asthma' may be under-represented in epidemiological studies.

Second, for every person who unambiguously has asthma and who needs to take regular medication, there are several who are close to the borderline. As a result, epidemiological data are extremely sensitive to how the line is drawn between the 'nearly asthmatic' and the 'just asthmatic'. Minor fluctuations in what is defined as asthma can have a major impact on prevalence estimates.

Third, greater awareness of asthma among health professionals may have uncovered formerly undiagnosed cases, or it may have changed the diagnostic criteria they use. The widespread availability of inhalers and new medications have increased the public profile of the condition still further, and this too may increase 'diagnostic transfer' of other respiratory conditions to the asthma category.

Fourth, the growing global concern with the environment put asthma in the limelight during the 1990s, when asthma prevalence rates were increasingly used as an indicator of air quality. The linking of asthma with air pollution inevitably changed the way that doctors, scientists and lay people defined and identified the condition. These perceptual changes may already have contributed to the apparent rise in asthma prevalence in urban environments. It will be interesting to note how current concerns with early childhood infection and exposure to allergens will affect popular and professional narratives of the condition and its causes. Will asthma in the twenty-first century be reconstructed as a disease of relative affluence?

Yet despite scientific advances in understanding asthma and greatly improving its treatment, we are no closer now than we were a century ago to identifying the environmental factors that cause asthma to develop or devising strategies to prevent it. Viewed from this perspective, the uncertainties involved in measuring the asthma 'epidemic' seem less significant than our ignorance about how to control it.

OBJECTIVES FOR CHAPTER 5

When you have studied this chapter, you should be able to:

5.1 Define and use, or recognise definitions and applications of, each of the terms printed in **bold** in the text.

5.2 Explain the main sources of difficulty in conducting epidemiological studies of asthma and, in the light of these problems, critically discuss the principal trends in asthma incidence, prevalence and mortality since the 1980s.

5.3 Describe the underlying biology of asthma, the ways in which an asthma attack might be triggered, and how the major types of medical treatment alleviate the symptoms.

5.4 Discuss the major hypotheses about what causes asthma to develop, highlighting areas of uncertainty for future research.

5.5 Illustrate the social and personal impact of asthma on adult patients and the parents of asthmatic children, and describe psychosocial models of how people may cope with the condition.

QUESTIONS FOR CHAPTER 5

1 (*Objective 5.2*)

A number of studies cited in this chapter estimated the prevalence of asthma in children on the basis of their parents' responses to a questionnaire. What reservation must be borne in mind when concluding from studies such as these that childhood asthma has risen over time? If you were designing a research study, how would you go about increasing your confidence that you could detect genuine changes in asthma prevalence rates?

2 (*Objective 5.3*)

Explain why IgE is a prime candidate for research into new treatments for asthma.

3 (*Objective 5.4*)

Atopic asthma is more common among children than among asthmatic adults in Western industrialised countries. How might this phenomenon be explained by the hygiene hypothesis?

4 (*Objective 5.5*)

What sources of financial difficulty might be experienced in a family where an adult or child is severely affected by asthma?

C H A P T E R   6

Schizophrenia

Study notes for OU students

Early in your study of this chapter (Section 6.2.1) you will be asked to listen to an audiotape band entitled 'Hearing voices'. In Section 6.3.5 you will be asked to read an article in *Health and Disease: A Reader* (Open University Press, third edition 2001), entitled 'Cross-cultural psychiatry' by Cecil Helman. A further optional Reader article, 'Media and mental illness' by Gregory Philo, is referred to in Section 6.8. This chapter builds on the discussion of the social construction of disease categories and the consequences for diagnostic uncertainty, which is a major theme of the first book in this series, *Medical Knowledge: Doubt and Certainty* (Open University Press, second edition 1994; colour-enhanced second edition 2001). It was written by Jacqueline Atkinson, a psychologist and Senior Lecturer in the Department of Public Health, University of Glasgow, with Daniel Nettle, Lecturer in Biological Psychology at The Open University.

6.1 Introduction

Schizophrenia probably causes more disquiet than any other disorder. It is found in all societies and, when using the same diagnostic criteria, at very similar rates. In acute episodes it resembles what has traditionally been described as 'madness'. It can be a one-off episode or a severely debilitating lifelong condition. At one time, schizophrenia filled more hospital beds than any other illness, but most patients now spend most of their life in the community and are treated there — a policy that has received almost as much criticism as institutionalisation once did. The cause of schizophrenia is unknown but hotly pursued, spanning genetics and family communication, brain structure and function, viruses and allergies, social pressures and political views. It is a battleground on which the ideological wars surrounding mental illness are fought, with myths and prejudices, disputed facts and opinions raised to the level of doctrine. But it is, most of all, a personal experience. No one approaches a subject like schizophrenia neutrally.

● What is likely to influence your understanding of schizophrenia?

■ A wide variety of factors are possible, including: the type of experience you have of it (for example, do you or does anyone you know have a diagnosis of schizophrenia?); your academic or professional background (for example, do you see yourself primarily as a scientist, a social scientist or a student of the humanities, are you a nurse or a social worker?); information you have gained from the media (for example, portrayals of schizophrenia in newspapers, books, films and television).

A person diagnosed as having schizophrenia will have a different view from the psychiatrist who makes the diagnosis. Family members — whether carers or not — will have yet another perspective, as will the person whose only experience comes from newspaper articles on yet another 'mental patient' attacking a stranger. For most people their only understanding of schizophrenia comes from the media and, as you will see later, this can be a highly misleading picture.

● Write down a list of words that you associate with schizophrenia and a second list of what you think the symptoms are. (This is not intended as a test of knowledge, and will be returned to at the end of the chapter.)

Some of the debates over schizophrenia are a microcosm of wider debates surrounding the nature of science. Science exists in a social context and some people believe the 'facts' that scientists uncover are socially constructed, reflecting the way scientists work, rather than objective truth.[1] Most people engaged in research on schizophrenia are probably psychiatrists, and it can be argued that they are dependent on schizophrenia being an accepted disease classification for the status and power of their profession. Following this line of argument, the psychologist Mary Boyle points out:

> Psychiatrists may not be as free to imagine alternative accounts of bizarre behaviour as were, say, physicists to imagine alternatives to Newton's theory. (Boyle, 1994, p. 403)

---

[1] The social constructionist view of medical knowledge is discussed in *Medical Knowledge: Doubt and Certainty* (Open University Press, 2nd edn 1994; colour-enhanced 2nd edn 2001), Chapter 7.

Whilst this may be true, similar arguments can be applied to others who have built their reputations (and thus, in part at least, their jobs) on attacking the medical concept of schizophrenia — as you will see in Section 6.6.

As you read this chapter you will be encouraged to consider the implications of different views of schizophrenia, since these influence decisions about treatment and management, the kinds of services provided and the wider social view of mental illness. For example, you will learn that there are variable criteria for deciding whether a person should be diagnosed as having schizophrenia. In the USA, diagnostic criteria have important implications because a formal diagnosis is necessary to get insurance coverage. The advice given to politicians and service planners is never neutral; prejudices and assumptions play as much a part as facts, as will be seen later in the chapter in the discussion of community care in the UK. No one can say with absolute certainty what schizophrenia is, what causes it, or how to cure it. There is no single answer to the questions that schizophrenia poses.

6.2 Schizophrenia: a personal experience

6.2.1 The personal perspective

First-hand accounts of people diagnosed as having schizophrenia probably bring us nearer to understanding what 'schizophrenia' means than anything else. Many experiences show similarities, but care should be taken to put reported events — particularly concerning treatment and diagnosis — in their historical context. As you will see later in this chapter, these aspects have changed considerably over time.

The first description is from the audiotape band 'Hearing voices', to which Open University students should now listen.[2] In the tape an account is given by Ron Coleman of his experiences of psychiatric services and a self-help group called *Hearing Voices* after he was diagnosed as having schizophrenia.

● In Section 2.3 of this book the creation of *softer social labels* to counteract stigma was described. How does Ron Coleman's experience reflect this?

■ He was labelled 'schizophrenic' by people in the formal health-care system. When he joined the Hearing Voices group he experienced the change of status to that of 'voice hearer' as helpful. For him, it marked a change towards acceptance by other people, and 'owning' the mental states he experienced, instead of the voices 'owning' him.

The stigma experienced by the person diagnosed as having schizophrenia can be distressing, as can the experience of psychiatric services. The symptoms are also distressing and frequently frightening, as the following account by Mary Barnes suggests:

> When I was bad, time seemed endless. To be able to think that in two, four, six hours, the feeling would lift, was not possible. It was so awful at the time, that there didn't seem to be any before or

---

[2] This audiotape has been recorded for Open University students studying this book as part of an undergraduate course; students should consult the relevant notes in the *Audiovisual Media Guide* before playing the tape.

after. The only possibility was to live one moment at a time. When really bad, I never spoke, knowing the only safe thing was to be very still, going into a sort of half-sleep, stupor state … people might try to talk to me, I knew better than to attempt to reply. Though I might moan or groan. It just had to lift before I could move, without stirring it worse … It, my anger, always did lift. But when caught in its grip I was still, immobile, dead. To me, at this time, IT coming out was very dangerous, it might kill anyone … To suffer myself, to stem my own rebellion, was the fight that at times became so intense within me that I hardly knew how to live with myself. (Barnes and Berke, 1971, pp. 129–30)

Figure 6.1 gives the most compelling insight into the experiences of a person who struggled with the symptoms of schizophrenia for over twenty years. It shows six self-portraits from a series of seventeen, painted by the artist Bryan Charnley between 11 April and 19 July 1991. The notes below each painting are from his diary. He began cutting back on his medication, knowing that he could expect a return of the symptoms of his schizophrenia (diagnosed in 1971), but wanting to work on a series of self-portraits *with* his illness rather than *in spite* of it. On 29 April 1991 he wrote:

The doctors just prescribe more and more drugs when the patient comes up with something he can't handle. What I think is interesting is that the drugs, no matter how high the dosage had no effect. What made the change was rational insight, the truth. The beauty of truth. The doctors of course will mutter the drugs just began to take effect but I do not believe this for an instant. I believe instead that the answer to my condition is rational insight but the doctors seem unwilling, or unable to help me here. Certainly many different schizophrenias exist and some cannot be attacked by rational insight for reason has broken down but why should everybody be lumped in the same druggy boat? I am overwhelmed by things I cannot understand. Understanding what was going on, the truth of the situation, would bring release. (Extract from Bryan Charnley's diary, 29 April 1991, by courtesy of his brother, Terence Charnley)

The impact of schizophrenia extends beyond the individual to the family and can have a devastating effect on those who live with, or care for, the person involved. This is illustrated in an account by Anne Deveson who is a writer, broadcaster and film-maker. Her son, Jonathan, diagnosed as having schizophrenia, died of a drug overdose in 1986 at the age of 24. She writes of her experience:

That same day I went to the Magistrate's Court to make application in person for the restraining order. I had to explain my reason for needing one. The magistrate looked at me over his glasses and said, 'But can't the boy get help? Why isn't he in hospital?' I said tartly that I wished that he would ask the hospital that same question. As I left the court, the police told me that because Jonathan did not have any fixed address, they might be unable to serve the order, which would mean it could not be enforced.

I returned to South Terrace alone, and felt the most terrible desolation. Georgia and Joshua had both been forced to leave home. Security guards were watching the house. Jonathan was still crazy. And I was helpless and frightened.

Figure 6.1 *Six Faces of schizophrenia: from a series of seventeen self-portraits made by Bryan Charnley between 11 April and 19 July 1991; the notes in quotation marks are taken from his diary. (Reproduced by kind permission of Terence Charnley, the artist's brother)*

20 April 1991: 'Very paranoid. The person upstairs was reading my mind and speaking back to me to keep me in a sort of ego crucifixion ... The large rabbit ear is because I was confused and extremely sensitive to human voices, like a wild animal.'

23 April 1991: 'I had come to the conclusion that most people around me had some extra sensory perception ability which gave them access to my mind ... I was like a blind man. Hence the crosses on the eyes. They also let me know verbally what they had picked up from my thoughts.'

18 May 1991: 'My mind seemed to be thought broadcasting very severely and it was beyond my will to do anything about it. I summed this up by painting my brain as an enormous mouth, acting independently of me.'

24 May 1991: 'Perhaps a broken heart is the cause of it all. Certainly it hurts ... The spiders legs on the right are to express my inhibitions and the feeling that comes over me as my thoughts surface and broadcast. Scary. I feel all the time now that I am getting nearer to a more acute expression of my schizophrenia'.

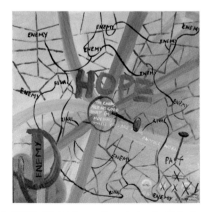

12 July 1991: There is no diary entry for this day. The words under 'HOPE' are adapted from a Bob Dylan song: they read THE CARDS ARE NO GOOD THAT I'M HOLDING UNLESS THEY ARE FROM ANOTHER WORLD.

19 July 1991: There is no diary entry for this day. This painting was on his easel when Bryan Charnley committed suicide on 29 July 1991.

Sometimes I slept at the house out of bravura: I would not be turned out of my own home. But I would wake in the night at the slightest rustle outside. The security guards' torches would flicker through my bedroom window and startle me so I would sit upright, pretending that I wasn't alarmed. Once, when the moon was flying high and I had been woken by a possum — or was it a cat? or was it my errant son? — I marched through the house in my bare feet shouting, 'Go away, Jonathan, go away! Leave me alone, Jonathan, leave me alone.' As I clambered back into bed I thought ironically of all those statements about mothers who clung to their children and would not cut the umbilical cord. God, I'd cut it, burn it, blow it up — anything to get rid of this burden that would never give me peace, and which left me so exhausted I did not know how I could face each day.

... February 1986. I began this year with a sense of profound melancholia. I felt haunted by the need to find some way of stopping Jonathan's deterioration but, because of my heavy work-load, I had little time to start another round of 'saving Jonathan'. It may sound foolish to write about 'saving Jonathan' after all those other abortive attempts but Jonathan needed saving.

... Now, so many years later when people say, 'But I don't know how you stood it', the answer is that you stand it because you have no option. You do hang on, precariously, to any small ledges of hope. You cling with your finger-nails, with your breath tightly held, and you cling, you bloody well cling. (Deveson, 1992, pp. 175, 245–7)

These passages give some indication of how devastating schizophrenia can be, not only to individuals but also to their families, but it would be wrong to suggest that the experience is always wholly bad, as some of the accounts on the audiotape revealed. Another positive example comes from Mark Vonnegut, son of the novelist Kurt Vonnegut, Jr., who was hospitalised in 1971, in Vancouver, with a diagnosis of schizophrenia. His book about his experience closes thus:

As well as being one of the worst things that can happen to a human being, schizophrenia can also be one of the richest and humanizing experiences life offers. Although it won't do much toward improving your condition, the ins and outs of your bout with schizophrenia are well worth figuring out. But if you concentrate on getting well for now, and come back to puzzling things out later, I guarantee you'll do a better job of it. Being crazy and being mistaken are not at all the same. The things in life that are upsetting you are more than likely things well worth being upset about. It is, however, possible to be upset without being crippled, and even to act effectively against those things ... There are great insights to be gained from schizophrenia, but remember that they won't do you or anyone else much good unless you recover. (Vonnegut, 1979, p. 274)

6.2.2 The user groups' perspective

Experience with schizophrenia and the psychiatric services has led some people to write their story. It has led many more to become involved in the **user movement**, a term that emerged in the 1990s to cover users of health and social-care services across a wide spectrum of conditions. In the mental health field, probably the best known user organisation in Britain is MIND (National Association for Mental Health), but there are many other national and local groups. **Empowerment** is a common goal for all, reflected in the emphasis in most organisations on issues of advocacy,[3] education and a right to define members' problems in their own way, including the use of their own 'labels'.

Labels may focus on a particular experience, as does the term 'voice hearer'. This does not replace a diagnosis, since everyone who hears voices would not receive a diagnosis of schizophrenia and everyone diagnosed as having schizophrenia does not hear voices. It does, however, remove the experience from the realm of medicine and offers other approaches to living with it. Other labels focus on current status, as does the term *survivor* (of the system or of the illness) used by the group Survivors Speak Out. Still others stay with the diagnosis (for example, the Manic-Depression Fellowship).

Mike Lawson, writing in 1991, when he was a director of International Self-Advocacy Alliance, vice-chair of MIND and an active member of Survivors Speak Out, reflects the political aspects common to much of the user movement:

> Power cannot be given, only advocacy and self-advocacy can ensure it is not taken away. Psychiatry is a sanctioned licence to remove power; self-advocacy and advocacy challenge and redress that imbalance. Power is essential to function and gain some autonomy and we regain our power through self-advocacy and advocacy …
>
> Reintegration does not mean to us taking on the values of the existing society. It means being able to function within that society, having a voice there, being heard and being able to work for change without persecution … The focus is moving to the political systems that oppress us rather than the individual who responds to that oppression in ways that are seen as 'sick'. (Lawson, 1991, pp. 69, 79)

● How does this perspective compare with the 'politics of disability' as discussed in Chapter 2 of this book?

■ The disavowal of 'disability' as a stigmatising label has involved identifying the cause of disability as being the physical and social environment, rather than the physical impairments of 'disabled' individuals.

Ron Coleman, whom you heard on the audiotape band 'Hearing voices', has written from a slightly different position to that of Lawson:

> I now had an understanding of why the voices were there, I was learning to accept that the voices might never go … I was still prone to being 'mad' at regular intervals and my life was still chaotic … My great self-discovery was that I still acted like a schizophrenic, I had given up the drugs but not the character … I was still a victim of my diagnosis … I realised that from then on I would have to accept responsibility for my own life, that I had to give up being a victim … I would find out all sorts of things about

---

[3] Advocacy involves volunteers or paid professional advocates who support health and social-services clients in obtaining appropriate care; it is discussed further in *Dilemmas in UK Health Care* (Open University Press, 3rd edn 2001), Chapter 4.

myself, including many that I would not like. For example, I discovered that I had used hospital as a bolt hole as soon as things got tough. I had also used my 'illness' as an excuse for some disgusting behaviour both on and off the ward. My illness was my power, it was the only power I had and, boy, did I learn to use it. (Coleman, 1995, p. 17)

● How does Ron Coleman's position differ from that of Mike Lawson?

■ Lawson is concerned to change external 'oppression', which he sees as responsible for the persecution of the people he represents. Coleman (while the audiotape shows him to be critical of the psychiatric system) is also concerned to change himself.

The changes initiated by the purchaser–provider split in the NHS[4] mean that most larger user organisations in the UK, are also now involved in providing services. This dual role poses a potential conflict of interests if a campaigning organisation is simultaneously highlighting the shortcomings of health and social service provision for users and carers, while bidding to the commissioners of those services for contracts of its own. Vociferous campaigning may not be acceptable in a service provider and, as charities, voluntary organisations are prohibited from any campaigning that is 'political'. Apparently straightforward projects may still be contentious. For example MIND's Yellow Card scheme encourages people taking prescribed drugs to report harmful effects to MIND, which then passes this information on to the Committee on Safety of Medicines. Doctors are supposed to report harmful effects through official 'yellow cards', but few returns are received, and MIND's scheme is intended to encourage awareness of such effects. It has, however, been criticised by some psychiatrists.

The National Schizophrenia Fellowship also provides services, running many drop-in centres and some of the very few respite services for people with mental health problems and for their carers. It has been actively campaigning for better community services to be in place when hospital beds are closed. It differs from other user groups in that it is an organisation predominately for carers, although most services are for users. This has, at times, led to tensions between the organisation and some user groups. Throughout the world, groups exist for carers of people diagnosed as having schizophrenia which have taken the National Schizophrenia Fellowship as their model.

SANE (Schizophrenia: A National Emergency) is neither part of the user nor carer movement. Started and run by the journalist Marjorie Wallace (Patron: HRH the Prince of Wales) it seeks to campaign in the media on various issues related to schizophrenia and mental illness. The organisation has repeatedly called for halts in the closure of mental hospitals, at least until more community services are in place. It also raises considerable sums for research and runs a telephone help line (Saneline). With no public funding (unlike, for example, both MIND and the National Schizophrenia Fellowship), all its funds come from private donations, industry and commerce and fund-raising events. In the 1980s it was involved in a dispute with MIND over the nature of one of its campaigns, which was seen as stigmatising people diagnosed as having schizophrenia.

[4] The internal market in health care which began in 1991 in the UK health system, and the shift to local commissioning of services after 1999, are discussed in *Caring for Health: History and Diversity* (Open University Press, 3rd edn 2001), Chapter 7.

As the views of consumers are increasingly sought by policy makers, providers and commissioners of health services, so user and carer organisations are solicited for their opinion. How representative their views are is open to debate but, since neither users nor carers are homogenous groups, a variety of opinions should be expected. Both the personal experiences of individuals and the political perspectives of users' and carers' organisations demonstrate diversity. They all, however, have in common the experience of living in a world where orthodox medical and scientific views of schizophrenia exert a powerful influence over peoples' thinking — even if this ultimately leads some people to reject the medical viewpoint. For this reason, in the next two sections of this chapter we seek an understanding of the medical and scientific view of schizophrenia, starting with the contribution of epidemiology.

6.3 Schizophrenia: a worldwide experience

6.3.1 Diagnostic differences between countries

Throughout this chapter the unfolding story of schizophrenia is one of claim and counterclaim, and epidemiological studies of schizophrenia are no exception. Studies are complicated by the problems surrounding cross-cultural definitions of the condition (note the similarities with difficulties in standardising asthma diagnoses, discussed in Chapter 5).

International research is dominated by the *International Pilot Study of Schizophrenia* (*IPSS*) which began in 1968. It was organised by the World Health Organisation and first reported in 1973 (WHO, 1973). The IPSS studied 1202 patients in nine centres: Aarhus (Denmark), Agra (India), Cali (Colombia), Ibadan (Nigeria), London (UK), Moscow (then in the USSR), Prague (then in Czechoslovakia), Taipei (Taiwan) and Washington DC (USA). Psychiatrists used an interview schedule called the *Present State Examination* (*PSE*) to interview and diagnose patients. The PSE is designed to ensure that patients are asked the same kinds of questions and the same significance is given to their responses. A computer program (called *Catego*) was developed to apply the same diagnostic rules to all information obtained by the psychiatrists, resulting in consistent diagnostic decisions.

One major and fairly controversial finding from this study was that the *core symptoms* of schizophrenia (discussed in the next section) are found with similar frequency throughout the world. Less surprising was the finding that there were differences in the way schizophrenia was diagnosed in different places. Since the PSE and Catego were developed in London it was to be expected that there would be good agreement between British psychiatrists and the diagnostic programme. In fact only two centres diagnosed schizophrenia substantially differently from the programme — Washington and Moscow. Both diagnosed *more* people as having schizophrenia, but for different reasons.

In the 1970s, American psychiatry — including diagnostic practice — was heavily influenced by psychoanalysis and the **psychodynamic approach**. This approach emphasises drives and motives and describes non-observable, unconscious processes within the mind as having an active influence or control on current behaviour, thought and emotion.[5] Such *intra-psychic* functions are inferred from symptoms, and greater emphasis is given to them than to the symptoms themselves. The

---

[5] The psychodynamic approach is described further in *Birth to Old Age: Health in Transition* (Open University Press, 2nd edn 1995; colour-enhanced 2nd edn 2001), Chapter 6.

psychodynamic approach led to a much broader definition of schizophrenia in the USA than that used in the UK. Many of the patients diagnosed as having schizophrenia in Washington would have been labelled 'neurotic' in London.

In contrast, in Moscow an approach to schizophrenia had developed that emphasised the course of the illness, and the level of *social adjustment* between episodes, more than the symptoms themselves. Thus the social component of the illness played a significant part in the diagnostic process in Moscow, which was not evident elsewhere. Clearly, there are opportunities for abuse of this emphasis in societies where deviations from the cultural norm are poorly tolerated. However, the IPSS only looked at diagnostic practice in Moscow, in clinicians trained in one particular school of psychiatry. There was evidence that elsewhere (Leningrad, now St Petersburg, for example) diagnostic practice was much closer to that in the UK.

Diagnostic practice has since changed in the USA, with the use of observable symptoms now being advocated, rather than psychodynamic concepts. The American Psychiatric Association in 1980 announced this official change with the publication of a new classification system for mental disorder (a more recent version of this system, DSM IV, is described later in this chapter, in Section 6.4). However, it takes time for diagnostic practices to change in the clinical setting and this, plus the time involved both to carry out and publish research, means that care must be taken when extrapolating from American data to British circumstances — particularly before about the mid-1980s. There are also variations *within* countries that depend on where a psychiatrist was trained and his or her age.

6.3.2 Effects of 'culture' on outcomes?

The second major finding subsequently to come out of the IPSS, which caused initial surprise, was that the *course* of schizophrenia, or its outcome, was better in what were described as the 'developing' countries compared with the 'developed'. Subsequent research has confirmed this finding, and the WHO has sought to determine the reasons (Jablensky *et al.*, 1992). The difference, it was concluded, was due to cultural features in developing countries: less reliance on medication, less pressure in rural societies, which have a place for people with mental illness in the work force, and the role and support of the extended family, were all seen as important.

These findings have been challenged, however, by researchers who question the methodology and highlight the many inherent difficulties in measuring, translating and comparing 'cultures' (for example, the work of American psychiatrists Robert Edgerton and Alex Cohen, 1994). The heterogeneity of centres in both 'developed' and 'developing' countries, is pointed out, along with the fact that many of the centres in the developing countries were predominately urban (the assumption usually being made that they are rural).

Edgerton and Cohen suggest that *gender* can explain most of the differences in outcome. Gender is a good predictor of outcome almost everywhere, with women having a milder course to their illness and a better prognosis than men, but gender differences are more than three times greater in developing countries. The explanation for this is unclear, but one possibility is that cultural factors may 'buffer' women from the most severe expressions of schizophrenia. Other studies point to family responses to the patient (Leff *et al.*, 1990), a topic that will be returned to later in this chapter.

Concentrating on the difference between Western and non-Western, or industrialised and non-industrialised countries, ignores the fact that everywhere schizophrenia can follow different courses with widely different outcomes. In industrialised societies approximately 30 per cent of people diagnosed as having schizophrenia remain chronically disabled, which is the same percentage as typically reported in non-industrialised societies. Even for these patients there can be a levelling-off process and a degree of recovery. For people experiencing a first episode of schizophrenia, a quarter in the West recover and remain well, compared with a half in developing countries.

6.3.3 The global picture

The WHO study mentioned earlier (Jablensky *et al.*, 1992) indicates rates of schizophrenia based on two definitions, the first being a *broad* definition (incorporating many symptoms), the second being *narrow* (incorporating fewer symptoms). The centre studied in Britain was Nottingham. What the researchers called *morbid risk* (the likelihood of developing the condition between the ages of 15 and 54 years) was given as 0.8 per cent for males and females combined in Nottingham, using the broad definition (i.e. 8 people per 1 000 in this age group can be expected to develop schizophrenia). Further details of Nottingham and the other centres are given in Table 6.1.

Table 6.1 Morbid risk (%) for age 15–54 years by broad and narrow case definition for schizophrenia.

	Broad definition			Narrow definition		
	male %	female %	all %	male %	female %	all %
Aarhus	0.68	0.51	0.59	0.33	0.20	0.27
Chandigarh (rural)	1.48	2.03	1.72	0.54	0.40	0.48
Chandigarh (urban)	1.04	1.21	1.10	0.22	0.42	0.30
Dublin	0.85	0.80	0.83	0.31	0.32	0.32
Honolulu	0.55	0.47	0.50	0.27	0.26	0.26
Moscow	1.08	1.17	1.13	0.39	0.54	0.47
Nagasaki	0.79	0.65	0.72	0.39	0.34	0.37
Nottingham	0.98	0.62	0.80	0.60	0.47	0.54

Source: Adapted from Jablensky *et al.* (1992) Schizophrenia: manifestation, incidence and course in different cultures, *Psychological Medicine*, monograph supplement 20.

● What do the data in Table 6.1 show? Look first at the broad definition, then the narrow definition, and finally consider gender differences.

■ Rates for males and females combined ('all'), using the broad definition, suggest that people are at the highest risk of developing schizophrenia in rural Chandigarh and at the lowest in Honolulu. The international differences are less marked for the narrow definition (in fact, they are only statistically significant for the broad definition). Far fewer people are diagnosed with schizophrenia under the narrow definition. Gender differences show a mixed pattern in different countries.

There are, then, some differences in rates between countries and between sexes, but more important is the impact of the *definition* on numbers. This indicates how important it is to know the definition of schizophrenia being used before trying to compare or interpret data in schizophrenia research. (Later in this chapter, Open University students will be referred to an article by Cecil Helman in *Health and Disease: A Reader* (Open University Press, 3rd edn 2001), which gives further examples of diagnostic differences between psychiatrists in the UK, USA, France and the former Soviet Union.)

6.3.4 Schizophrenia in the UK and Ireland

The low priority generally given to research in psychiatry is nowhere more evident than in the epidemiology of schizophrenia. Few large-scale studies have been conducted and methodological problems abound. The media frequently report that the lifetime risk of developing schizophrenia in Western populations is 1 in 100. In fact it is slightly under this in the UK and further translating this easily remembered statistic into meaningful prevalence estimates is beset with problems.

The general consensus is that the prevalence of schizophrenia in the UK is stable over time. This is in contrast to some other mental illnesses, like depression and eating disorders, for which there are rising rates of diagnosis. However, even establishing the stability of the diagnosis of schizophrenia is not straightforward. Figure 6.2 shows the number of episodes of treatment within England's National Health Service (NHS), diagnosed as schizophrenia between 1990 and 1998.

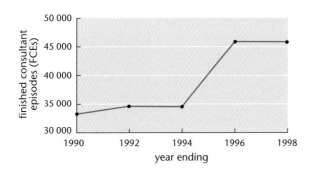

● What does the sharp rise between 1994 and 1996 in Figure 6.2 suggest?

■ This pattern is unlike the constant slight increase of a disease whose prevalence is genuinely on the increase. More likely, some change in the way schizophrenia is recorded and classified occurred between 1994 and 1996, which led to a greater number of cases receiving the schizophrenia 'label'.

Figure 6.2 *Treated episodes of schizophrenia in NHS hospitals in England, 1990–98. Note 'episodes' of in-patient stay exceed the number of patients, since some will be admitted more than once in a year. (Based on data from the* Hospital Episode Statistics System, *supplied by the Department of Health, personal communication)*

The international classification system for diseases and disabilities changed for some conditions in 1993, when the tenth revision of this system (called ICD-10) was published.[6] In ICD-10, the classification of the core diagnostic criteria for schizophrenia altered and disorders at its margin were included under this disease category for the first time. The effect of this *diagnostic transfer* on the apparent prevalence of schizophrenia is illustrated in Figure 6.2, providing a further illustration of the effect that changes in diagnostic criteria can have on disease rates. (In Chapters 4 and 5, a similar point was made in relation to HIV/AIDS and asthma.)

[6] This classification system is still known as 'ICD' reflecting its original title, the *International Classification of Diseases* which applied up to ICD-9; however, the 10th revision took a new title, the *International Statistical Classification of Diseases and Related Health Problems*. Note that ICD-10 was not adopted in the UK for many conditions — including asthma — until 2001.

Disease rates at the population level cannot reveal much about possible risk factors for different groups, distinguished for example on the basis of demographic variables such as age, sex and social class, or a whole range of other factors. The OPCS (Office for Population Censuses and Surveys) carried out a series of surveys in 1993 and 1994 into psychiatric morbidity in Britain. The first report to be published (OPCS, 1995) concerned 10 000 adults aged between 16 and 64 years, living in private households.

Since the number of people diagnosed as having schizophrenia was small, people with this diagnosis were grouped together with people having other diagnoses of mental disorder, including *manic-depressive psychosis* and *schizo-affective disorder* (together commonly termed the **functional psychoses**). This spectrum of related disorders had a yearly prevalence rate[7] of 4 per 1 000, with no difference between the sexes. Prevalence rates showed only small differences with age, but were highest in 30–34-year-old women and 55–64-year-old men.

Increased prevalence of functional psychoses in men was statistically associated with being widowed, being economically inactive (i.e. not seeking work) and living alone. Increased prevalence in women was associated with being divorced, unemployed (which includes those who are 'looking after the home or family') and being a lone parent. In both sexes, increased prevalence was associated with having educational qualifications of 'A' level or above, being in social class V, living in rented accommodation and living in a flat (which includes a room in a house or a bed-sit). Psychoses, along with most other mental disorders, were twice as prevalent in urban as in rural populations.

●   Do these associations suggest that the factors identified by the OPCS study *cause* psychoses? Explain why or why not.

■   A statistical association cannot prove causality. It cannot rule out the possibility that some other factor is *confounding* the result by independently increasing the risk of schizophrenia *and* increasing the risk of (for example) being unemployed or divorced. It is also possible that the pattern of social and demographic factors identified in the OPCS study are a *result* of mental illness.[8]

The association between schizophrenia and low social class is difficult to disentangle, as the following study illustrates. Mulvany *et al.* (2001) investigated the relationship in people diagnosed with schizophrenia in Dublin, compared with matched controls. The occupational social class of each patients' father was used as the class indicator, in view of the relatively young age of onset of schizophrenia. They found no increased risk of developing the condition in the lower social classes, and in fact there was a slight increased risk of schizophrenia in the highest social-class group. However, the main finding was in the age at which people first presented for treatment. For patients whose father was in the highest social class, the average age of first hospital admission for schizophrenia was 24.8 years, compared with 33.1 years for those whose father was in the lowest social class. There was no evidence that the age of onset of schizophrenia differed between social classes.

---

[7] In this study, prevalence was estimated during a *period* of a year (rather than a *point*, such as a day) because the prevalence of these disorders is so low. Period prevalence was discussed in Chapter 5 of this book.

[8] The difference between causal relationships and associations, and the issue of causal direction, are explored more fully in *Studying Health and Disease* (Open University Press, 2nd edn 1994; colour-enhanced 2nd edn 2001), Chapters 5 and 8.

● What do these results suggest might be contributing to the greater prevalence of schizophrenic illness among people in lower social classes in most population studies?

■ In the Dublin study, there seems to be a delay of (on average) 8 years in commencing treatment when the affected person comes from a household in the lowest social class compared with those in the highest social class. Earlier treatment may give a better chance of recovery, so treatment delay may contribute to the poorer outcome among people with schizophrenia in lower social classes.

6.3.5 Cross-cultural diagnosis in the UK

Within multicultural societies, there are particular difficulties with the diagnosis of mental illnesses. At this point, students of the Open University should read the article by Cecil Helman entitled 'Cross-cultural psychiatry', which appears in *Health and Disease: A Reader* (Open University Press, 3rd edn 2001).

● According to the research cited by Helman, what may influence the perceptions of psychiatrists considering a diagnosis of mental illness in people from a different cultural tradition?

■ Initial diagnosis could be made wrongly without consideration of cultural differences. The experiences and beliefs that count as bizarre in one cultural context might not be considered abnormal in another. It is therefore important for the psychiatrist to distinguish between controlled, socially sanctioned beliefs and experiences within the patient's culture, and uncontrolled, socially abnormal beliefs and experiences.

In the UK, African-Caribbean people have higher rates of diagnosed schizophrenia than do the white population. The rate among African-Caribbeans born in the UK is even higher than for immigrants (Helman cites one study in which it was nine times greater). This 'excess' of schizophrenia does not occur in other ethnic groups, for example the Asian population. There is no convincing evidence that differences in the prevalence of the disorder stem from differences in genetic predisposition between the ethnic groups. The determinants are much more likely to be environmental.

One possibility is that the effect is *indirectly* connected with ethnicity, mediated through other social factors that are also concentrated in the African-Caribbean population. For example, the African-Caribbean population is mainly an urban one, and schizophrenia is more common in urban than in rural areas. People diagnosed with schizophrenia are concentrated in the lower socio-economic classes, and the African-Caribbean population is still economically disadvantaged in the UK. Thus it could be that the apparent ethnicity effect is really an effect of social deprivation, which overlaps with ethnic origin. Thus, one interpretation of the schizophrenia excess is what Littlewood and Lipsedge (1989, quoted in the Reader article by Helman) refer to as psychiatrists 'disguising disadvantage as disease'.

However, this interpretation is not straightforward, since the association between lower social class and schizophrenia may be largely a *consequence* of the disease, rather than its cause.

● How might a concentration of schizophrenia in people in lower social classes come about as a result of the disease?

■ People with schizophrenia-related problems have difficulties in jobs and education. They often end up in sporadic or unskilled jobs, or unemployed, and thus are judged to be in low social classes. Drifting down the social scale as a consequence of chronic illness is an example of *social selection*.[9]

There is not much evidence that low social class of origin (i.e. the parents' social class) makes the disease more likely. In fact there are many cases of schizophrenia coming from the professional classes. Thus, the fact that many African-Caribbeans come from lower social classes seems unlikely to constitute a sufficient explanation for their excess of schizophrenia.

It has been suggested that the experience of being part of a disadvantaged minority in society is a stressor that could precipitate schizophrenia (Eaton and Harrison, 2000). This hypothesis has gained support from studies showing that the prevalence of mental health problems in ethnic minorities is affected by the local density of people of that ethnicity. Where a neighbourhood contains a high density of members of a minority group, mental health problems are rarer than where there are only a few members of that minority (Halpern and Nazroo, 2000). This effect has been demonstrated for schizophrenia among people of African-Caribbean and African origin at the level of electoral wards in South London (Boydell *et al.*, 2001), and presumably reflects the negative effects of lacking social support and 'feeling different'.

These studies also suggest, ironically, that those African-Caribbeans who move to more affluent neighbourhoods (where their concentration is lower), risk experiencing worse mental health than those in poorer areas — the opposite of the pattern seen in the white community. It may also partly explain the excess of psychiatric problems in the African-Caribbean, as opposed to the Asian population, as the latter is much more clustered geographically within the UK.

Finally, to return to the themes raised by Cecil Helman in the Reader article, it is also possible that the excess of African-Caribbean schizophrenia is the result of diagnostic practices as much as objective illness. Young black men are more likely than whites to be detained involuntarily under the Mental Health Act, and more likely than whites to be given a diagnosis of schizophrenia (Koffman *et al.*, 1997). This is despite the fact that studies that have looked within the community at the prevalence of symptoms that might be considered indicative of schizophrenia have not found a strong association with ethnicity.

● Consider the preceding discussion and the article by Helman: sum up why there might be an over-representation of schizophrenia among people from ethnic minorities in the UK.

■ Cultural differences may lead to the labelling of behaviour that seems 'odd' as illness. The psychiatrist fits the patient's experience into that of Western medicine, which is compounded by the effects of indirect discrimination regarding treatment. Furthermore, mental illness may be precipitated by material deprivation, social isolation and social difference, all of which are

[9] Social selection as one explanation for social class differences in health are discussed in *World Health and Disease* (Open University Press, 3rd edn, 2001), Chapter 10.

disproportionately common in the experience of ethnic minorities. A further possibility not yet investigated, is that delay in seeking treatment among certain ethnic groups may be a factor (as in Mulvany *et al.*'s study of social-class effects).

In summary, epidemiologists who try to measure schizophrenia are beset by many problems of definition. These arise for various reasons, notably the difficulties in agreeing stable diagnostic criteria that can be applied across time and cultures in an unbiased way, and the difficulties of interpreting trends in official statistics. Difficulties with diagnosis are also experienced by clinicians even when faced with a patient from the same culture and background as the doctor, and it is to clinical diagnosis that we now turn.

6.4   Schizophrenia: a clinical entity

Schizophrenia is both an individual experience and a defined clinical entity and, as such, can be understood as both an illness and a disease.[10] If we examine the concept historically we can say either that schizophrenia *itself* has changed or that the *description* of schizophrenia has changed: the two statements make different assumptions. In this section the way in which clinicians have attempted to describe schizophrenia as a disease will be outlined.

When the German psychiatrist Emile Kraepelin developed his classification of mental disorders at the end of the nineteenth century, he introduced the term *dementia praecox* to describe a severe, chronic, deteriorating condition (dementia) that started early in life (praecox). This concept of the disorder was redefined by the Swiss psychiatrist Eugen Bleuler in 1911 (translated 1950), who coined the term **schizophrenia** (from the Greek words for 'split mind' to signify a splitting off from reality). Bleuler altered Kraepelin's original description to reflect the observation that the outcome was not always negative, but the term has created the misleading public impression that people diagnosed as having schizophrenia tend to switch between two 'personalities', one apparently normal and the other violent. (We return to the misrepresentation of schizophrenia in public opinion at the end of this chapter.)

Since Bleuler's time, the description of schizophrenia has undergone numerous revisions, and thus descriptions of the illness and research on it as a clinical entity must be put in an historical and geographical context. Some people have taken the position that schizophrenia did not exist before industrialisation, claiming that it is a modern illness caused by the pressures of modern living. This is, however, a rather extreme view. More likely schizophrenia did exist — clear descriptions of psychoses exist in earlier centuries — but it could have been described differently and/or included in other conditions. Descriptions of the conditions that are now called catatonia and dementia, for example, have existed for much longer than these medical labels. It is not uncommon in other areas of medicine for apparently new diseases to emerge, just as in the early 1980s AIDS was diagnosed, apparently for the first time (Chapter 4 of this book), but it had probably existed in Africa for decades as 'slim disease'.

[10] The distinction between illness and disease was discussed in Chapter 1 of this book, and more extensively in *Medical Knowledge: Doubt and Certainty* (Open University Press, 2nd edn 1994; colour-enhanced 2nd edn 2001), Chapter 2.

6.4.1 Symptoms of schizophrenia

There is clearly a necessity to describe a set of **core symptoms** that always indicate schizophrenia. However, finding symptoms that are both necessary and sufficient to diagnose schizophrenia is no easy task.[11] Of importance today are two major classification systems, known as DSM IV and ICD-10. DSM IV is the *Diagnostic and Statistical Manual of Mental Disorders*, fourth revision (published by the American Psychiatric Association, 1994), and is the system developed in the USA. We mentioned ICD-10 earlier in the chapter; the *International Statistical Classification of Diseases and Related Health Problems*, tenth revision (published by WHO, 1993), is used more in Britain and elsewhere in Europe. For research purposes, however, DSM IV has proved to be more popular, although ICD-10 is intended to be used for cross-cultural work.

Both systems describe schizophrenia as a disease in which aspects of the person's thinking, perception and personality become distorted, the central aspect of which is a distortion of reality. The person experiences difficulty in distinguishing between their internal subjective experiences and the external, 'real' or objective world, as their normal mental processes break down. ICD-10 describes this:

> The disturbance involves the most basic functions that give the normal person a feeling of individuality, uniqueness and self-direction. (WHO, 1993, p. 86)

Central to this disturbance are such experiences as *hallucinations*, which may occur in any of the senses. The most common are auditory hallucinations, often in the form of voices giving a running commentary on the person's behaviour or discussing the individual between themselves. These voices often threaten or make commands. *Delusions* may also occur, defined as an unshakeable belief that is considered false or bizarre in the surrounding social context. It may be something completely impossible, for example when a person describes him or herself as being controlled by rays from outer space, or more mundane and plausible, such as the mistaken belief in a partner's infidelity. The person may see him or herself as pivotal in all that is happening, and ordinary insignificant events have enormous personal meaning. Delusions of persecution are common, such as the person believing that MI5 or the KGB is out to get him. In these cases, the schizophrenia may be described as *paranoid*.

A third category of symptom is known as *thought disorder*. The person's thinking looks to others to be vague, inconsistent, following a non-linear path (called *knight's move thinking*) and is generally obscure, resulting in incoherent or irrelevant speech. This can be compounded by the introduction of new words made up by the individual (*neologisms*), or even a new written language (Figure 6.3 overleaf). The senses may be disturbed to make colours or sounds seem peculiarly vivid or altered in some way, and trivial features of objects, situations or concepts become more important than the whole. *Catatonic* behaviour, which includes bizarre movement disturbances, may be present. Inappropriate emotions may occur, for example laughing when sad or at serious moments.

Hallucination, delusion and thought disorder make up the so-called **positive symptoms** of schizophrenia. They are 'positive' in the sense that they *add* something to normal experience in such a way as to make it unreal and confused.

---

[11] Similar problems beset the diagnostic criteria for hysteria, as explained in *Medical Knowledge: Doubt and Certainty* (Open University Press, 2nd edn 1994; colour-enhanced 2nd edn 2001), Chapter 6.

Figure 6.3 *Writing produced by a person diagnosed as having schizophrenia. (Source: Curran, D. and Partridge, M., 1969,* Psychological Medicine, *Churchill Livingstone)*

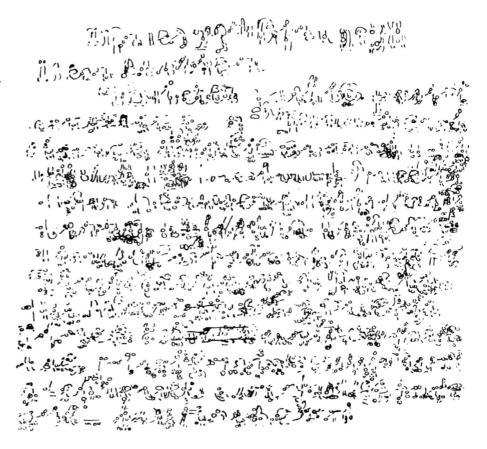

The **negative symptoms**, on the other hand, represent a *lack* of normal behaviour. They include *apathy* and *lack of motivation* which show themselves as loss of interest, aimlessness and what some family members may see as 'laziness'. Speech may be slow and lacking in content, and the individual becomes self-absorbed. The person may exhibit *emotional blunting* in that they no longer express the full range of human emotions. Not surprisingly all this can lead to social withdrawal and lowering of social performance. It is these negative symptoms, which are seen to alter the personality of the individual, that are possibly the most distressing for the person with the illness and their family and friends. Intellectual capacity is not affected, although performance may be, as a consequence of the behaviour described above and problems with concentration and memory.

Schizophrenia need not follow a chronic or deteriorating course as was once believed inevitable. It varies from complete (or very nearly complete) recovery to a continuous illness, or the illness may involve episodic acute relapses with a greater or lesser degree of deficit due to negative symptoms.

The description of schizophrenia as a clinical entity thus sets out to categorise a variety of behaviours as symptoms and to find in them some recognisable pattern, which can then be treated systematically. Once the core symptoms of schizophrenia have been defined, the question then arises whether it is both valid and reliable as a clinical entity. It is certainly true that the presentation of schizophrenia varies greatly from person to person. It is also true that the symptoms, considered singly, are not unique to schizophrenia. Sporadic hallucination, for example, is quite common amongst those who are stressed, ill in other ways, or under the influence of drugs, and is also found amongst otherwise healthy people. Disordered thought and negative symptoms are clearly continua rather than clear discontinuities between schizophrenia and normality. There is no single test, either psychological or biological, that divides everyone with schizophrenia from everyone else. Nonetheless, most psychiatrists believe that the set of core symptoms, taken together, delineate a robust and valid clinical entity.

6.4.2 Schizophrenia: a neurological entity?

Part of the mystery of schizophrenia is the difficulty in understanding how such strange phenomena as hallucinations can suddenly occur, without the brain being damaged, in a person who has been functioning 'normally' for decades. Much of the problem people have had in thinking about schizophrenia stems from the notion that the bizarre thought process or behaviour is a sudden aberration, without immediate cause, in a previously healthy and articulate person.

Since the early 1990s, however, evidence has been amassing that for most cases of schizophrenia, there is lifelong, if subtle, neurological impairment. A study by Elaine Walker and her colleagues at Emory University, found that those who would go on to develop schizophrenia could be reliably identified from the home videos their parents had filmed, even though the schizophrenia was typically not diagnosed for another twenty years (Walker and Levine, 1990). In this and other more recent studies, those who later developed schizophrenia were generally found to be clumsy, to have delays reaching developmental and scholastic milestones (like the onset of speech and motor control), to perform poorly in IQ tests and at school, and to be impaired in problem-solving tasks that require sustained attention.

Researchers have consistently found that differences such as these between people who go on to develop schizophrenia, and those who do not, have already emerged in the first few years of life. These findings led to the formulation of what is known as the **neurodevelopmental hypothesis** of schizophrenia. This states that the pathology is an abnormal trajectory of development of the nervous system, starting at birth or even before, of which hallucination and delusion are just two rather extreme manifestations. The neurodevelopmental hypothesis does not *explain* schizophrenia so much as give us a new way of thinking about it.

●   What aspects of schizophrenia does the neurodevelopmental hypothesis fail to explain?

■   Developmental delays, motor problems and cognitive deficits occur in many people from an early age, most of whom do not go on to develop schizophrenia. In other words, none of the neurodevelopmental problems of people diagnosed with schizophrenia are specific to this condition, so we still need an account of why some but not all of those who show them go on to experience hallucinations, delusions and the other classical symptoms.

Nonetheless, the neurodevelopmental hypothesis marks an important shift in scientific thinking about schizophrenia. Instead of hallucination and delusion being the iceberg whose sudden appearance in warm seas we have to explain, they are seen as the tip of a lifelong trajectory of impaired development of the nervous system. However, thinking of schizophrenia as a disorder of nervous-system development does not explain why this abnormal trajectory of development occurs in the first place.

6.5 Explaining schizophrenia

There are, across the world, thousands of researchers looking for the cause of schizophrenia. Over 2 000 new articles appear in the scientific literature each year. So far, although many theories have been proposed — the major contenders are discussed below — none explains everything about its aetiology. There are suggestions, hypotheses, 'facts' which seem to hold true for a while before being succeeded by new explanations and different 'facts'. Researchers as diverse as geneticists and sociologists contribute their ideas. Others look less for the cause and concentrate on factors that seem to influence the course and outcome of the illness. Whatever the approach, care must be taken not to confuse statistical associations with evidence of causal connections.

Individual researchers have their own preferred approaches to explaining schizophrenia, but it is fair to say that it is unlikely that any 'single factor' theory will ever be adequate. Many factors conspire to lead to schizophrenia, and it is possible that the set of factors will vary from person to person. The only point on which all researchers can agree is that however much research is already being done, more is needed.

6.5.1 Genetic approaches

An hereditary factor in schizophrenia was suggested by Kraepelin at the very dawn of schizophrenia research at the end of the nineteenth century, but at that time genetic knowledge was not advanced enough to allow genes associated with specific diseases to be identified. Since the 1980s, with genetic techniques advancing rapidly, many research groups have searched for genetic variants that might be carried by people who develop schizophrenia. Though as many as a dozen different candidate genes have been proposed, none has been shown to be present in all and only those in whom the disorder is diagnosed.

Nonetheless, there must be a role for genes in schizophrenia. People who are close kin to someone diagnosed as having schizophrenia have a far greater lifetime risk of developing the illness than the risk for the general population. A synthesis of the evidence from family studies is shown in Figure 6.4. The risk of the disease increases dramatically from around 1 per cent of people with no schizophrenic relatives, to around 9 per cent with one schizophrenic sibling, to almost 50 per cent with a schizophrenic identical twin. Such a pattern strongly suggests an hereditary factor is involved. This conclusion is further reinforced by the fact that adopted children show a pattern of risk that corresponds to their biological rather than their adopting families, even if they have been removed from their biological parents within hours of birth.

However, the pattern of inheritance from one generation to the next is incompatible with the action of a single faulty gene, as is found in cystic fibrosis or Huntington's disease.[12] In schizophrenia, it is more likely that many genetic factors combine to give everyone a level of risk, from very high to very low. Whether this genetic risk progresses to disease depends upon the environment and life experiences.

● What evidence does Figure 6.4 provide for the importance of non-genetic factors in the development of schizophrenia?

[12] The genetic bases of cystic fibrosis and Huntington's disease are discussed in *Human Biology and Health: An Evolutionary Approach* (Open University Press, 3rd edn 2001).

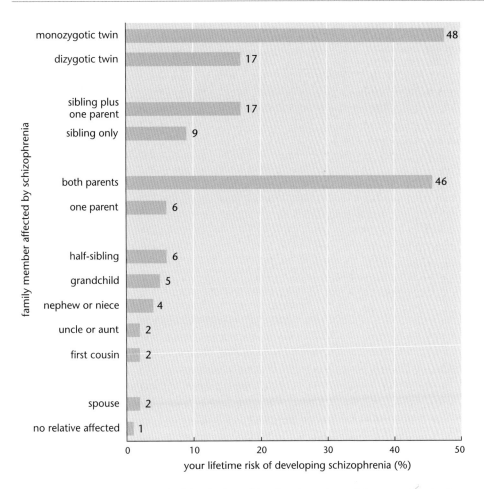

Figure 6.4 *Average lifetime risk of developing schizophrenia, estimated from a synthesis of European studies of kinship effects conducted between 1920–1987. (Data derived from Gottesman, I., 1991,* Schizophrenia Genesis, *W.H. Freeman and Company; diagram adapted from Nettle, D., 2001,* Strong Imagination: Madness, Creativity and Human Nature, *Oxford University Press, Figure 3, p. 53)*

■ The diagram shows that the disease cannot be purely genetic in origin. Even when two people share exactly the same genes, as identical twins do, the probability of them having the same outcome for schizophrenia is only around 50 per cent. The difference between identical twins where one has schizophrenia and the other does not cannot be due to differences in their genes, so it must be due to variations in their environment and life experiences.

6.5.2 Neurobiological approaches

As we said earlier, schizophrenia is categorised in psychiatry as a *functional psychosis*. These are serious psychological disorders that arise without obvious damage to the brain. Functional psychoses are usually contrasted with *organic psychoses*, where there is an identifiable abnormality in the brain, caused by an accident, by toxins, or by the ageing process. No differences between the brains of those with schizophrenic symptoms and those without were found until the 1970s, which fuelled the controversy of interpretation surrounding the disease. Was it a brain disorder at all, or a category of illness entirely constructed by society?

Since the late 1970s, however, evidence of subtle brain changes in people with schizophrenia has begun to amass. The picture is still very unclear, and no single change has been found that is reliably associated with either the predisposition to schizophrenia, or the disease itself. It is not that there is no evidence of differences between the brains of people who develop schizophrenia and other brains — in fact, the opposite picture is true. Using brain scanning techniques and post-mortem analysis, large numbers of statistically significant differences between the brains of people diagnosed with schizophrenia and controls without the condition have been identified. (These differences have been comprehensively reviewed by Heinrichs, 2001.)

The brains of people with schizophrenia have been found to be smaller and more symmetrical than average, to have enlarged cerebral ventricles (fluid-filled spaces, see Figure 6.5) at their centre, to have less dense cell packing in many areas of the brain, to have unusual patterns of cell connection in parts of the cerebral cortex (the outer layer of the brain), and to be unusual in many other ways. Chemical changes have been detected too, again using both post-mortem analysis and scans of functioning brains (Figure 6.6).

The brain uses a complex range of chemical signalling molecules called neurotransmitters, of which one in particular — *dopamine* — has been implicated in schizophrenia. The **dopamine hypothesis** of schizophrenia is based on indirect evidence, for example, dopamine-blocking drugs reduce the positive symptoms of schizophrenia in most users. This suggests that the condition involves some imbalance in the functioning of dopamine and related chemicals. Several studies have indeed found evidence that this is the case.

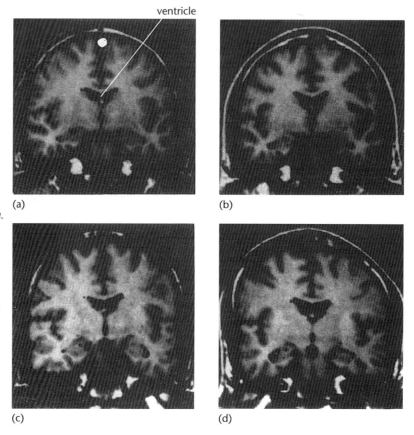

Figure 6.5 *Magnetic resonance images (MRI) of the brains of two sets of identical twins. In each case only one twin has a diagnosis of schizophrenia. The ventricles at the centre of the brain in the affected twins (b) and (d) are larger than those in the unaffected twins (a) and (c). (Source: Suddath, R. L. et al., 1990, Anatomical abnormalities in the brains of monozygotic twins discordant for schizophrenia,* New England Journal of Medicine, *322, p. 791)*

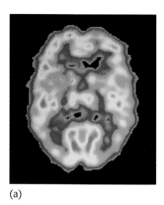 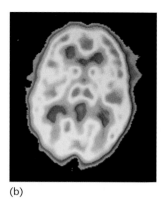

(a)   (b)

Figure 6.6 *An illustration of differences in the neurological activity in the brain of (a) a person diagnosed with schizophrenia while experiencing symptoms, who had never been treated with anti-psychotic drugs; and (b) a person with no psychiatric history. The artificially added colours indicate areas of high (red) and low (blue/purple) uptake of glucose by activated brain cells. (Photo: Dr Monty Buchsbaum/ Peter Arnold Inc./Science Photo Library)*

This situation is almost unique in the search for the physical basis of disease; the problem is not that no differences can be found, but that there are so many differences. However, none of the differences are very great. For every putative difference that has been found, there is overlap and variability between people diagnosed with schizophrenia and control groups. Some people who are not diagnosed as ill fall in the 'schizophrenic' range, and some people with schizophrenia fall in the 'normal' range. Just as with the symptoms and the neurological precursors of schizophrenia, such results suggest a complex model is needed when thinking about the condition. There may be no single discrete characteristic that separates those who develop schizophrenia from those who do not. Rather, there is a suite of interlinked psychological, biological and biochemical changes in schizophrenia, none of which on its own represents a discontinuous break from normal human variation.

6.5.3 Interpersonal and social approaches

Psychodynamic approaches

Psychodynamic explanations for schizophrenia are focused on the upbringing of the child. From Freida Fromm-Reichmann, who coined the term 'schizophrenogenic mother' (1948), to Gregory Bateson, who developed the theory of 'double-bind relationships' (Bateson *et al.*, 1956), schizophrenia was seen as the result of problems within the family, either of communication or relationships. A 'double bind' is an intolerable situation of being given conflicting messages by a parent, so that whatever the child did would be wrong.

● The major and most common criticism of this body of work concerns cause and effect. How might these be confused?

■ Even if families of people diagnosed as having schizophrenia are different from other families, it is not clear that this is a cause of the illness rather than a result of living with someone who has 'pre-schizophrenic' tendencies. You saw in Section 6.4 that many of the difficulties faced by people with schizophrenia onset early in life, and might thus cause problems in relationships long before the condition is formally diagnosed.

Early family studies tended to concentrate on the mother to the exclusion of other relationships. Although most of the later theories include the role of the father, few address the issue of why 'this child' rather than another in the family should develop schizophrenia.

The psychodynamic and social-relationship approaches to explaining schizophrenia have been vaunted as being more concerned with the patient as a person than is the case with biomedical explanations. They have, however, had devastating consequences for a different group, namely the families of people with schizophrenia. Parents were blamed for causing their child's illness. Although some therapists tried to engage the family in therapy, in others the 'patient' was encouraged to loosen contact with the family. In some cases, visiting the patient in hospital was forbidden. A review by psychologist Jacqueline Atkinson (the principal author of this chapter) and Denise Coia, a psychiatrist (1995), revealed that some families remained deeply suspicious of professionals because of the way they were blamed for causing the illness. There were also professionals left with a lingering sense of unease about families and who thus dismissed them and their concerns.

Expressed emotion

The mid-1970s heralded what could be described as a minor revolution with respect to families and their relationship with schizophrenia. Two British researchers, Julian Leff, a psychiatrist, and Christine Vaughn, a clinical psychologist, decided to look at the way the expression of emotions in families affected the development of schizophrenia (Vaughn and Leff, 1976a, b). They developed the concept of **expressed emotion (EE)** — a measure of the emotional atmosphere in a family — and focused on two aspects: *critical comments* and *emotional over-involvement*, which includes over-protectiveness.

Assessing EE involves both the content of speech and non-verbal aspects. Thus, from examples given by Leff and Vaughn (1985), 'I wish he could hold down a job — any job would do' would not be rated as a critical comment unless a critical tone was also present. There must be a clear and unambiguous statement by the relative of dislike, disapproval or resentment of the behaviour of the person with schizophrenia or some characteristic, as in 'When I see her sitting all day long, it aggravates me. I figure she's decaying. And I don't like it.' Rejecting comments would include statements such as 'I washed my hands of her'. Over-involvement is detected by both the reported behaviour of the relative and their behaviour at interview. It includes exaggerated emotional responses, self-sacrificing and devoted behaviour, and extremely over-protective behaviour. A very clear version is given in this exchange:

> In response to the question 'Would you like her to have a boyfriend?' the mother replied, 'She's not interested in marriage, no. I don't really want her to marry, I would miss her. Anyway, marriages aren't very happy, are they? No, I'm happy to have her home; she would never listen to anybody else if not me.' (Leff and Vaughn, 1985, p. 55)

High levels of EE seem to contribute to increased relapse rates in people diagnosed as having schizophrenia, particularly when face-to-face contact in the family is high (more than 35 hours per week) and the person does not take medication. Interventions to reduce relapse have thus focused on all three aspects (EE, contact time and medication), although more attention has been paid to developing family interventions to reduce EE in relatives than to reduce contact. High EE is believed to be related to increased relapse through raising the stress levels to which the person diagnosed as having schizophrenia is exposed. Some studies measuring physiological arousal have also demonstrated this association.

Expressed emotion has been a very popular and powerful concept, particularly in Britain, but it is worth noting that not all families of a person with schizophrenia show high EE, so interventions to reduce it are not universally applicable. Research has suggested that EE is not a stable trait, but that it fluctuates in families over time, and thus a measure of EE is only ever a 'snapshot' of the family. There is no clear evidence as to factors that influence changes in EE, and studies of fluctuations over time generally report a subsequent *decrease* in EE where high EE was initially recorded. These findings, combined with some critics' perception of EE as a harking back to 'blaming the family', have led to suggestions that professionals should talk about high EE *settings* or environments and not high EE *families*. Recent research considering EE levels among staff and patients in residential settings echoes this point; high EE is not confined to relatives.

●   Earlier you saw theories criticised on the grounds that they failed to disentangle cause and effect. How could this be applied to the work on EE?

■   As with other theories of family relationships, it is unclear whether high EE pre-dates the development of schizophrenia or is a response to it. (This question has not been resolved, although reducing EE reduces relapse.)

Life events and other stressors

Other explanations in this vein focus on the individual's social and physical environment, suggesting that the development of schizophrenia is related to the role of these factors in raising levels of stress. However, a review of the role of **life events**[13] in influencing schizophrenia, by psychiatrists Ross Norman and Ashak Malla in Canada (1993a, b), concludes that people with schizophrenia do *not* have higher levels of life events than people with other psychiatric disorders, and only minimally higher stressors than the general population. This suggests that life events are not a primary *cause* of schizophrenia. There is evidence, however, that life events are correlated with changes in symptoms over time among people who have already been diagnosed as having schizophrenia.

It is commonly believed that urban living is stressful and therefore higher rates of mental illness are found in cities. There might be several reasons why this should be so. On the one hand, environmental stressors could directly contribute to schizophrenia: the disintegration of community structures could strengthen the tendency towards social isolation of a person with schizophrenic predisposition. On the other hand, social selection theory suggests that schizophrenia causes the individual to 'drift' into inner city areas, where there is cheap bed-sit accommodation and a collection of other marginalised individuals amongst whom the person with schizophrenia is less likely to be stigmatised.

6.5.4 An integrated approach to explanation

None of the individual theories reviewed so far is free of problems. As a consequence, an *integrated* approach has developed, which recognises the potential contributions of all these factors as well as their potential limitations. This has resulted in a

[13] The impact on mental health of life events such as births, deaths and marriages, change of job or house, sudden major loss or other trauma, etc. are discussed briefly in *Studying Health and Disease* (Open University Press, 2nd edn 1994; colour-enhanced 2nd edn 2001), Chapter 5, and is a recurring theme in *Birth to Old Age: Health in Transition* (Open University Press, 2nd edn 1995; colour-enhanced 2nd edn 2001).

vulnerability model of schizophrenia. Vulnerability to schizophrenia is conceived as a relatively permanent trait in the individual, almost certainly biological in origin. For schizophrenia to become manifest, however, levels of environmental stress are required to reach the threshold of each individual's level of vulnerability in order to trigger an episode. Thus, episodes of schizophrenia are temporary states when symptoms recur and are interspersed with periods of remission. Remission may be more or less complete; or negative symptoms may continue most of the time with episodes being more an exacerbation of positive symptoms.

This model is important for two reasons. First, it is a genuine attempt to unify biological and environmental factors in explaining schizophrenia as a multifactorial disorder. Second, it has encouraged health professionals to concentrate on factors that contribute to *relapse* rather than the traditional focus on the underlying *causes* of the condition. These are important developments with implications for clinical practice, which redirect activity towards finding interventions to prevent relapse rather than initial episodes. This opens the way for more psychosocial interventions in schizophrenia and for seeing the treatment of schizophrenia as something other than the preserve of psychiatrists through medication. Biological vulnerability remains, however, a theoretical construct with no way (as yet) of measuring it directly.

6.6 Schizophrenia: a social and political entity

6.6.1 The anti-psychiatry movement

Although the approaches to explanation described above differ dramatically in their conceptualisation of schizophrenia, they do (by and large) agree that schizophrenia is at least a problem worthy of *medical* attention, even if not a true physical illness. Not everyone would agree with this. The 1960s and 1970s saw the rise of the **anti-psychiatry movement**, which denied the very existence of mental illness. In reality there were two distinct strands to this movement, linked only by a rejection of the medical model of psychiatry and treatment by drugs. The two people who are best known in this area (although both had strong objections to the 'anti-psychiatry' label), are Thomas Szasz, an American professor of psychiatry, and the late R. D. (Ronnie) Laing, a Glaswegian psychiatrist who became a cult figure in the 1970s.

Through a number of books, Szasz has systematically denied the existence of both neurotic and psychotic illness as disease states, in the sense that measles or cancer are diseases. He argues that if there is no physical trauma or lesion, there is no physical illness or need for medical involvement. Szasz (1979) also believes that there are ethical and political questions to be answered in *medicalising* schizophrenia by calling it a disease. He questions whether the psychiatrist has the right to diagnose and treat someone who has not asked for it, and he also questions whether a diagnosis is an invasion of privacy. He sees the psychiatrist as re-labelling the person's 'intimate personal possessions, such as their dreams and their opinions', in such a way that the person is redefined as a 'schizophrenic patient'.

Szasz does not, however, suggest that antisocial behaviour is ignored or excused, but says that society already has other ways of dealing with this, through ethics, legal systems and politics. Szasz argues that behaviour labelled as schizophrenic is merely antisocial behaviour, 'misbehaviour' or other unusual behaviour, which society (or the individual) doesn't like or doesn't understand and then finds easier to deal with by labelling it as illness. If it is so labelled, people who display anti-social behaviour can be treated (involuntarily if necessary), constrained and controlled, and the medical label can stay with them all their lives. Szasz also suggests that the

> psychotic and psychiatrist, are locked in an embrace of mutual coercion, confusion, and confirmation. (Szasz, 1979, p. 197)

Szasz seeks other, more 'everyday' explanations for behaviour defined as symptoms of mental illness. He prefers to describe 'thought disorder' as 'crazy talk' (1993), and then suggests that this is no different to the phenomenon of 'speaking in tongues' (or *glossolalia*) sometimes experienced in religious fervour.

If Szasz seeks to demolish 'the sacred symbol of psychiatry', Laing added to the mystique of schizophrenia. His early work, *The Divided Self* (1960), describes schizophrenia as a special strategy that a person invents in order to live in an unliveable situation, namely their family and the demand to be something other than oneself. Schizophrenia is then described not as a psychological problem of *intra*-personal functioning, but as a problem of *inter*-personal relationships.

Later in his career, Laing moved away from psychiatry altogether and declared schizophrenia to be 'a *political event*' (1967). He differed from Szasz in that, rather than labelling certain behaviours to be a problem for society, he labelled society itself as being the problem. To Laing, schizophrenia was not a *breakdown* of a functioning person, but a *breakthrough* to a new, and more positive, state. If society is evil, then the mad are virtuous; if society is restrictive and coercive, then the insane are seeking new ways to experience reality and may have new insights to offer the rest of us.

It is often argued that the rise in our understanding of the neurobiological basis of schizophrenia, which has taken place since around 1980, makes the arguments of Laing and Szasz outdated. After all, if the brains of people who develop schizophrenia are different from other members of the population, how can the disease be purely a social and political construction?

● How could recent knowledge of the neurobiology of schizophrenia have the opposite effect and reinforce the anti-psychiatry movement's critique of schizophrenia as a 'disease'?

■ The many differences between the brains of people with schizophrenia and other brains can only be demonstrated as small statistical differences between the two populations. They cannot reliably distinguish between a 'schizophrenic' and a 'normal' individual. The neurobiological studies show people with schizophrenia to be mainly towards one end on a continuum of brain structure and function, which overlaps with the 'normal' range. Such findings do not of themselves justify calling those who are different 'diseased'.

6.6.2 Responses to Szasz

Most psychiatrists and psychologists would dispute the views of the anti-psychiatry movement. Psychologists Richard Bentall and David Pilgrim (1993) have responded in detail to some of its charges. Although disputing the concept of schizophrenia as a discrete disease entity, they point to a continuum of behaviour with psychotic symptoms lying at one extreme. They focus on the unintelligibility of such behaviour, and suggest that whether or not the negative valuing of some behaviour as 'illness' is appropriate, it should not stop attempts to understand it.

The psychiatrist Julian Leff (1993) points out the inherent differences between speaking in tongues and the type of speech produced in schizophrenic disorder. The former are strings of sound which are not recognisable as language, the latter are recognisable words but in an order with no recognisable meaning. The former usually lasts a matter of minutes, possibly hours, whereas schizophrenic speech can last days, months, occasionally years. (A similar analysis is given in the Reader article by Cecil Helman, referred to earlier in the chapter.)

The best justifications for the invocation of the language of disease are humanitarian, not biological ones. Schizophrenia causes great human suffering. There is good evidence that early and appropriate treatment, using an integrated approach, can alleviate the condition in at least a proportion of people (as will be discussed in Section 6.7).

Critics of Szasz's views are concerned that they lead to the ignoring of human distress:

> ... Szasz's attempt to neatly mark off the manifestations of 'physical' and 'mental' illness is seriously misleading, mainly because it fails to provide a basis for helping people whose distress, however it is caused, might be relieved by physical or psychological interventions. (Bentall and Pilgrim, 1993, p. 75)

> Szasz's arguments ... are inhumane, since they deny the possibility of help for a condition which claims the life of one in ten sufferers. (Leff, 1993, p. 78)

6.6.3 Anti-psychiatry and the treatment conundrum

Both Laing and Szasz's views highlight the difficulty in abandoning the 'schizophrenia as illness' model. If people diagnosed as having schizophrenia are not 'ill', how are they to be treated? Szasz's position is that if there is no mental illness there is nothing to treat. However, there is a contradiction in Laing's views on the 'otherness' of schizophrenia, which nevertheless requires 'something', if not to treat it, then to allow it full expression.

If people with schizophrenia are no different from everybody else, then there is no need to plead mitigating circumstances or lack of responsibility. They can be sent to prison for committing unlawful acts in the same way as other criminals. How, though, to deal with behaviour which is troublesome to others (antisocial), but not sufficient to break the law or warrant a custodial sentence? If they don't work should they be subject to the same rules and regulations as other unemployed people? Whether treated by psychiatry or abandoned as 'not ill', such people will tend to be marginalised by society, both socially and economically.

In Italy in 1978, a group of psychiatrists from the far left, supported by the Communist Party, forced the government to repeal the Mental Health Laws and to stop any more admissions to mental hospitals. This was a neo-Marxist response to what was seen as the marginalisation of psychiatric patients (amongst others) by capitalist society. (A full account is given by Michael Donnelly, 1992.) There were real problems reintegrating such people into society without sufficient community resources.

The integrated approach to explaining schizophrenia has been mirrored in an integrated approach to treatment, to which we now turn. It recognises the important part played by medication but also recognises that drugs alone are unlikely to be the answer. People with schizophrenia and their carers also need a variety of other interventions and supports.

6.7 Treating schizophrenia

If diagnosing schizophrenia is controversial, then treating it is equally so, and it is important to separate reality from myth and from the past. For many people, psychiatric treatment is summed up by the film *One Flew Over the Cuckoo's Nest*, which includes heavy and forced medication, the use of surgery to affect psychological states (psychosurgery), controlling, insensitive or brutal staff, locked wards and long periods of hospitalisation. Although it might be a very powerful indictment of the worst of psychiatric treatment, the book by Ken Kesey on which the film was based was published in 1962 and relates to the psychiatric hospitals of the 1950s. The buildings may have remained the same, but many of the procedures and management strategies have since changed.

Psychosurgery is now extremely rare: in the UK it requires more than one medical opinion and cannot be performed without the patient's consent, even if he or she is an 'involuntary' patient detained under the Mental Health Act. It is used mainly for severe, intractable depression and obsessive compulsive disorders. Electroconvulsive therapy (ECT) is infrequently used for people diagnosed as having schizophrenia, and then only for severe depressive symptoms or catatonic states. This is not to say that there are no longer, and never will be, any unpleasant staff or involuntary medication, but it is not the norm. Nor is it the norm for most patients with schizophrenia to be kept in hospital for long periods of time, nor in locked wards.

Medication is the primary source of treatment for people diagnosed as having schizophrenia and, for most patients, forms the foundation of the treatment plan on which other interventions are built. Although important, drugs are rarely successful alone; other interventions are equally useful and will be discussed in what follows.

6.7.1 Medication

Neuroleptic drugs

The 1950s saw a revolution in the treatment of schizophrenia with the introduction of the *neuroleptic drugs* (or neuroleptics, also known as *anti-psychotic* drugs; examples include chlorpromazine, Largactil). These drugs form a diverse group of chemical compounds, but are normally grouped together because of their clinical effect. They are used with all types of psychosis, not just schizophrenia.

The typical neuroleptics block dopamine neurotransmission, which, as you saw earlier, is part of the evidence for the dopamine hypothesis of the aetiology of schizophrenia. They are used to treat the *positive* symptoms of schizophrenia, but do not affect the *negative* symptoms and are not curative. They bring about a marked decrease in acute symptoms in 60–70 per cent of patients, and often a shorter period of chronic symptoms. The long-term course and outcome of schizophrenia is probably improved when treated by *maintenance* neuroleptics (designed to maintain patients in a reasonable state of mental health), but there remain some questions about this. Patients who have a slow onset of illness show less improvement.

The neuroleptics have harmful side effects. These include unwanted, involuntary movements and twitches (mimicking Parkinson's disease), particularly of the mouth and tongue, and a 'restlessness' which is muscular in origin rather than psychological. *Dysphoria* is a distressing subjective state common among people on neuroleptics, who describe themselves as being generally 'ill-at-ease'. Some of these effects are irreversible. The harmful effects of neuroleptics can generally be managed by giving the lowest appropriate dose of the drug, together with anti-Parkinsonian medication.

However, the impact of the harmful side effects of these drugs on some patients should not be underestimated and this contributes to reluctance to take them. Other reasons for refusing them include an unwillingness or inability to accept the illness or a general dislike of continued medication. Most patients who take neuroleptics do so for long periods to help prevent recurrences of the illness and to manage 'florid' symptoms (symptoms that are particularly visible).

Compliance with instructions to take medication can be low in schizophrenia, but this is also true of other long-term conditions and some acute illnesses as well. The reluctance of many people to finish a prescribed course of antibiotics because they are 'feeling better' is well known.

Following the introduction of the neuroleptics, the next stage of the revolution in drug therapy for schizophrenia was the introduction in the late 1960s of the long-acting *depot phenothiazines* (for example, fluphenazine, decanoate or Modecate). These slow-release drugs are given by injection every two to four weeks, usually by a community psychiatric nurse, either at an out-patient clinic or at the patient's home. Although some patients are grateful not to have to remember to take their medication every day, others have seen the depot medications as depriving them of responsibility and choice.

Atypical anti-psychotic drugs

During the 1980s, a new generation of drugs was introduced — the so-called *atypical anti-psychotic drugs*, sometimes also called 'novel', because they are chemically unlike the previous anti-psychotic drugs. Their definition is vague and they come from a number of different pharmacological groups. Clozapine was the first of these to be used widely, particularly for people diagnosed with chronic schizophrenia who are 'drug resistant' (i.e. have not responded to other anti-psychotic medications). It underwent trials in Europe in the mid-1970s, but was withdrawn in the USA (it had never been available in the UK) when several patients developed a potentially fatal blood condition (agranulocytosis). However, a double-blind trial[14] in the 1980s (Kane *et al.*, 1988) demonstrated its superiority over chlorpromazine for 'drug resistant' patients, and it was reintroduced in the USA and licensed in the UK. It is only given under close supervision because it requires frequent blood tests. Other newer anti-psychotic drugs include respiridone and olzanapine.

The atypical anti-psychotic drugs have fewer harmful effects than the older neuroleptics (for example, they do not produce *dysphoria*), and they have some beneficial effects on the *negative* symptoms of schizophrenia, unlike the older drugs.

Current drugs, then, have greater potential in the control of symptoms of schizophrenia, but also have a number of drawbacks. Compliance is often poor, the effects are inconsistent and some patients derive little benefit from medication, or believe the harmful effects outweigh the potential benefits. The neurological and psychological aspects of the side effects of these drugs may make rehabilitation more difficult and may, indeed, be the very signs that mark someone out as being 'a psychiatric patient'. Despite the problem of agranulocytosis with clozapine, the fact that many otherwise 'drug resistant' patients respond positively to it means that the atypical anti-psychotics do hold out some hope for improvements in drug therapy.

---

[14] Double-blind trials to establish the efficacy of new drugs compared with existing treatments are discussed in *Studying Health and Disease* (Open University Press, 2nd edn 1994; colour-enhanced 2nd edn 2001), Chapter 8.

6.7.2 Psychosocial interventions

As you have seen, much drug therapy is aimed predominately at the *positive* symptoms of schizophrenia. Although positive symptoms are distressing and incapacitating, it is often the more chronic *negative* symptoms that are most handicapping and disabling in terms of people enjoying a reasonable quality of life. Most **psychosocial interventions** are thus aimed at preventing deterioration and teaching empowering strategies such as new skills to manage the illness or aid daily living and rehabilitation — both social and vocational — and restoring skills lost through illness. Many of these interventions come under the general heading of **behavioural programmes**.

Behavioural programmes directed at improving social skills have expanded considerably from the early 1970s, and now encompass a wide repertoire of interventions and outcomes. They tend to have names such as 'training in community living' or 'survival skills workshops'. Many are unstructured, but the most successful are tailored to the special needs of their members and use specific behavioural techniques, such as those developed by Robert Liberman, a California-based psychiatrist.

Liberman has probably done the most to develop what is now generally termed 'skills training' for severely mentally ill people. He advocates a *modular* approach: each module is divided into a number of skills areas, and the same methods of instruction are used in each module. These include the use of manuals, video-assisted modelling, role-playing and rehearsal, problem-solving and exercises in 'real-life' situations. Since people with schizophrenia are believed to have cognitive dysfunctions that interfere with learning, there is an emphasis on repetition and 'over-learning' (i.e. learning beyond the level at which knowledge or skills will be applied, to allow for some 'fall back' of performance). Modules in Liberman's programme include Medication Management, Symptom Management, Recreation for Leisure, and Grooming and Hygiene. Liberman contends that strict adherence to the full programme is necessary for patients to show improvements and generalisation of skills to new situations. To this end a training programme for trainers has been provided (Liberman *et al.*, 1993).

Other types of psychosocial interventions include various group therapies, stress management, problem-solving and specific behavioural and cognitive techniques to manage particular problems or symptoms, for example, auditory hallucinations. Empowerment is a key goal.

A rapidly developing area is *cognitive behavioural therapy* (or CBT) combined with standard drug treatments for people with schizophrenia. CBT is based on the premise that the unwanted feelings and behaviours can be altered by changing the person's patterns of thinking. It helps people to challenge their own delusional beliefs by encouraging rational self-questioning (e.g. 'How do I know that people are talking about me? Could they be talking about something else?'). CBT is a demanding technique for both clients and therapists and does not suit everyone; experienced therapists are scarce and the financial costs are high, but a systematic review of randomised trials of CBT in treatment programmes for schizophrenia showed some beneficial effects on reduced relapse rates (Jones *et al.*, 2001).

Running in parallel with, or as part of, many of these interventions are **educational programmes**, which give people information about their illness and its management. This is very often a central part of programmes aimed at getting patients to comply with their medication. Programmes vary in the balance they achieve between 'coercing' participants into becoming 'better patients', and giving the necessary information to enable participants to exercise informed choice and greater responsibility in the management of their condition.

An educational approach can simply mean giving people (carers as well as people diagnosed as having schizophrenia) information about schizophrenia, often relating this to coping strategies or medication compliance. It can also be used in a much wider sense whereby an 'educational approach' is contrasted with a 'therapeutic approach'. The educational approach looks at 'skill deficit' and people previously defined as 'patients' or 'clients' become students, learners or participants; 'therapists' become teachers, tutors or group leaders. In an effort to promote the 'student' image, manuals or workbooks are often used. **Psycho-education**, it has been suggested, expands these educational approaches to include social and psychological support and possibly counselling (Atkinson and Coia, 1995).

Although the majority of psychosocial interventions show positive outcomes for participants, these can be fairly short-lived unless some form of ongoing intervention or support is provided. For many patients, learning daily living and social skills is not a one-off, all-or-nothing intervention, but something that requires continued support and encouragement to use, if they are not to be overtaken by negative symptoms again. Many programmes report a variety of unexpected benefits, which were not formally assessed: these include participants becoming generally more assertive, responsive and responsible as the groups progress. This may be due as much to the style of the intervention as the skills being taught. Changes in the behaviour and attitudes of therapists are often observed, or reported by the therapists, and these allow patients to take more initiative for themselves.

Therapies are often presented as either/or (e.g. medication or psychosocial intervention) and seen as tied to a particular view of schizophrenia. In reality this need not be so and a **multi-intervention approach** can be used. People advocating this approach argue that the belief that schizophrenia is a biologically based illness does not preclude the need for psychosocial interventions along with drug therapy. The family does not have to cause or even contribute to schizophrenia to benefit from involvement in family programmes. What is important is to develop individual care programmes to suit individual needs.

Current clinical guidelines give testimony to the importance now placed on psychosocial interventions (SIGN, 1998) and the requirement for these to be provided along with drug therapy (Clinical Standards Board for Scotland, 2001). In England, one of the first National Service Frameworks (NSFs) dealt with mental health and included standards for effective services for people with severe mental illness (Department of Health, 1998).

6.7.3 Family interventions

Despite the interest in the family's role in the development and course of schizophrenia, until the 1980s little effort was put into involving the family in therapy or other interventions. Where schizophrenia had been redefined as a problem in family communication or roles, then family therapy was offered with the aim of treating the dysfunctional family rather than the individual patient. This trend was reinforced by research on levels of expressed emotion (EE) in families and its correlation with relapse.

● What trends in health and social care in the UK from the 1990s may have led to the increasing interest in involving families in interventions?

■   Two factors have been most influential: first, the rise of self-help groups, the user movement and carer organisations; and second, the policy of community care, which relies on families as informal carers.

Psycho-education forms the backbone of **family interventions**, whether they are group- or individual-based. Families showing critical high expressed-emotion behaviour (high EE) tend to have negative attitudes to schizophrenia and also to the patient, who is often held to be to 'blame' for his or her illness. Such families tend to believe that the patient could behave differently if he or she wanted to. Indeed it may be that it is resolving these beliefs, rather than high EE as such, that is central to effective family interventions. Those involved in psycho-education, therefore, try to understand the family members' beliefs and work with them. The evidence shows that simply presenting information or 'facts' is not enough to change beliefs or behaviour. Amongst other aspects, families are helped to understand what *is* and, importantly, what is *not* within the voluntary control of the person with schizophrenia, how their behaviour may influence outcome, and the role and function of other treatment and management interventions (Leff and Vaughn, 1985).

Not all family intervention programmes are the same. A slightly different approach was taken by psychiatrist Ian Falloon and his colleagues (1993), who used problem-solving techniques with families, focusing on stress management to influence the family environment.

Family-based interventions usually take *relapse* by the person diagnosed as having schizophrenia as their primary outcome measure, and there is good evidence that these programmes do reduce relapse rates. Set against this, however, is the problem of encouraging family involvement. Take-up rates are often low and drop-out high, with families not always seeing the relevance of the interventions. Take-up rates are higher when families are approached at a time of crisis, either at first episode of schizophrenia or subsequent relapse. Family sessions based in the family's home also seem to maintain family involvement. Involving families as early as possible in the illness also seems to be important in contributing to success. This may be because the families are actively looking for help and information and have not yet become cynical about the services on offer, or demoralised by their problems. (Other reasons are suggested in the Reader article by Goffman associated with Chapter 2 of this book.)

Although carers' organisations frequently demand more involvement of relatives in management and decision-making, clearly the family intervention programmes currently on offer do not appeal to all families. Little attention has been paid to the views of people diagnosed as having schizophrenia, whose families are involved in these programmes.

●   What tensions do you think may arise if people diagnosed as having schizophrenia are not included in family intervention programmes?

■   The 'patient' may feel marginalised or that their privacy is being invaded. On the other hand, if relatives are acting as carers they may feel entitled to information and help that will make them more effective in that role.

Some family intervention programmes do have elements that focus largely on the carer's problems and aim to reduce *their* stress rather than that of the person with schizophrenia. A greater emphasis on outcomes for carers rather than patients would alter the 'tone' of the programmes and might make them more acceptable.

Rather than an intervention to change them or help them cope better, what some families want, however, is something that removes the source of stress. This could be anything from a cure for schizophrenia to better day-care services, supported housing, appropriate vocational rehabilitation and sheltered employment opportunities.

The emphasis on carers and their role in supporting family members with schizophrenia has led to some services developing to support carers in their own right, rather than the outcome being aimed at the person who is ill (Atkinson and Coia, 1995). The need for staff to be trained to work with relatives is acknowledged.

6.7.4 Community care

The formal introduction of community care by the *NHS and Community Care Act*, 1990 (enacted April 1993) was the logical outcome of a movement which had been under way in the UK since the 1960s.[15] The result has been that most hospital treatment for schizophrenia is now for episodes when the patient is very acutely ill, and in-patient stays are usually between six and twelve weeks. A small minority of patients require longer-term hospital care and an even smaller number will be detained involuntarily under a section of the Mental Health Act. The local authority has the leading responsibility for community care, but in practice the lead agency can be either social services or the health authority, depending on the area. In 1998, data from a large sample of General Practices in England and Wales, covering 2.6 per cent of the total population, showed that on average GPs were treating 2.0 males and 1.7 females with schizophrenia per 1000 patients on their lists (age-standardised rates; Office for National Statistics, 2000, Table 5A6).

The lead agency is responsible for commissioning services from both the statutory and voluntary sectors. As a result, self-help organisations such as the National Schizophrenia Fellowship and MIND have also become service providers. A variety of new services are offered, including drop-in centres, employment projects, support for carers, telephone help-lines, as well as traditional day centres and accommodation projects. The need for social and recreational facilities has been recognised, along with the more traditional 'therapeutic' services. Voluntary organisations are often able to provide innovative services responding directly to users' needs and normally have user or carer representatives on the board of management. Moving into service provision has, however, meant that the nature of the organisations is changing from small self-help groups relying on mutual support to multimillion pound businesses (Atkinson and Coia, 1995). But the policy of community care enabled carers' organisations to reiterate their members' needs to be taken seriously as primary carers and to demand supporting services.

Although most people probably accept that treating patients in the community is more appropriate than long-stay institutionalisation, there is concern that some individuals fall through the gaps in the various service provisions and that there may be a need for some kind of safety net. The media tend to highlight the problems of community care rather than the successes, publicising examples of people who cannot get the services or treatment they need, or who end up homeless or perpetrate acts of violence on others. Probably the best known case is that of Jonathan Zito, who was stabbed to death on the London Underground in December 1992 by Christopher Clunis, who was suffering from schizophrenia. Zito's wife,

---

[15] The history of community care policies in the UK is discussed in *Dilemmas in UK Health Care* (Open University Press, 3rd edn 2001), Chapter 8.

Jayne, has kept the names of both men, and the problems inherent in community care, in the public eye through her campaigning work and the formation of the Zito Trust. This organisation was set up in July 1994 with the aim of supporting those whose lives have been affected by the failure of community care to prevent acts of violence by mentally ill people.

In the same month as the Zito murder, another person with a schizophrenia diagnosis, Ben Silcock, went into the lion's enclosure at London Zoo and was mauled. The presence of a family with a video camera raised a personal tragedy to a media event (Figure 6.7). What was a gift for cartoonists became a trigger for Virginia Bottomley, then Secretary of State for Health, to suggest that the Mental Health Act needed to be reviewed and provision made for some form of community treatment or supervision order. Amid controversy, *supervision registers* were introduced in England in 1994. *The Mental Health (Patients in the Community) Act 1995* introduced community supervision and community care orders, although it did not attempt to make treatment compulsory for patients in the community.

At the time of writing (2002) proposals are in place in both England and Wales and in Scotland to produce new Mental Health Acts (Department of Health, 2000; Scottish Executive, 2001). These reviews of the legislation have suggested the need for some form of community based order, which would allow patients to be treated compulsorily in the community — often referred to as *community detention* (Atkinson and Patterson, 2001). Concern has been expressed, particularly by some user groups, that people should not be compelled to receive treatment whilst living in the community; others see it as a positive step to enable people with mental disorders to be maintained outside hospital for as long as possible. There is concern from both sides, however, that community services may not always be equal to the potential demands that will be made on them.

The prediction of being a danger (to self or others) is very difficult, the best predictor being previous dangerous behaviour. In a retrospective survey by Elizabeth King (1994) of 17 men diagnosed as having schizophrenia who committed suicide, only four had given any warning of their intention. People diagnosed as having

Figure 6.7 *Ben Silcock enters the lion's den at London Zoo. (Photo: Philip Hollis/Rex Features)*

schizophrenia are much more likely to harm themselves than others. A review by Caldwell and Gottesman (1990) suggests that between 10–13 per cent of such people kill themselves and that suicide is the most common cause of premature death in this group.

There are no data showing the percentage of people diagnosed as having 'current' schizophrenia who kill someone else, but the statistics indicate that it is far lower than the proportion who kill themselves. A national report (National Confidential Inquiry, 2001) investigated suicides and homicides[16] by people with a diagnosis of mental illness (including schizophrenia and other diagnoses). It found that 5 per cent of all the homicides in England and 2 per cent of those in Scotland were committed by a person who had been diagnosed with schizophrenia at some point in their lives. At the time of the homicide, 15 per cent of the perpetrators in England and 5 per cent in Scotland had symptoms of some sort of mental illness.

By contrast, of people who committed suicide in Britain, the same study showed that approximately a quarter had been in contact with mental health services in the previous year. Younger people who committed suicide were more likely to have a history of schizophrenia, personality disorder, drug or alcohol misuse and violence. People with schizophrenia who commit suicide are more likely to be unemployed and unmarried. About a quarter of people who commit suicide do so within three months of being in hospital.

Community care guidelines require all patients leaving hospital to have a *care programme* clearly drawn up, with an identified key worker, following a comprehensive assessment of needs. In reality this does not always happen, as the suicide rates demonstrate. Areas that are often inadequate are housing and employment opportunities and alternatives to paid employment.

6.8   Schizophrenia: public opinion and the media

Schizophrenia affects less than 1 per cent of the adult population in the UK, and most people have no direct experience of how the condition manifests in reality. Yet public expectations of individuals with a serious mental illness are generally characterised by fear and antagonism.

There has been some evidence that attitudes in the 1990s began changing towards greater acceptance. For example, a study by a group of psychiatrists in England, led by Ian Brockington, showed that the public fear and intolerance of mentally ill people had receded, at least on the surface, although it remained in 'a substantial minority of the community' (Brockington *et al.*, 1993). However, this study was based on expressed attitudes during research interviews, not on observed behaviours, and people may have been motivated to present tolerant views because these were felt to be socially acceptable.

Additionally, genuine 'good intentions' held in a state of comparative ignorance and inexperience may give way in the face of reality. In Brockington's study, although two-thirds of those interviewed at first said they would be prepared to marry someone with a mental illness, this dropped to only 6 per cent after being shown descriptions of mentally ill people. Responses after the description may have been closer to reality, and suggested that only between a third and half the population

[16] 'Homicide' is a wider term than 'murder' and includes verdicts of manslaughter, infanticide, unfit to plead, and not guilty by reason of insanity.

would live next door to, work with or join the same club as someone with a mental illness. Although on average older people were more intolerant than younger, the *most* intolerant group were those under 25 years.

Possibly the best way of assessing how the community treats people with a mental illness, however, is to look at the prevalence of harassment. Research comparing the amount of harassment in the community experienced by people with mental health problems showed that they were subjected to significantly more harassment, compared to others (National Schizophrenia Fellowship (Scotland), 2001).

● Think back to Chapter 2. What psychological processes might be involved in forming these public perceptions?

■ It was argued that stigma is the result of the *projection* of fundamental anxieties onto the person thus stigmatised, who is perceived as presenting a threat to the *ontological security* of others.

Earlier in this chapter we referred to the publicity surrounding the murder of Jonathan Zito by a man diagnosed with schizophrenia in December 1992, the same month as Ben Silcock's incursion into the lion's enclosure at London Zoo. Events such as these are extremely rare, but they tend to be reported in the media as though they are 'typical' of the behaviour of people with a serious mental illness such as schizophrenia. How far the media shape attitudes and behaviour is a controversial issue, especially when applied to acts of violence. Despite some sympathetic portrayals — for example, the 2002 film 'A Beautiful Mind' on the effects of schizophrenia on the life of Nobel-prize winning mathematician, John Forbes Nash Jr. — the media's record on images of mental illness is generally stigmatising.

Fictional portrayals of mental illness frequently mix reality with enough fantasy to make a good story. Schizophrenia has often been misrepresented, even unrecognisable, especially in thrillers and horror films. The following description comes from the 1977 Warner Brothers film *Schizo*, for which the publicity poster, the video cover and the opening words read:

> When the left hand doesn't know who the right hand is killing, you're dealing with a SCHIZO ... Schizophrenia, a mental disorder, sometimes known as multiple or split personality ... an alternation between violent and contrasting behaviour patterns.

Most films that use 'schizophrenia' encourage the public to believe that it means 'split personality' — that the person is some kind of Jekyll and Hyde — or use the term as a description of anyone who is generally 'mad', or as a scaring-enough label in itself to generate fear in the audience. These are very useful concepts for a film producer, but a major handicap for anyone trying to set up supported housing in a community, let alone trying to live in such housing. This is not to say that more positive portrayals of schizophrenia do not exist, but they are few and far between. More commonly, however, the label 'schizophrenia' is thrown into the plot to explain why someone is violent, kills or is otherwise antisocial or beyond understanding.

A study of the tabloid press and television by the Glasgow University Media Group (1993a), led by Gregory Philo, categorised representations according to whether

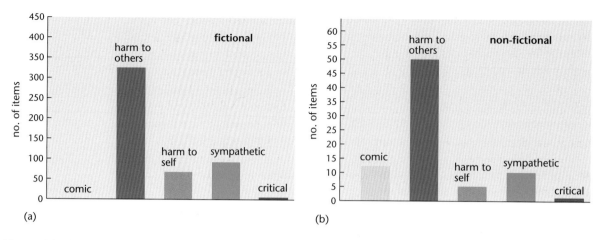

Figure 6.8 *(a) Fictional, and (b) non-fictional representations of mental illness. Analysis of television, newspapers and magazines during one month in 1993 showed that the greatest number of representations of people with mental illness involved them harming others. (Source: Glasgow University Media Group, 1993a,* Mass Media Representations of Mental Health/Illness. Report for the Health Education Board for Scotland, *Glasgow University Media Group, Glasgow, Appendix 3 and Appendix 4, pages unnumbered)*

they described people with mental illness as harming others, harming themselves, behaving in a comical way, or were largely sympathetic or critical (Figure 6.8). The researchers found the overwhelming majority of both fictional and non-fictional representations of people with mental illness concerned them harming others. This is despite the reality that people with mental illness who harm anyone are most likely to harm themselves. In a sample of the general population, these researchers found that 40 per cent believed that serious mental illness was associated with violence, and cited media representations as the source of this belief (Glasgow University Media Group, 1993b).

When the researchers examined the responses of audiences to media representations of mental illness, other worrying findings emerged. Unlike other topics, where the impact of personal experience generally outweighs the influence of media reports, this did not hold true for mental illness. Some respondents who had limited, but *positive*, experience of mental illness discounted or ignored their experience in the light of contradictory media messages. One woman, for example, who had done some voluntary work in a psychiatric hospital said:

> The actual people I met weren't violent — that I think they are violent, that comes from television, from plays and things … None of them were violent — but I remember being scared of them, because it was a mental hospital — it's not a very good attitude to have but it is the way things come across on TV, and films — you know, mental axe murderers and plays and things — the people I met weren't like that, but that is what I associate them with. (Glasgow University Media Group, 1993b, p. 32)

Two further concerns were identified in later research reported by this group. (Open University students may wish to read the article 'Media and mental illness' originally published in 1999 by Gregory Philo; it is reproduced in *Health and Disease: A Reader*, Open University Press, 3rd edn 2001, and is optional reading for this chapter.) One was the prevalence of violent fantasies expressed by members of the general public when asked to imagine how they would have reacted to a mentally ill character, who had recently been portrayed in a popular TV 'soap opera'. Respondents were more likely to have said they would have 'killed her' or 'kicked hell out of her' than to have sought psychiatric help for her. The second concern was the negative effect of media representations of people with schizophrenia on the individuals with this diagnosis themselves. In addition to the problems arising from their illness, they also worried about what their neighbours must think of them, and feared the stigmatisation and avoidance of contact that would result when the diagnosis became known.

Concerns about the way in which mental illness is misrepresented in the media has led to groups as divergent as the Royal College of Psychiatrists and the Schizophrenia Media Agency (a user group) campaigning and working with the media to improve their reporting.

It is an interesting exercise, which you may like to try, to keep a note of all the references to mental illness in the newspapers you read, including the local ones, for a month. This can reveal a great deal about media messages on mental illness. Removing the words 'mental patient' where crimes are reported can show that the story appears less 'newsworthy'. Such stories are often not followed up, and frequently newspapers only report that someone with a history of mental illness has been charged, not whether they were found guilty, or what happens to them.

6.9   Conclusions

●   Go back to the list of words you wrote down at the beginning of this chapter which you associated with schizophrenia, and your list of its symptoms. What, if anything, has changed?

Depending on your point of view, schizophrenia is either a clearly defined mental illness or a vague concept which keeps slipping away. Some people believe passionately that it is a biological disease with its roots in brain abnormalities. Others believe, equally passionately, that as an entity it does not exist and that so-called 'psychotic behaviours' have other explanations. Some say that the family environment is central — others that the family is largely irrelevant; some that drugs are fundamental to management; others that drugs cause more problems than they solve. Yet others argue that people with schizophrenia often can't help their actions and therefore need to be protected or controlled; this is countered with the argument that people with schizophrenia should have all the rights of other citizens and accept the responsibilities that come with them.

Schizophrenia remains a confusing and tantalising chimera for researchers and a potentially devastating experience for those who have it or care about someone who has it. Whatever our views and beliefs we should not lose sight of the distress of people with schizophrenia — whether through the condition, or their treatment in 'the system'. Maybe the best way to end is to repeat the (very) old joke, first told to the principal author of this chapter by a patient many years ago:

Schizophrenia? I'm in two minds about it.

OBJECTIVES FOR CHAPTER 6

When you have studied this chapter, you should be able to:

6.1 Define and use, or recognise definitions and applications of, each of the terms printed in **bold** in the text.

6.2 Describe the symptoms and prognosis of schizophrenia and distinguish the features identified in a clinical diagnosis from those in lay descriptions.

6.3 Discuss the problems encountered in comparing people diagnosed as having schizophrenia across time and between geographical locations.

6.4 Describe the different approaches to explaining the causes of schizophrenia and how they are reflected in different approaches to treatment.

6.5 Discuss the issues involved in treating people diagnosed as having schizophrenia either in the community or in hospitals.

6.6 Recognise the influence of individual perspectives and experiences, and media representations, on personal and public attitudes to schizophrenia.

QUESTIONS FOR CHAPTER 6

1   (*Objective 6.2*)

Distinguish between the *positive* and *negative* symptoms of schizophrenia according to clinical diagnoses. How do they compare with lay descriptions of the condition?

2   (*Objective 6.3*)

Is schizophrenia an illness of Western industrialised countries? What evidence is there to shed light on this question, and what are the reasons for interpreting epidemiological data with caution?

3   (*Objective 6.4*)

To what extent have beliefs about the causes of schizophrenia influenced approaches to treatments?

4   (*Objective 6.5*)

Mental health laws in the UK allow for the compulsory detention and treatment in hospital of persons considered to be a danger to themselves or others by virtue of their mental illness. Imagine that, following the example of radical psychiatrists in Italy in the 1970s, a group of professionals in the UK proposes that these laws should be abolished. Others argue in favour of closing mental hospitals. What arguments could be made for and against these developments?

5   (*Objectives 6.2 and 6.6*)

One of your closest friends comes to tell you he or she has just got engaged to someone who has been diagnosed as having schizophrenia. They are looking for your support. What factors would you try to take into account when discussing the possible prognosis? What misconceptions about schizophrenia might you have to dispel?

CHAPTER 7

Pain and suffering

Study notes for OU students

This chapter is the fifth case study, but it also refers to the wider framework of this book and the discussion in Chapters 1 and 2 of the construction of personal and medical narratives to explain physical and mental disorders. During your study of Section 7.4.3 you should listen to an audiotape entitled 'Being in pain', after consulting the notes associated with it in the *Audiovisual Media Guide*. During Section 7.5.3 you will be asked to read an article contained in *Health and Disease: A Reader* (Open University Press, third edition 2001) by Sally Macintyre and David Oldman called 'Coping with migraine'. This chapter was written by Clive Seale, Professor of Medical Sociology at Goldsmiths' College, University of London, with Basiro Davey, Senior Lecturer in Health Studies, Department of Biological Sciences, The Open University.

7.1 Introduction

> A doctor administered a lethal injection to an elderly dying woman to end her suffering, Winchester crown court was told yesterday … Mrs Boyes was suffering from severe rheumatoid arthritis … By August 16 she was seriously ill, suffering great pain and discomfort which was not relieved by large doses of pain killers … [she] had no reasonable prospects of ever living an independent life again … on August 10 she told her youngest son she had had enough and did not want to carry on … The drugs were not controlling her pain and once she screamed out and was severely distressed. [The prosecution said] 'By this time … Dr Cox himself was considerably affected by the condition of his patient and decided he must bring her suffering to an end.' … Staff nurse Christina Eeles said … that on the morning Mrs Boyes died Dr Cox had been distressed at the pain she was suffering. She had screamed with pain. The screams had sounded like those of a wounded animal. (*Guardian*, 1992, 11 September, p. 2)

The word 'pain' comes from the Latin *poena*, a penalty, signifying that we experience it like a punishment for illness or injury. This is clearly the case in the above depiction of almost unimaginably severe pain, and the effect it had on people who felt responsible for alleviating it. In everyday life, pain and suffering are rarely experienced so severely, or with such a devastating loss of hope. Many pains are quite minor and easily 'treated' by words of sympathy or over-the-counter remedies, so that they become part of a routine background of minor troubles. Short-term pain can even be seen as having a certain value in prompting us to 'take it easy' or guard an injury.

This chapter will consider some extreme examples of pain and suffering because, rather like the experiments conducted by Harold Garfinkel to disrupt 'normality', which you read about in Chapter 2, these reveal underlying strategies for *repairing reality* that are usually taken for granted. In particular, we focus on the experience of *persistent* (chronic) pain, which continues long after short-term (acute) pain has gone away. Chronic pain disturbs people's routine strategies for dealing with suffering and makes them fragile. We also explore the role of medicine in people's attempts to alleviate and understand the meaning of suffering.

During this chapter you will be invited to reflect back on the case studies of rheumatoid arthritis, HIV and AIDS, asthma and schizophrenia, which all demonstrate varieties of human suffering and the varying success of medicine in its alleviation. In particular, rheumatoid arthritis shows the disruptive effect of chronic *physical* pain. Pain, though, can also be *social*, as in the stigma of AIDS and a variety of other stigmatised conditions (discussed in Chapter 2), and *emotional*, as in the fears and anxieties associated with asthma. Schizophrenia exerts a profoundly disruptive effect on mental processes, with consequences for social and emotional pain. For the purposes of this chapter, physical, social and emotional pain will be discussed as three components of the broader phenomenon of human suffering.

The chapter begins by proposing that the experience of pain has the potential to 'unmake' the usual capacity of people to participate in a meaningful world. Medical treatments are then depicted as helping people to construct *personal illness narratives* (as well as giving physical relief), which enable them to repair the damage to their world by giving a meaning and an explanation for their pain.

Different theories of pain are summarised to illustrate how biological explanations can contribute to medical narratives (defined in Chapter 1). Because they have the support of a powerful social institution — medicine — these narratives carry great weight and often dominate the personal narratives that people construct to explain their illness or distress. Some medical narratives encompass more dimensions of the experience of suffering than others, as you will see later in this chapter.

The chapter ends by reviewing historical and cross-cultural evidence about variability in experiences and explanations for pain and suffering.

7.2   The making and unmaking of the world[1]

Human social life can be understood in part as a continuous, jointly organised struggle to 'forget' the crude fact that as individuals all our thoughts, our hopes, our plans and our participation in culture depend in the last analysis on the physical integrity of our bodies. The experience of illness, then, is a reminder of the limitations of bodily existence and often involves a sense of *marginality*, where people are forced to retire from this joint human endeavour.

● Can you think of examples of marginality from the earlier case studies?

■ Rheumatoid arthritis often stops people from taking part in social activities that require physical mobility; the social stigma of AIDS can exclude groups already marginalised by sexual stigmas; asthma can make children feel 'different' at school; the disruption of thoughts and emotions in schizophrenia places many sufferers outside 'normal' social participation.

Not all of the above examples are directly caused by physical limitations. For example, the degree to which schizophrenia is a physical disease excites great controversy. The excluding effect of stigma can be understood as a type of *inflicted* social pain, that sometimes builds an additional layer of suffering onto the experience of illness. Yet all of these situations demonstrate how illness can separate a person from others so that, in the words of the American sociologist Richard Hilbert, whose work with chronic pain sufferers will be described later:

> ... [they are] continuously approaching the amorphous frontier of non-membership. They are falling out of culture. (Hilbert, 1984, p. 375)

To be 'in culture' means sharing a world of meaning with others. People's understanding of who they are is a matter of constant negotiation, seen starkly in the struggles over self-identity that occur in adolescence.[2] Provisional self-interpretations are tested out and validated in the external social world through continuing 'conversations' with others. In such conversations — which may literally be the experience of face-to-face talk, but which can also be interaction with cultural products such as the media, books, art, music and so on — people seek to construct meaningful *narratives* of the self.

---

[1] The title of this section is taken from Scarry, E. (1985) *The Body in Pain: The Making and Unmaking of the World*, Oxford University Press, Oxford.

[2] An account of adolescence along these lines is given in *Birth to Old Age: Health in Transition* (Open University Press, 2nd edn 1995, colour-enhanced 2nd edn 2001), Chapter 6.

● What role do personal illness narratives play in the experience of rheumatoid arthritis, and what sources do people draw on to construct them?

■ Through 'narrative reconstruction' people with rheumatoid arthritis construct explanations of why they have the disease, drawing on events and circumstances in their lives that seem significant. This process helps them to deal with their uncertainties about its daily course, including variations in their experience of pain. Such personal illness narratives draw on both lay and scientific accounts.

The process of constructing and reconstructing narratives of the self can be understood as a **world-making activity**, contributing to *ontological security* (see Chapter 2) by repairing damage from encounters with perceived threats to existence. In order to maintain a sense of optimism and purpose about continuing in life, people need 'explanations' for suffering. Religion, in its origins, provided a structure of explanations that people could readily appropriate into their own internal world-making activity. Religious explanations are known as *theodicies*, as they seek to justify suffering as the will of God (*theo*, God; *-dicy*, justice). In modern times, many people turn to science (and particularly medicine) for explanations that are alternative to those of religion. Most obviously, belief systems of both religious and scientific types seek to provide explanations for death, the ultimate marginal situation, intimately linked with the limitations of bodily existence, where the individual's 'falling out of culture' is complete. Theodicies that explain death can be understood as attempts to remake a fractured world.

Theodicies also enable the surrender of the self to society. Rituals, in which allegiance to particular belief systems is enacted, whether religious or medical, transform an *individual* event into an episode in the history of *society*, thereby asserting a connectedness of the individual with others and giving continuity between generations. As the sociologist Peter Berger has put it, rituals create a type of 'sheltering canopy' over 'even those experiences that may reduce the individual to howling animality' (Berger, 1973, p. 63).

Marginalising experiences, such as that of illness, disrupt world-making activity and contribute to the **unmaking of the world**. The experience of illness or physical pain means that the body ceases to be a vehicle for the expression of the self, for example when it is draped with fashionable clothes, or used to indicate emotions ('body language'), or shaped by diet or exercise to indicate 'health' or 'fitness'. Pain makes the body strange and the self 'watches' the body which is now acting *against* it. This is illustrated in the words of one sufferer from chronic pain:

> ... [there are] those moments too when I think it's ... I'm outside myself, this whole thing I've got to deal with is ah, a decayed mass of tissue that's just not any good, and I, I'm almost looking at it that way again; as if my mind were separated ... I guess. I don't feel integrated. I don't feel like a whole person. (Good, 1994, p. 123)

At the extreme, such self-estrangement can lead to a collapse of ontological security and self-destructive acts.

In acts of 'world making', people collectively create structures of meaning. Thus they agree to designate certain individuals (for example, priests, doctors) as having a particular expertise, and to interpret certain of their actions as an exercise of that expertise. When meanings are routinely agreed by large numbers of people they 'thicken' and 'harden', so becoming *objectified* in social institutions such as the church, education or medicine. These are then reflected back to people to supply them with meanings that appear 'given' and are handed down through childhood socialisation as 'truths'. Most obviously, this is the case with the institution of religion in traditional societies. But science and, in particular medicine, now provide people with institutionalised meanings for dealing with pain and suffering. Medicine in these terms can be understood as a *grand narrative* (Chapter 1), in which patients are offered opportunities to be scripted into a jointly produced 'story'.

- ● The 'story' offered by medicine to the sufferer is not always a welcome one. Can you think of any examples of this from the book so far?

- ■ The medical narrative of rheumatoid arthritis may, on occasion, contain the message 'You'll just have to learn to live with it' (Chapter 3). The diagnosis of epilepsy or HIV may be deeply disturbing over and above the physical symptoms, because they can carry stigmatising connotations (Chapters 2 and 4). People diagnosed as having schizophrenia may resist the medical label, preferring softer social labels such as that of 'voice hearer'; they may also resist genetic explanations in favour of environmental causes that offer greater hope of personal control over the condition (Chapter 6).

Thinking of medicine as a 'narrative' does not imply a relativist position, where narratives can be constructed with no reference to whether they accurately describe an independently existing reality. Medical narratives may be concerned with technical measures that have real physical impact, alleviating certain pains very effectively (for example, the simple act of carrying an inhaler at all times can relieve the fear of an asthma attack). Additionally, medical narratives can be experienced as both helpful and unhelpful by sufferers. This is illustrated towards the end of the following discussion of the experience of chronic pain.

7.3 The experience of pain

Pain occurs in different intensities, ranging from the transient mild pain of a knock or a scratch, to the acute pains of childbirth or toothache. A common feature of **acute pain** is that those who suffer it expect that it will eventually go away. Acute pain is usually associated with a well-defined source of tissue damage, for example a cut or burn, or the powerful muscle contractions experienced in labour. Once the physical damage heals or the muscles relax, the pain will generally disappear.

However, in **chronic pain** the expectation of resolution is violated. This situation is outside the realm of most people's experience, although there are some chronic pains which are experienced by a significant proportion of the population, such as lower back pain. Here, pain may persist without obvious tissue damage or, as in rheumatoid arthritis, recur or intensify for no apparent reason. Unlike acute pain, which may be interpreted as a 'warning' to change behaviour in order to avoid further pain, chronic pain appears to serve no such useful purpose. It therefore poses significant problems of meaning to people who suffer it.

Additionally, one of the key problems facing the person with pain is to communicate its nature to others. Language is the means by which people place their subjective thoughts into culture and jointly engage in world-making activity. Extreme pain is often expressed in primitive, pre-linguistic groans, cries and shrieks. To place the subjective experience of pain in culture, a common language for communicating pain experience must be created. Here again, the chronic pain sufferer is faced with particular problems, as the legitimacy of a pain without an identifiable physical cause may be questioned by others.

> Some people thought it was a joke, they thought I was just trying to get [something] over on everybody. Like my father, he didn't really think I had that much pain. (Hilbert, 1984, p. 367)

Variations in the experience of pain from day to day are subjectively experienced for reasons that may be mysterious; for people who live with or treat a person with chronic pain, the language of the sufferer is their only evidence for the existence of pain. Managing the disclosure of pain therefore has certain parallels with the problems experienced by those managing the disclosure of invisible stigmas.

7.3.1 Chronic pain and the 'unmaking' of the world

Richard Hilbert interviewed 22 people with chronic pain in order to gain an understanding of the problems they faced. When pains began, people initially used their existing knowledge of 'normal' acute pain to interpret the experience. It was only when the pain did not go away that they realised they were facing a qualitatively different experience:

> I'm an athlete and a coach and very active, and so I was used to pain, and thought 'Well, I just kind of injured my tailbone a little bit.' And I thought it'd go away. I never *dreamed* what it would end up being.
>
> When my leg went numb in March of '77, then … it really hit me. I almost flipped out, in a sense, because I knew that there it was again, and it would be like a sore tooth. It would never go away. That's when it really threw me in an emotional turmoil — [a] crisis. (Hilbert, 1984, p. 367)

The lack of an adequate explanation was profoundly disturbing:

> I honestly don't know what it is. And *that's* pretty frustrating a lot of times. Just the fact that *I* don't know what it is, you know. I've been frustrated with that. Well, what *is* this goddamn thing? Why do I *have* these headaches? (Hilbert, 1984, p. 368)

'Brian', interviewed by Byron Good, an American anthropologist, describes the world-destroying qualities of his pain:

> Sometimes, if I had to visualise it, it would seem as though there there's a ah … a demon, a monster, something very … horrible lurking around banging the insides of my body, ripping it apart. And ah, I'm containing it, or I'm trying to contain it, so that no one else can see it, so that no one else can be disturbed by it. Because it's scaring the daylights out of me, and I'd assume that … gee, if anybody had to, had to look at this, that … they'd avoid me like the plague. So I redouble my efforts to … say … I'm gonna be perfectly contained about this whole thing. And maybe the less I do, the less I make myself known, and the less I … venture out … or display any, any initiative, then I won't let the, this junk out. It seems like there's something very, very terrible happening. I have no control over it. (Good, 1994, pp. 121–2)

There are striking similarities between this account and those of the people with schizophrenia you read about in Chapter 6. Like those who hear voices from inside, so Brian's pain is personified as an internal demon or monster that he is trying to contain. He expresses the fear of stigma if his efforts at containment fail and the monster is revealed to others. Hilbert's respondents made similar points about the difficulties of containment and in judging when and how much to reveal:

> When you're with somebody else and you really want to participate with them and get to know them or whatever ... you would like to be able to give whoever the guy is your total attention for five minutes, and if in fact your attention is somewhere else you're going to end up ... being a little anti-social. You know, I don't ... go out much.

> They act like I've done something to them, like I've lied to them somehow. Like somehow I've done something wrong to them.
> (Hilbert, 1984, pp. 371–2)

● Think back to the explanation of the psychological roots of stigma in Chapter 2. In what sense might the complainer of chronic pain be 'doing something wrong' to those around him or her?

■ In Chapter 2 it was argued that the desire to be 'normal' was linked to the preservation of a basic sense of security (*ontological security*) about being in the world. People with deformities, or who stand outside 'normality', can be experienced as threatening to the security of others, and are therefore stigmatised. Chronic pain sufferers demonstrate an abnormal pain experience, for which onlookers cannot find an adequate explanation; this provokes deep anxieties that can lead to the person in pain being shunned.

People experiencing conditions characterised by chronic pain, then, are potentially isolated, marginalised without resources to make sense of their condition, and unable to find others with whom to share their experience. Once again, you should remember that this depicts the extreme end of an extreme condition. Not all pains are like this, or else it would be hard to imagine any of us continuing optimistically for long! The purpose of describing such an extreme is to show starkly what lies beneath more minor sufferings and their treatments, where the 'fall from culture' hardly begins before powerful reparative work occurs. Even for people with extreme troubles, there exist a variety of opportunities to pull back from despair and remake their worlds. It is to this that we now turn.

7.3.2 Healing and 'remaking' the world

One view of healing is that it is devoted to the removal of suffering. This may be achieved by straightforward technical means that, for example, anaesthetise pain or remove its cause. This understanding masks another feature of healing, which is brought into sharp relief when technical means are inadequate, as in chronic pain. Here, healing can be understood as the search for an adequate *narrative* (by the healer as well as the patient) with which to bestow meaning on suffering. As Byron Good has put it:

> One of the central efforts in healing is to symbolise the source of suffering, to find an image around which a narrative can take shape.
> (Good, 1994, p. 128)

The pursuit of relief and the search for meaning go hand in hand, and the sufferer and the medical system may play a part in both. The case of Brian, interviewed by

Byron Good, shows a succession of searches for an adequate narrative. Two were offered to Brian by the medical system. One focused on the physical level:

> Three successive physicians, treating him for congestion and pain in his ears and head, heard a clicking and popping sound in his jaw, suggested he might be suffering from 'temporomandibular joint disorder' or TMJ, and recommended restorative dentistry ... Thus began a reinterpretation of all of his pain ...
>
> I was a little sceptical at first ... [but then] I began to think this is something that may have a physical basis. (Good, 1994, p. 120)

Another narrative emphasised psychological causation:

> I spent a period of three months when I was two years of age [in an orphanage] ... it might have just come in right at that time ... that stripped me of any parental attachment ... [it was] something that damaged my feelings in the process. (Good, 1994, p. 119)

Both surgery and psychotherapy, however, failed to alleviate the pain, and by their failure indicated to Brian their inadequacy as narratives. When interviewed, Brian found relief in art:

> For him, it seems, [art] is a symbolic form of world making ... when language fails as a medium of self extension ... 'there are times when I ... can find expression in the art ... If I have a shrieking person inside me, someone that's yelling and screaming and trying to get out, sometimes I don't do it concretely. You know, I don't do it verbally ... it comes out in the painting'. (Good, 1994, p. 129)

Pain and suffering have frequently inspired artists such as Edvard Munch, an expressionist painter who sought to convey basic features of the human condition in his work. To this end, many of his themes drew on images of illness, suffering and death, as in his famous painting 'The Scream'. The use of non-verbal imagery as a means of communicating experiences of pain and suffering has also been encouraged in cancer hospitals (Figure 7.1) and in hospices, where patients seek to depict their feelings about terminal cancer. For example, one patient

> ... depicts his pain surrounding him totally as he lies stretched out on his bed. He described the whorled figure to us as the 'knotted muscles' of tension. He is cut off from the world by it. [His pain was subsequently relieved in a hospice.] (Saunders, 1978, p. 10)

Another patient felt 'constantly at the mercy of some kind of demolition squad' (Saunders and Baines, 1983, p. 12).

7.3.3   The meaning of a diagnosis

The moment of diagnosis can be of intense importance to people experiencing inexplicable illness, because of its potential to include the experience in a powerful institutionalised narrative. A medically sanctioned explanation in the case of one person interviewed by Hilbert, for example, was crucial in reassuring him that he was experiencing his body 'correctly':

> When the doctor called me in and told me what I had, I remember, I was so *delighted* to know that I had something that I didn't even

(a)

(b)

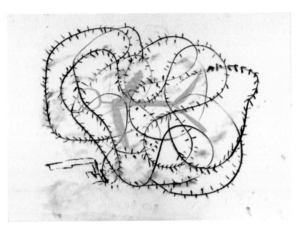

(c)

Figure 7.1 *Three images produced by people with cancer. (a) After a mastectomy and a severe infection in the reconstructed breast, the painter expresses both her physical pain and her powerful feelings about her current situation. (b) This painting expresses the emotional turmoil of learning that the cancer has returned after several years in remission. (c) 'Total Pain', a representation of the whole, painful experience of coping with the diagnosis and treatment of colon cancer. (Source: with kind permission of the Art Therapy Department, The Royal Marsden NHS Trust, London)*

hear what he said … Even if they'd have told me I had *cancer*, I wouldn't have cared. Really! I had just got to the point where I was desperate to be told that I had something. Cause I *knew there was something wrong* but I didn't know *what*. And the doctors couldn't find anything. And that's really hell … It meant there was nothing wrong with my head. That I wasn't a — you know — a hypochondriac, that I wasn't imagining all this stuff, because I was beginning to *believe* it. (Hilbert, 1984, p. 368)

In the case of pain, whether a patient has 'something' or 'nothing' can thus be of crucial importance in the sufferer's search for an adequate narrative giving meaning to their personal experience. The history of medical knowledge, however, shows that it constantly changes, with new divisions of disease categories replacing old ones, and shifting views about the relative importance of mind and body offer clinicians a changing basis for diagnostic labels.[3] In the case of chronic pain, there have been major shifts in the medical understanding of its nature, as the following section demonstrates. This means that a variety of medically sanctioned narratives are now available, some of them offering more opportunities than others to patients seeking to remake worlds disrupted by pain.

[3] Changes in medical knowledge over time, and across cultures, are discussed in *Medical Knowledge: Doubt and Certainty* (Open University Press, 2nd edn 1994; colour-enhanced 2nd edn 2001), and *Caring for Health: History and Diversity* (Open University Press, 3rd edn 2001).

7.4   Medical narratives for pain

Two major biological theories have dominated explanations of the phenomenon of pain, which have led to different approaches to treatment and to the construction of different medical narratives. Here we examine each in turn, before discussing the concept of *total pain*, developed in response to the needs of people with terminal cancer, as a narrative that contains elements derived from both medical and other sources.

7.4.1   Specificity theory

The earliest of the two biological theories explaining pain is known as **specificity theory**, shown at its simplest in the ideas of the seventeenth-century philosopher René Descartes. Figure 7.2 shows his (1664) concept of the pain pathway.

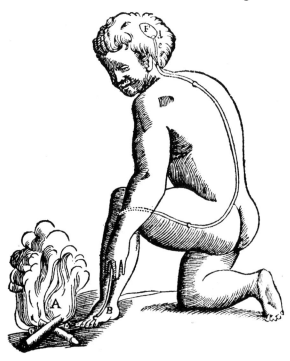

It starts from the basic assumption that pain is experienced because of *specific* messages generated in response to tissue damage, which are sent from the *periphery* (in Figure 7.2, nerve endings in the skin) to the **central nervous system** (the brain and spinal cord). In this model, the nervous system is seen as a 'hard-wired' electrical circuit, like a telephone exchange. The brain — or rather a specific part of it designated the 'pain centre' — is depicted as the *recipient* of signals from the damaged area. Specificity theory rests on a very firm distinction made by Descartes between the mind and the body (so-called *mind–body dualism*). Pain is designated as a bodily event, to which the mind reacts.

With advances in microscopy and other laboratory techniques in the nineteenth and twentieth centuries, specificity theory was developed in various ways. It was shown that pain signals from the periphery (**superficial pain**), and from the joints and internal organs (**deep pain**), travel along specialised nerve fibres with sensory endings devoted to recording only sensations of pain, rather than (say) warmth, cold or touch. These nerve endings generate a stream of electrical impulses when a stimulus locally exceeds the 'pain threshold', for example a blow or burning heat. The electrical signals travel along small-diameter *afferent fibres* (afferent means 'travelling inwards'), from the damaged area towards the brain, and are no different from the waves of impulses carried by all other nerve cells.

Figure 7.2   *René Descartes' concept of the pain pathway, which he described thus: 'If for example fire (A) comes near the foot (B), the minute particles of this fire, which as you know move with great velocity, have the power to set in motion the spot of the skin of the foot which they touch, and by this means pulling upon the delicate thread (c c) which is attached to the spot of the skin, they open up at the same instant the pore (d e) against which the delicate thread ends, just as by pulling at one end of a rope one makes to strike at the same instant a bell which hangs at the other end.' (Source: Oeuvres des Descartes, 1664)*

It also became clear that there was not a single unbroken 'telephone wire' connecting the site of damage to the brain (in contrast to Descartes' model). Many junctions exist in the pathway: the afferent pain fibres take the signals only as far as the spinal cord, where they trigger *transmission* cells, which in turn relay the pain signals up the spinal cord and across more junctions with nerve cells in the brain. At each of these junctions (or *synapses*), the signal is carried across the gap by chemical messengers called **neurotransmitters**. As the electrical impulses arrive at the junction, they cause the release of molecules of neurotransmitter, which diffuse across the gap and bind to receptors on the next nerve cell in the circuit, triggering new electrical impulses which are conducted on towards the brain. There are many different kinds of neurotransmitters but none are unique to the pain pathway.

Medical treatment based on specificity theory seeks to identify the physical origins of pain and the pathways by which it travels, and to intervene in these circuits to alleviate pain. For example, the surgical procedures shown in Figure 7.3, block transmission or even cut nerves between the pain site and the brain, but inevitably they also result in some unwanted damage to the patient's functional abilities. However, when such treatments are successful, they reinforce the medical narrative of pain as a purely 'bodily' event.

Unfortunately the basic premise of specificity theory — that once the nerve endings of a pain fibre are triggered by tissue damage, the message travels unaltered to the brain — cannot explain some contradictory facts about the experiences of people with chronic pain. Most dramatically, cutting a nerve pathway does not always achieve the same effect as cutting off a telephone. The pain sensation commonly reasserts itself, as if emanating from the same troublesome location as before. Additionally, a given level of stimulus does not correlate with a given level of experienced pain, as it should if the message travels 'straight through' to the brain from the pain site; in reality, the 'pain threshold' seems to vary even in the same person.

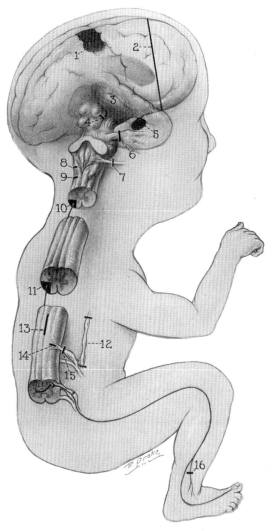

Figure 7.3 *Schematic diagram illustrating various surgical procedures designed to alleviate pain. Specificity theory has led surgeons to make interventions to block or cut physical pathways of pain. The numbers refer to points where the nerve pathways may be severed. (Source: MacCarty, C. S. and Drake, R. L., 1956, 'Neurosurgical procedures for the control of pain',* Proceedings of Staff Meetings of the Mayo Clinic, **31**, *facing p. 211)*

This is not merely a scientific problem: a patient who complains of pain whose origin cannot be found in the body runs the risk of being designated at worst a malingerer, or at least someone with a psychological disturbance. The description of nerve fibres, neurotransmitters and pathways derived from specificity theory is essentially correct, but something more is needed to explain the puzzles of felt pain and provide a more supportive medical narrative for patients.

7.4.2 Gate-control theory

In the 1960s, a psychologist, Ronald Melzack, and a neurophysiologist, Patrick Wall, developed a 'gate-control' theory, which represented a major development in the understanding of pain (Melzack and Wall, 1965). Although it has been modified in its details since it was first published, there is broad agreement about the general outline. Before we look at it in more detail, we need to explore some of the major problems it sought to resolve. Any comprehensive theory of pain needs to explain the puzzling features listed in Box 7.1 overleaf. (There are others, which are beyond the scope of this chapter.)

Box 7.1   Puzzles in the experience of physical pain

1   Rubbing the area of a painful blow (e.g. a knocked knee) generally relieves the pain.

2   Conversely, intense pain can sometimes be experienced when only a light stimulus is applied to an affected area, e.g. putting a burnt finger into lukewarm water.

3   Extremely serious injuries are sometimes accompanied by no pain sensation in the immediate aftermath of the trauma; this has been observed in injuries sustained on the battlefield, and in sports injuries occurring at crucial stages of an important contest.

4   Placebo analgesics (dummy pills given to patients who believe they are taking genuine painkillers), produce significant pain relief; additionally, patients who are in the most pain are those who experience the greatest placebo effect, which is the opposite of what you might expect to occur.

5   Pain can sometimes occur when there has been no apparent injury, or it continues long after an injury has apparently healed; it may even be felt in a 'phantom' limb years after it has been amputated.

6   Surgical intervention to cut or disable nerves transmitting pain sensations from a site of injury frequently fails to stop the experience of pain.

Most people will not have experienced the phenomena in Box 7.1, but their study has proved worthwhile in understanding the genesis of the more routine pains that most of us recognise. **Gate-control theory** — summarised in Figure 7.4 — offers a basis for understanding these (and other) puzzles. The theory starts in the same way as specificity theory, in that nerve endings are triggered by a painful stimulus and transmit signals in the form of electrical impulses along small-diameter afferent fibres towards the spinal cord. But Melzack and Wall proposed that mechanisms in the spinal cord then act like a 'gate', which can prevent the incoming impulses from stimulating the spinal cord cells and thus from transmitting pain signals along the ascending pathway to the brain (Figure 7.4a). Only when the gate is 'open' can the brain receive and record sensations of pain (Figure 7.4b).

Melzack and Wall also proposed ways in which the permeability of the gate could be altered (Figure 7.4c), in an important departure from specificity theory. In their model, the transmission cell in the spinal cord is not a simple 'relay station' passing on an unchanged message about pain. Instead, it is part of a complex 'pain-suppression network', which also involves *intermediate* cells in the spinal cord. When the intermediate cells are activated, they stimulate the transmission cells to 'close' the gate. Two major sources of input to the intermediate cells were identified, which could reduce or prevent pain sensations from reaching the brain — one originating from the painful area of the body and one originating in the brain itself. Figure 7.4c represents these inputs as (left) signals arriving at the intermediate cells along large-diameter afferent fibres, which are triggered by gentle mechanical stimulation (e.g. rubbing) in the painful area; and (right) signals descending from the brain, triggered by mental processes (thoughts, emotions, etc.).

By the end of the twentieth century, further research had revealed many more interactions than those shown in Figure 7.4c, and the neurophysiological mechanisms by which the stimulation of one nerve cell can *inhibit* the activity of another were well understood. The details are not part of this discussion, but you

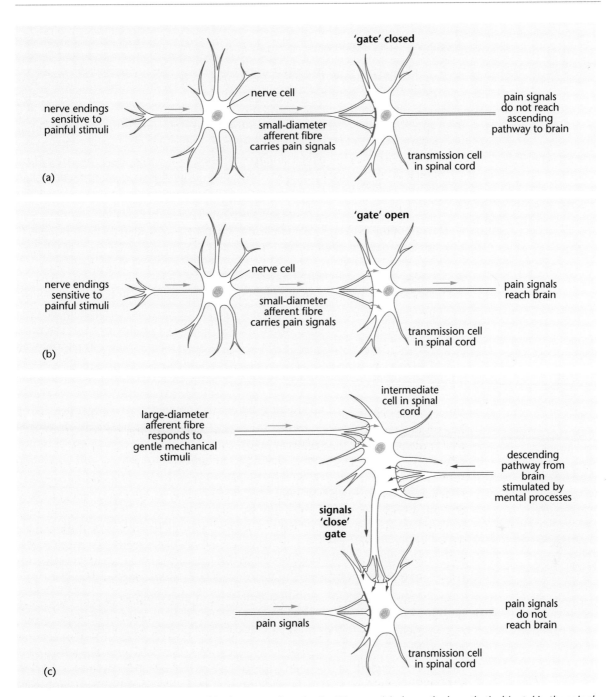

Figure 7.4   *The concept of gate control in the perception of pain. Diagram (a) shows the hypothetical 'gate' in the spinal cord closed, preventing the transmission of pain signals carried by small-diameter afferent fibres from the periphery to the brain. In (b) the 'gate' is open, and signals from the periphery stimulate transmission cells in the spinal cord to relay pain signals to the brain. Diagram (c) shows how the 'gate' may be closed by messages relayed by intermediate nerve cells, originating either from (left) large-diameter afferent fibres stimulated by gentle mechanical pressure in the periphery, or (right) descending signals from the brain.*

should be aware that the normal functioning of the whole nervous system — not just the components involved in pain perception — relies on the *summation* of billions of stimulatory and inhibitory inputs, modulated one against another, achieving the exquisitely fine gradations of sensation, mood and movement that most of us enjoy.

Gate-control theory has had important implications for understanding the puzzles of pain and how to relieve it.

● Look back at Box 7.1. How could puzzle 1 be explained in terms of gate-control theory, as represented in Figure 7.4?

■ Large-diameter afferent fibres are stimulated by gentle mechanical stimuli (Figure 7.4c). Relief of pain obtained by rubbing the area may be due to the partial closing of the gate in the transmission cells when large-diameter fibres stimulate intermediate cells in the same pain-suppression circuit. The pain signals transmitted to the brain are reduced as a consequence.

● Which of the puzzles of pain in Box 7.1 could be explained by the influence of mental processes altering the transmission of pain signals in the spinal cord?

■ Puzzles 3 and 4. In situations of extreme danger or excitement, such as battlefields or sports contests, the pain of an injury may not be recorded in the brain because the mental processes stimulated by the surrounding context close the gate in the spinal cord, via the descending pathway from the brain (Figure 7.4c). Similarly, the expectation of pain relief aroused in people who take a placebo can close the gate, and the effect is strongest if they are in considerable pain and therefore most anxious for it to work.

The idea of a gate opens up the possibility that the central nervous system has a degree of autonomy from the periphery in *creating* the perception of pain. In particular, the central nervous system performs a summation of a variety of stimuli from different sources, prioritising the perception of some stimuli and relegating others to a preconscious level. Thus, summation can be used to explain puzzle 3, by suggesting that in some contexts the perception of pain is not prioritised. Whether pain is experienced or not, and if so to what degree, is therefore influenced by what *else* is going on in the person's environment, interpreted broadly to include both the immediate physical surroundings and the psychological and cultural climate of the individual. As Melzack and Wall state:

> The effects of mood, culture, experience and expectation fall into place as part of a unified and integrated system and not as mysteries to be pushed aside or assigned to a totally separate mechanism of the mind. (Melzack and Wall, 1988; reprinted 1991, pp. 182–3)

The understanding that the brain could influence the perception of pain led to the discovery of pain-suppression mechanisms that could be triggered by psychological states. For example, during episodes of pain (and indeed stresses of other kinds), messages from the brain direct the release of *endorphins* and other naturally occurring *opioids* (molecules with a similar action to morphine). These substances act as **analgesics**, that is they selectively reduce the perception of pain without diminishing other sensations. They act on the brain itself, blocking the recording of incoming pain stimuli, and they are involved in the complex mechanisms that close the 'gate' in the spinal cord. Some of these natural opioids are also released during exercise and altered mental states, such as meditation.

Once the general principles of gate-control theory were accepted, additional features were added to explain several other puzzles in Box 7.1. For example, under certain circumstances the gate in the transmission cells can remain 'open' permanently and they continue to generate electrical signals and relay them to the brain long after the original stimulation from the periphery has ceased. This could explain the persistence of pain long after injury and also 'phantom limb' pain (puzzle 5). Cutting peripheral nerves would not affect the persistent abnormal activity of these transmission cells, thus explaining some (though not all) failures of such surgery (puzzle 6). That only leaves puzzle 2, which leads us to a discussion of what causes chronic intractable pain in diseases such as rheumatoid arthritis, and how it may be treated.

7.4.3 Treating chronic pain

Pain that persists long after a physical injury has healed is a relatively rare phenomenon. Chronic pain is most often the result of an unremitting injury (e.g. lower back pain), or progressive tissue damage caused by an advancing cancer or by an inflammatory disease such as rheumatoid arthritis. In all these conditions, a persistent state of inflammation is set up in the affected area, which causes the release of many different irritant chemicals, including a group called the *prostaglandins*. One effect of these substances locally is that they alter the sensitivity of the nerve endings that respond to painful stimuli, lowering the 'pain threshold' so that even a gentle stimulus may be enough to trigger an extreme sensation of pain. This state is called **hyperalgesia** and it is also experienced during the mild inflammation that is part of the normal healing process around a minor injury. This is the solution to puzzle 2 in Box 7.1.

A number of different approaches to pain control have been developed, which build on an understanding of hyperalgesia and the gate-control model of pain perception outlined above. For example, drugs that reduce inflammation will also reduce the experience of pain. Two of the commonest over-the-counter remedies for pain — aspirin and paracetamol — are both anti-inflammatory drugs, whose principal action is to block the release of prostaglandins. Narcotic drugs such as morphine and pethidine block pain signalling centrally, in the brain and spinal cord, in the same way as endorphins and other naturally occurring opioids.

Transcutaneous electrical nerve stimulation (TENS) achieves some pain reduction in about 60 per cent of people with acute pain by applying weak electrical stimulation to the skin in an affected area. TENS is often used to relieve back pain during childbirth, and has also proved successful in some cases of chronic pain. (At this point, Open University students should ideally play the audiotape entitled 'Being in pain', after first consulting the notes associated with it in the *Audiovisual Media Guide*. It begins with Patrick Wall, one of the originators of the gate-control model, describing how the theory was developed and how it led to new approaches to pain control. This is followed by interviews with a senior doctor and several patients attending a pain-control clinic.)

● What applications of gate-control theory have led to new treatments for pain, according to Wall?

■ TENS was developed as a direct application of the theory, by using weak electrical stimulation to 'close the gate' in just the same way as rubbing the affected area may relieve milder pains. (The mechanism is illustrated in Figure 7.4c; you may be interested to know that the centuries-old technique of acupuncture analgesia is thought to work in the same way.) Wall also emphasises the importance of gate-control theory in establishing that psychological and behavioural programmes could be effective pain-control strategies, if they altered people's attitude to their pain.

● How is this aspect of gate-control theory applied in the Liverpool pain-management programme featured on the audiotape?

■ The programme emphasises psychological rather than medical or surgical treatment, and helps patients to develop *cognitive*, *affective* and *behavioural* skills in learning to take more control over their pain. As patients become more active and self-reliant in treating their own pain by modifying their attitude and lifestyle, they also report feeling less anxious and depressed even when the physical pain itself does not diminish.

7.4.4 From biological theory to medical narrative

At the outset of this chapter, we emphasised that different *biological* theories of pain lead to different *medical narratives* to explain it, which in turn offer different material that people can draw on to make a 'meaningful' personal narrative of their pain. Specificity theory led to a medical narrative in which pain was simply a 'bodily' phenomenon, a consequence of physical mechanisms. When this model was in the ascendancy, patients whose experience did not fit the theory (as in the puzzles in Box 7.1), could not construct a meaningful explanation for their pain that fitted the prevailing medical narrative. They were seen as 'anomalies' who deviated from the norms of pain theory.

Gate-control theory released doctors and patients alike from the straightjacket of seeing the body and mind as separate systems. Matters that previously were relegated to the purely physical category of 'reflex' are now understood as amenable to influence from the conscious mind:

> If we pick up a hot cup of tea in an expensive cup we are not likely to simply drop the cup, but jerkily put it back on the table, and *then* nurse our hand. (Melzack and Wall, 1988, reprinted 1991, p. 193)

It also proposed mechanisms to explain *how* psychological phenomena can play an important role in determining our subjective experience of pain. In so doing, it constructed a new medical narrative that was both scientifically respectable and 'meaningful' to patients whose experience of pain had previously been a distressing puzzle. There are still controversies and pain mechanisms as yet unexplained by gate-control theory, but it has allowed a large variety of external factors to be brought to bear on the control of pain: the immediate physical environment, our evaluation of sources of threat and pleasure, our personalities, our conscious calculations about the consequences of courses of action, and indeed our cultural conditions.

7.4.5 The concept of total pain

It should by now be clear that the delineation of a separate sphere of experience called 'physical pain', and its separation from emotional and social pain is less easy to maintain in cases where pain is chronic. Just as this insight has arisen from study of rarer and more extreme cases (such as the 'puzzles' in Box 7.1), so the concept of **total pain** and its alleviation derives from work with people at an extreme point in life: those with terminal illness. It represents a medical narrative which attempts to help people who are experiencing suffering at, perhaps, its most extreme.

Total pain is a concept used by some professionals associated with hospice care to describe the suffering that may be experienced as people approach death, and to provide a rationale for their treatment and care. Cicely Saunders and Mary Baines (1983), doctors working in St Christopher's Hospice, London, have distinguished four elements to total pain: physical, emotional, social and spiritual.

Much effort in hospices has been devoted to investigating pharmacological and other methods for treating *physical* pain, for example advocating the use of high dosages of morphine without introducing irrelevant fears about drug dependency. In this respect, hospice care has drawn on the development of gate-control theory, and Patrick Wall was himself involved in the work of St Christopher's Hospice. However, hospices also seek to address the other aspects of total pain. Noting that a patient's mental distress is likely to be linked to his or her experience of physical pain, Saunders and Baines also observed that the effective treatment of one often relieves the other. Thus drug treatments for physical pain also relieve mental distress.

Listening to people's fears and concerns in a sympathetic manner is also a means of addressing the *emotional* pain of dying, which can in turn influence people's perceptions of their physical pain. The definition of *social* pain used by Saunders and Baines includes the distress of a dying person's family and friends. Hospice care seeks to attend to their needs too, for example by providing specific services to help people with their bereavement. Other aspects of social pain refer to anxieties about how the family will cope with practical matters after the death, for example childcare or financial hardship. The identification of *spiritual* pain reflects the religious background of some hospice practitioners, who seek also to maintain a religious narrative to give meaning to dying.

Although not specifically mentioned in the concept of 'total pain', hospice care has sometimes been characterised as treating the *pain of stigma*. Hospices arose partly in response to the stigmatisation of dying people in hospitals, who were (and perhaps still sometimes are) discharged, avoided or shut away in side rooms because they represented failure for the medical model of practice oriented towards cure. Hospice care, in the context of this chapter, can be understood as an attempt to construct a narrative of treatment and care that not only relieves physical pain, but also stresses the values of emotional and social *accompaniment* at a time of life where people are dying — or, in the words we used earlier, making a complete exit from culture.[4]

7.5 Negotiating treatment

Treatment for pain can be understood as a matter of negotiation between the personal world of the patient, and the technical or scientific world of the doctor or other healer. The first task in this negotiation is to come to an agreed definition of the problem, which in the case of pain is dependent on the creation of a shared language to communicate about subjective experiences. Issues of personal as opposed to medical responsibility for controlling the pain underlie negotiations over treatment, as you will see shortly.

7.5.1 Communicating about pain

Christian Heath, a sociologist interested in the dynamics of medical consultations, has presented evidence to suggest that, from one moment to another, people's expression and experience of pain may be determined by the particular psychosocial

[4] Hospice care is discussed in *Birth to Old Age: Health in Transition*, (Open University Press, 2nd edn 1995; colour-enhanced 2nd edn 2001), Chapter 13.

context, in a way that is consistent with the theories outlined by Melzack and Wall. Heath (1989) made videotape recordings of several consultations in which patients' pains were a topic. Through detailed analysis of the minutiae of the interaction, including the timing of pauses, manipulation of painful parts by the doctor, and analysis of exactly when 'pain cries' were emitted in the sequence of talk, Heath demonstrated that these occur only at *socially appropriate* moments. Patients managed the twin task of giving emotional expressions to their pain so as to 'prove' that it is there, and of withholding these cries when a more objective information-giving stance is required by the doctor. Box 7.2 contains an extract from one of these consultations.

Box 7.2   An example of 'socially appropriate' expression of pain

Dr: Just show me where that pain was will you?

P: It's just there, just on that bone.

Dr: Yes, yes, yes. Is it sort of like inside or just …

P: Seems on the inside — *oooh* [patient points towards his chest].

Dr: Yes.

P: *ooh*, it is there tender.

Dr: Yes, yes.

P: What is it doctor if you don't think that's a rude question, is it?

Dr: Well I don't think it's a rude question. I mean I think it just you know I think it is probably pain from your heart.

(Adapted from Heath, 1989, p. 120)

The first pain cry (*oooh*) is accompanied by the patient pointing towards his chest; neither he nor the doctor touched the chest. Clearly, the expression of pain occurs at the moment when it was 'required' by the ongoing interaction, that is to say, at the moment when it was needed as 'evidence'.

● What alternative explanations could there be for this precise timing of pain cries?

■ (a) The patient could be expressing a pain he did not have, or exaggerating it; (b) alternatively, he could be restraining himself from expressing a severe pain and 'letting it out' when given permission to do so; or (c) he could be subjectively experiencing the pain according to the moment-to-moment demands of the interaction.

One of the major difficulties in trying to understand pain is that we cannot know exactly how other people experience their pain. However, it is at least possible, given the theory of gate control and summation of a variety of stimuli arriving simultaneously, that (c) is the correct explanation. The central nervous system may be capable of changing its priorities for the perception of pain according to quite subtle changes in the flow of a conversation — 'allowing' the pain sensations to reach consciousness only at socially appropriate moments.

7.5.2 A shared language for pain

It was stated earlier that pain is often expressed in pre-linguistic cries; the lack of a shared language for communicating varieties of pain experience contributes to its isolating effect and allows stigmatising perceptions to develop. Significantly, the scientists who developed and elaborated the theory of gate control have also been prominent in attempts to construct linguistic devices that convey the subjective experience of pain in an accurate and valid way. Figure 7.5 shows the *McGill–Melzack Pain Questionnaire*, developed to measure different qualities of the pain experience.

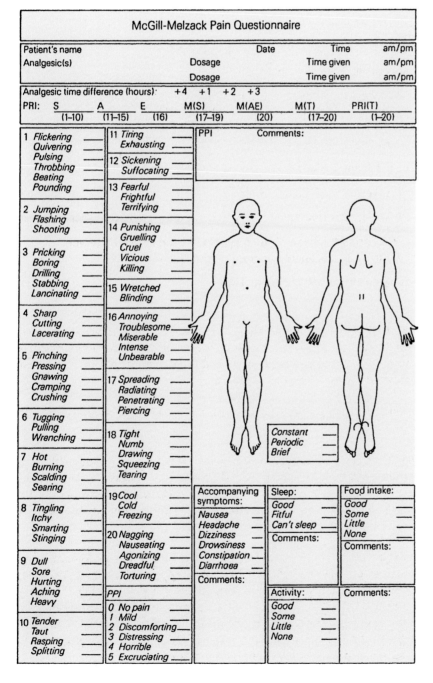

Figure 7.5 *The McGill–Melzack Pain Questionnaire. From each of the applicable sections, the sufferer chooses the word that best describes the current feelings and sensations evoked by the pain. The questionnaire allows people to assess separately various sub-classes of pain, e.g. sensory (S: numbers 1–10), affective (A: 11–15), evaluative (E: number 16) and miscellaneous (M: 17–20) categories. From the individual responses, a Pain Rating Index (PRI) can be calculated, based on the numerical values previously ascribed to each word. The Present Pain Index (PPI) is a single assessment of overall pain severity. (Source: based on the original version of the McGill–Melzack Pain Questionnaire described in Melzack, 1975, and reproduced in Melzack and Wall, 1988, p. 40)*

Table 7.1 is based on careful research into the language used by people to describe different sources of pain. It shows how six different pain syndromes were associated with particular words and has proved successful in helping to communicate clinically relevant information. One study (Dubuisson and Melzack, 1976) showed that, on the basis of the words chosen by patients with eight different pain syndromes, a computer was able to identify correctly the cause of the pain in 77 per cent of cases. When the sex of the patients and the location of the pain were included, all cases were correctly classified.

Table 7.1   Descriptions characteristic of clinical pain syndromes.

Menstrual pain (N = 25)	Arthritic pain (N = 16)	Labour pain (N = 11)	Disc disease pain (N = 10)	Toothache (N = 10)	Cancer pain (N = 8)
Sensory					
cramping (44%)	gnawing (38%)	pounding (37%)	throbbing (40%)	throbbing (50%)	shooting (50%)
aching (44%)	aching (50%)	shooting (46%)	shooting (50%)	boring (40%)	sharp (50%)
		stabbing (37%)	stabbing (40%)	sharp (50%)	gnawing (50%)
		sharp (64%)	sharp (60%)		burning (50%)
		cramping (82%)	cramping (40%)		heavy (50%)
		aching (46%)	aching (40%)		
			heavy (40%)		
			tender (50%)		
Affective					
tiring (44%)	exhausting (50%)	tiring (37%)	tiring (46%)	sickening (40%)	exhausting (50%)
sickening (50%)		exhausting (46%)	exhausting (40%)		
		fearful (36%)			
Evaluative					
	annoying (38%)	intense (46%)	unbearable (40%)	annoying (50%)	unbearable (50%)
Temporal					
constant (56%)	constant (44%)	rhythmic (91%)	constant (80%)	constant (60%)	constant (100%)
	rhythmic (56%)		rhythmic (70%)	rhythmic (40%)	rhythmic (88%)

Note that only those words chosen by more than one-third of the patients are listed and the percentage of patients who chose each word is shown in parentheses. The word 'rhythmic' is one of three words ('rhythmic/periodic/intermittent') used in different versions of the McGill–Melzack Pain Questionnaire (Melzack, 1975). (Source: Melzack, R. and Wall, P. D., 1988, *The Challenge of Pain,* reprinted 1991, p. 42)

As confidence in the validity of instruments such as those shown in Figure 7.5 and Table 7.1 builds in medical settings, so confidence increases in the ability to convey hitherto incommunicable experiences. This has the potential to combat the isolation experienced by people with chronic pains by offering a shared language. However, the limitations of using measures of pain devised by 'outsiders' rather than determined by patients themselves must be borne in mind, as the discussion of rheumatoid arthritis (Chapter 3) made clear.

7.5.3 Taking responsibility

Although medicine offers powerful institutionally based narratives for people experiencing pain and suffering, people are not simply 'written into' such narratives as if they were passive recipients of a 'script'. People actively *appropriate* medical narratives, sometimes choosing between a variety of conflicting scripts in negotiation with various medical practitioners.

● Which conflicting scripts for people with chronic pain (such as Brian, interviewed by Byron Good) have been reviewed in this chapter?

■ Specificity theory and gate-control theory offer people (through their interaction with doctors and others who 'represent' these narratives) different scripts in terms of their explanations and treatments for chronic pain. Locating pain as having a physical or psychological cause involves a choice between scripts; each at various times was accepted by Brian as he sought an explanation for his chronic pains.

The issue of personal responsibility is a theme that runs through many negotiations between doctors and patients with pain. Medical settings may initially be approached by patients with the expectation that the doctor will take responsibility for seeking a solution to their pain. Sometimes this may literally involve 'writing a script', as where the doctor issues a drug prescription. However, in many cases the interaction that proceeds is not as simple as that. To explore these issues Open University students should now read the article by Sally Macintyre and David Oldman, 'Coping with migraine'.[5]

● What treatments were experienced by Sally Macintyre?

■ She lists a variety of treatments: at first she used a drug to handle the migraine attacks. She was reluctant to accept psychological therapies as they threatened her feelings about herself. Eventually, Valium helped with her anxieties about attacks and helped her to begin to modify aspects of her life, such as her diet and the wearing of dark glasses. She now regards herself as an 'expert' in using her GP as a resource for her to manage her own treatment.

● What treatments were experienced by David Oldman?

■ His mother treated his migraine attacks with the home remedies of bed rest, a dark room and a hot-water bottle. With varying degrees of success, he sought to build this pattern of withdrawal into his life to control attacks. Like Sally Macintyre, he too selectively uses drugs obtained from his doctor.

---

[5] An edited extract from Macintyre and Oldman (1977) appears in *Health and Disease: A Reader* (Open University Press, 3rd edn 2001).

Sally Macintyre, in particular, describes her experiences with doctors as a series of negotiations over treatments, some being acceptable to her, others being unacceptable. David Oldman appears to have had a somewhat easier time in reaching an eventual position which, for both these people, displays a strong sense of personal responsibility for controlling the illness. Both can be seen as having appropriated elements of medical narratives in writing a personal narrative that gives meaning to, and offers a degree of control over their pains.

7.6 Stoicism

The emphasis in hospice care and in pain clinics on recognising and treating pain in others involves the construction of medical narratives that emphasise sensitivity to the subjective experience of those affected. Heightened sensitivity of this type (empathy) is commonly characterised as a caring or compassionate approach in modern culture and attracts considerable approval, so that it may be seen as having a widespread *social value.*

Figure 7.6 *A member of the Rufias sect in Erbil, Iraq, demonstrates his religious conviction and endurance by stoical acceptance of pain from ritual piercing of the body. (Photo: Sedat Aral/Rex Features)*

However, the institutionalised promotion of care and compassion, involving an encouragement to speak and care about suffering, is a relatively recent historical phenomenon — at least on the large scale represented by the construction of systems of health care. The alternative value of **stoicism** is one which was more widespread in the past, and may be characteristic of some traditional cultures today. In common parlance, it is associated with the 'stiff upper lip' and avoidance of resort to medicine.

There is evidence to suggest cross-cultural and historical variability in people's tolerance to pain and suffering. Cross-cultural aspects are illustrated, once again, by some rather dramatic examples. Indian fakirs appear to be able to induce a state of hypnotic analgesia when they walk across beds of hot coals or lie on nails; piercing the body with knives and skewers is occasionally displayed on stage, involving a similar state of mind. Certain ritual occasions induce in individuals, who have reached a sufficiently trance-like state, an ability to tolerate damage that would normally cause intense pain (Figure 7.6).

7.6.1 Declining tolerance to pain?

It is likely that in the past there were higher levels of stoicism. This is demonstrated by the discovery, in a variety of archaeological sites, of skulls with holes cut into the top associated with a fairly common operation done in the past, described here by Melzack and Wall:

> In East Africa, men and women undergo an operation — entirely without anaesthetics or pain-relieving drugs — called 'trepanation', in which the scalp and underlying muscles are cut in order to expose a large area of the skull. The skull is then scraped by the doktari [doctor] as the man or woman sits calmly, without flinching or grimacing, holding a pan under the chin to catch the dripping blood. Films of this procedure are extraordinary to watch because of the discomfort they induce in the observers, which is in striking contrast to the apparent lack of discomfort in the people undergoing the operation. There is no reason to believe that these

people are physiologically different in any way. Rather, the operation is accepted by their culture as a procedure that brings relief of chronic pain. (Melzack and Wall, 1988, p. 17)

● In Chapter 2 you saw that Elias argued that a 'civilising process' had made people more sensitive to, and more ashamed of, bodily functions. How might this theory be applied to historical changes in perceptions of pain?

■ The same process may have made people more sensitive to pain. Whereas before pain was not remarked upon, now it is a focus of attention. Sensitivity to others' pains, institutionalised in the activities of health-care workers, may have increased sensitivity to one's own pains.

If such a change has occurred, gate-control theory would suggest that subjective experiences of pain would have been *less* common in the past for a given level of physical stimulus. Stoicism is another word for effective mental control over pain sensation, not simply a suppression of the desire to express distress. In the terms used earlier in this chapter, stoicism involves effective resistance to the unmaking of the world by pain. This means that higher levels of injury can be tolerated before the remaking of the world by religious, medical or other narratives becomes necessary.

7.6.2 Killing pain

The encouragement in modern culture towards a heightened sensitivity to pain leads on the one hand to its widespread discussion and inclusion in medical narratives, and on the other to a decreased tolerance for pain. This reduction in stoicism leads to dependence on technical methods for killing pain. The philosopher and theologian Ivan Illich (1976) develops this argument, saying that Western *medicalised*[6] culture is one where the general problem of human suffering has increasingly been interpreted as simply a matter of *physical* pain. The solution to pain in such a culture is to provide an anaesthetic for the slightest occasion and make remedies for pain available as commodities. Pain relief has come to be regarded as a right. Thus, Illich argues, we live in an 'anaesthetic society' in which we flee from pain by trying to kill it as soon as it appears.

Melzack and Wall, for example, although their theory allows for approaches that involve learning to live with pain, otherwise represent the sort of view of which Illich is critical: they consider it to be an appropriate goal to move towards a pain-free world:

> There is no question that our new understanding is leading to our goal of abolishing pain … The challenges before us are clear: to conquer pain and suffering in all their forms … [We must] combine all the available resources to allow the nervous system to move toward a normal, pain-free mode of operation. (Melzack and Wall, 1988, reprinted 1991, pp. 213, 273, 295)

Even if this were possible, it is debatable whether such a world would be a very pleasant place in which to live. John Hick (1977), a theologian, contemplated just such a world as proposed by the eighteenth-century philosopher David Hume.

---

[6] Medicalisation, and the contribution of Ivan Illich to the debate about its impact, is discussed in *Medical Knowledge: Doubt and Certainty* (Open University Press, 2nd edn 1994; colour-enhanced 2nd edn 2001). An article by Illich, ' The epidemics of modern medicine', also appears in *Health and Disease: A Reader* (Open University Press, 3rd edn 2001).

In opposition to Hume, Hick points out that pain is a warning signal that is essential for our survival in the material environment. Occasional cases of people who are congenitally unable to feel pain reveals that these individuals lead very dangerous lives, frequently damaging themselves very seriously. In addition, the removal of pain would radically alter the nature of human existence. As Hick argues,

> A soft unchallenging world would be inhabited by a soft unchallenged race of men [sic] (Hick, 1977, p. 307).

The alternative, which Illich believes is characteristic of societies that have not experienced medicalisation, is to *include* pain as a part of the 'performance of suffering'. Pain is seen as an inevitable part of life, albeit unpleasant, but one that paradoxically means that the pleasures of life are experienced more fully when they occur. Illich also harks back nostalgically to a time when pain was contained in a religious narrative, making it more easy to accept.

It is undoubtedly the case that responses to acute pain in Western culture generally take the form outlined by Illich, as evidenced by the increasing use of analgesics, epidural anaesthesia and Caesarean section in childbirth. However, this chapter has demonstrated that, in the case of chronic pain and the 'total pain' of dying, new medical narratives are now available that incorporate both the acknowledgement and acceptance of pain and suffering, and the goal of eradicating it.

7.7 Conclusion

This chapter has demonstrated the value of an interdisciplinary approach to understanding the experience of pain and suffering. In so doing, a picture of pain as both a physiological and a psychosocial experience has emerged, and its position in the spectrum of distress commonly referred to as 'suffering' has been explored.

Central to the experience of pain is the search for an explanation that will turn the perception of chaos and the experience of isolation into one of order and inclusion in social life. Medical efforts have been depicted as institutionalised narratives, which can be drawn upon with varying degrees of success by people experiencing pain and suffering. Recent shifts in medical thinking have created more all-embracing narratives with a greater potential for inclusion and healing of hitherto mysterious conditions.

At the same time, these broader medical narratives, seen in gate-control theory and its associated treatments, and in hospice care, can be understood as part of a wider historical process in which the modern experience of illness and care is located. Modern conditions encourage us to pay great attention to suffering, particularly suffering of the body, and paradoxically this may mean that we increase the likelihood that we will find it overwhelming and seek relief in 'anaesthetics'. The tension between killing pain, suffering pain and learning to live with it is central to the modern experience of illness.

OBJECTIVES FOR CHAPTER 7

When you have studied this chapter, you should be able to:

7.1 Define and use, or recognise definitions and applications of, each of the terms printed in **bold** in the text.

7.2 Demonstrate how and why people who are suffering physical, emotional and social pain seek to give their experience meaning and legitimate it in the eyes of others.

7.3 Discuss the ways in which specificity theory and gate-control theory lead to different treatments for pain, and different medical narratives to explain it; comment on the implications of these theories in attempts made by people to give chronic pain a meaning.

7.4 Distinguish the specifically modern aspects of pain and suffering in Western culture from those that seem to have been current in earlier times.

QUESTIONS FOR CHAPTER 7

1 (*Objective 7.2*)

Small children with quite minor scratches often cry inconsolably until a plaster is applied by a sympathetic adult, at which point their attention may then switch to more pleasurable activity. How could the concepts of 'making' and 'unmaking' the world help to explain this? What component of suffering is appealed to by the adult who says 'Don't make such a fuss: it's only a scratch'?

2 (*Objective 7.2*)

Richard Hilbert concludes his study of people with chronic pains by stating:

> The mere addition of 'chronic pain syndrome' to the lexicon of sufferers is a treatment of sorts. (Hilbert, 1984, p. 376)

Why might the mere naming of a syndrome by medicine be tantamount to treating it?

3 (*Objective 7.3*)

People who are suffering from severe chronic pain may experience significant relief from taking a placebo pill which they believe to be a genuine pain-killer. How does gate-control theory provide them with a medical narrative for this phenomenon and from what stigmatising accusations are they protected as a consequence?

4 (*Objective 7.4*)

The diaries of the Reverend Ralph Josselin (1616–1683) discuss health and illness in his family over a forty-year period. The sociologist Deborah Lupton notes:

> They were unwell, or at least uncomfortable, most of the time, due to continual colds and occasional bouts of ague, eye and skin disorders, and in the case of Josselin's wife Jane, fifteen pregnancies and at least five miscarriages. Of the ten live births to the Josselins, five children predeceased their father. Worms, rickets, boils, measles and smallpox were suffered by the children, while Ralph Josselin himself suffered pain, swelling and ulceration in his left leg for the

eleven years before his death, and inflammation of the navel for almost four years ... While there were expectations that people sick enough to be confined to bed should stay in bed, be waited on and take medicine if required, it was expected that people well enough to be out of bed should bear their discomfort and carry on with their normal duties ... [the family] almost never consulted physicians and surgeons, but relied on their own knowledge or that of others such as friends, nurses and part-time healers for treatment ... the Josselins believed that God's will was of the ultimate importance in determining the outcome of an illness. (Lupton, 1994, p. 82, summarising a study of the diaries made by Beier, 1985)

How does the modern experience of pain and suffering in Western culture differ from this?

CHAPTER 8

Experiencing and explaining disease: some conclusions

Study notes for OU students

If you have time while reading this chapter, an optional article in *Health and Disease: A Reader* (Open University Press, third edition 2001) will enhance your understanding of stigmatisation and discrimination as a major theme of this book; it is 'Pride against prejudice: "lives not worth living" ' by Jenny Morris. At the end of this chapter, as a revision exercise, you will be asked to listen to an audiotape band, 'Living with epilepsy', which gives you the opportunity to apply the perspectives developed in earlier chapters to another and quite different disorder. This final chapter also marks the conclusion of the *Health and Disease* series, so the authors briefly look back over the territory covered by students of the Open University course of which this is the last of eight books. This chapter was written by Clive Seale, Professor of Medical Sociology at Goldsmiths' College, London University, and Basiro Davey, Senior Lecturer in Health Studies in the Department of Biological Sciences, The Open University.

8.1 Introduction

This book has described certain consistent features of the *experience* of illness and disability, and of the dominant *explanations* for disease in both lay and professional accounts. Every chapter has pointed to ways in which the experiential and explanatory domains interact and exert profound influences on each other. In assembling material for this book, the authors have drawn on the findings of a variety of academic disciplines, including biology, epidemiology, clinical medicine and the social and behavioural sciences. We have also incorporated personal anecdotes, fragments of news reporting, and portrayals of illness in the entertainment media.

In this final chapter, we summarise the main themes of the book, which — for the sake of clarity — we have organised under two headings: 'Doubt and certainty' and 'Inclusion and exclusion'. Other methods of grouping the material are possible and, indeed, other interpretations of 'what this book is about' may have occurred to you as you read it — an outcome that we warmly welcome. Health and illness, disease and disability are not fixed entities, as we noted in Chapter 1, and each of us adds to the fluidity of meaning attached to these terms. However, we maintain that the major themes identified in this book have a certain universality: they can be found at different times and in different places and cultures, wherever humans experience ill-health and attempt to explain and alleviate pain and suffering. We reinforce this assertion by noting — briefly — the expression of these themes in accounts of illness, disease or disabling states other than those already discussed in earlier chapters of this book.

At the very end of this chapter, we offer a few concluding remarks for the *Health and Disease* series as a whole.

8.2 Doubt and certainty

It is no accident that the 'label' we have chosen to stand for one group of themes in this final book in the series, is also part of the title of its first book.[1] Doubt and certainty — and the tension between them — have helped to link the various books in the series as they spanned huge distances of time, space and culture.

8.2.1 Personal knowledge

In this book, Chapter 2 brought the tension between doubt and certainty in our personal worlds to the foreground. It argued that any doubts about continuing in existence pose such a threat to the human psyche that we act — individually and collectively — to create an illusion of certainty. Illness, according to social theorists, such as Anthony Giddens, undermines our *ontological security*, as well as disrupting the familiar mental and physical states we associate with 'normal' health. Recourse to the *grand narratives* of orthodox medical treatment, traditional therapies, prayer, psychoanalysis, or whatever else holds out hope of a cure, is prompted by the desire to banish threatening doubts and restore a degree of certainty and control, as well as by the desire to be free from pain and disability.

Part of the experience of illness and injury is the need to answer the existential questions we have posed throughout this book: 'Why me? Why now? What next?'

---

[1] *Medical Knowledge: Doubt and Certainty* (Open University Press, 2nd edn 1994; colour-enhanced 2nd edn 2001).

These questions arise even for a trivial illness, a common cold for example — was it due to staying out too late in cold air, or getting stressed at work, or was it just our bad luck to encounter another 'bug' doing the rounds, which a couple of days' rest will resolve? Finding answers takes on real urgency when the illness is chronic, painful, severely disabling (either mentally or physically), incurable, or potentially fatal, as all the case studies in this book have illustrated. As Chapter 1 described, the search for certainty in a world 'unmade' by such an illness typically leads to the construction of a *personal illness narrative*, a meaningful story that explains the illness in a way that 'makes sense' to the person who constructed it. Such narratives often involve the reconstruction and reinterpretation of past events, now seen to be part of the underlying history of the present disorder.

In schizophrenia, where the condition affects thought processing itself, reaching a satisfactory personal construction of the illness may be a particularly difficult task. Questions of 'Why me?', Why now?' may be 'answered' in ways that others find unbelievable — for example, 'voices' may be heard as real or emanating from sources that appear to others to be imaginary.

Professionals who seem able to offer authoritative explanations for an illness are likely to be sought as allies in constructing a meaningful narrative. Medical knowledge and the treatment practices associated with it contribute to a grand narrative about human suffering, which people draw upon to give meaning to the potentially chaotic and mysterious process of being ill, disabled, or in chronic pain. It helps to 'remake the shattered world' if a *medical label* can be tied to a person's symptoms, investing it with a reassuring legitimacy. Several of the personal accounts in this book have expressed the relief of being told by a doctor that distressing symptoms were due to an identifiable disease. The anxiety that one may be thought a 'malingerer' or 'hypochondriac' is relieved by a medical diagnosis, which can restore the patient's *moral reputation*.

The ability of medicine to do all these things helps to explain its power as a cultural icon in modern industrialised societies. The 'moral' aspect is particularly apparent when a medical diagnosis is applied to someone with a mental illness. As the Reader article by Goffman[2] and the chapter on schizophrenia show, mental illness presents a basic threat to *social norms* of conduct, which others often find more difficult to condone than in the case of deviations from the norm due to a physical illness.

But illness is more than a matter of abstract psychology and social constructs. It faces us with pressing physical realities. Common to all the conditions described in this book is the experience of uncertainty about the progression of the disease, and its likely consequences for an individual's life. Rheumatoid arthritis, HIV disease, asthma and schizophrenia are all relatively unstable, fluctuating or episodic conditions, and people who are affected by these conditions face a daily uncertainty about the severity of their symptoms. There may be long periods of remission, followed by an unpredictable relapse. As a person living with HIV says:

> One of the cruellest ruses of the virus is letting you think the good
> times are the real times. (Quoted by Small, 1995, p. 103)

Uncertainty, then, preoccupies many people with the conditions reviewed in the case studies chosen for this book. It also concerns their families, friends and colleagues. The uncertainties associated with the illness have an impact beyond

---

[2] 'The insanity of place' in *Health and Disease: A Reader* (Open University Press, 3rd edn 2001) was set reading for Open University students during Chapter 2 of this book.

the individuals designated as 'sufferers', profoundly altering the lives of others around them. For example, the parents of a child with severe asthma can agonise over whether to rush to a hospital if a bout of wheezing occurs in the night; holidays may have to be cancelled at the last minute, broken sleep and worry can become routine. The families of adults whose chronic back pain leads to job loss cannot know if the financial insecurity is temporary or permanent. The children of people living with HIV are often very anxious about how they will cope when their parent becomes too sick to take care of them.

But most illness episodes do not rob the affected person of the ability to cope, at least to some degree. People are not usually the passive recipients of what a disease dictates, and uncertainty is actively counteracted with skills developed from past experiences of illness.

● Can you recall an example from earlier in this book?

■ Sally Macintyre and David Oldman described how they came to deal with the uncertainty of migraines.[3] They built up expertise in self-care, recognising the signs of a coming attack and taking action at the appropriate time to pre-empt a worsening of symptoms.

But novel, fluctuating or puzzling symptoms raise doubts about 'What to do for the best?' It may be difficult to decide whether to seek medical help in determining whether the symptoms are serious or even 'real'. Delay may stem from anxiety about having one's worst fears confirmed (as in the case of an HIV test), or out of a concern not to waste the doctor's time by 'making a fuss about nothing'. After all, most illness episodes resolve without medical help or are successfully self-treated. Part of the anxiety among lay people about whether they should seek professional help for an illness that cannot be pinned down may arise from the belief that medicine is an exact science and that doctors only like to deal with certainties. This book, along with others in this series, has sought to illustrate the tenuousness of this belief. People with chronic ailments may worry that they will lose the goodwill of health professionals if they seek help too often, and may try to cope alone rather than risk the GP's heart sinking as they walk into the surgery again.

● What other reasons can you suggest for delay in seeking medical help?

■ People may realise that there is no point in seeking help because the treatment is too costly for a health service to afford (e.g. HAART drugs in low-income countries) or because it is inaccessible (e.g. too far away). Or they may not realise that help is available and would be given to them if they came forward (e.g. the delay among poorer families in seeking help for a schizophrenic member may be due to assumptions like these).

But delay may also mean that medical intervention comes too late to prevent an otherwise avoidable attack or deterioration of the condition — a dilemma acutely expressed in Chapter 5 by the parents of children with asthma, and in Chapter 6 by the worse outcomes for people with schizophrenia whose treatment is begun 'late'.

---

[3] 'Coping with migraine', in *Health and Disease: A Reader* (Open University Press, 3rd edn 2001) was referred to in Chapters 5 and 7 of this book.

8.2.2 Professional knowledge

The sphere of professional knowledge that has figured most prominently in our discussion of doubt and certainty is biomedicine — that is, medical knowledge based on biological research into the structures and functions of the body. In addition to establishing the legitimacy of an illness, a medical diagnosis holds out the hope of more tangible certainties for the patient. The doctor may be able to say what caused the condition, how it is likely to progress or be resolved by treatment, and what can be done to prevent it from occurring again. Medicine can be technically effective in reducing suffering, by alleviating pain or anxiety, or treating the underlying causes of the symptoms. Medicine on this level is a remarkable human achievement in which many health-care workers are justifiably proud to play their part. But 'certain knowledge' is relatively uncommon in modern medicine, as the disorders we chose as case studies for this book amply demonstrate.

● What were the main areas of medical uncertainty highlighted in earlier chapters?

■ The disease processes themselves are generally well *described* in rheumatoid arthritis (RA), HIV disease and asthma, but remain a mystery in schizophrenia and in many cases of chronic pain. The underlying *cause* of HIV disease is known to be a virus, but there is considerable uncertainty about what 'triggers' the inflammation in RA and asthma, and what produces persistent pain in the absence of injury; the causes of schizophrenia are utterly obscure. All the conditions featured in this book have a *variable* course, sometimes progressing and at other times remitting, without any consistent explanation. Despite a medical consensus about the *range* of treatment options, there is still some disagreement about which therapies are most effective, none yet produce a *cure*, and available drugs and surgical interventions can have serious adverse *side effects*. There are no medical strategies for *preventing* any of these conditions.

These uncertainties limit the extent to which medical knowledge can alleviate suffering, and they also reduce the power of medical narratives as sources of comfort and reassurance for patients. The principal doubts in scientific medicine stem from the inability of basic biological research to *explain* disease processes rather than simply describe them.

● How does the example of HIV and AIDS illustrate a 'failure' of biological research to supply vital medical knowledge (at least up to 2002)?

■ The HIV was identified in 1983 and its mode of binding to host cells and replication within them was established in the next few years. But despite this knowledge, almost two decades later there was little progress in developing protective vaccines and no drugs that eradicate HIV from the body. (The 'successes' have been new therapies to treat opportunistic infections, drugs that prevent mother-to-baby transmission of HIV, and social research leading to interventions that reduce the spread of HIV.)

This situation is in contrast to that of asthma. Biological knowledge about the mechanisms that lead to allergies, inflammation and bronchoconstriction has enabled treatment strategies to be devised, which enable most asthmatic people to live normal lives. However, there is continuing biological uncertainty about what causes asthma to develop in the first place, so as yet little can be done to prevent it.

Perhaps the most intriguing area of uncertainty in academic and professional knowledge concerns the *definition* of a disease entity, which reliably distinguishes it from the range of variation in 'normal' states of health and from other states of disease. The diagnostic criteria that, for example, distinguish asthma from 'wheezing' are necessarily imprecise: they may vary from one country to another, change over time, and be subject to disagreement between individual doctors.

● How does the example of schizophrenia illustrate the interaction between diagnostic criteria and epidemiological data on trends in the condition in the UK?

■ When the diagnostic criteria for schizophrenia changed in 1993 as a consequence of the tenth revision of the international classification of diseases (ICD-10), the number of episodes of hospital admission for schizophrenia jumped to a higher level (Figure 6.2) — an example of diagnostic transfer.

As the list of opportunistic infections accepted as indicative of HIV-related disease has grown, so larger numbers of individuals have been recorded as having AIDS. The numbers leapt when tubercular pneumonia was added to the list — a decision that increased the prevalence of recorded AIDS among Western drug injectors and some populations in developing countries. Examples such as these illustrate the reasons for uncertainty about whether published data on the incidence and prevalence of a disorder are reliable and indeed comparable over time and between different locations.

However, these uncertainties should not be allowed to obscure the fact that within a particular medical tradition (for example, Western biomedicine or Ayurvedic medicine), a consensus about the principal signs and symptoms of a certain disease generally exists among practitioners, or can be achieved through collaboration.

● The published prevalence of schizophrenia in different countries has shown considerable variation in the past. What was the outcome when the same 'narrow' definition of schizophrenia was applied in several sites around the world?

■ Apparent differences in prevalence were greatly reduced and the rates became similar, even in countries with markedly different cultures. This finding casts doubt on the hypothesis that schizophrenia is a product of cultural pressures.

Epidemiologists have contributed to scientific understanding of the causes of many diseases, by demonstrating varying prevalence rates in particular subgroups within and between populations. This is most obviously illustrated by HIV and AIDS and their association with people exposed to sexual or blood-borne routes of infection. Epidemiological research on asthma is beginning to identify the environmental triggers for attacks (if not the underlying causes of susceptibility to these triggers).

● What insight into the underlying causes of RA has epidemiological research provided?

■ Demonstrating that prevalence is higher among women than men, but falls during pregnancy or with use of oral contraceptive pills, has strongly suggested a role for the female hormone oestrogen in the aetiology of RA.

However, considerable doubts about the causes of RA remain, and an equivalent uncertainty has been emphasised in other case studies in this book. For example, schizophrenia is one of many conditions in which the '*nature–nurture*' debate has been fiercely contested in professional circles. The majority view since the 1990s is that schizophrenia is a disorder of chemicals in the brain, rather than an expression of dysfunctional family relationships — a view that was more prominent in the 1970s. In the twenty-first century, the rapid developments in human genetics may resurrect an interpretation of schizophrenia as an inherited condition — a belief that research in previous decades failed to prove.

Inevitably, the dominant medical understanding of a disease at a particular time and place influences the treatments that are considered 'best practice', while relegating others to the 'fringe'. It is not always the case that medical knowledge accumulates and treatments are refined and improved on the basis of scientific evidence. Medical 'fashions' can influence treatment strategies, and the wonder drug of one period can fall from favour, as occurred with steroids in the treatment of RA, and may yet occur in relation to HAART for people with HIV. There is no shortage of examples to demonstrate tension between doubt and certainty in all areas of professional knowledge about health and disease.

8.2.3 Public knowledge

Changes in the professional understanding of a certain disease have also had a major impact on what seems to be 'public knowledge' about it. As the earlier chapters in this book have illustrated, every disease has a *social history*, which has influenced the ways that health professionals, lay people, governments, international health organisations such as the WHO, and the media think and write about it, fund and research it, treat and legislate to control or prevent it. For example, AIDS was originally thought of as an immune deficiency disorder among gay men, and in some accounts it was brought about by frequent sexually transmitted infections, extensive use of 'social' drugs, and a high-stress 'fast-lane' lifestyle.

●   On current worldwide epidemiological evidence, how should HIV and AIDS more accurately be described?

■   As a heterosexually transmitted infection most closely associated with material disadvantage and other sources of vulnerability (for example, the relative powerlessness of women to command their own sexual safety).

Thus, the social history of HIV and AIDS continues to evolve and there is no way of predicting what the next developments will be.

External forces can change the importance of a disease in public perceptions in a relatively short period, as occurred with RA in the inter-war years in Britain. Anxieties about the basic fitness of troops in wartime and the returning workforce in peacetime have proved to be potent stimulators of biomedical research in a number of debilitating conditions, including RA. This example illustrates how a disease can emerge from neglect to prominence on medical and governmental agendas, and be fundamentally altered in the eyes of the general public. A further example of a disease that may be undergoing social reconstruction is asthma — widely believed to be a consequence of rising industrial pollution in the 1980s and 1990s. It may turn out to have a different interpretation placed upon it in the twenty-first century in which relative affluence and rising standards of domestic hygiene have a more prominent explanatory role. What seems certain now, may not remain so indefinitely.

The assertion that all diseases are — at least in part — *socially constructed* should not be taken to mean that the pain and suffering they produce is not real. However, it does suggest that the *nature* of the social construction influences the experience of illness for those affected by it, as HIV and AIDS have convincingly demonstrated. The influence of society and culture extends beyond the boundaries of identifiable diseases into less-defined realms of pain and suffering. In Chapter 7, it was argued that there are *cultural thresholds* which have changed over time, altering the perception and meaning of pain, and reactions to it.

● How has the meaning and hence the experience of physical pain changed in Western culture, according to the analysis in Chapter 7?

■ The accepted public understanding of pain in modern society is as a *bodily* state, produced by physical damage or malfunction, which a person cannot control and should not have to endure. In the past, people may have been more stoical about pain, and interpreted it in a wider *spiritual* framework which viewed some forms of suffering as potentially valuable.

Some commentators (for example, Ivan Illich) have argued that the boundaries of what is now considered 'unacceptable' discomfort or disability have become so widely drawn in Western culture that medicine — as the panacea for all ills — has achieved a dangerous level of power over human lives.[4] The increasing sophistication of lay knowledge about medical matters, and its pervasiveness in modern culture (for example via the Internet), may encourage patients to pressurise doctors into recognising their symptoms and validating them with new disease labels. And although some ancient disease categories may be fading away (hysteria, for example[5]), the rate of acquisition of new ones may be exceeding the rate of loss. For example, conditions such as post-viral fatigue syndrome, repetitive strain injury, post-traumatic stress disorder and attention deficit hyperactivity disorder did not exist as recognised disease labels until the 1990s. This evolution towards a growing number of apparently new diseases in modern times illustrates the uncertainty about what constitutes 'normal health' and where the line should be drawn between health and disease. It also brings us to the second constellation of themes identified in this book, under the general title of 'Inclusion and exclusion'.

8.3 Inclusion and exclusion

It seems to be a feature of human societies that a distinction is made between what is considered 'normal' in terms of physical and mental functioning, emotional and spiritual well-being, and what falls outside this norm into the realm of illness or disability. There may be cultural differences in how the norm is constructed, and even within one culture there are likely to be differences between what is considered to be normal health for people of different genders, ages and ethnic groups.

However, despite these variations, most members of a society share a common understanding of what it means to be well or sick, able-bodied or physically impaired.

---

[4] The medicalisation thesis propounded by Illich, and its limitations, are discussed in *Medical Knowledge: Doubt and Certainty* (Open University Press, 2nd edn 1994; colour-enhanced 2nd edn 2001), Chapter 8. An article by Illich, 'The epidemics of modern medicine', appears in *Health and Disease: A Reader* (Open University Press, 3rd edn 2001).

[5] Hysteria is the subject of an historical case study in *Medical Knowledge: Doubt and Certainty* (Open University Press, 2nd edn 1994; colour-enhanced 2nd edn 2001), Chapter 6.

Of itself, this distinction need not form a barrier between people, but observation of contemporary societies and a study of human history shows that it generally does. Something in the human psyche seems to draw a line between 'us' (the well) and 'them' (the unwell). This tendency can be detected in acts of stigmatisation and discrimination against ill or disabled people, and also in the superiority attributed to 'expert' professional accounts of these states, from which the lay perspective is generally excluded and often denigrated.

8.3.1 Stigmatisation and discrimination

As we noted earlier, illness and disability are reminders of the fragility of our bodies and minds and of the inevitability of death. People who are ill or disabled can provoke quite fundamental insecurities in others. The anxiety has to be coped with somehow, and two strategies were described in Chapter 2.

- What are they and what are their consequences?

- One strategy is to assuage the anxiety by attempting to alleviate the suffering of ill or disabled people, to form an alliance with them, and to champion their right to be *included* in mainstream society. Another method of coping with the discomfort is by *projecting* the 'unpleasure' onto those who seem to have aroused it. It is as though ill or disabled people have committed an offence — 'the sick' are blamed for upsetting the ontological security of 'the well', and are rejected and *excluded* from society as a punishment.

The inclusion strategy has led to substantial support for civil rights and other activist organisations committed to the welfare and *normalisation* of people with physical and mental illness or impairment. For example, the campaign for equity of access to treatment for HIV-related disorders has social justice as its guiding principle. The exclusion strategy leads to the *stigmatisation* of illness and disability, and *victim-blaming* of those who are affected by it. They may experience active *discrimination* in many areas of life, such as employment, housing, life insurance and access to health services and social support.

- On the basis of what you have read in this book, and from your own experience, what features of an illness or disability seem most likely to provoke these negative reactions?

- Physical disfigurement, mental disability, high mortality rate, contagiousness, sexual route of transmission, high prevalence in an already stigmatised group (for example, injecting-drug users), violent or culturally 'inappropriate' behaviour.

These features were illustrated most powerfully in this book by HIV disease and schizophrenia, although people in chronic pain also report a degree of stigmatisation. Additionally, the depiction of people with HIV acquired from blood products or in the womb as 'innocent' victims reflects stigmatising assumptions that the rest are 'guilty'. Newspaper headlines and films often portray schizophrenic people as inherently dangerous predators who stalk innocent bystanders with murderous intent; in reality, self-harm and suicide are by far the most likely outcomes of violence by mentally disturbed individuals. Even if non-violent, the actions of a person with a mental disturbance can seem *deliberately* to offend social norms and will be met with rejection.

The exclusion of certain categories of ill or disabled people from mainstream society can, in its most extreme form, lead to the view that they should be excluded from life itself. A disabled-rights activist, Jenny Morris (1991), has written about the ease with which able-bodied people assume that someone with severe physical impairments has a 'life not worth living'.[6] She argues that the stigmatisation and discrimination experienced by severely handicapped people can be so great that their quality of life becomes too low to sustain with grace and dignity. If exclusion from everything that maintains the desire to live is prolonged, the person may conclude that their life is indeed not worth living. Morris cites several cases in the USA where a physically handicapped person has applied to the courts for the right to assisted euthanasia, and though denied this right, the court ruled that the wish to die was *rational* given the level of disability. Morris asks:

> The question is, in such a context, is the wish to die a so-called rational response to physical disability? Or is it a desperate response to isolated oppression? (Morris, quoted in Davey *et al.* 2001, p. 120)

One response to the excluding power of stigmatisation is to create a new society of people who have an illness or handicap in common (the *own*), together with their 'stigma champions' (the *wise*). Within this alternative social circle, the 'abnormal' becomes the norm. Self-help groups exist for a wide range of conditions, including all those illustrated in this book. They not only help their members cope with the activities of daily living, but also develop and present to outsiders a less stigmatising message about the condition. For example, people with facial disfigurements have formed a powerful alliance called 'Changing Faces' to help overcome stigma.[7] One self-help group for people with schizophrenia (featured in Chapter 6) refers to its members as 'voice hearers', supplying them with a less-stigmatising social label for their condition which acknowledges the reality of their experiences.

People are often excluded by the medical label that a doctor has applied to them: a person's individuality and uniqueness may be subsumed beneath a term such as 'schizophrenic' or 'asthmatic'. It is as though the person becomes equated with the disease and everything is viewed through this filter — a phenomenon that Erving Goffman saw as the disease assuming a *master status*. Medical labels have frequently been challenged as stigmatising in themselves, and this charge has extended to some of the explanations for certain diseases that have been provided by scientific research. Medicine may be an ally in the search for recovery and for personal meaning in the face of illness, but it also supplies powerful professional narratives which can be experienced as stigmatising.

This process could be illustrated by any of the conditions discussed in this book, but schizophrenia offers an instructive example. People who are diagnosed as schizophrenic may find particular medical explanations for the condition deeply stigmatising.

● Suggest how a genetic explanation for schizophrenia might be received, and contrast this with the effects of locating the causes of the condition in family interactions.

[6] Open University students should read her article 'Pride against prejudice: "lives not worth living" ' in *Health and Disease: A Reader* (Open University Press, 3rd edn 2001) if time is available.

[7] The Open University TV programme 'More than meets the eye', associated with Chapter 2 of this book, focuses on people with facial disfigurements.

■ The attribution of schizophrenia to faulty genes could induce feelings of inferiority and helplessness that nothing can ever be done to alter one's inheritance; the parents of schizophrenic children may suffer shame that they 'passed on' the condition. Alternatively, the family of a schizophrenic person may be deeply offended by theories that their ways of relating to each other have driven one of them to a mental breakdown; they may prefer a genetic explanation which 'absolves' them from direct blame.

Many illnesses are not considered particularly stigmatising by people on the outside looking in. The clearest examples in this book are RA and asthma. But affected individuals may experience what is known as *felt stigma* — an expectation or anxiety that others may be repelled or rejecting, which powerfully affects their self-esteem and confidence even in the absence of direct discrimination. People may also feel shame if they are unable to fulfil the tasks normally associated with their *social role*, or perform the usual activities of self-care such as washing and dressing. There may be a retreat from the world as illness threatens the capacity to participate in 'normal' social life, often forcing people to reconsider their relationships and reorder their lives.

In the modern world, relationships have increasingly come to depend on forward planning. Maintaining plans is made very difficult by chronic illness. An arrangement to see friends may have to be cancelled at the last minute, making particular demands on their tolerance. People with unpredictable or disabling conditions, and their carers, may experience a shrinking set of social contacts as a result of their apparent inconsistency and inability to reciprocate.

> By far the hardest thing about caring for a wife with Alzheimer's disease, says Tom, is the loneliness ... At weekends, he can spend hours exchanging no words with anyone ... [A friend] comes round for a chat on Saturdays ... Other friends, though, do not come any more. (Burton-Jones, in Davey *et al.* 1995, p. 81)

This common experience can result in unwelcome feelings of dependency on those contacts who do 'make an effort' to maintain the relationship. Casual acquaintanceship is hard to sustain and the person becomes reliant on family and old friends, with all the attendant embarrassment about becoming a 'burden' on those who are under most obligation to care. Chronically ill or disabled people are usually only too well aware of the extra workload and social discrimination that may be falling on their carers.

And finally, as we have illustrated many times, inadequacies in the formal support mechanisms provided by the health and social services, in employment and in other aspects of daily life, is a form of discrimination in itself. The effects of these inadequacies are not equally distributed, but act to divide 'haves' from 'have nots' in different social strata within countries, and separate economically powerful countries from those in the developing world. The outcome often distances chronically ill or handicapped people even further from mainstream society.

8.3.2 Lay accounts and professional accounts

A basic analytic distinction which has run through this book (and others in the series) is between *illness* and *disease,* as described here by the medical anthropologist, Leon Eisenberg:

> To state it flatly, patients suffer 'illnesses', physicians diagnose and treat 'diseases' ... illnesses are *experiences* of disvalued changes in

states of being and in social function; diseases, in the scientific paradigm of modern medicine, are *abnormalities* in the *structure* and *function* of body organs and systems. (Eisenberg, 1977, p. 11)

This distinction marks the boundary between the *lay* and *professional* sectors of health care. The medical and scientific view of disease can be seen as a sort of parallel system to that of lay peoples' constructions of illness, but they do not have equal status.

Scientific medicine is supposed to be based on consistent and objective measurement under carefully controlled conditions; the possibility of bias is reduced to the minimum by the selection of random or representative samples of experimental subjects and controls, the use of placebos where appropriate, and the evaluation of outcome by people who are 'blind' to which subjects received which intervention.[8] Practitioners of all the professional disciplines represented in this book — epidemiologists, clinicians and medical scientists, sociologists, psychologists, and so on — strive to acquire knowledge about health and disease through the application of scientific research methods.

Against this literally 'disciplined' approach, the accumulation of hearsay and folklore, personal anecdotes, media reporting and TV dramas, which contributes to many lay accounts of illness, presents a striking contrast. The usage made by lay people of professional, disease-based explanations and treatments can be highly selective; they are intermingled with ideas and remedies from many other sources. Although the richness of lay narratives of illness and the importance of strategies for self-care have not been lost on sociologists and anthropologists as a research topic in their own right, the lay perspective is frequently excluded from consideration by medical practitioners and other health-care workers. When a person is transformed into a patient, his or her beliefs have traditionally been seen as irrelevant distractions, unless they coincide with the medical model and can be manipulated to encourage compliance with treatment.

Yet the assumed superiority of professional over lay accounts denies what we established earlier: that medical knowledge, even in the well-developed scientific context of Western societies, contains rather more doubts than certainties. Medical treatments sometimes do not work, or are harmful. The narrative provided by medicine can itself be stigmatising and serve to exclude people from society.

Until relatively recently in the history of scientific medicine, the patient was not acknowledged as an 'expert' in his or her own illness, and was excluded from participation or negotiation in most aspects of medical care. This situation is gradually changing: medical schools now have classes in communication skills, social awareness and patients' rights on the syllabus, and practitioners are increasingly advocating *patient-centred* medicine. Researchers have begun to devise *patient-derived* outcome measures for evaluating interventions to alleviate rheumatoid arthritis, which are based on criteria provided by patients. Thus, instead of imposed criteria such as 'can walk upstairs unaided', people can set highly individual criteria of their own: for example 'can take my dog for a walk again' or 'can lift my grandson onto my lap'. The success or failure of any intervention is then judged against these criteria by the person receiving the treatment, rather than by the doctor who prescribed it.

---

[8] These and other aspects of scientific research methodology, including clinical trials, are discussed in *Studying Health and Disease* (Open University Press, 2nd edn 1994; colour-enhanced 2nd edn 2001), Chapter 8.

Medical sociologists have also been involved in systematic measurement of the psychosocial impact of disease, increasingly as part of multidisciplinary teams that include health practitioners and patients. Considerable efforts have been made to evaluate the consequences of certain conditions — notably rheumatoid arthritis and HIV disease — for peoples' relationships and social lives. In this respect, medicine has begun to explore the patients' varied world of *illness*, breaking somewhat from the narrower concern only with their *disease*. Attempts to include lay people more actively in their health care are certainly increasing and may one day be commonplace.

● In the audiotape band for Open University students associated with Chapter 6, Ron — a man who has suffered from schizophrenia for most of his life — recounts a shift from exclusion to inclusion in his experiences of treatment. Summarise it briefly.

■ He describes his feelings about being given a series of unwelcome forced injections early in his illness, and being locked on wards with nurses who would not talk to him about his voices for fear of 'colluding' with his delusions. He has since broken away from a view of himself as a victim of medical treatment, and has come to see psychiatrists as people who genuinely want to help him and who might be his allies. The change has been gradual, but Ron thinks it is due to a shift in attitudes among professionals in mental health care; they now listen more to the patient's perspective and can themselves learn from the people they treat. Significantly, Ron links this with a broader societal acceptance of mental illness, linked to a reduction in the stigma associated with mental disturbance and a greater recognition of our common humanity.

Religion in European societies once exercised an all-pervasive influence on peoples' attempts to give meaning to fundamental existential questions of life, death and the purpose of suffering. Religion requires allegiance, trust and faith, rewarding these attributes with the promise that a meaningful life is possible for all, and punishing heretics with excommunication and exclusion. It can be argued that medicine in modern society exhibits somewhat similar characteristics, and plays a similar excluding or including role. It has been one of our aims in writing this book to bring the worlds of lay experience and professional explanations for health and disease closer together.

8.4   Conclusion to the series

You have now reached the end of this book, and (if you are an Open University student) the end of the series of eight books that together form the *Health and Disease* undergraduate course. This is, in a sense a ceremonial moment, marking the completion of a phase in the lives of those of you who have studied all the books from beginning to end. This is the sort of moment when tourist guides shake hands and wait for their tip, head teachers stand up and say a few inspiring words, vice chancellors don their gowns and rustle in their pockets to look for last year's speech, and the audience shuffle restlessly because they know that whatever is said at such a moment is going to sound quite vacuous.

This is the nature of such ceremonies and rituals in modern society. They generally fail to command much respect or generate much emotion. But let us see what can be done nevertheless.

The first book in the course, *Medical Knowledge: Doubt and Certainty*, began by introducing the metaphor of a *journey* to evoke a sense of embarking on something new that might change your thinking about illness, medicine and health care. Another metaphor — this time derived from an academic source (as is appropriate to the sources we now hope you are using to think about health and disease) — is that of the *rite of passage*. This concept is derived from the work of an early anthropologist, Arnold van Gennep (1909), who coined the term to indicate the purpose of rituals that mark passages from one stage of life to the next in traditional societies.

Van Gennep noted that events like birth, initiation into adult status, marriage and death are often marked by a series of three types of ritual, starting with *rites of separation*. Here the person is removed from a previously occupied state. The first book of this course specifically set out to 'remove you' from the cultural assumption of medical certainty and introduce you to sources of doubt about the medical process — some of which may not have occurred to you previously. It introduced a series of critiques about the socially constructed nature of medical knowledge, aimed at further disrupting the unquestioning faith in the objectivity and beneficence of medical institutions and the doctors they trained, which used to characterise attitudes among the lay public in the UK. The purpose was to help you stand back from any assumptions you may have brought with you, in order to view the world of health and disease as *anthropologically strange*.

Van Gennep's second set of rites are known as *rites of transition*. The period in which these rites occur is characterised by confusion about right and wrong. It is a time when the loss of the previous status is felt as disturbing, and where new knowledge is actively sought in order to construct a new identity or understanding of the world. This is the point, in traditional societies, where instruction in the duties of new social roles are given by magicians, priests or healers. In a sense, this is the sort of experience we hope that you will have had as you progressed through the eight books in this series.

The second book, *Studying Health and Disease*, was designed to give you an understanding of how academic 'narratives' of health and disease are constructed, showing you the methods used by researchers in different disciplines and pointing to their strengths and often neglected limitations. The third book, *World Health and Disease*, sought to help you gain a worldwide perspective on problems that you might hitherto have only considered in a British or European context. It also continued the exploration of historical trends in patterns of illness and the sources of inequalities in health experience between and within societies. The fourth book, *Human Biology and Health: An Evolutionary Approach*, invited you to explore biological understandings of health and disease in some depth, focusing particularly on the interaction of biological evolution and human culture. Such a perspective has rarely been attempted in biological texts.

Together, the first four books constitute the foundation on which an understanding of the last four books is built. In the second half of the series our primary purpose was to integrate the various disciplines presented in books 1–4, through a series of case studies. The fifth book, *Birth to Old Age: Health in Transition*, involved you in a sequential consideration of the life course from a contemporary UK perspective, in which the contribution of different academic disciplines to the understanding of health issues at each stage of life was emphasised. The realm of psychological processes and inner experience was given prominence, together with the influence of social construction in shaping how we feel about growing up and growing old.

Next came two books concerned with health care, starting with *Caring for Health: History and Diversity*. This historical account traced the development of the British health system from 1500 to 2001, but it also considered the worldwide influence of Western colonial powers on health care in the former colonial territories of European states. Other important themes were the role of women as key providers of lay and nursing care, the evolution of professional boundaries in the health sector, and the changing status of primary care and public health as professional disciplines. The seventh book, *Dilemmas in UK Health Care*, was concerned with present-day dilemmas in the organisation and delivery of health care in the UK through the NHS, including the debate about rationing and waiting lists, the organisation of health worker hierarchies, the impact of new medical technologies and structures such as community care, and the possibilities and limitations of disease prevention and social welfare strategies to reduce inequalities in health. In this final book, *Experiencing and Explaining Disease*, you have been invited to use the knowledge you have acquired to develop a new understanding of what it is to be ill and to explain and to treat disease.

What have we just done? The last few paragraphs have summarised the topics contained in eight books and suggested a framework in terms of rites of passage in which their study might be placed. This is the nature of ceremonial moments. They do not offer new knowledge, but act as invitations to the audience to review and reformulate what you know already. They help to crystallise tracts of experience. If you have read these books in sequence, with care and attention, this cryptic listing of their titles and contents will evoke some memories for you of the process you have been through, and may help you see it as a coherent sequence.

The authors of this text now stand aside to allow you to complete the final rite yourself — what van Gennep called a *rite of incorporation*. In this phase, individuals use their new knowledge to construct their own, personal understanding of the position they now have reached. We hope that studying these books will have enhanced your capacity to develop many new perspectives on matters of health and disease.

OBJECTIVE FOR CHAPTER 8

When you have studied this chapter, you should be able to:

8.1 Summarise the main themes of this book, using examples from earlier chapters to illustrate them, and interpret new material on relevant topics in terms of those themes.

There are no 'bold' terms in Chapter 8, but many of the key terms that were introduced in earlier chapters have been incorporated into the discussion and this should have helped to consolidate your understanding of their meanings and usage.

Objective 8.1 is tested in a revision exercise set out on p. 260.

REVISION EXERCISE FOR CHAPTER 8
(*Objective 8.1*)

Listen to the audiotape band entitled 'Living with epilepsy', which has been prepared for Open University students completing the course in *Health and Disease*. This tape presents part of an interview with Jill, a young woman who developed epilepsy in her teens, and her mother, Rose. They describe their experiences of the illness and the reactions of others outside the family, including health professionals and employers.

Interpret this material in terms of the themes of this book, identifying as many aspects as you can find on the tape. Note that this exercise will further develop your skills of *qualitative data interpretation*. We suggest that you listen to the tape twice: first, straight through to get an overview, and second, using 'stop–start' to allow time to make notes. Decide before you begin whether to use the same 'headings' for groups of themes that we used in this chapter (see the Chapter contents list on p. 245), or to reorganise the themes into another scheme of your own.

When you have finished making notes and organising themes into a coherent sequence, write a short report (under 500 words) of your analysis. Illustrate your main points with suitable phrases quoted from the transcript of the audiotape as 'evidence' to support your interpretation.

When you have finished this exercise, turn to the 'Answers to questions' at the end of this book, where you will find some notes on this revision exercise under Chapter 8.

References and further sources

References

Adams, S., Pill, R. and Jones, A. (1997) Medication, chronic illness and identity: the perspective of people with asthma, *Social Science and Medicine*, **45**(2), pp. 189–201.

American Psychiatric Association (1994) *Diagnostic and Statistical Manual of Mental Disorders*, American Psychiatric Association, Washington.

Anderson, G. G. and Cookson, W. O. C. M. (1999) Recent advances in the genetics of allergy and asthma, *Molecular Medicine Today*, **5**, pp. 264–73. (This journal has since been renamed *Trends in Molecular Medicine*.)

Anderson, H. R., Atkinson, R., Limb, E. S. and Strachan, D. P. (1996) Epidemic of asthma was not associated with episode of air pollution, *British Medical Journal*, **312**, pp. 1606–7.

Arndt, C. and Lewis, J. (2001) The HIV/AIDS pandemic in South Africa: sectoral impacts and unemployment, *Journal of International Development*, **13**, pp. 427–50.

Arnett, F. C., Edworthy, S. M., Bloch, D. A. *et al.* (1988) The American Rheumatism Association 1987 revised criteria for the classification of rheumatoid arthritis, *Arthritis and Rheumatism*, **31**, pp. 315–24.

Atkinson, J. M. and Coia, D. A. (1995) *Families Coping with Schizophrenia: A Practitioner's Guide to Family Groups*, Wiley, Chichester.

Atkinson, J. M. and Patterson, L. E. (2001) *Review of the Literature Relating to Mental Health Legislation*, Scottish Executive Central Research Unit, Edinburgh.

Atkinson, R. W., Anderson, H. R., Strachan, D. P. *et al.* (1999) Short-term associations between outdoor air pollution and visits to accident and emergency departments in London for respiratory complaints, *European Respiratory Journal*, **13**(2), pp. 257–65.

Atkinson, R. W., Anderson, H. R., Sunyer, J. *et al.* (2001) Acute effects of particulate air pollution on respiratory admissions – Results from the APHEA2 project, *American Journal of Respiratory and Critical Care Medicine*, **164**(10), pp. 1860–66.

Badley, E. M. and Wood, P. H. N. (1979) Attitudes of the public to arthritis, *Annals of the Rheumatic Diseases*, **38**, pp. 97–100.

Barnes, M. and Berke, J. (1971) *Mary Barnes: Two Accounts of a Journey Through Madness*, McGibbon and Kee, London.

Baruch, G. (1982) *Moral tales: interviewing parents of congenitally ill children*, unpublished PhD thesis, University of London.

Bateson, G., Jackson, D. D., Haley, J. and Weakland, J. (1956) Towards a theory of schizophrenia, *Behavioural Science*, **1**, pp. 251–64.

Beattie, A., Gott, M., Jones, L. and Sidell, M. (eds) (1993) *Health and Wellbeing: a Reader*, Macmillan, Basingstoke.

Becker, G., Janson-Bjerklie, S., Benner, P., Slobin, K. and Ferketich, S. (1993) The dilemma of seeking urgent care: asthma episodes and emergency service use, *Social Science and Medicine*, **37**(3), pp. 305–13.

Beier, L. (1985) In sickness and in health: a seventeenth century family's experience, in Porter, R. (ed.) *Patients and Practitioners: Lay Perceptions of Medicine in Pre-industrial Society*, Cambridge University Press, Cambridge.

Bentall, R. and Pilgrim, D. (1993) Thomas Szasz, crazy talk and the myth of mental illness, *British Journal of Medical Psychology*, **66**, pp. 69–76.

Berger, P. (1973) *The Social Reality of Religion*, Penguin Books, Harmondsworth. (First published in 1969 as *The Sacred Canopy*, Faber and Faber.)

Berwick, D. (2001) We all have AIDS (editorial), *Washington Post*, June 26, p. A17.

Bird, S. M. and Brown, A. J. L. (2001) Criminalisation of HIV transmission: implications for public health in Scotland, *British Medical Journal*, **323**, pp. 1174–7.

Black, N., Boswell, D., Gray, A. Murphy, S. and Popay, J. (1984) *Health and Disease: A Reader*, 1st edn, Open University Press, Milton Keynes.

Bleuler, E. (1950) *Dementia Praecox, or the Group of Schizophrenias*, Zimkin, J. (trans.), International Universities Press, New York.

Boydell, J., van Os, J., McKenzie, K. *et al.* (2001) Incidence of schizophrenia in ethnic minorities in London: ecological study into interactions with environment, *British Medical Journal*, **323**, pp. 1336–38.

Boyle, M. (1994) Schizophrenia and the art of the soluble, *The Psychologist*, **7**, pp. 399–404.

Brighton, S. W., Harpe, A. L., Staden, D. J. *et al.* (1988) The prevalence of rheumatoid arthritis in a rural African population, *Journal of Rheumatology*, **15**, pp. 405–8.

Brockington, I. F., Hall, P., Levings, J. and Murphy, C. (1993) The community's tolerance of the mentally ill, *British Journal of Psychiatry*, **162**, pp. 93–9.

Burt, J. and Stimson, G. V. (1993) *Drug Injectors and HIV Risk Reduction: Strategies of Protection*, Health Education Authority, London.

Burton-Jones, J. (1992) *Caring for the Carers*, Scripture Union, London; an edited extract appears as 'Tangled feelings: an account of Alzheimer's disease' in Davey, B., Gray, A. and Seale, C. (eds) (1995) *Health and Disease: A Reader*, 2nd edn, Open University Press, Buckingham.

Bury, M. (1982) Chronic illness as biographical disruption, *Sociology of Health and Illness*, **4**, pp. 167–82.

Bury, M. (1991) The sociology of chronic illness: a review of research and prospects, *Sociology of Health and Illness*, **13**(4), pp. 451–68.

Caldwell, C. B. and Gottesman, I. I. (1990) Schizophrenics kill themselves: a review of risk factors for suicide, *Schizophrenia Bulletin*, **16**, pp. 571–90.

Campbell, C. and Mzaidume, Y. (2002) How can HIV be prevented in South Africa? A social perspective, *British Medical Journal*, **324**, pp. 229–32.

Campbell, M. J., Cogman, G. R., Holgate, S. T. and Johnston, S. L. (1997) Age specific trends in asthma mortality in England and Wales, 1983–95: results of an observational study, *British Medical Journal*, **314**, pp. 1439–41.

Cane, R. S., Ranganathan, S. C. and McKenzie, S. A. (2000) What do parents of wheezy children understand by 'wheeze'? *Archives of Disease in Childhood*, **82**, pp. 327–32.

Cantor, D. (1991) The aches of industry: philanthropy and rheumatism in inter-war Britain, in Barry, J. and Jones, C. (eds) *Medicine and Charity Before the Welfare State*, Routledge, London.

Cantor, D. (1992) Cortisone and the politics of drama, in Pickstone, J. V. (ed.) *Medical Innovations in Historical Perspective*, Macmillan, London.

Cantor, D. (1993) Cortisone and the politics of empire: imperialism and British medicine, 1918–1955, *Bulletin of Medical History*, **67**, pp. 463–93.

Carricaburu, D. and Pierret, J. (1995) From biographical disruption to biographical reinforcement: the case of HIV-positive men, *Sociology of Health and Illness*, **17**, pp. 65–88.

Cates, C. (2001) Chronic asthma, *British Medical Journal*, **323**, pp. 976–9.

CDC (2001) *HIV/AIDS Surveillance Report*, **13**(1), Centers for Disease Control and Prevention, Atlanta, Georgia; available at http://www.cdc.gov/hiv/stats/hasr1301.pdf (accessed March 2002).

CDSC (2001) *HIV and AIDS in the UK: An epidemiological review, 2000*, Communicable Disease Surveillance Centre, Public Health Laboratory Service, London; available at http://www.phls.co.uk/facts/HIV/HIVreport.pdf (accessed March 2002).

Charmaz, K. (1987) Struggling with a self: identity levels among the chronically ill, in Roth, J. A. and Conrad, P. (eds) *Research in the Sociology of Health Care*, **6**, JAI Press, Greenwich, CT.

Charmaz, K. (1997) Identity dilemmas of chronically ill men, in Strauss, A. and Corbin, J. (eds) *Grounded Theory in Practice*, Chapter 2, Sage, London; an edited extract also appears in Davey, B., Gray, A. and Seale, C. (2001) *Health and Disease: A Reader*, 3rd edn, Open University Press, Buckingham.

Chun, T. W., Davey, R. T. Ostrowski, M. *et al.* (2000) Relationship between pre-existing viral reservoirs and the re-emergence of plasma viremia after discontinuation of highly active anti-retroviral therapy, *Nature Medicine*, **6**(7), pp. 757–61.

Clinical Standards Board for Scotland (2001) *Clinical Standards: Schizophrenia*, Clinical Standards Board for Scotland, Edinburgh; also available at www.clinicalstandards.org (accessed January 2002).

Coleman, R. (1995) How I stopped being a victim, *Openmind*, **75**, p. 17.

Committee on the Medical Effects of Air Pollutants, and Department of Health (1995) *Non-Biological Particles and Health*, HMSO, London.

Cunningham, L. S. and Kelsey, J. L. (1984) Epidemiology and musculoskeletal impairments and associated disability, *American Journal of Public Health*, **74**, pp. 574–9.

Curran, D. and Partridge, M. (1969) *Psychological Medicine*, Churchill Livingstone.

Da Silva, J. A. and Hall, G. M. (1992) The effect of gender and sex hormones in rheumatoid arthritis, *Baillieres Clinical Rheumatology*, **6**, pp. 196–219.

Davey, B., Gray, A. and Seale, C. (eds) (1995) *Health and Disease: A Reader*, 2nd edn and (2001) 3rd edn, Open University Press, Buckingham.

Deighton, C., Surtees, D. and Walker, D. (1992) Influence of the severity of rheumatoid arthritis on sex differences in Health Assessment Question Scores, *Annals of Rheumatic Diseases*, **51**, pp. 473–5.

Department of Health (1998) *National Service Framework: Mental Health*, The Stationery Office, London; also available at http://www.doh.gov.uk/nsf/mentalhealth.htm (accessed February 2002).

Department of Health (2000) *Reforming the Mental Health Act*, White Paper, The Stationery Office, London; also available at www.doh.gov.uk/mentalhealth (accessed January 2002).

Department of Health (various years) *Hospital Episode Statistics*, HMSO, London.

Descartes, R. (1664) *L'homme*, translated by Foster, M. (1901) *Lectures on the History of Physiology During the 16th, 17th and 18th Centuries*, Cambridge University Press, Cambridge.

Deveson, A. (1992) *Tell Me I'm Here*, Penguin, London.

Dixon, S., McDonald, S. and Roberts, J. (2002) The impact of HIV and AIDS on Africa's economic development, *British Medical Journal*, **324**, pp. 232–4.

Donnelly, M. (1992) *The Politics of Mental Health in Italy*, Routledge, London.

Dow, L., Fowler, L., Phelps, L. *et al.* (2001) Prevalence of untreated asthma in a population sample of 6 000 older adults in Bristol, UK, *Thorax*, **56**, pp. 472–6.

Downs, S. H., Marks, G. B., Sporik, R., Belosouva, E. G., Car, N. G. and Peat, J. K. (2001) Continued increase in the prevalence of asthma and atopy, *Archives of Disease in Childhood*, **84**, pp. 20–3.

Dubuisson, D. and Melzack, R. (1976) Classification of clinical pain descriptions by multiple group discriminant analysis, *Experimental Neurology*, **51**, pp. 480–7.

Eaton, W. and Harrison, G. (2000) Ethnic disadvantage and schizophrenia, *Acta Psychiatrica Scandinavica Supplement*, **102**, pp. 38–43.

Edgerton, R. B. and Cohen, A. (1994) Culture and schizophrenia: the DOSMD challenge, *British Journal of Psychiatry*, **164**, pp. 222–31.

Eisenberg, L. (1977) Disease and illness: distinctions between professional and popular ideas of sickness, *Culture, Medicine and Psychiatry*, **1**, pp. 9–23.

Elder, R. (1973) Social class and lay explanations for the etiology of arthritis, *Journal of Health and Social Behaviour*, **14**, pp. 28–38.

Elias, N. (1978) *The Civilizing Process: The History of Manners*, Blackwell, Oxford.

Elias, N. (1982) *The Civilizing Process: State Formation and Civilization*, Blackwell, Oxford.

Falloon, I. R. H., Laporta, M., Fadden, G. and Graham-Hole, V. (1993) *Managing Stress in Families: Cognitive and Behavioural Strategies for Enhancing Coping Skills*, Routledge, London.

Finkel, D. (2000) Few drugs for the needy: in impoverished Malawi, one man faces the odds, *The Washington Post*, 1 November, p. A01; an edited extract also appears under the title 'Costs of treating AIDS in Malawi and America', in Davey, B., Gray, A. and Seale, C. (eds) (2001) *Health and Disease: A Reader*, 3rd edn, Open University Press, Buckingham.

Fitzpatrick, R., Ziebland, S., Jenkinson, C. and Mowat, A. (1992) A generic health status instrument in the assessment of rheumatoid arthritis, *British Journal of Rheumatology*, **31**, pp. 87–90.

Fleming, A., Crown, J. and Corbett, M. (1976) Early rheumatoid arthritis, *Annals of the Rheumatic Diseases*, **35**, pp. 357–60.

Fleming, D. M., Sunderland, R., Cross, K. W. and Ross, A. M. (2000) Declining incidence of episodes of asthma: a study of trends in new episodes presenting to general practitioners in the period 1989–98, *Thorax*, **55**, pp. 657–61.

Flowers, P. (2001) Gay men and HIV/AIDS risk management, *Health*, **5**, pp. 50–75.

Freud, S. (1961, first published 1920) Beyond the pleasure principle, in *The Standard Edition of the Complete Works of Sigmund Freud*, Vol. 18, Hogarth Press, London.

Fries, J., Spitz, P. and Young, D. (1982) The dimensions of health outcomes: the Health Assessment Questionnaire, disability and pain scales, *Journal of Rheumatology*, **9**, pp. 789–93.

Fromm-Reichmann, F. (1948) Notes on the development of treatment of schizophrenics by psychoanalytic psychotherapy, *Psychiatry*, **11**, pp. 263–73.

Gabbay, J. (1982) Asthma attacked? Tactics for the reconstruction of a disease concept, pp. 23–48 in Wright, P. and Treacher, A. (eds) *The Problem of Medical Knowledge*, Edinburgh University Press, Edinburgh.

Garfinkel, H. (1963) A conception of, and experiments with, 'trust' as a condition of stable concerted actions, in Harvey, O. J. (ed.) *Motivation and Social Interaction*, Ronald Press, New York.

Garrett, T. (1998) One year on therapy and counting ... Doses taken: 1,460; Doses missed: 0, *The Body* (an Internet information resource on HIV and AIDS) available at http://www.thebody.com (accessed March 2002); an edited extract also appears under the title 'Costs of treating AIDS in Malawi and America', in Davey, B., Gray, A. and Seale, C. (eds) (2001) *Health and Disease: A Reader*, 3rd edn, Open University Press, Buckingham.

Giddens, A. (1989) *Sociology*, Polity Press, Cambridge.

Giddens, A. (1991) *Modernity and Self-identity: Self and Society in the Late Modern Age*, Polity Press, Cambridge.

Glasgow University Media Group (1993a) *Mass Media Representations of Mental Health/Illness: Report for the Health Education Board for Scotland*, Glasgow University Media Group, Glasgow.

Glasgow University Media Group (1993b) *Media Representations of Mental Health/Illness: Audience Reception Study: Report for the Health Education Board for Scotland*, Glasgow University Media Group, Glasgow.

Goffman, E. (1968) *Stigma: Notes on the Management of Spoiled Identity*, Pelican Books, London.

Goffman, E. (1969) The insanity of place, *Psychiatry: Journal for the Study of Interpersonal Processes*, XXXII (No. 4); an edited extract appears in Davey, B., Gray, A. and Seale, C. (eds) (2001) *Health and Disease: A Reader*, 3rd edn, Open University Press, Buckingham.

Good, B. (1994) *Medicine, Rationality and Experience*, Cambridge University Press, Cambridge.

Gottesman, I. I. (1991) *Schizophrenia Genesis*, Freeman, New York.

Gray, D. (1983) 'Arthritis': variation in beliefs about joint disease, *Medical Anthropology*, **7**, pp. 29–46.

Green, G. and Platt, S. (1997) Fear and loathing in health care settings reported by people with HIV, *Sociology of Health and Illness*, **19**(1), pp. 70–92.

Greenhalgh, T. and Hurwitz, B. (1999) Why study narrative? *British Medical Journal*, **318**, pp. 48–50.

Guardian (1992) Doctor denies attempt to kill suffering patient, 11 September, p. 2.

Gupta, G. R. (2002) How men's power over women fuels the HIV epidemic, *British Medical Journal*, **324**, pp. 183–4.

Halpern, D. and Nazroo, J. (2000) The ethnic density effect: results from a national community survey of England and Wales, *International Journal of Social Psychiatry*, **46**, pp. 34–46.

Hardey, M. (1999) Doctor in the house: the Internet as a source of lay health knowledge and the challenge to expertise, *Sociology of Health and Illness*, **21**(6), pp. 820–35; an edited extract appears in Davey, B., Gray, A. and Seale, C. (eds) (2001) *Health and Disease: A Reader*, 3rd edn, Open University Press, Buckingham.

Hart, G. and Flowers, P. (1996) Recent developments in the sociology of HIV risk behaviour, *Risk, Decision and Policy*, **1**, pp. 153–65.

Heath, C. (1989) Pain talk: the expression of suffering in the medical consultation, *Social Psychology Quarterly*, **52**(2), pp. 113–25.

Heinrichs, R. W. (2001) *In Search of Madness: Schizophrenia and Neuroscience*, Oxford University Press, Oxford.

Helman, C. (1990) *Culture, Health and Illness*, Wright, London.

Helman, C. (2000) Cross-cultural psychiatry, Chapter 10 in *Culture, Health and Illness: An Introduction for Health Professionals*, 4th edn, Arnold, London; an edited extract appears in Davey, B., Gray, A. and Seale, C. (eds) (2001) *Health and Disease: A Reader*, 3rd edn, Open University Press, Buckingham.

Hick, J. (1977) *Evil and the God of Love*, Macmillan Press, London.

Higgins, B. G., Francis, H. C., Yates, C. J. *et al.* (1995) Effect of air pollution on symptoms and peak expiratory flow measurements in subjects with obstructive airways disease, *Thorax*, **50**, pp. 149–55.

Hilbert, R. (1984) The acultural dimensions of chronic pain: flawed reality construction and the problem of meaning, *Social Problems*, **31**(4), pp. 365–78.

Holland, J., Ramazanoglu, C., Scott, S., Sharpe, S. and Thompson, R. (1991) Between embarrassment and trust: young women and the diversity of condom use, in Aggleton, P., Hart, G. and Davies, P. (eds) *AIDS: Responses, Intervention and Care*, Falmer Press, Lewes.

Holt, P. G., Sly, P. D. and Björkstén, B. (1997) Atopic versus infectious diseases in childhood: a question of balance? *Pediatric Allergy and Immunology*, **8**, pp. 53–8.

Hoskins, G., McCowan, C., Neville, R. G. *et al.* (2000) Risk factors and costs associated with an asthma attack, *Thorax*, **55**(1), pp. 19–24.

Illich, I. (1976) *Limits to Medicine; Medical Nemesis: the Expropriation of Health*, Penguin, Harmondsworth.

Imrie, J., Stephenson, J. M., Cowan, F. M. *et al.* (2001) A cognitive behavioural intervention to reduce sexually transmitted infections among gay men: randomised trial, *British Medical Journal*, **322**, pp. 1451–6.

ISAAC Steering Committee (1998) Worldwide variations in the prevalence of asthma symptoms: the International Study of Asthma and Allergies in Childhood (ISAAC), *European Respiratory Journal*, **12**, pp. 315–35.

Jablensky, A., Sartorius, N., Ernberg, G. *et al.* (1992) Schizophrenia: manifestation, incidence and course in different cultures, *Psychological Medicine*, monograph supplement 20.

Jacob, D. L., Robinson, H. and Masi, A. T. (1972) A controlled home interview study of factors associated with early rheumatoid arthritis, *American Journal of Public Health*, **62**, pp. 1532–7.

Jacobsson, L. T. H., Frithiof, M., Olofsson, Y. *et al.* (1998) Evaluation of a structured multidisciplinary day care program in rheumatoid arthritis — A similar effect in newly diagnosed and long-standing disease, *Scandinavian Journal of Rheumatology*, **27**(2), pp. 117–24.

Janson, C., Anto, J., Burney, P. *et al.* (2001) The European Community Respiratory Health Survey (ECRHS): what are the main results so far? *European Respiratory Journal*, **18**, pp. 598–611.

Jawaheer, D., Seldin, M. F., Amos, C. I. *et al.* (2001) A genomewide screen in multiplex rheumatoid arthritis families suggests genetic overlap with other autoimmune diseases, *American Journal of Human Genetics*, **68**, pp. 927–36.

Jeffery, R. (1979) Normal rubbish: deviant patients in casualty departments, *Sociology of Health and Illness*, **1**(1), pp. 90–108; an edited version appears in Davey, B., Gray, A. and Seale, C. (eds) (2001) *Health and Disease: A Reader*, 3rd edn, Open University Press, Buckingham.

Jones, C., Cormac, I., Mota, J. and Campbell, C. (2001) Cognitive behaviour therapy for schizophrenia (Cochrane Review). In: *The Cochrane Library*, 1, Oxford; available at http://www.cochraneconsumer.com/index.asp?SHOW=Search, then type in 'schizophrenia' (last accessed March 2002).

Jones, K. P., Bain, D. J. G., Middleton, M. and Mullee, M. A. (1992) Correlates of asthma morbidity in primary care, *British Medical Journal*, **304**, pp. 361–4.

Kaipiainen-Seppanen, O., Aho, K. and Laakso, M. (1996) Shifts in the incidence of rheumatoid arthritis towards elderly patients in Finland during 1975–1990, *Clinical Experimental Rheumatology*, **14**, pp. 537–42.

Kane, J., Honigfeld, G., Singer, J. and Meltzer, H. (1988) Clozapine for the treatment-resistant schizophrenic: a double-blind comparison with chlorpromazine, *Archives of General Psychiatry*, **45**, pp. 789–96.

Katsouyanni, K., Touloumi, G., Samoli, E. *et al.* (2001) Confounding and effect modification in the short-term effects of ambient particles on total mortality: results from 29 European cities within the APHEA2 project, *Epidemiology*, **12**(5), pp. 521–31.

Kaur, B., Anderson, H. R., Austin, J. *et al.* (1998) Prevalence of asthma symptoms, diagnosis, and treatment in 12–14-year-old children across Great Britain (international study of asthma and allergies in childhood, ISAAC, UK), *British Medical Journal*, **316**, pp. 118–24.

Kelly, J. A., St Lawrence, J. S., Stevenson, L. Y. *et al.* (1992) Community AIDS/HIV risk reduction: the effects of endorsements by popular people in three cities, *American Journal of Public Health*, **80**, pp. 1483–9.

Kesey, K. (1962) *One Flew Over the Cuckoo's Nest*, Methuen, London.

King, E. (1994) Suicide in the mentally ill: an epidemiological sample and implications for clinicians, *British Journal of Psychiatry*, **165**, pp. 658–63.

Kippax, S., Crawford, J., Connell, B. *et al.* (1992) The importance of gay community in the prevention of HIV transmission: a study of Australian men who have sex with men, in Aggleton P., Davies P. and Hart, G. (eds) *AIDS: Rights, Risk and Reason*, Taylor and Francis, London.

Kleinman, A. (1988) *The Illness Narratives: Suffering, Healing and the Human Condition*, Basic Books, New York.

Klipple, G. L. and Cecere, F. A. (1989) Rheumatoid arthritis and pregnancy, *Rheumatic Disease Clinics of North America*, **15**, pp. 213–39.

Koffman, J., Fulop, N. J., Pashley, D. and Coleman, K. (1997) Ethnicity and use of acute psychiatric beds: one-day survey in North and South Thames regions, *British Journal of Psychiatry*, **171**, pp. 238–41.

Kotarba, J. and Seidel, J. (1984) Managing the problem patient: compliance or social control? *Social Science and Medicine*, **19**(12), pp. 1393–400.

Laing, R. D. (1960) *The Divided Self: A Study of Sanity, Madness and the Family*, Tavistock, London.

Laing, R. D. (1967) *The Politics of Experience*, Penguin, Harmondsworth.

Lamptey, P. R. (2002) Reducing heterosexual transmission of HIV in poor countries, *British Medical Journal*, **324**, pp. 207–11.

Launer, G. (1999) A narrative approach to mental health in general practice, *British Medical Journal*, **318**, pp. 117–9.

Lawrence, J. (1970) Rheumatoid arthritis—nature or nurture? *Annals of the Rheumatic Diseases*, **29**, pp. 357–9.

Lawson, M. (1991) A recipient's view, in Ramon, S. (ed.) *Beyond Community Care: Normalisation and Integration Work*, Macmillan, London.

Leff, J. (1993) Comment on crazy talk: thought disorder or psychiatric arrogance by Thomas Szasz, *British Journal of Medical Psychology*, **66**, pp. 77–8.

Leff, J. P. and Vaughn, C. E. (1985) *Expressed Emotion in Families: Its Significance for Mental Illness*, Guilford Press, New York.

Leff, J., Wig, N. N., Bendi, H. *et al.* (1990) Relatives' expressed emotion and the course of schizophrenia in Chandigarh: a two-year follow-up of a first-contact sample, *British Journal of Psychiatry*, **151**, pp. 166–73.

Liberman, R. P., Wallace, C. J., Blackwell *et al.* (1993) Innovations in skill training for the seriously mentally ill: the UCLA Social and Independent Living Skills modules, *Innovations and Research*, **2**, pp. 43–60.

Littlewood, R. and Lipsedge, M. (1989) *Aliens and Alienists: Ethnic Minorities and Psychiatry*, 2nd edn, Penguin, Harmondsworth; an edited extract entitled 'Ethnic minorities and the psychiatrist' appears in Davey, B., Gray, A. and Seale, C. (eds) (1995) *Health and Disease: A Reader*, 2nd edn, Open University Press, Buckingham.

Locker, D. (1983) *Disability and Disadvantage: the Consequences of Chronic Illness*, Tavistock, London.

Lukes, S. (1973) *Emile Durkheim: His Life and Works*, Penguin, Harmondsworth.

Lupton, D. (1994) *Medicine as Culture: Illness, Disease and the Body in Western Societies*, Sage, London.

MacCarty, C. S. and Drake, R. L. (1956) Neurosurgical procedures for the control of pain, *Proceedings of Staff Meetings of the Mayo Clinic*, **31**, pp. 208–14.

MacGregor, A., Riste, L., Hazes, J. and Silman, A. (1994) Low prevalence of rheumatoid arthritis in Black Caribbeans compared with Whites in inner city Manchester, *Annals of the Rheumatic Diseases*, **53**, pp. 293–7.

Macintyre, S. and Oldman, D. (1977) Coping with migraine, in Davis, A. and Horobin, G. (eds) *Medical Encounters*, Croom Helm, London; an edited extract also entitled 'Coping with migraine' appears in Davey, B., Gray, A. and Seale, C. (eds) (2001) *Health and Disease: A Reader*, 3rd edn, Open University Press, Buckingham.

Maddison, A. (2001) *The World Economy: A Millennial Perspective*, Development Centre of the Organisation for Economic Co-operation and Development (OECD), Paris.

Mangge, H., Hermann, J. and Schauenstein, K. (1999) Diet and rheumatoid arthritis — a review, *Scandinavian Journal of Rheumatology*, **28**(4), pp. 201–9.

MAP Network (2000) *Durban MAP Symposium Report: The Status and Trends of HIV/AIDS in the World*, MAP (Monitoring the AIDS Pandemic) Network Secretariat, Harvard University, Boston; Introduction available at http://www.unaids.org/hivaidsinfo/statistics/june00/map/map%5Fstats%5F2000%5Fintro.doc; Abstract available at http://www.unaids.org/hivaidsinfo/statistics/june00/map/map%5Fstats%5F2000.doc (accessed March 2002).

Mason, J., Weener, J., Gertman, P. and Meenan, R. (1983) Health status in chronic disease: a comparative study of rheumatoid arthritis, *Journal of Rheumatology*, **10**, pp. 763–8.

McKeganey, N. and Barnard, M. (1992) *AIDS, Drugs and Sexual Risk*, Open University Press, Buckingham.

McLean, J., Boulton, M., Brookes, M. *et al.* (1994) Regular partners and risky behaviour: why do gay men have unprotected sex? *AIDS Care*, **6**, pp. 331–41.

Meenan, R., Gertman, P. and Mason, J. (1980) Measuring health status in arthritis: the Arthritis Impact Measurement Scales, *Arthritis and Rheumatism*, **23**, pp. 146–52.

Melzack, R. (1975) The McGill pain questionnaire: major properties and scoring methods, *Pain*, **1**, pp. 277–99.

Melzack, R. and Wall, P. (1965) Pain mechanisms: a new theory, *Science*, **150**, pp. 971–9.

Melzack, R. and Wall, P. (1988) *The Challenge of Pain*, Penguin Books, Harmondsworth; reprinted 1991.

Morris, J. (1991) *Pride Against Prejudice: A Personal Politics of Disability*, The Women's Press, London; an extract appears as 'Pride against prejudice: "lives not worth living"' in Davey, B., Gray, A. and Seale, C. (eds) (2001) *Health and Disease: A Reader*, 3rd edn, Open University Press, Buckingham.

Mugerwa, R. D., Kaleebu, P., Mugyenyi, P. *et al.* (2002) First trial of the HIV-1 vaccine in Africa: Ugandan experience, *British Medical Journal*, **324**, pp. 226–9.

Mulvany, F., O'Callaghan, E., Takei, N., Byrne, M., Fearon, P. and Larkin, C. (2001) Effect of social class at birth on risk and presentation of schizophrenia: case-control study, *British Medical Journal*, **323**, pp. 1398–401.

Myer, L., Mathews, C. and Little, F. (2001) Condom gap in Africa is wider than study suggests (Letter), *British Medical Journal*, **323**, p. 937.

National AIDS Trust (2000) *Attitudes Towards HIV and AIDS,* results of a MORI poll conducted on behalf of NAT; cited in Terrence Higgins Trust (2001), *Prejudice, Discrimination and HIV,* Terrence Higgins Trust, London.

National Asthma Campaign (2000) Greater Expectations? Findings from the National Asthma Campaign's representative study of the needs of people with asthma in the UK, *Asthma Journal,* **5**(3), Special Supplement.

National Asthma Campaign (2001a) Out in the Open: Asthma Audit 2001, *Asthma Journal,* **6**(3), Special Supplement; also available at http://www.asthma.org.uk/AsthmaAudit.pdf (accessed February 2002).

National Asthma Campaign (2001b) Prescriptions potential health risk for people with asthma, Press Release 2 July 2001; available at http://www.asthma.org.uk/newspr34.html (accessed March 2002).

National Confidential Inquiry (2001) *Safety First. Five Year Report of the National Confidential Inquiry into Suicide and Homicide by People with Mental Illness,* Department of Health, London; also available at http://www.doh.gov.uk/mentalhealth/safetyfirst/safetyfirst.pdf (accessed February 2002).

National Schizophrenia Fellowship (Scotland) (2001) *Give us a break. Exploring harassment of people with mental health problems,* National Schizophrenia Fellowship (Scotland), Edinburgh; some information is also on their website at www.nsfscot.org.uk (accessed January 2002).

Nettle, D. (2001) *Strong Imagination: Madness, Creativity and Human Nature,* Oxford University Press, Oxford.

Newman, S., Fitzpatrick, R., Revinson, T., Skevington, S. and Williams, G. (1995) *Understanding Rheumatoid Arthritis,* Routledge, London.

Nicoll, A., Hughes, G., Donnelly, M. *et al.* (2001) Assessing the impact of national anti-HIV sexual health campaigns: trends in the transmission of HIV and other sexually transmitted infections in England, *Sexually Transmitted Infections,* **77**, pp. 242–7.

Nijhof, G. (1995) Parkinson's disease as a problem of shame in public appearance, *Sociology of Health and Illness,* **17**(2), pp. 193–205.

Nocon, A. and Booth, T. (1990) *The Social Impact of Asthma,* University of Sheffield, Sheffield; an edited extract appears as 'The social impact of childhood asthma', in Davey, B., Gray, A. and Seale, C. (eds) (2001) *Health and Disease: A Reader,* 3rd edn, Open University Press, Buckingham.

Norman, R. M. G. and Malla, A. K. (1993a) Stressful life events and schizophrenia. I: A review of the research, *British Journal of Psychiatry,* **162**, pp. 161–5.

Norman, R. M. G. and Malla, A. K. (1993b) Stressful life events and schizophrenia. II: Conceptual and methodological issues, *British Journal of Psychiatry,* **162**, pp. 166–74.

Oakley, A. (1985) *The Sociology of Housework,* 2nd edn, Basil Blackwell, Oxford.

Oliver, M. (1993) Re-defining disability: a challenge to research, in Swain, J., Finkelstein, V., French, S. and Oliver, M. (eds) *Disabling Barriers—Enabling Environments,* Sage, London.

ONS (2000) *Key Health Statistics from General Practice 1998,* Series MB6, No. 2, Office for National Statistics, The Stationery Office, London; available at http://www.statistics.gov.uk/nsbase/downloads/theme_health/Key_Health_Stats_1998.pdf (accessed February 2002).

ONS (2001) *Mortality Statistics: Cause. Review of the Registrar General on Deaths by Cause, Sex and Age, in England and Wales, 2000,* Office for National Statistics Series DH2 No.27, The Stationery Office, London; available at http://www.statistics.gov.uk/downloads/theme_health/DH2_27/DH2_27.pdf (accessed February 2002).

OPCS (1995) *OPCS Survey of Psychiatric Morbidity in Great Britain. Report 1. The Prevalence of Psychiatric Morbidity among Adults living in Private Households,* HMSO, London.

Parker, J., Frank, R., Beck, N. *et al.* (1988) Pain in rheumatoid arthritis: relationship to demographic, medical and psychological factors, *Journal of Rheumatology*, **15**, pp. 433–7.

Parsons, T. (1951) *The Social System*, Free Press, Glencoe, Illinois.

Partridge, M. R. (2001) The profile of respiratory conditions: why government action is necessary, *Thorax*, **56**, pp. 744–5.

Patton, C. (1990) *Inventing AIDS*, London, Routledge.

PHLS (2002) *HIV and AIDS Reporting Section (HARS) Slide Set*, Public Health Laboratory Service, London; available at http://www.phls.co.uk/facts/HIV/hiv.htm (accessed February 2002).

Pincus, T. and Callahan, L. F. (1986) Taking mortality in rheumatoid arthritis seriously—predictive markers, socio-economic status and comorbidity (Editorial), *Journal of Rheumatology*, **13**, pp. 841–5.

Pincus, T. and Callahan, L. F. (1994) Association of low formal education level and poor health status: behavioral, in addition to demographic and medical, explanations?, *Journal of Clinical Epidemiology*, **47**, pp. 355–61.

Piot, P. (2000) Global AIDS epidemic: time to turn the tide, *Science*, **288**, pp. 2176–8; an edited extract also appears in Davey, B., Gray, A. and Seale, C. (eds) (2001) *Health and Disease: A Reader*, 3rd edn, Open University Press, Buckingham.

Pope, C. A. and Dockery, W. (1992) Acute health effects of PM_{10} pollution on symptomatic and asymptomatic children, *American Review of Respiratory Diseases*, **145**, pp. 1123–8.

Prout, A. and Deverall, K. (1995) *MESMAC—Working with Diversity, Building Communities*, HEA/Longman, London.

Reisine, S., Goodenow, C. and Grady, K. (1987) The impact of rheumatoid arthritis on the homemaker, *Social Science and Medicine*, **25**, pp. 89–95.

Renzoni, E., Forastiere, F., Biggieri, A. *et al.* (1999) Differences in parental- and self-report of asthma, rhinitis and eczema among Italian adolescents. SIDRIA collaborative group, *The European Respiratory Journal*, **14**(3), pp. 597–604.

Rhodes, T. (1994) *Risk, Intervention and Change: HIV Prevention and Drug Use*, Health Education Authority, London.

Richardson, A. and Bolle, D. (1992) *Wise Before Their Time: People with AIDS and HIV Talk about their Lives*, HarperCollins, London.

Rigby, A. S. (1992) HLA haplotype sharing in rheumatoid arthritis sibships: risk estimates in siblings, *Scandinavian Journal of Rheumatology*, **21**, pp. 68–73.

Rigby, A. S., Silman, A. J., Voelm, L. *et al.* (1991) Investigating the HLA component in rheumatoid arthritis: an additive (dominant) mode is rejected, a recessive mode is preferred, *Genetic Epidemiology*, **8**, pp. 153–75.

Robinson, I. (1990) Personal narratives, social careers and medical courses: analysing life trajectories in autobiographies of people with multiple sclerosis, *Social Science and Medicine*, **30**(11), pp. 1171–86.

Rosenhan, D. L. (1973) On being sane in insane places, *Science*, **179**, pp. 250–8.

Royal Pharmaceutical Society of Great Britain and Department of Health (1997) Compliance to Concordance, available at http://www.concordance.org (accessed February 2002).

Saunders, C. M. (1978) *The Management of Terminal Disease*, Edward Arnold, London.

Saunders, C. M. and Baines, M. (1983) *Living with Dying: The Management of Terminal Disease*, Oxford University Press, Oxford.

Scambler, G. (1984) Perceiving and coping with stigmatizing illness, in Fitzpatrick, R., Hinton, J., Newman, S., Scambler, G. and Thompson, J. (eds) *The Experience of Illness*, Tavistock, London.

Scambler, G. and Hopkins, A. (1988) Accommodating epilepsy in families, in Anderson, R. and Bury, M. (eds) *Living with Chronic Illness: The Experience of Patients and their Families,* Unwin Hyman, London.

Scarry, E. (1985) *The Body in Pain: The Making and Unmaking of the World,* Oxford University Press, Oxford.

Schliekelman, P., Garner, C. and Slatkin, M. (2001) Natural selection and resistance to HIV, *Nature,* **411**, pp. 545–6.

Scottish Executive (2001) *Renewing Mental Health Law,* Scottish Executive, Edinburgh; also available at www.scotland.gov.uk/health/mentalhealthlaw (accessed January 2002).

Shearer, A. (1981) *Disability: Whose Handicap?,* Basil Blackwell, Oxford; an edited extract also entitled 'Disability: whose handicap?' appears in Black, N., Boswell, D., Gray, A., Murphy, S. and Popay, J. (eds) (1984) *Health and Disease: A Reader,* 1st edn, Open University Press, Milton Keynes.

Shelton, J. D. and Johnston, B. (2001) Condom gap in Africa: evidence from donor agencies and key informants, *British Medical Journal,* **323**, p. 139.

Sibbald, B. (1988) Patient self care in acute asthma, *Thorax,* **44**, pp. 97–101.

SIGN (1998) *Psychosocial Interventions in the Management of Schizophrenia,* Scottish Intercollegiate Guidelines Network, Edinburgh; also available at www.show.scot.nhs.uk/sign/guidelines/fulltext/30/index.html (accessed January 2002).

Silman, A. J. (1988) Has the incidence of rheumatoid arthritis declined in the United Kingdom? *British Journal of Rheumatology,* **27**, pp. 77–8.

Silman, A. J. (1991) Is rheumatoid arthritis an infectious disease? *British Medical Journal,* **303**, pp. 200–1.

Silman, A. J., MacGregor, A. J., Thomson, W. *et al.* (1994) Twin concordance rates for rheumatoid arthritis: results from a nationwide study, *British Journal of Rheumatology,* **32**, pp. 903–7.

Silverman, D. (1993) *Interpreting Qualitative Data: Methods for Analysing Talk, Text and Interaction,* Sage, London.

Small, N. (1995) Living with HIV and AIDS, in Davey, B., Gray, A. and Seale, C. (eds) (1995) *Health and Disease: A Reader,* 2nd edn, Open University Press, Buckingham.

Smolen, J. S. and Steiner, G. (1998) Are autoantibodies active players or epiphenomena? *Current Opinion in Rheumatology,* **10**(3), pp. 201–6.

Snadden, D. and Belle Brown, J. (1992) The experience of asthma, *Social Science and Medicine,* **34**(12), pp. 1351–61.

Solomon, L., Robin, G. and Walkenburg, H. A. (1975) Rheumatoid arthritis in an urban South African negro population, *Annals of Rheumatic Diseases,* **34**, pp. 128–35.

Sontag, S. (1978) *Illness as Metaphor,* Penguin Books, Ltd. Chapter 4 is reprinted under the title 'Illness as metaphor' in Davey, B., Gray, A. and Seale, C. (eds) (2001) *Health and Disease: A Reader,* 3rd edn, Open University Press, Buckingham.

Sontag, S. (1991) *Illness as Metaphor: AIDS and its Metaphors,* Penguin, Harmondsworth.

Spector, T. M. and Hochberg, M. C. (1990) The protective effect of the oral contraceptive pill on rheumatoid arthritis: an overview of the analytic epidemiological studies using meta-analysis, *Journal of Clinical Epidemiology,* **43**, pp. 1221–30.

Stedman, J. R. and Bush, T. (2000) Mapping of Nitrogen Dioxide and PM_{10} in the UK for Article 5 Assessment, AEA Technology Environment, Harwell.

Stephens, J. C., Reich, D. E., Goldstein, D. B. *et al.* (1998) Dating the origin of the CCR5–Delta32 AIDS-resistance allele by the coalescence of haplotypes, *American Journal of Human Genetics*, **62**, pp. 1507–15.

Stimson, G. V. (1976) General practitioners' 'trouble' and types of patient, in Stacey, M. (ed.) *The Sociology of the National Health Service*, University of Keele Sociological Review, Monograph no. 22, University of Keele.

Strachan, D. P. (1989) Hay fever, hygiene and household size, *British Medical Journal*, **299**, pp. 1258–9.

Strachan, D. P. (2000) Family size, infection and atopy: the first decade of the 'hygiene hypothesis', *Thorax*, **55** (Supplement 1), pp. S2-S10.

Suddath, R. L., Christison, G. W., Torrey, E. F. *et al.* (1990) Anatomical abnormalities in the brains of monozygotic twins discordant for schizophrenia, *New England Journal of Medicine*, **322**, pp. 789–94.

Sullivan, F., Eagers, R., Lynch, K. and Barber, J. (1987) Assessment of disability caused by rheumatic diseases in general practice, *Annals of Rheumatic Diseases*, **46**, pp. 598–600.

Szasz, T. (1979) *Schizophrenia: The Sacred Symbol of Psychiatry*, Oxford University Press, Oxford.

Szasz, T. (1993) Crazy talk: thought disorder or psychiatric arrogance? *British Journal of Medical Psychology*, **66**, pp. 61–7.

Taylor, P. C., Williams, R. O. and Maini, R. N. (2001) Immunotherapy for rheumatoid arthritis, *Current Opinion in Immunology*, **13**, pp. 611–16.

Terrence Higgins Trust (2000) *Give Us a Job? Barriers to Employment for People with HIV*, Terrence Higgins Trust, London.

Terrence Higgins Trust (2001) *Prejudice, Discrimination and HIV*, Terrence Higgins Trust, London.

Thompson, P. W. and Pegley, F. S. (1991) A comparison of disability measured by the Stanford Health Assessment Questionnaire disability scales (HAQ) in male and female rheumatoid outpatients, *British Journal of Rheumatology*, **30**, pp. 298–300.

Times Higher Education Supplement (1995) Proof of plan for child radiation tests, 27 January, p. 3.

Tugwell, P., Bombardier, C., Buchanan, W. *et al.* (1987) The MACTAR Patient Preference Disability Questionnaire: an individualized functional priority approach to assessing improvement in physical disability in clinical trials in rheumatoid arthritis, *Journal of Rheumatology*, **14**, pp. 446–51.

Tugwell, P., Bombardier, C., Buchanan, W. *et al.* (1990) Methotrexate in rheumatoid arthritis: impact on quality of life assessed by traditional standard-item individualized patient preference health status questionnaires, *Archives of Internal Medicine*, **150**, pp. 59–62.

UK Collaborative Group on Monitoring the Transmission of Drug Resistance (2001) Analysis of prevalence of HIV-1 drug resistance in primary infection in the United Kingdom, *British Medical Journal*, **322**, pp. 1087–8.

UNAIDS/WHO (2000) 'A global view of HIV infection at the end of 1999' (poster), UNAIDS/WHO, Geneva; available at http://www.unaids.org/epidemic_update/report/JC404-Poster-Report.jpg (accessed March 2002).

UNAIDS/WHO (2001) *AIDS Epidemic Update: December 2001*, Joint United Nations Programme on AIDS and the World Health Organisation, Geneva; available at http://www.unaids.org/worldaidsday/2001/Epiupdate2001/Epiupdate2001_en.pdf (accessed March 2002).

van Gennep, A. (1960) *The Rites of Passage*, University of Chicago Press, Chicago (first published 1909).

Vandenbroucke, J. P., Valkenberg, H. A., Boersma, J. W. *et al.* (1982) Oral contraceptives and rheumatoid arthritis: further evidence for a protective effect, *Lancet*, **ii**(8303), pp. 839–42.

Vaughn, C. E. and Leff, J. P. (1976a) The influence of family and social factors on the course of psychiatric illness, *British Journal of Psychiatry*, **129**, pp. 125–37.

Vaughn, C. E. and Leff, J. P. (1976b) The measurement of expressed emotion in the families of psychiatric patients, *British Journal of Social and Clinical Psychology*, **15**, pp. 157–66.

Verbrugge, L. M., Gates, D. M. and Ike, R. W. (1991) Risk factors for disability among US adults with arthritis, *Journal of Clinical Epidemiology*, **44**, pp. 167–82.

von Mutius, E., Martinez, F. D., Fritzsch, C. *et al.* (1994) Prevalence of asthma and atopy in two areas of West and East Germany, *American Journal of Respiratory and Critical Care Medicine*, **149**, pp. 358–64.

Vonnegut, M. (1979) *The Eden Express*, Bantam, New York.

Walker, E. F. and Levine, R. J. (1990) Prediction of adult-onset schizophrenia from childhood home-movies of the patients, *American Journal of Psychiatry*, **147**, pp. 1052–6.

Watney, S. (1989) The subject of AIDS, in Aggleton, P., Hart, G. and Davies, P. (eds) *AIDS: Social Representations, Social Practices*, Falmer Press, Lewes.

Watters, J. (1996) Americans and syringe exchange: routes of resistance, in Rhodes, T. and Hartnoll, R. (eds) *AIDS, Drugs and Prevention*, Routledge, London.

Weeks, J. (1990) Post-modern AIDS?, in Gupta, S. (ed.) *Ecstatic Antibodies: Resisting the AIDS Mythologies*, Rivers Oram, London.

Wiener, C. (1975) The burden of rheumatoid arthritis: tolerating the uncertainty, *Social Science and Medicine*, **9**, pp. 97–104.

Wiles, N., Symmons, D. P. M., Harrison, B. *et al.* (1999) Estimating the incidence of rheumatoid arthritis. Trying to hit a moving target? *Arthritis and Rheumatism*, **42**(7), pp. 1339–46.

Williams, G. (1984a) *Interpretation and Compromise: Coping with the Experience of Chronic Illness*, unpublished PhD thesis, University of Manchester.

Williams, G. (1984b) The genesis of chronic illness: narrative reconstruction, *Sociology of Health and Illness*, **6**, pp. 175–200.

Williams, G. (1986) Lay beliefs about the causes of rheumatoid arthritis: their implications for rehabilitation, *International Rehabilitation Medicine*, **8**, pp. 65–8.

Williams, G. (1987) Disablement and the social context of daily activity, *International Disability Studies*, **9**, pp. 97–102.

Williams, G. (1993) Chronic illness and the pursuit of virtue in everyday life, in Radley, A. (ed.) *Worlds of Illness: Biographical and Cultural Perspectives on Health and Disease*, Routledge, London.

Williams, G. and Wood, P. (1986) Common-sense beliefs about illness: a mediating role for the doctor, *Lancet*, **ii**, pp. 1435–7.

Williams, G. and Wood, P. (1988) Coming to terms with chronic illness: the negotiation of autonomy in rheumatoid arthritis, *International Disability Studies*, **10**, pp. 128–32.

Williams, S. J. (1993) *Chronic Respiratory Illness*, Routledge, London.

Wilson, C., Tiwana, H. and Ebringer, A. (2000) Molecular mimicry between HLA-DR alleles associated with rheumatoid arthritis and Proteus mirabilis as the aetiological basis for autoimmunity, *Microbes and Infection*, **2**(12), pp. 1489–96.

Wolfe, F. and Cathey, M. (1991) The assessment and prediction of functional disability in rheumatoid arthritis, *Journal of Rheumatology*, **18**, pp. 1298–306.

Wood, P. and Badley, E. (1986) The epidemiology of individual rheumatic diseases, pp. 59–142 in Scott, J. T. (ed.) *Copeman's Textbook of the Rheumatic Diseases, Volume 1* (6th edn), Churchill Livingstone, London.

World Health Organisation (1973) *The International Pilot Study of Schizophrenia*, WHO, Geneva.

World Health Organisation (1993) *The ICD-10 Classification of Mental and Behavioural Disorders: Clinical Descriptions and Diagnostic Guidelines*, WHO, Geneva.

World Health Organisation (2000) *Blood safety – for too few*, Press release WHO/25, 7 April 2000, World Health Organisation, Geneva; available at http://www.who.int/inf-pr-2000/en/pr2000–25.html (accessed March 2002).

Yamey, G. and Rankin, W. W. (2002) AIDS and global justice (editorial), *British Medical Journal*, **324**, pp. 181–2.

Yelin, E., Henke, C. and Epstein, W. (1987) The work dynamics of the person with rheumatoid arthritis, *Arthritis and Rheumatism*, **30**, pp. 507–12.

Further sources

Chapters 1 and 8

Greenhalgh, T. and Hurwitz, B. (eds) (1998) *Narrative Based Medicine*, BMJ Books, London. The contributions in this book illuminate the therapeutic value of a narrative approach to medicine, in which patients and health professionals share their 'stories' about the illness. Five of the chapters were later adapted for publication in the *British Medical Journal* (volume 318) in consecutive weeks beginning on 2nd January 1999, and can be accessed electronically at www.bmj.com by date using the search/archive function. A special issue of the *British Medical Journal* (**324**, 13 April 2002) containing articles debating the pros and cons of medicalisation is also highly recommended.

Chapter 2

Goffman, E. (1968) *Stigma: Notes on the Management of Spoiled Identity*, Pelican Books, London (reprinted most recently in June 1995 and still in print). This is Goffman's classic analysis of the consequences of stigma for peoples' management of their relationships with other people. Controlling the flow of information about stigmatising attributes becomes a central preoccupation for individuals as they seek to avoid unwelcome discrimination.

Shakespeare, T. (1994) Cultural representations of disabled people: dustbins for disavowal, *Disability and Society*, **9**(3), pp. 283–301. This is a classic article in which Tom Shakespeare explores the politics of stigma in relation to disability. A more recent newspaper article by the same author appears in *Health and Disease: A Reader* (Open University Press, 3rd edn 2001), entitled 'Brave New World II', in which he explores the possibility that new genetic knowledge will reinforce the representation of disabled people as 'defective'. He also appears briefly in 'More than meets the eye', the Open University TV programme associated with this book.

Williams, S. (1987) 'Goffman, interactionism and the management of stigma in everyday life', in Scambler, G. (ed.) *Sociological Theory and Medical Sociology*, Tavistock, London. In this chapter, Simon Williams outlines the key ideas of Goffman in a clear and concise way, and explains their relevance for the sociological study of health and illness. Although now out of print, this book is well worth obtaining through a public library.

Chapter 3

Medical information written for a lay audience is available in the booklets and fact sheets published free by ARC, the Arthritis Research Campaign. Information on all forms of arthritis, including rheumatoid arthritis, treatments, and adaptations to cope with aspects of daily living, such as diet and driving, can be downloaded free from their excellent website at http://www.arc.org.uk, or write with a stamped self-addressed envelope to: ARC Publications, PO Box 177, Chesterfield, Derbyshire, S41 7TQ.

Another useful website is Veritas Medicine, which publishes information on the outcomes of clinical trials in a wide range of conditions; the specific link to information about rheumatoid arthritis can be found at http://www.veritasmedicine.com/d_index.cfm

Newman, S., Fitzpatrick, R., Revenson, T., Skevington, S. and Williams, G. (1995) *Understanding Rheumatoid Arthritis*, Routledge, London. Two of the authors, Ray Fitzpatrick and Gareth Williams, are also co-authors of Chapter 3 of this book. The volume brings together the available evidence from sociology and psychology concerning the impact of rheumatoid arthritis on individuals and their families, and examines the processes whereby individuals cope and adjust to the problems raised by a chronic disease.

Klippel, J. H. and Dieppe, P. A. (1998) *Rheumatology,* 2nd edn, Mosby, London, is a huge medical textbook aimed at practitioners, but may be useful to anyone who is seeking more detailed clinical description and discussion, if you are familiar with the relevant medical terminology or can use a medical dictionary. It costs almost £200, so consult a library copy! The 3rd edition is due for publication at the end of 2002, with a new editor (Hochberg), but other details as above.

Silman, A. J. and Hochberg, M. C. (2001) *Epidemiology of the Rheumatic Diseases*, 2nd edn, Oxford University Press, Oxford, is a specialist textbook for readers with a background in the subject area and is a comprehensive source on the genetics and epidemiology of RA. More accessible in academic terms, but harder to find (because it is out of print, so must be ordered through a library) is Wood, P. and Badley, E. (1986) 'The epidemiology of individual rheumatic disorders', pp. 59–142 in Scott, J. T. (ed.) *Copeman's Textbook of the Rheumatic Diseases, Volume 1* (6th edn), Churchill Livingstone, London.

Chapter 4

There are an enormous number of Internet sites carrying information on every aspect of HIV and AIDS. Here are a few of the most comprehensive, but they all give links to other websites you can follow up (all were last accessed in March 2002):

UNAIDS, the United Nations website for HIV/AIDS offers a huge range of international and country-specific epidemiological data, posters, diagrams and charts, press releases and conference reports at http://www.unaids.org

Regularly updated epidemiological data for the UK can be found on the Public Health Laboratory Service (PHLS) website at http://www.phls.co.uk/facts/HIV/hiv.htm

The Centers for Disease Control and Prevention (CDC)'s website at http://www.cdc.gov/hiv/pubs/facts.htm publishes comprehensive data and analysis for the USA.

The Terrence Higgins Trust at http://www.tht.org.uk, the leading UK charity for people living with HIV/AIDS, offers a wide-ranging collection of information and support networks, particularly for gay and bisexual men, women and ethnic minorities affected by HIV/AIDS in the UK.

'The Body' is an American HIV/AIDS information resource for people living with HIV/AIDS, at http://www.thebody.com. A glossary of terms related to HIV/AIDS is at http://www.critpath.org/research/gloss-vh.htm.

HIV/AIDS has been one of the most extensively published topics in books and articles since the 1980s, and more are appearing all the time. As we go to press in 2002, here are a few titles we strongly recommend:

Adler, M. (ed.) (2001) *ABC of AIDS*, 5th edn, BMJ Books, London. This regularly updated paperback is the most concise and widely respected reference text for health care workers. Each short chapter is written by internationally recognised experts, and topics include a history of the epidemic, diagnosis, treatment of opportunistic infections in developed and developing countries, anti-retroviral drug therapies, palliative care and pain control, hospital and community-based care and counselling, and personal accounts of living with HIV.

Aggleton, P., Hart, G. and Davies, P. (eds) (1999) *Families and Communities Responding to AIDS*, Taylor and Francis, London. This collection of accounts illustrates how families (nuclear, extended and refugee families) and communities around the world have responded to people with AIDS in their midst, and examines the features that promote positive support or make stigmatisation and rejection more likely.

Bloor, M. (1995) *The Sociology of HIV Transmission*, Sage, London, is an accessible account of medical sociology's contribution to the understanding of HIV in the UK. Drawing on qualitative research among injecting drug users and male sex workers, it reviews the emergence of HIV infection and the policy response to HIV prevention. It also contains a useful chapter on theories of risk behaviour, which shows how different social science paradigms conceptualise risk.

British Medical Journal (2002) Special theme issue 'Global Voices on the AIDS Catastrophe', volume 324, 26 January, contains a wide range of articles with particular emphasis on the need for social justice as the guiding principle in tackling the epidemic. For example, Lamptey, P. R. (pp. 207–11) 'Reducing heterosexual transmission of HIV in poor countries', stresses the need to decrease vulnerability — particularly among adolescent girls, sex workers, and displaced people; Macintyre, J. and Gray, G. (pp. 218–21) 'What can we do to reduce mother-to-child transmission of HIV?', considers the major barriers to implementation of anti-retroviral treatments in low-income countries; Dixon, S., McDonald, S. and Roberts, J. (pp. 232–4) 'The impact of HIV and AIDS on Africa's economic development', refers to the disproportionate loss of skilled workers. Available at http://bmj.com/collections/specials.shtml (accessed March 2002).

Fee, E. and Fox, D. (eds) (1992) *AIDS: The Making of a Chronic Disease*, University of California Press. Still in print, this book illuminates how studying the social history of public health policy during epidemics in the past can inform contemporary understandings of social and medical responses to HIV and AIDS. It includes chapters on history and epidemics (Guenter Risse), enforcement of public health (Roy Porter, Dorothy Porter), medical responses to sexually transmitted disease (Allan Brandt, Elizabeth Fee), and the social construction of sexuality since AIDS began (Paula Treichler, Dennis Altman).

Guest, E. (2002) *Children of AIDS: Africa's Orphan Crisis*, Pluto Press, London. Africa is home to 95 per cent of the world's 13 million AIDS orphans. This paperback is a collection of stories from some of them in South Africa, Uganda and Zambia. They reflect the children's feelings of stigma, their hopes and fears for the future, their gratitude for the care given by grandparents, siblings and foster parents, and their experiences of institutional support and international aid.

Rhodes, T. and Hartnoll, R. (eds) (1996) *AIDS, Drugs and Prevention*, Routledge, London, brings together a range of international contributions on the research, theory and practice of developing community-based HIV prevention. Chapters include a focus on: sexuality (Graham Hart, Sheila Henderson), prostitution (Marina Barnard), drug injecting (Robert Power, Steve Koester), sexual behaviour change (Tim Rhodes, Benny Jose), and community and activist HIV prevention (Cindy Patton, Wayne Wiebel, Jean-Paul Grund).

Smith, R. A. (ed.) (2001) *Encyclopaedia of AIDS: A Social, Political, Cultural and Scientific Record of the HIV Epidemic*, Penguin Books, London, is a weighty but cheaply priced paperback of contributions from 175 experts over 300 topics on everything from the global epidemiology, biomedical science, prevention, treatment, social support, politics, ethics and the law.

Watney, S. (2000) *Imagine Hope: AIDS and Gay Identity*, Routledge, London. Since the early 1980s, Simon Watney has been writing about the representation of HIV and AIDS in the mass media and its effect on the identities associated with being a gay man in Western society. In this book he chronicles the changing course of the epidemic and the shifts in public and private responses to it from the perspective of gay men.

Weiss, R., Adler, M. W. and Rowland-Jones, S. L. (2001) *The Changing Face of HIV and AIDS*, Oxford University Press, Oxford, is a series of expert reviews aimed at updating clinicians and scientists with an interest in the biomedical aspects of HIV-related disease and its management.

Chapter 5

The National Asthma Campaign is the leading UK charity at Providence House, Providence Place, London N1 0NT, or 2a North Charlotte Street, Edinburgh EH2 4HR; they publish research reports, information for people living with the effects of asthma, and details of support networks, available from their website at http://www.asthma.org.uk or by post. The Lung and Asthma Information Agency (LAIA) at St Thomas' Hospital Medical School reports on UK asthma trends at http://www.sghms.ac.uk/depts/laia/laia.htm (last accessed March 2002).

The progress of the major international studies to determine the environmental causes or triggers of asthma, including air pollution, can best be followed by using the following terms in Internet searches: APHEA (Air Pollution and Health: a European Approach); ECRHS (European Community Respiratory Health Survey); and ISAAC (International Study of Asthma and Allergies in Childhood).

The literature on asthma is dominated by hundreds of self-help guides for people with asthma or the parents of asthmatic children, including many that take alternative approaches to medical management. The orthodox medical viewpoint is most accessibly presented in Rubin, B. K., Newhouse, M. T. and Barnes, P. J. (1998) *Conquering Childhood Asthma*, B. C. Decker Inc., Hamilton, Ontario and London.

Bryar, R. and Bytheway, B. (eds) (1996) *Changing Primary Health Care*, Blackwell Science, Oxford. Accounts of a series of projects intended to develop primary health care in the valleys of South Wales. As with many other illnesses, an increasing emphasis is being placed upon the role of GPs and community nurses in the treatment of asthma. Chapters by Ajay Thapar, and by Duncan Williams and Beth Griffiths, describe two local projects intended to improve the effectiveness of asthma care by the primary health care team.

Rona, R. J. (2000) Asthma and poverty, *Thorax*, **55**(3), pp. 239–44, presents a thoughtful review of the social distribution of asthma, particularly among children. *Thorax* is the leading academic journal for asthma research and offers limited access to non-subscribers online at http://thorax.bmjjournals.com ; however, some articles are free to download, including Rona's review cited above.

The debates about the 'hygiene hypothesis' are well represented by its originator, David P. Strachan (2000) Family size, infection and atopy: the first decade of the 'hygiene hypothesis', *Thorax*, **55**(Suppl. 1), pp. S2–S10; see also two opposing editorials in the *American Journal of Critical Care Medicine* (2001), **164**, pp. 1106–9, entitled 'The increase in asthma can/cannot be ascribed to cleanliness', by Erika von Mutius and by Thomas Platts-Mills *et al.*

Chapter 6

There are a number of charities specifically concerned with schizophrenia, all excellent sources of information on a wide range of topics including theories about causation, epidemiology, treatment and community support. All the Internet sites that follow have links to other useful resources (last accessed March 2002).

The National Schizophrenia Fellowship (England and Wales), 30 Tabernacle Street, London EC2A 4DD or 28 Castle Street, Kingston-Upon-Thames, Surrey KT1 1SS, or on the Internet at http://www.nsf.org.uk (England and Wales) and http://www.nsfscot.org.uk (Scotland).

SANE (Schizophrenia A National Emergency), 1st Floor, Cityside House, 40 Adler Street, London E1 1EE (also offices in Bristol and Macclesfield), or at http://www.sane.org.uk/default.htm

The 'Hearing Voices' Network, 91 Oldham Street, Manchester, M4 1LW, and at http://www.hearing-voices.org.uk

MIND, the National Association for Mental Health, Registered Office 15–19 Broadway, London, E15 4BQ, has local offices nationwide; details at http://www.mind.org.uk

The following books and articles are recommended: Andreasen, N. C. (2000) Schizophrenia: The fundamental questions, *Brain Research Reviews*, **31**, pp. 106–12. A summary of current understanding of the disorder and an analysis of the many unresolved issues about schizophrenia at the start of the new millennium.

Atkinson, J. M. and Coia, D. A. (1995) *Families Coping with Schizophrenia: A Practitioner's Guide to Family Groups*, Wiley, Chichester. Written by a psychologist and a psychiatrist, this book offers a background to the involvement of families in schizophrenia — both as carers, and in terms of family influences on the aetiology of schizophrenia. The authors examine the provision of services for carers, focusing particularly on the development of groups for relatives for both education and support, including the development of self-help groups throughout the world.

Bentall, R. P. (ed.) (1992) *Reconstructing Schizophrenia*, 2nd edn, Routledge, London, challenges the concept of schizophrenia from biological, historical and social perspectives and presents new insights including into psychological approaches to therapy. All the authors are psychologists working in the UK.

Heinrichs, R. W. (2001) *In Search of Madness: Schizophrenia and Neuroscience*, Oxford University Press, Oxford. A systematic summary and evaluation of all the evidence for neurobiological abnormalities in schizophrenia.

Jablensky, A., Sartorius, N., Ernberg, G. *et al.* (1992) Schizophrenia: manifestation, incidence and course in different cultures, *Psychological Medicine, monograph supplement 20*. This monograph recounts an international study by the WHO into schizophrenia throughout the world. It is interesting for its detailed description of the research, as well as the findings it presents. The authors discuss the conclusions that may be drawn from such work, along with many of the problems inherent in it.

Littlewood, R. and Lipsedge, M. (1997) *Aliens and Alienists*, 3rd edn, Routledge, London. In this revised edition of a classic text, the authors combine theoretical perspectives from psychiatry and social anthropology to examine the distribution of mental illness among ethnic minorities and black Britons in the UK. They review the development of transcultural psychiatry and argue that racist bias has resulted in inadequate and poorly researched treatment of mental-health problems in people from ethnic minorities.

Nettle, D. (2001) *Strong Imagination: Madness, Creativity and Human Nature*, Oxford University Press, Oxford, tackles the question of why madness exists. Daniel Nettle shows that there is, as long suspected, a link between madness and creative genius and argues that the traits that lie behind madness have evolved because they have psychological benefits as well as psychological costs.

O'Hagan, M. (1996) Two accounts of mental distress, in Read, J. and Reynolds, J. *Speaking Our Minds: An Anthology*, Palgrave Macmillan, London. Extracts from Mary O'Hagan's journal are intercut with extracts from her medical notes made during the same period in hospital for a severe psychotic illness. A slightly edited version appears in Davey, B., Gray, A. and Seale, C. (2001) *Health and Disease: A Reader*, 3rd edn, Open University Press, Buckingham.

The Sainsbury Centre for Mental Health (1998) *Acute Problems: A Survey of the Quality of Care in Acute Psychiatric Wards*, The Sainsbury Centre, Kings College, London University. This assessment of patient's needs in acute psychiatric wards and the extent to which those needs were met, concludes with short accounts of patients' experiences. An edited extract appears in Davey, B., Gray, A. and Seale, C. (2001) *Health and Disease: A Reader*, 3rd edn, Open University Press, Buckingham.

Chapter 7

Bendelow, G. A. and Williams, S. (1995) Transcending the dualisms: towards a sociology of pain, *Sociology of Health and Illness*, **17**(2), pp. 139–65. This article reviews sociological perspectives on pain.

Good, M. J. D., Brodwin, P. E., Good, B. J. and Kleinman, A. (eds) (1994) *Pain as Human Experience: An Anthropological Perspective*, University of California Press. The authors use case studies drawn from anthropological investigations of people in chronic pain and the work of pain clinics in the USA, to contrast the cultural shaping of the language of suffering in the words of people experiencing pain, with the language of medical and psychological theorizing.

Melzack, R. and Wall, P. (1996) *The Challenge of Pain*, Penguin Books, Harmondsworth. The most recent edition of this accessible paperback, by the originators of 'gate-control' theory, outlines the major biological theories of pain and their implications for treatment.

Wall, P. (1999) *Pain: The Science of Suffering*, Weidenfeld and Nicholson, London. In this very clearly written book, written towards the end of his life when he was suffering from prostate cancer, Patrick Wall explains pain perception and chronic pain, and examines its philosophical basis as well as our physiological experience. He also assesses possible treatments for chronic pain, ranging from drugs and surgery, through relaxation techniques and exercise, to acupuncture and herbalism.

Internet database (ROUTES)

A large amount of valuable information is available via the Internet. To help OU students and other readers of books in the *Health and Disease* series to access good quality sites without having to search for hours, the OU has developed a collection of Internet resources on a searchable database called ROUTES. All websites included in the database are selected by academic staff or subject-specialist librarians. The content of each website is evaluated to ensure that it is accurate, well presented and regularly updated. A description is included for each of the resources.

The URL for ROUTES is: http://routes.open.ac.uk/

Entering the OU course code U205 in the search box will retrieve all the resources that have been recommended for *Health and Disease*, including all the Internet sites given above. Alternatively if you want to search for any resources on a particular subject, type in the words which best describe the subject you are interested in.

Answers to questions

Chapter 1

1 The social construction of CHD has gradually changed from a belief that it means a sudden, fatal 'heart attack' to a greater understanding that it is a chronic debilitating condition, often associated with pain (angina), which restricts the daily lives of a large proportion of the older population. The public perception of CHD in the 1970s and 1980s incorporated ideas about 'aggressive' personality types who were supposed to be most at risk, and created a myth that top businessmen were most likely to develop it. By the 1990s, the association of CHD with men in lower-social-class occupations was well established and the condition began to be reconstructed as a disease due to poverty, stress, low self-esteem and smoking. The attribution of 'blame' to smokers who develop CHD has subsequently emerged as an issue, with some health professionals arguing that scarce resources should not be wasted on treating smokers who will not quit. (An article 'Should smokers be offered coronary bypass surgery?' appears in *Health and Disease: A Reader*, Open University Press, 3rd edn 2001.)

2 He draws on Bible stories from the New Testament, the parable (not paradox) of the prodigal son, and from the Old Testament, the 'fall' of Adam and Eve from the garden of Eden, illustrating the influence of religious narratives on his understanding of why he became ill. He has made sense of his diabetes as his 'salvation', a condition that saved his life by forcing him to change to a healthier lifestyle.

Chapter 2

1 Suicide is often due to a failure to sustain *ontological security*, the resultant despair and anxiety so overwhelming the individual that the only way to end the feeling is the complete anaesthesia of death. In wartime people group together against a common enemy, upon whom the bad feelings that might otherwise lead to suicide are *projected*. The enemy is a receptacle for fundamental insecurities and anxieties, and is thus *stigmatised* as evil. (Of course, the enemy may in fact *be* evil, but the psychological effect remains the same.) This promotes feelings of togetherness and security amongst the *membership* of both sides.

Everyday conversations depend on sustaining agreements about what counts as normality, part of which can involve drawing boundaries between normality and abnormality. People who are not of 'normal' appearance may threaten ontological security by reminding others of the limitations of their own bodily existence. However, unlike enmity in wartime, it is morally unacceptable in modern conditions to ascribe character defects to disabled people, although it is becoming increasingly acceptable to condemn prejudice and stigma. This enables a more egalitarian sharing of ontological security.

2 The account shows Roberta Galler seeking to disavow a *master status* as a disabled person ('I wanted to be known for *who* I am and not just by what I physically cannot do'). This was done by *covering* her *discredited* status ('I became the "exceptional" woman, the "super-crip", noted for her independence').

She avoided contact with others with disabilities (the *own*) because this threatened her own security. Such avoidance of people who are stigmatised is an example of *enacted* stigma.

3   'Compensation neurotic' is not a medical diagnosis, but is based on an evaluation of the moral character of patients as malingerers, complaining about pain for ulterior motives. This typification gives a stigmatised identity to the patient. The use of such a label may arise from the need of doctors to simplify their task by placing 'problems' into a single category that can then be ignored. 'Problem pain patient' may be a category serving a similar purpose, though it may simply be an initial attitude before diagnosis of the nature of the problem begins. Medical diagnosis involves categorisation and labelling, but not with a stigmatising intent. However, certain disease labels may subsequently attract stigma or arguably rest upon stigmatising assumptions, as the anti-psychiatrists claimed in the case of mental illness categories. Typifications, however, are more likely to be stigmatising from the outset, and by intent.

Chapter 3

1   Failure to perform the tasks associated with fulfilling customary social roles leads people to feel that their status and importance in the social arena has been damaged and that the quality of their relationships has been diminished. Difficulties of this kind may lead to depression, anxiety and social isolation, and to feelings of loss of control and self-worth.

2   Benefits have to be weighed against the multiple risks of side effects, any benefit may take a considerable time to show, different measures of outcome will show different benefits, and what is a benefit in clinical terms may not be seen to be so by the patient. The relapsing and remitting course of the disease means that it is difficult to be sure that an improvement is due to a given drug. These factors combine to make the prolonged follow-up required for scientific evaluation very difficult to implement. Moreover, the unpredictable benefits of treatment and possible adverse side effects, along with the psychological effects of having RA (such as depression and anxiety), may have important consequences for a patient's willingness to comply with lengthy spells of out-patient treatment, which place enormous demands on an individual's time and resources. Compliance is important for realistic evaluation of the effectiveness of particular drug regimens.

3   Much of the problem in studying the aetiology of RA arises from the nature of the disease itself. It has a relatively low incidence, an onset which is often insidious and difficult to fix to a given date, and a chronic 'waxing and waning' course which is often modulated by years of drug treatment. Studying individuals remote in time from the onset of disease may provide little information about its original cause, or causes. A further problem is that RA as a disease entity remains incompletely clinically defined; there are variations between individuals in the speed of progression of the disease and in their physical, histological and serological features (e.g. approximately 20 per cent of RA patients do not have rheumatoid factor in their blood). Finally, as biological knowledge of the condition accumulates, the possibility becomes stronger that a number of different factors — genetic, infectious, hormonal, immunological — may all be involved in a complex causal interaction which may vary from person to person.

4   Several common features of lay illness beliefs are illustrated in this account, perhaps most obviously the emphasis on 'stress' as a cause of her illness. But you should also note that:

(i)   She has developed a *personal* causal model of her illness, in which she identifies the interaction of stresses in her family life and her own personality and methods of coping with stress;

(ii)   Her account shows signs of *narrative reconstruction* in which past events and experiences, that were not considered to be significant at the time, have subsequently become incorporated into a meaningful story of why she became ill (e.g. 'I'm quite certain that the last straw was my husband's illness');

(iii)   She hints at a possible *teleological analysis* of her illness (i.e. does it have a purpose?), when she talks about suppressing her feelings, her personal identity and her aspirations ('Where have I got to? There's nothing left of me'). Although she does not make the point directly, she implies that the illness made her focus on herself as an individual after too many years of identifying herself as 'a mother and wife'.

5   (a)   A strength of asking standardised questions is that answers from different studies are easier to compare and results are easier to analyse and report. A weakness is that some individuals' main concerns or difficulties are not reflected in the questions and are thus neglected in reports.

(b)   Conversely, the strength of a personalised questionnaire is to maximise sensitivity to individuals' own personal concerns. The weakness is that such data are much more time-consuming to collect and harder to analyse and compare with other studies.

Chapter 4

1   In the first few weeks after HIV enters the body, the virus proliferates unchecked and concentration in the blood rises to a small peak before the person's immune system adapts sufficiently to mount an attack, which brings the viral load down again to barely detectable levels. During the latent period, which varies from about two to ten years, an equilibrium appears to be struck between the rate at which new virus particles replicate and appear in the bloodstream, and their rate of destruction by the immune system. But eventually, unless effective anti-retroviral treatment intervenes, the virus 'escapes' from control by the immune system and the viral load in the blood soars and the person develops symptoms of HIV-related illness. When people on HAART regimens with no detectable HIV in their blood stopped taking the drugs, the virus concentration 'rebounded' very quickly to high levels. This indicates that HIV had persisted in reservoirs outside the circulatory system (for example, in the bone marrow, lymph nodes or brain), where the HAART drugs kept virus replication at a low level, but it rapidly accelerated as soon as the drugs were stopped.

2   Vaccines work by 'priming' the immune system to recognise and attack the infectious agent more effectively, and ideally to produce a sterilising immune response (i.e. one that eradicates it completely). HIV is able to evade this response partly because it replicates inside the cells of its host, which gives it some protection from the host's attack, it preserves its genes from destruction by 'splicing' them into the DNA of the cell it infects, and it produces huge numbers of virus particles (about 10 billion a day), which swamp the host's

immune defences. Vaccine design is further complicated by the fact that HIV genes mutate very frequently, producing new variants. Thus, an effective vaccine would have to contain fragments of all the existing or potential mutants that might arise, in order to prime the recipient's immune system to respond more effectively to whichever strains he or she encounters.

Trials of candidate vaccines in developing countries have been criticised on ethical grounds as exploiting the less-stringent controls that may apply there, and using volunteers as 'guinea pigs' for tests that would not be allowed in Western countries. Conversely, campaigners have accused Western research institutes of unethical behaviour in carrying out most trials in their own populations, when 90 per cent of HIV infections occur in developing countries. There has also been concern that fully informed consent to participate in vaccine trials may be too difficult to achieve, given the complex biology of HIV and its effects on the body. Misunderstandings could have fatal outcomes: for example, volunteers who mistakenly believe the trial injection will give them some protection from HIV may place themselves at greater risk of exposure. The random allocation of some participants to receive a placebo injection has also been criticised as unethical, since they cannot benefit from any protection the trial vaccine might confer, but the trial is useless without a placebo group.

3   There are two main limitations to information-giving strategies. First, informed individuals may not have access to the practical means to act on the basis of their knowledge. Injecting drug users, for example, may know that the sharing of syringes is risky, but may not be able to obtain new ones; safer-sex practices may be taught in places where condoms are not available or affordable. Second, even if the practical means are available, information to individuals cannot achieve behaviour change if it is opposed by a peer group or by more powerful members of the community. If, for example, it is not considered socially 'normal' or 'acceptable' to use condoms with a long-term sexual partner, this makes the negotiation of condom use — particularly by women — considerably more difficult. The same problem arises when the clients of sex workers insist on unprotected penetrative sex and economic disadvantage makes it impossible to refuse.

4   The pharmaceutical companies have objected to the free distribution of HAART drugs to the millions of people with HIV in low-income countries, claiming that their profits will fall to such an extent that research and development into new drugs will have to slow down. It costs over £500 million to develop a new drug and bring it onto the market, so the argument is made that progress towards finding a cure for HIV will take much longer if HAART drugs are distributed free. A further objection is that adherence to HAART regimens must be absolute and consistent, probably for life, to reduce the evolution of drug-resistant strains of HIV. If these drugs are distributed free in countries where the infrastructure to support adherence is missing, then the pace at which new drug-resistant strains evolve could accelerate so quickly as to make current HAART drugs ineffective. Campaigners for distribution of free treatment with HAART drugs have countered these arguments on grounds of equity and social justice, claiming it is ethically indefensible for rich countries to deny access to therapies that have been shown to reduce symptoms and prolong life.

5   *Ontological security* refers to a basic sense of trust and optimism about personal survival. Perceived threats to that sense of security arouse great anxiety, which may be dealt with by *projecting* anger onto anyone who seems to have provoked

it. These 'others' are thus excluded from the tribe of 'normals'. Mass advertising campaigns have tended to reinforce the 'otherness' of people infected with HIV, who are represented as threatening the lives of 'normal' people. There are historical precedents for this reaction in public responses to sexually transmitted infections in the past (e.g. syphilis), and in the persistent association of homosexuality in most Western countries with sin, sickness and death. The political climate of the 1980s, when HIV was identified in the USA and the UK, was characterised by the promotion of 'family values', in opposition to the perceived social and economic excesses of the 1960s and 1970s. This political agenda reinforced the representation of people with HIV as a threat to the 'moral order' of society.

Chapter 5

1   The problem with studies that rely solely on 'parent-reported' symptoms of asthma is that public awareness of asthma has been increasing over time. A questionnaire given to parents in the 1970s may have elicited fewer reports of (say) 'child wheezing at night' than parents reported in the 1990s, simply because parents have paid more attention in recent years to wheezing as a potential danger signal of asthma. This difficulty could be reduced by simultaneously collecting objective data on the children's lung function (e.g. by taking peak-flow measurements) and seeing if this correlates with parental reports. Studies that use scientifically defined measures of asthma could also include an experimental intervention, such as measuring peak flow before and after the child inhaled a blast of cold air (as in the East and West German comparisons by Erika von Mutius and colleagues, 1994).

2   IgE is a type of antibody produced inappropriately and in elevated amounts in atopic individuals when they encounter common environmental allergens, such as the droppings of house-dust mites and plant pollens. It binds to mast cells, which are particularly abundant in the respiratory tract and around the eyes. The next time the triggering allergen is inhaled, it is 'captured' by the IgE on the mast cells, and this in turn causes the mast cells to release inflammatory chemicals. Over time, persistent inflammation results in the airway walls becoming thickened, clogged with mucus and prone to bronchoconstriction. Atopic asthma could, in theory, be alleviated if IgE levels could be reduced. (In fact, clinical trials began in the late 1990s of anti-IgE-antibodies, that is, antibodies that bind to the IgE molecules and prevent them from binding to the mast cells.)

3   If the hygiene hypothesis is correct, children born in Western industrialised countries in the last few decades are more prone to atopic asthma than today's adults because they have grown up in more 'hygienic' domestic environments than their parents experienced. They had less contact during early life with other children, and so were less exposed to the mild respiratory infections that may 'educate' the naive immune system towards recognition of infectious agents as targets for immune responses in the future. Modern Western children are also exposed to higher levels of domestic allergens due to improved living standards; for example the widespread installation of central heating and fitted carpets has promoted the infestation of house-dust mites. The exposure to allergens from domestic pets in these enclosed environments may also have increased in recent generations. In the absence of priming by mild infection in early childhood, persistent exposure to airborne allergens during development

may educate the immune system of susceptible individuals inappropriately, so they become more prone to allergies and atopic asthma.

4   The most obvious source of financial difficulty is loss of income from employment: unpaid leave may have to be taken from work; a part-time or lower-paid job may have to be accepted, perhaps to avoid an occupational trigger for asthma; a parent may decide not to return to work in order to look after an asthmatic child; in extreme cases a job may be lost altogether. In addition, there may be extra expenses on heating, non-allergenic bedding, trips to the GP or hospital, and on prescription charges.

Chapter 6

1   The main *positive* symptoms can be described under headings of distortions of thinking (e.g. thought broadcast, delusions, incoherent and irrelevant speech), distortions of perceptions (e.g. hallucinations), disturbances of volition (e.g. 'I was made to …') and disturbances of movement (e.g. catatonia). Disturbances of personality are usually a consequence of *negative* symptoms, such as withdrawal, apathy, loss of interest, emotional blunting, slow speech and self-absorption. Lay versions of schizophrenia usually emphasise unpredictability and violence, especially to others, but in reality, violence is uncommon and most frequently results in *self*-harm.

2   International comparisons are often invalid due to different criteria being applied to measure schizophrenia. For example, Table 6.1 illustrates the international variation when a broad definition of schizophrenia is taken, with inhabitants of Chandigarh in India apparently being at highest risk of developing schizophrenia. When the International Pilot Study of Schizophrenia (IPSS) tried to impose a stable 'narrow' definition, it found that the core symptoms of schizophrenia occurred in similar frequency throughout the world. Both these findings contradict the view that schizophrenia is an 'illness of Western industrialised countries'. However, the *course* and the *outcome* of schizophrenia are better in 'developing' rather than 'developed' countries, possibly due to differences in social organisation and support — giving some credence to the statement in the question.

3   In the continuing absence of any conclusive evidence of a single cause for schizophrenia, the dominant model of the condition refers to multiple interacting factors that will vary from person to person, but typically include both biological and psychosocial contributions. Two consequences of this understanding of the condition are that approaches to intervention have gradually migrated towards a *multi-intervention approach*, and treatments for schizophrenia now largely aim to influence the *course* of the disease rather than its *cause*. For example, psychosocial interventions to reduce high expressed emotion (EE) in the family of a person diagnosed with schizophrenia are aimed at preventing relapse. Treatment with the new generation of atypical antipsychotic drugs aims to control symptoms and reduce relapse, and hopes have faded that blocking dopamine pathways in the brain would remove the original cause of the illness. Additionally, neither a belief that schizophrenia is largely the result of genetic make-up, nor a belief in environmental causes, detracts from the fact that patients and families may benefit from a variety of treatment interventions including education and skills development.

286 Experiencing and Explaining Disease

4   Arguments in favour of retaining the compulsory detention and treatment legislation would include the point that they protect the public and may help individuals who are unable to look after themselves. Closing mental hospitals in favour of community care may be a laudable aim, but it could be argued that — in the absence of adequate support 'in the community' — it may do more harm than good. Arguments against retaining compulsory detention and treatment might mirror Szasz's view that dangerous individuals should be dealt with under the criminal law. Protecting the individual from harm by compulsory supervision and treatment can be viewed as paternalistic and an infringement of civil liberties, as well as undermining the autonomy of people with mental illness to take charge of their own lives. Long-term institutionalisation may disable people from coping in the community.

5   You might want to weigh up information such as how long ago the person was diagnosed and how he or she has coped since then, and whether or not the symptoms have stabilised (with or without medication). Other factors that contribute to a good prognosis include being female, in employment, living in a developing country, living with a low 'expressed emotion' family, and having no other members of the person's family with a diagnosis of schizophrenia or another psychotic disorder. Schizophrenia is a variable condition and some people 'do well' in that they recover or are able to live a fairly 'normal' life. Depending on the circumstances, it might be possible to make some estimate of prognosis. You might want to dispel misconceptions about schizophrenia producing a 'split personality' with violent tendencies, to counteract personal prejudice, deep-seated anxieties or media misrepresentations of the condition.

Chapter 7

1   Small children are inadequately socialised into institutionalised routines for defending against the insecurity engendered by pain, for which they depend on their parents or other caretakers. A minor injury can appear as a frightening event, posing problems about the physical integrity of the body that a small child is not yet able to confront. Parental attention 'remakes' this sudden fracturing (unmaking) of the world, the application of a plaster serving to 'explain' the injury to the child and restoring security. The adult who says 'it's only a scratch' is appealing to a concept of physical suffering, divorced from the emotional and social aspects addressed by the 'unnecessary' plaster.

2   It is profoundly disturbing to suffer from conditions where a physical cause is difficult to identify, where symptoms are hard to communicate, and for which neither lay views nor medical science have an explanation. People may experience difficulty in persuading others of the legitimacy of their complaint, and the lack of a commonly accepted meaning for their condition may produce fear and isolation. The naming of a condition by an authoritative source of knowledge such as medicine can therefore allay such anxieties and make people feel that their condition is shared and potentially within the bounds of normal human experience. This may happen even in the absence of any valid medical explanation or effective medical treatment.

3   Gate-control theory provides a scientific basis for the placebo effect by establishing the ability of signals descending from the brain to close the 'gate' in the spinal cord and reduce the sensation of pain. The belief that the pill will

bring relief, coupled by the strong desire to reduce severe pain, activates the descending pathway. The provision of a medical narrative for the placebo effect protects the patient from accusations that they were 'fooled' into reporting less pain, or that they must have been malingering before they took the dummy pill.

4   The sort of suffering that the Josselins experienced would nowadays be regarded as exceptional and tragic in Western cultures, where there is more widespread recourse to organised medicine to 'kill' pain and cure the source of suffering, and less reliance on religious explanations. There is now less tolerance of discomfort and a greater expectation that medical knowledge can explain its origin. Nevertheless, there exist some causes of pain and suffering — such as chronic illness and death — for which medicine has no cure, and sometimes no adequate explanation. Modern medical management of these conditions emphasises guided self-reliance, for example, as taught in the pain control clinic featured on the audiotape band 'Being in pain'.

Chapter 8

Notes on the revision exercise 'Living with epilepsy'

These notes are not meant to be an exhaustive analysis of everything that could have been said about the material on the audiotape band 'Living with epilepsy'. We have picked out a number of the ways in which it illustrates major themes of this book, as summarised in Chapter 8. You may well have noted others. We have used the same headings as in Chapter 8, but we warmly congratulate you if you developed your own scheme for analysing and interpreting the quantitative data.

Doubt and certainty

Personal knowledge   Jill and Rose describe their confusion and anxiety when her symptoms began, as they tried to work out what was happening. Jill says 'I started to think "Well, maybe I'm going mad. My friends aren't having this happen to them." ' When the diagnosis was finally made, mother and daughter expressed relief at the certainty: 'at least it had a label', which to some extent has protected Jill's moral reputation by convincing people that her symptoms were real. Rose describes her daughter's terror of her symptoms in the first couple of years, in which the medical and practical implications of epilepsy were not explained to her.

Professional knowledge   No medical explanation has ever been found for why Jill became epileptic at the age of 15, and doctors don't seem to have been sure how to treat her condition, given the number of different drugs she has been prescribed. (You may be interested to know that in part of the interview which was not included in this tape, Jill briefly outlines her 'personal illness narrative', attributing her epilepsy to the after-effects of an operation to remove her appendix.)

Public knowledge   Jill's experience suggests that there is considerable uncertainty and ignorance in the public understanding of epilepsy; people have thought that she ought to look 'different' or that epilepsy is due to cancer or having a 'rotten' brain, and shown surprise that she has achieved a high educational standard (an Open University degree, followed by a Masters). Some have assumed that she is not safe to 'be with people'.

Inclusion and exclusion

Stigmatisation and discrimination   There are numerous examples of this theme on the tape. Onlookers assumed Jill was drunk or a drug addict (two other stigmatised 'identities') when she was having an epileptic fit, or had anorexia when her medication caused sickness and weight loss. She has been discriminated against in employment, losing a Saturday job in a sweet shop, which she had held for years before her diagnosis, and being told she could sort jumble but not do voluntary work with children. She was eventually asked to leave school and be educated at home. Jill also describes her experience of the *master status*, in which everything about her becomes interpreted and understood in terms of her epilepsy. She asserts her identity: '*I'm* not epileptic. My *fits* are epileptic'.

Lay accounts and professional accounts   The dominance of professional accounts, and their power to stigmatise, is illustrated by the doctor who told Jill she would be considered 'possessed' in the USA. His list of famous but dead people who were also epileptic pushed her further into a marginalised group. Her treatment has been driven by the medical model of epilepsy as a *disease*, and does not appear to have included her as an equal partner in coping with the *illness*: 'To the medical profession it's just a condition. I was never given any help socially to adapt'. Medication originally increased her exclusion as a result of its side effects, although it later enabled her to rejoin society. Exclusion from school and work meant Jill became isolated from her friends, and Rose also speaks of her isolation: 'All our lives were very restricted ... I didn't go outside the door, I couldn't leave her'. The lay account of epilepsy has also contributed to Jill's exclusion from society: her family were over-protective and held her back from developing a social life. She has since fought her way back to inclusion, and now runs the local branch of a self-help group which aims to increase public understanding of epilepsy and counteract the stigmatisation associated with it.

Acknowledgements

Grateful acknowledgement is made to the following sources for permission to reproduce material in this book:

Figures

Frontispiece Mother at her Child's Sickbed by Christian Krogh, 1884, source: © 1996 Nasjonalgalleriet, Oslo, photo J. Lathion; *Figure 1.1* BBC Photo Library; *Figure 1.2* The Freud Museum, London; *Figure 2.1 The Doubting Thomas* by Leendert van der Cooghen, 1610–1681, © Royal Cabinet of Paintings, Mauritshuis, The Hague; *Figure 2.2* Ian Simpson/ Photofusion; *Figure 2.3* Gideon Mendel/Network Photographers; *Figure 2.4 and 3.2b* Dr P. Marazzi/Science Photo Library; *Figure 2.5* David Hartley/Rex Features; *Figure 3.2a* CNRI/ Science Photo Library; *Figure 3.3a and 3.4* Courtesy of the Arthritis Research Campaign; *Figure 3.3b* Wellcome Trust Medical Photo Library; *Figure 3.5* Williams, G. H. and Wood, P. H. N. (1986) 'Common-sense beliefs about illness: a mediating role for the doctor', *Lancet*, ii, p. 1435–1437, © by The Lancet Ltd 1986; *Figure 3.6* Silman, A. J. (1988) 'Has the incidence of rheumatoid arthritis declined in the United Kingdon?' *British Journal of Rheumatology*, **27**, pp. 77–78, Oxford University Press; *Figure 3.7* Linos, A., Worthington, J. W., O'Fallon, M. *et al.* (1980) 'The epidemiology of rheumatoid arthritis in Rochester, Minnesota: A study of incidence, prevalence and mortality', *American Journal of Epidemiology*, **111**, pp. 87–98, The Johns Hopkins University School of Hygiene and Public Health; *Figure 3.8* John Callan/Shout; *Figure 4.1* Reproduced by kind permission of the NAMES Project (UK), photo: Patsy Wilson; *Figure 4.2* Courtesy of the National Institute for Biological Standards and Control; *Figure 4.3* Reproduced by kind permission of the Terence Higgins Trust; *Figures 4.4 and 6.2* Crown copyright material is reproduced under Class Licence Number C01W0000065 with the permission of the Controller of HMSO and the Queen's Printer for Scotland; *Figure 4.6a and b* NIBSC/Science Photo Library; *Figure 4.7* Worpole, I. (1988) from 'HIV infection: the clinical picture' by Robert R. Redfield and Donald S. Burke, *Scientific American*, October 1988, International edition; *Figure 4.8* Elizabeth Rivers; *Figures 4.9 and 4.10* Reproduced by kind permission of the Joint United Nations Programme on HIV/AIDS (UNAIDS); *Figure 4.11 Global Population Profile 2000*, US Bureau of the Census, International Programs Center; *Figures 4.12, 4.14 and 4.15* Public Health Laboratory Service: Communicable Disease Surveillance Centre; *Figure 4.13 The Status and Trends of the HIV/AIDS Epidemics in the World*, Monitoring the AIDS Pandemic (MAP) Network; *Figure 4.16* Tony Woodcock/Open University; *Figures 5.1 and 5.7c* Mike Levers/Open University; *Figures 5.3, 5.5 and 5.12* Barnes, P. J. and Godfrey, S. (1975) *Asthma*, Martin Dunitz Ltd; *Figure 5.4* Barnes, P. J. and Newhouse, M. T. (1994) *Conquering Asthma*, Decker Periodicals; *Figure 5.8* 'Out in the Open', *The Asthma Journal*, Special Supplement **6**(3), National Asthma Campaign; *Figure 5.9* Marcus Enoch; *Figure 5.10* Stedman, J. R. and Bush, T. (2000) 'Mapping of Nitrogen Dioxide and PM_{10} in the UK for Article 5 Assessment', AEA Technology Environment; *Figure 5.11* Pope, C. A. and Dockery, W. (1992) 'Acute health effects of PM_{10} pollution on symptomatic and asymptomatic children', *American Review of Respiratory Diseases*, **145**, p. 1124, © American Lung Association; *Figure 5.13c* National Asthma Campaign; *Figure 6.1* Reproduced by kind permission of Terence Charnley, the artist's brother; *Figure 6.3* Curran, D. and Partridge, M. (1969) *Psychological Medicine,* Churchill Livingstone; *Figure 6.4* Gottesman, I. (1991) *Schizophrenia Genesis*, W. H. Freeman and Company and Nettle, D. (2001) *Strong Imagination: Madness, Creativity and Human Nature*, Oxford University Press; *Figure 6.5* Suddath, R. L. *et al.* (1990) 'Anatomical abnormalities in the brains of monozygotic twins discordant for schizophrenia', *New England Journal of Medicine*, **322**(12), p. 791, copyright 1990, Massachusetts Medical Society; *Figure 6.6* Dr Monty Buchsbaum/Peter Arnold Inc./Science Photo Library; *Figure 6.7* Philip Hollis/ Rex Features; *Figure 6.8 Mass Media Representations of Mental Health/Illness. Report for the Health Education Board for Scotland*, (1993) Glasgow University Media Group; *Figure 7.1* With kind permission of the Art Therapy Department, The Royal Marsden NHS Trust; *Figure 7.3* MacCarty, C. S. and Drake, R. L. (1956) 'Neurosurgical procedures for the control of pain',

Index

Entries and page numbers in orange type refer to key words which are printed in **bold** in the text. Indexed information on pages indicated by *italics* is carried mainly or wholly in a figure or a table.